The Changing Role of Nationality in International Law

The book explores the current role of nationality from the point of view of international law, reassessing the validity of the 'classical', state-centered, approach to nationality in light of the 'new' role the human being is gradually acquiring within the international legal order. In this framework, the collection assesses the impact of international human rights rules on the international discourse on nationality and explores the significance international (including private international) law attaches to the links individuals may establish with states other than that of nationality. The book weighs the significance of the bond of nationality in the context of regional integration systems, and explores the fields of international law in which nationality still plays a pivotal role, such as diplomatic protection and dispute settlement in international investment law. The collection includes contributions from legal scholars of different nationalities and academic backgrounds, and offers an excellent resource for academics, practitioners and students undertaking advanced studies in international law.

Alessandra Annoni is a Researcher in International Law at the University of Catanzaro, Italy. She teaches Public International Law, Private International Law and a Jean Monnet Module on European Migration Law. Her research interests include International Humanitarian Law and Human Rights Law.

Serena Forlati is Associate Professor of International Law at the University of Ferrara, Italy. Her current research interests focus on public international law, especially international human rights and international dispute settlement.

Routledge Research in International Law

Available:

International Law and the Third World
Reshaping justice
Edited by Richard Falk, Balakrishnan Rajagopal and Jacqueline Stevens

International Legal Theory
Essays and engagements, 1966–2006
Nicholas Onuf

The Problem of Enforcement in International Law
Countermeasures, the non-injured state and the idea of international community
Elena Katselli Proukaki

International Economic Actors and Human Rights
Adam McBeth

The Law of Consular Access
A documentary guide
John Quigley, William J. Aceves and Adele Shank

State Accountability under International Law
Holding states accountable for a breach of jus cogens norms
Lisa Yarwood

International Organisations and the Idea of Autonomy
Institutional independence in the international legal order
Edited by Richard Collins and Nigel D. White

Self-Determination in the Post-9/11 Era
Elizabeth Chadwick

Participants in the International Legal System
Multiple perspectives on non-state actors in international law
Jean d'Aspremont

Sovereignty and Jurisdiction in the Airspace and Outer Space
Legal criteria for spatial delimitation
Gbenga Oduntan

International Law in a Multipolar World
Edited by Matthew Happold

The Law on the Use of Force
A feminist analysis
Gina Heathcote

The ICJ and the Development of International Law
The lasting impact of the Corfu Channel case
Edited by Karine Bannelier, Théodore Christakis and Sarah Heathcote

UNHCR and International Refugee Law
From treaties to innovation
Corinne Lewis

Asian Approaches to International Law and the Legacy of Colonialism
The law of the sea, territorial disputes and international dispute settlement
Edited by Jin-Hyun Paik, Seok-Woo Lee, Kevin Y. L. Tan

The Right to Self-determination Under International Law
"Selfistans," secession, and the rule of the great powers
Milena Sterio

Reforming the UN Security Council Membership
The illusion of representativeness
Sabine Hassler

Threats of Force
International law and strategy
Francis Grimal

The Changing Role of Nationality in International Law
Alessandra Annoni and Serena Forlati

Forthcoming titles in this series include:

International Law, Regulation and Resistance
Critical spaces
Zoe Pearson

The Cuban Embargo under International Law
El Bloqueo
Nigel D. White

The Changing Role of Nationality in International Law

Edited by
Alessandra Annoni and Serena Forlati

Routledge
Taylor & Francis Group
LONDON AND NEW YORK

First published 2013
by Routledge
2 Park Square, Milton Park, Abingdon, Oxon OX14 4RN

Simultaneously published in the USA and Canada
by Routledge
711 Third Avenue, New York, NY 10017

Routledge is an imprint of the Taylor & Francis Group, an informa business

British Library Cataloguing in Publication Data
A catalogue record for this book is available from the British Library

Library of Congress Cataloguing in Publication Data
A catalog record for this book has been requested

ISBN: 978-0-415-53545-8 (hbk)
ISBN: 978-0-203-43697-4 (ebk)

Typeset in Garamond
by Wearset Ltd, Boldon, Tyne and Wear

Contents

Notes on contributors ix
Preface xi
List of abbreviations xiii

1 *Staatsvolk* and homogeneity: from Weimar to the *Maastricht* decision of the German Federal Constitutional Court and beyond 1
HOLGER P. HESTERMEYER

2 Nationality as a human right 18
SERENA FORLATI

3 Statelessness in the context of state succession: an appraisal under international law 37
FRANCESCO COSTAMAGNA

4 Nationality of individuals in public international law: a functional approach 54
ALICE SIRONI

5 Nationality and diplomatic protection: a reappraisal 76
ANNEMARIEKE VERMEER-KÜNZLI

6 Nationality and freedom of movement 96
FRANCESCA DE VITTOR

7 Nationality and political rights 117
DELIA RUDAN

8 Nationality and social rights 135
ALESSANDRA ANNONI

9 Determining the nationality of companies in ICSID arbitration 153
GIULIA D'AGNONE

10 Nationality and regional integration: the case of the European Union 169
PIERLUIGI SIMONE

11 The evolving role of nationality in private international law 193
PIETRO FRANZINA

12 Conclusions 210
FRANCESCO SALERNO

Index 215

Notes on contributors

Alessandra Annoni (Ph.D), Researcher in International Law, University of Catanzaro, Italy.

Francesco Costamagna (Ph.D), Researcher in European Union Law and Lecturer in International Law, University of Turin, Italy.

Giulia D'Agnone, Ph.D Candidate in International and European Law, University of Macerata, Italy.

Francesca De Vittor (Ph.D), Researcher in International Law and Lecturer in International Law and International Organizations Law, University of Macerata, Italy.

Serena Forlati (LL.M, Ph.D), Associate Professor of International Law, University of Ferrara, Italy.

Pietro Franzina (Ph.D), Associate Professor of International Law, University of Ferrara, Italy.

Holger P. Hestermeyer (LL.M, Ph.D), Head of the Otto Hahn Group on 'Diversity and Homogeneity', Max Planck Institute of Comparative Public Law and International Law, Heidelberg, Germany.

Delia Rudan, (Ph.D), Teaching Assistant in International Human Rights and International Law, University of Ferrara, Italy.

Francesco Salerno, Chair of International Law, University of Ferrara, Italy. Member of the International Institute of Human Rights, Strasbourg, France.

Pierluigi Simone (Ph.D), Researcher in International Law and Lecturer in EU Law, University of Rome 'Tor Vergata', Italy.

Alice Sironi (Ph.D), Officer at the International Organization for Migration, Geneva, Switzerland.

Annemarieke Vermeer-Künzli (M.A., Ph.D), Assistant Professor, Amsterdam Center for International Law, University of Amsterdam, The Netherlands.

Preface

Alessandra Annoni and Serena Forlati

Today, no less than in the past, nationality is crucial in construing individuals' legal relationships with states at national and international levels, their personal identities, and their capacity to integrate into a given society. It is thus no wonder that the topic has attracted wide attention by scholars of different backgrounds.

Nationality is also an issue that lies at the crossroads among different legal systems: constitutional law, international law, international human rights law, private international law, as well as regional integration systems. This book aims at exploring the current role of nationality from a legal perspective, and specifically from the point of view of international law. In this area, the approach to nationality and its regulation has undergone significant changes: as several chapters in this book confirm, the 'new' role the human being is gradually acquiring within the international legal order has led to a shift from the 'classical', state-centered approach to nationality, while not leaving that approach completely aside.

The impact of human rights rules on the international discourse on nationality is twofold. First of all, it is reflected in the development of international rules that are gradually eroding the traditional idea according to which the definition of conditions for acquiring nationality falls within the exclusive domestic jurisdiction of states, in an attempt to limit cases of statelessness and to ensure everyone the 'right to a nationality'. Moreover, the recognition of a set of rights to be enjoyed by every human being, irrespective of nationality or immigration status, tends to overcome the differences in treatment between nationals and non-nationals, including stateless persons and refugees.

From a different perspective, the shift of the attention onto individuals and the protection of their interests has prompted international law to look beyond the bond of nationality, thus enhancing the significance of the links individuals may establish with states, other than that of nationality. These developments – which also affect private international law – are all the more evident in the context of regional integration systems, especially within the European Union, where the bond of nationality is a gateway to acquiring the status of European citizen, which grants access to an autonomous set of rights.

Nationality, however, still plays a pivotal role in many fields of international law, such as that of diplomatic protection. In this context, 'factual links' may come into consideration only in exceptional circumstances, e.g., in respect of stateless persons and refugees, and in cases of multiple nationalities, when a claim is brought by one state of nationality against another state of nationality.

Although this book addresses the various aspects of nationality regulation mainly from the perspective of individuals, one chapter is devoted to a specific facet of the legal regulation of nationality of companies, namely its determination in the framework of international investment law. We felt that in this context, more than in others, it might be worth exploring the relevance of any factual elements that justify the setting aside of formal attribution of nationality for the purposes of international law.

The first opportunity to work jointly on the topic of nationality was with the organization, together with Pietro Franzina, of the VIII Italian Meeting of Young International Lawyers, devoted to 'Funzioni e limiti della cittadinanza rispetto ai fenomeni di mobilità internazionale degli individui' and of a related seminar, on 'Citizenship and Democracy' (Ferrara-Rovigo, 8–9 October 2010). While this book is an autonomous project, and has lost, in particular, the inter-disciplinary approach that was a main feature of those events, we would like to thank all those who took active part in that stimulating debate, which led us to think that an effort to reappraise the notion and the role of nationality in the specific perspective of international law could be worthwhile. Our book does not claim to address all the international legal issues connected to nationality, but it will hopefully offer some food for thought in this respect.

We also thank Adrienne Lester-Fitje and Laura Salvadego for their help in the proofreading phase, and Katie Carpenter and Steven Gutierrez of Routledge for their support. Last but not least, we gladly acknowledge the contribution of Pietro Franzina in framing the concept of this project and in the first phases of its development: thank you Pietro.

Ferrara, August 2012

List of abbreviations

1930 Convention	Convention on Certain Questions relating to the Conflict of Nationality Laws
1951 Convention	Convention relating to the Status of Refugees
1954 Convention	Convention relating to the Status of Stateless Persons
1961 Convention	Convention on the Reduction of Statelessness
1992 Convention	Council of Europe Convention on Participation of Foreigners to Public Life at Local Level
1999 Draft Articles	ILC Draft Articles on Nationality of Natural Persons in Relation to the Succession of States
2006 Convention	Council of Europe Convention on the Avoidance of Statelessness in relation to State Succession
2006 Draft Articles	ILC Draft Articles on Diplomatic Protection
2012 Draft Articles	ILC Draft Articles on Expulsion of aliens, provisionally adopted on first reading by the Drafting Committee
ACERWC	African Committee of Experts on the Rights and Welfare of the Child
ACHPR	African Charter on Human and Peoples' Rights
ACHR	American Convention on Human Rights
AComHPR	African Commission on Human and Peoples' Rights
ACRWC	African Charter on the Rights and Welfare of the Child
ArCHR	Arab Charter on Human Rights (revised)
BIT	Bilateral Investment Treaty
CAT	Committee against Torture
CEDAW	Convention on the Elimination of All Forms of Discrimination against Women
CEDW	Committee on the Elimination of Discrimination against Women
CERD	Convention on the Elimination of All Forms of Racial Discrimination
CESCR	Committee on Economic, Social and Cultural Rights
CETS	European Treaty Series (until 2003)/Council of Europe Treaty Series (as of 2004)

CIS Convention	Commonwealth of Indepentent States – Convention on Human Rights
CMW	Committee on the Protection of the Rights of All Migrant Workers and Members of Their Families
CoE	Council of Europe
CRC	Convention on the Rights of the Child
CRPD	Convention on the Rights of Persons with Disabilities
CSCE	Conference on Security and Co-operation in Europe
CtERD	Committee on the Elimination of Racial Discrimination
CtRC	Committee on the Rights of the Child
EC	European Community
ECHR	European Convention on Human Rights
ECJ	Court of Justice of the European Communities (until 30 November 2009)/Court of Justice (as of 1 December 2009)
ECLSMW	European Convention on the Legal Status of Migrant Workers
ECN	European Convention on Nationality
EComHR	European Commission of Human Rights
ECR	European Court Reports
ECSR	European Committee of Social Rights
ECtHR	European Court of Human Rights
ESC	European Social Charter (revised)
EU	European Union
EU Charter	Charter of Fundamental Rights of the European Union
EWCA	England and Wales Court of Appeal
FC	Full Court
GC	Grand Chamber
HRC	Human Rights Committee
IACHR	Inter-American Court of Human Rights
ICCPR	International Covenant on Civil and Political Rights
ICESCR	International Covenant on Economic, Social and Cultural Rights
ICJ	International Court of Justice
ICRMW	International Convention on the Protection of the Rights of All Migrant Workers and Members of Their Families
ICSID	International Centre for Settlement of Investment Disputes
ICSID Convention	Convention on the Settlement of Investment Disputes between States and Nationals of Other States
ILC	International Law Commission
ILO	International Labour Organization
ILOAT	Administrative Tribunal of the International Labour Organization

LNTS	League of Nations Treaty Series
Mercosur	Southern Common Market
OAS	Organisation of American States
PCIJ	Permanent Court of International Justice
PIL	Private international law
Protocol of San Salvador	Protocol to the American Convention of Human Rights in the Area of Economic, Social and Cultural Rights
SADC	Southern African Development Community
SFRY	Socialist Federal Republic of Yugoslavia
TEC	Treaty establishing the European Community
TEEC	Treaty establishing the European Economic Community
TEU	Treaty on European Union
TFEU	Treaty on the Functioning of the European Union
UAE	United Arab Emirates
UDHR	Universal Declaration of Human Rights
UKSC	United Kingdom Supreme Court
UN	United Nations
UNAT	United Nations Administrative Tribunal
UNESCO	United Nations Educational, Scientific and Cultural Organization
UNGAOR	United Nations General Assembly Official Records
UNHCR	United Nations High Commissioner for Refugees
UNRIAA	United Nations Reports of International Arbitral Awards
UNTS	United Nations Treaty Series
VCLT	Vienna Convention on the Law of Treaties
Venice Commission	European Commission for Democracy through Law
WGM	UN Sub-Commission on the Promotion and Protection of Human Rights, Working Group on Minorities

Except where otherwise indicated, the case law quoted in the text is available online at the following links:

ECJ	http://curia.europa.eu
ECtHR	http://hudoc.echr.coe.int
IACHR	www.corteidh.or.cr/
ICJ	www.icj-cij.org
UN Treaty Bodies	www.ohchr.org/EN/HRBodies/Pages/HumanRightsBodies.aspx

1 *Staatsvolk* and homogeneity

From Weimar to the *Maastricht* decision of the German Federal Constitutional Court and beyond

Holger P. Hestermeyer[1]

Introduction

What is it that makes a people? What is the identity of a nation? These questions have been asked by philosophers, sociologists, and lawyers alike ever since the birth of the modern nation-state in the eighteenth and nineteenth century.[2] As Italy celebrates its 150th birthday,[3] spoiled by a movement that is oscillating between separatism and decentralization, and Europe proceeds on its path towards an 'ever closer union'[4] that demonstrates an annoying resilience to all attempts at attaching the comfortingly familiar labels of 'state', 'federalism', and 'citizenship' to it, the debate about identity – European, national, or regional – has been renewed. Advocates for nation-states over the European project couch their arguments in terms of identity, as do advocates of the contrary.

This contribution does not pretend to present the debate in all its complexity. Instead, it will highlight a tiny aspect of it: the debate about homogeneity of the *Staatsvolk* (or people), popular in the Weimar republic and still referred to by the Federal Constitutional Court in its *Maastricht* judgment. Homogeneity in this meaning alleges that there is some sociological tie, a common language, history, or common traditions, uniting the *Staatsvolk*. This contribution will recount the discussion about homogeneity of the *Staatsvolk* both during the Weimar Republic and today, and then draw on studies in behavioural and cognitive sciences to argue that it is not the absence of such a tie, as some state, but its arbitrariness that makes homogeneity a meaningless criterion. It is reasonable to assume that the German Constitutional Court would agree, as it seems to have laid the criterion of homogeneity of the *Staatsvolk* to rest in the *Lisbon* decision.

Jellinek and the *Staatsvolk* as an element of the state

Georg Jellinek, writing in 1900, as a professor of the University of Heidelberg, identified the *Staatsvolk* as one of three elements defining a state: territory, government, and *Staatsvolk*.[5] His account of the state was the subject of much debate and criticism in the Weimar period. Over time, however, his description became, and today still is, the standard definition of a state,[6] with others diverging in detail only. Thus, Dionisio Anzilotti would have added independence from a superior power to the three elements[7] and Article 1 of the 1933 Montevideo Convention on Rights and Duties of States adds the 'capacity to enter into relations with other states'.[8]

Identifying the *Staatsvolk* as a necessary element of a state seems obvious to the point of being a truism. Long before Jellinek formulated the now standard definition of the modern state, philosophers had discussed the importance of the people in and for the state. But the identification of the people as at the core of what makes a state raises the question of what exactly constitutes that people. Intuitively, it would seem that not just any random group of people could form a *Staatsvolk*. But what is the tie binding a group of people into such a *Staatsvolk*? Jellinek's answer pointed towards another of his elements of the state: government. He postulated that the people are simultaneously the subject of the government and its object. A people's identity as the subject of government binds that people together as a collective, and as such, members of the people are the subjects (and beneficiaries) of public rights recognized by the state.[9]

Staatsvolk and homogeneity

Many writers did not find this to be a satisfactory description of a *Staatsvolk*. Since antiquity, writers have invoked the need for close relations among the citizens of a state. Plato argued that there was nothing more important for a state than unity and nothing more dangerous than division. He proposed drastic methods,[10] such as dissolving traditional families and imposing communal relationships with women and children, to achieve a state in which citizens could rightly think of each other as relatives.[11] Aristotle regarded closer ties among the *Staatsvolk* as necessary for forming a fully functioning society and state. He wrote:

> [A] state is a community of households and families leading a good life together, i.e. a community for the purpose of complete and autarkic life. That cannot be realized if the members do not live in one and the same place and do not intermarry. That is why in states family bonds, tribal alliances, common sacrifices and communal events are formed. Only friendship can achieve this, as the decision to live together is characteristic of friendship.[12]

The close ties among the *Staatsvolk* discussed by Plato and Aristotle are inspired by, and can only be understood in the context of, the type of state the Greeks considered to be exemplary: the *Polis*, the Greek city-state. Even though many translators today translate the word as state, the comparison is somewhat forced: only three *Poleis* had a population of more than 20,000 citizens. A *Polis* of 1,000,000 amounted, for Aristotle, to a self-evidently absurd suggestion.[13]

With the growth of states beyond the proportions imaginable to Greek philosophy, the ties among members of a modern *Staatsvolk* must be weaker than those aspired to by Plato or Aristotle. Modern cognitive and anthropological research seems to indicate rather strict limits of the number of people with whom close social relationships can be maintained.[14] The alternative proposed by many writers was that a people must, in some shape or form and to some extent, be homogenous. The proposition obtained powerful jurisprudential support when the German Federal Constitutional Court considered homogeneity a characteristic of a *Staatsvolk* in its *Maastricht* judgment. In the decision, the Court examined the compliance of the Maastricht Treaty on European Union (TEU) with German constitutional law. It argued that Europe's indirect legitimization via the population of nation states, the *Staatsvölker*, imposes limits on integration:

> States require their own fields of competencies of sufficient importance, in which the respective *Staatsvolk* can develop and articulate itself in a process of political decision-making both legitimized and controlled by itself and thus give legal expression to those things that unite it, relatively homogenously, spiritually, socially and politically.[15]

The statement sparked much controversy in German legal academia. One of the reasons was that it was referenced to an article by Hermann Heller,[16] a German-Jewish legal scholar of the Weimar era,[17] who had only called for social homogeneity of a *Staatsvolk*. The Federal Constitutional Court's ideas about homogeneity rather seemed to stem from another source, Carl Schmitt,[18] whose history of anti-Semitism and arguments in defence of Nazi policies[19] in the 1930s made him an authority that could not be quoted.

Homogeneity and *Methodenstreit*

To avoid any possible confusion it must be pointed out that German constitutionalists use the term 'homogeneity' in two entirely different contexts. As the 'principle of homogeneity', the term refers to the requirement of structural similarity of different levels of government in federal states or integration systems. Thus, the German Basic Law in Article 28(1) demands that '[t]he constitutional order in the *Länder* must conform to the principles of a republican, democratic and social state governed by the rule of law within the meaning of this Basic Law.'[20] This Article discusses a different use of the term, namely homogeneity as a sociological requirement of some commonality among the citizens of a state.

Weimar era scholars remain central to that concept of homogeneity. As one of their fundamental disagreements was about the correct methodology, their discussions entered history under the buzzword *Methodenstreit*, or literally a conflict about methods. The historic backdrop of the debate was the politically instable Republic of Weimar. Having lost the First World War at an enormous cost (1.8 million dead, 4.2 million injured, 0.6 million prisoners of war, not to speak of economic costs) Germany's monarchic government was swept into history. Germany became a republic, and was declared so twice – by the social democrat Philipp Scheidemann and the socialist Karl Liebknecht. Wedged between right-wing and left-wing radicals, the Weimar Republic experienced upheaval and instability entirely unknown to today's Germans. That upheaval is vital for understanding the period and its intellectual debates.

The instability can be illustrated by a short overview of events in the early years of the Republic. January 1919 saw the army and right-wing paramilitaries break up a left-wing attempt at revolution, as well as the murder of the socialists Rosa Luxemburg and Karl Liebknecht. In February, the minister president of Bavaria, Kurt Eisner, was shot to death and a communist government seized power illegally, executing its political enemies. The military intervened, having already subdued uprisings in the Ruhr, Berlin, and other areas of Germany. The new Constitution, adopted in July 1919, did not stabilize the situation and the 1920 coup attempt by military officers, known as the *Kapp-Putsch*, forced the government to flee. Even after the failure of the *Putsch*, the Republic remained in crisis, as demonstrated by the use of troops in the Ruhr area to fight a Red Army formed by left-wing militants; the assassination of the former Finance Minister Matthias Erzberger in 1921, and of the Foreign Minister Walther Rathenau in 1922 by right-wing radicals; the occupation of the Ruhr by France and Belgium in 1923, to enforce reparation claims; and Adolf Hitler's failed coup in Munich in 1923.[21]

Traditional legal positivism fared poorly in this environment and Jellinek's understanding of the state came under severe attack. Hans Kelsen favoured purging legal methodology from other (e.g. sociological) influences[22] and regarded the state merely as a system of laws.[23] Offended by the dissociation of the state and reality in the works of Kelsen, and influenced by the philosophical thoughts of Theodor Litt,[24] Rudolf Smend characterized the state as an intangible, but real, structure in a constant process of renewal that he called integration. Integration can be achieved by three means: through persons, through acts aiming at social synthesis, and through material goals of the state, such as rights.[25]

Schmitt also advocated a more sociological approach. He regarded positivism and the validity of norms as limited to normal situations,[26] and thought of decisions as a better theoretical basis for the legal system than norms.[27] His *Verfassungslehre*, published in 1928, further developed his thinking on the state and on democracy. Schmitt identifies equality as one of the core principles of the democratic state. But democratic equality is not equality of everyone, but equality of the members of the *Staatsvolk*. Only these members can vote, and only these members are equal participants of the democratic state. Equality is thus, according to Schmitt, a principle that only applies to those participating in the material content of equality. This material content can differ from democracy to democracy: ancient Greeks automatically assumed that only free Hellenic citizens were apt to participate in democracy. Machiavelli and Montesquieu required *vertu*. English levellers did not mean to extend liberties to papists or atheists, and the American colonies limited their liberties to the religiously similarly inclined. The modern nation-state, according to Schmitt, bases democracy on national homogeneity. A nation is a people with a particular political self-identification, which can be based on several elements, such as language, history, traditions, memories, political aspirations, and hopes. Where the nation becomes the basis for democratic identity, lack of homogeneity, according to Schmitt, becomes something abnormal and a threat to peace. Schmitt proposes several possible 'solutions': controlling immigration, as in the United States; ruling over territories with heterogeneous populations without annexation, as done by the United States in the case of some Latin American territories; laws against foreign infiltration or foreign control of industry such as Article 27 of the Mexican Constitution of 1917; or tools of citizenship laws, such as withdrawing citizenship.[28] Finally, Schmitt suggests the peaceful separation of the non-homogenous part, and assimilation, or 'disposing of the foreign part by suppressing it, resettling it or similar radical means'[29] as exemplified by Greece and Turkey in 1923.

One cannot read these passages without the chilling awareness of how Schmitt's words dovetail with the Nazi policies of discrimination and murder of 'undesirable' minorities. Other authors strongly opposed Schmitt's position. Already in 1925, Kelsen had published his *Allgemeine Staatslehre* in which he rejects the notion that the *Staatsvolk* is a psychologically homogenous group. He does not question strong emotional group ties of individuals among national, religious, class, or political lines, but emphasizes that none of these coincide with the community formed by a state, but both separate citizens of the same state and tie citizens of one state to those of other states. The *Staatsvolk*, according to Kelsen, does not exist separately and independently from the normative order. It is that order that ties the citizens together to form the *Staatsvolk*.[30] More sociological than Kelsen,[31] and rejecting the *Reine Rechtslehre*,[32] Heller defined the state as an organization with sovereign power over territory.[33] He keenly observes that commonalities in heritage, language, religion, customs, art, and science are highly important for the construction of a people. But Heller goes on to state that none of these commonalities are consistently present in all peoples, nor are they sufficient for determining what makes a people. Neither is a *Staatsvolk* defined purely along subjective lines, as summed up by Ernest Renan's characterization of the people as a 'plébisicite de tous les jours.'[34] A *Staatsvolk*, for Heller, is part of a lived reality, perpetuated by individuals renewing an intangible web of traditions. It becomes a nation if it is further developed into a political body that is trying to maintain its specificity by way of a relatively uniform political will. The reality of a people, for Heller, is pluralism rather than unity, such as pluralism of political currents, pluralism of ethnicities, and pluralism of economic and religious thought. The reality of a state can even unite people speaking different languages into one unit.[35] Heller did, however, regard social homogeneity as necessary to enable democratic parliamentary discourse.[36]

But the voices of reason did not prevail and the radicalized ideology of Nazi Germany could, during the first years of its rule,[37] count on the ambitious Schmitt as a prompter.[38] In *Staat*, *Bewegung*, *Volk*, a triad influenced by Italian fascism, he repeats his call for homogeneity, regarding pluralism as a risk exposing the state to liberal or Marxist ideas. Homogeneity, including racial homogeneity, now also becomes a guarantee of the similarity between the people and its leader.[39] From there, it was only a small step to Schmitt's conference on 'Judaism and jurisprudence' in which he called for a 'cleansing' of libraries and restrictions on citations of Jewish authors.[40]

Homogeneity in today's debate

Germany has changed dramatically since the days of the Weimar Republic. Rather than a state in constant crisis, Germany has become a model of stability, located on a continent that has been living in peace for over 60 years. Rather than a state pursuing the murderous policies of the Nazis, it is a state that has atoned for, and is still atoning for its past. Two developments have given a new meaning to the debate about homogeneity of the *Staatsvolk* under these changed circumstances: the European Union (EU)'s perceived threat to the nation-state from the supranational level and the changing structure of German society resulting in a debate about integration of immigrants. The EU has laid siege on old concepts of sovereignty and the powers of a state. Immigration has changed the structure of the people living in Germany. An emigration country in the first half of the twentieth century, Germany became an important target for immigration starting in the mid-1950s. By 1968, it had attracted 1.9 million foreigners, and today there are 6.7 million foreigners living in Germany. The notion of what it means to be German has changed, too; 8.5 million German citizens now have a migration background. Thus, 19.6 per cent of the population living in Germany have some form of migration background.[41]

Relevance of the notion of Staatsvolk

The concept of a people remains relevant both for constitutional and for international law. In constitutional law, authors continue to regard the *Staatsvolk* as one of the three elements of a state. It is also particularly relevant for the concept of democracy: *Staatsvolk* is the *demos* required to establish democratic rule. As a matter of positive constitutional law, the term 'German people' appears several times in the Basic Law. The preamble states that the German people is the *pouvoir constituant* and Article 20(2) makes clear that it is the people[42] that exercises its authority through elections, and is the source from which all state authority is derived. Members of the German Bundestag are representatives of the whole people (Article 38(1)) and the Basic Law ceases to apply when the German people freely adopts a new constitution (Article 146). The Basic Law does not define the term 'German people'. But it does define the notion of 'German' in Article 116 stating that, unless otherwise provided, a German is

> a person who possesses German citizenship or who has been admitted to the territory of the German *Reich* within the boundaries of 31 December 1937, as a refugee or expellee of German ethnic origin [in the original German the term *deutscher Volkszugehörigkeit* seems broader] or as the spouse or descendant of such person.

Article 116 also provides for the restoration, on application, of citizenship of former German citizens deprived of their citizenship on 'political, racial or religious grounds' between 30 January 1933, and 8 May 1945. The intricate wording of the provision is due to the complex historic situation for which it had to offer a solution; Germany had to undo Nazi Germany's policy of depriving Germans of their citizenship, e.g. on racial and religious grounds. At the same time it had to find a solution for refugees from territories with a long and difficult history of German settlements abused particularly by the Nazis, e.g. for territorial claims. They were now expelled or fled from the revenge of those who had suffered severely under the Nazis.[43] Recourse to German *Volkszugehörigkeit*, a status of being German without German citizenship, was a part of that solution – and invokes the idea of a German nationality.[44] Section 6(1) of the Law on the Affairs of Displaced Persons and Refugees[45] defined German *Volkszugehörigkeit* as the commitment to the German *Volkstum*, affirmed by certain characteristics such as ethnicity, language, education, and culture.[46] At least one commentator hence regards Article 116 of the Basic Law as the *locus* for stating that the German Constitution adheres to a notion of a culturally or ethnically characterized people, the notion of a homogeneity of the people.[47] Today, this sub-group of German refugees, known as 'status Germans', do not have any practical relevance.[48] What is more, the German law on citizenship has made significant strides towards combining elements of *jus sanguinis* and *jus soli*, moving away from former ethnocentric notions of citizenship.[49]

In public international law, the notion of people is of vital importance for the right to self-determination. Articles 1(2) and 55 of the Charter of the United Nations (UN) explicitly espouse the principle of self-determination of peoples, and Article 1(3) both of the International Covenant on Civil and Political Rights[50] and of the International Covenant on Economic, Social and Cultural Rights[51] recognize a right of self-determination. The principle has also been included in the Declaration on Friendly Relations[52] and mentioned in several cases decided by the International Court of Justice (ICJ).[53] Even though the right of a people to self-determination has gained recognition, there is no agreement on the definition of 'people' and state practice does not seem to give any clear and consistent indication of the precise characteristics that turn a group into a people.[54] Both the ICJ's advisory opinion on Kosovo's declaration of independence, which carefully avoids clarifying the right to self-determination,[55] and the debate about the *Estatuto* of Catalonia and its use of the word 'nation'[56] show that any such definition would raise hot-button issues that actors would rather not touch.

Staatsvolk *and homogeneity in the constitutional debate*

Paul Kirchhof, a former judge at the Federal Constitutional Court and judge *rapporteur* in the *Maastricht* case is one of the best-known proponents of the nation-state. For Kirchhof it is the nation-state that allows the individual to accept and confront the diversity of a foreign culture through the security provided by the nation-state's own culture and traditions. This security of one's own culture and – beyond that – the material security provided by a social state relies on a network of rights and obligations binding citizens together. To form a democratic state capable of such ties, the people forming it, according to Kirchhof, need some homogeneity. A *Staatsvolk* requires 'a community conscious of its togetherness, characterized by a commonality of values [. . .] joined largely by language, culture and religion'.[57] Josef Isensee adds that the legal unity and the legal equality provided by citizenship can only function properly if based on this factual homogeneity of the citizens.[58] Ernst Wolfgang Böckenförde, too, regards the relative homogeneity of the people as a pre-constitutional condition of a functioning democracy.[59]

The theoretical approach to what constitutes a people has a direct impact on the conception of a united Europe. For proponents of a relatively homogenous nation-state, European integration cannot mean abandoning the idea of the nation-state, but rather respect for the particularities of each nation combined with openness towards the others. The development of a democratic united Europe would require a relevant cultural homogeneity on a European level. This, for Kirchhof, is impossible, given the diversity of languages in the EU.[60]

Other scholars strongly contest this position. The former judge of the Federal Constitutional Court Brun-Otto Bryde argues that the constitutional rights of the German Basic Law guarantee diversity, and hence defeat a concept of homogeneity,[61] a homogeneity that – as Ingolf Pernice points out – as a sociological fact does not exist in any modern democracy.[62] Much like a thorough, recent doctoral thesis focusing in particular on the homogeneity criteria history and language, rejecting the former as largely artificially created and the latter as based on a misunderstanding of how communication is conducted in modern societies with connected sub-networks, these authors reject the concept of homogeneity of the *Staatsvolk*.[63] Armin von Bogdandy holds a roughly comparable position: he concedes that a community cannot function if split into antagonistic religious, ethnic, or social groups, but he rejects a homogeneity requirement for a society to function.[64] Such a requirement is equally rejected by Joseph Weiler. He insists on the possibility of multiple understandings of what is sufficient to constitute a *demos*, including permitting multiple ethno-cultural identities.[65]

These and other commentators also fear the practical implications of a homogeneity requirement in the realm of EU law. Christian Tomuschat noted that such a requirement leads into a dead end for EU reform: authors advocating the need for a homogeneous people as a *demos* cut off all avenues to remedy the perceived democracy deficit of the EU by denying the theoretic ability of the EU to ever be democratic.[66] Why the theoretical conceptualization of democracy in a nation-state should prevent a more democratic EU, based on a slightly different practical implementation of democracy, is not explained by proponents of the necessity of a homogenous state.[67] Von Bogdandy provides some content for this different implementation by stating that Europe can be built based on a contract theory between individuals of possibly conflicting interests, a construction that offers Europeans the opportunity to participate in European politics – with the possibility that the EU and its legal framework might ultimately create a European identity.[68] Weiler seems to regard even the concession of a possible development of a European identity as a nod to notions familiar from nation-states that goes too far. Supranationality, according to him, does not imply that there will be a European people in the same sense as there are French, German, or Italian peoples. The EU should not be understood in the old terms of a nation-state, but as a *demos* consisting of several peoples, and as a supranational community modifying the excesses of nation-states.[69]

The emptiness of homogeneity

What is one to make, then, of the notion of homogeneity in the face of this debate? Is it the hallmark of a nation-state necessary to permit an individual to develop as a *zoon politikon*? Or is it simply a mistaken sociological assumption of the composition of a people? To understand what homogeneity means for the formation of social groups, it is helpful to look at studies of the cognitive sciences on group formation and group stabilization.[70] Those studies suggest that the categorization of people into groups is hardwired into the human brain. The human brain groups people together constantly as a mechanism to cope with the complexity of every day life, to predict behaviour of others, and guide one's own behaviour. Individuals can simultaneously belong to an infinite number of these groups: a person can be Italian, a piano player, and a male. We attach certain expectations to certain groups, so-called stereotypes. These stereotypes can change over time and bear only a very tenuous relationship to true facts about the group. Rather, they are based on facts about how people relate to this group. Expectations of group behaviour can solidify in a process of self-identification of individuals with the group and adoption of the expected behaviour, thereby again reinforcing the stereotype both within and outside the group that similar behaviour has to be expected from members of the group.

It is common societal practice to reject stereotypes. However, stereotyping is a necessary and even subconscious process to cope with the complexity of the world. It should be encouraged to challenge wrong stereotypes, but stereotypes cannot be entirely prevented. The extent of the subconscious process of stereotyping was illustrated by an experiment in which Asian-American women, having been reminded of the fact that they are Asian, performed better on maths tests than those reminded that they are females, conforming with the US stereotype that Asians are supposedly good at maths and women supposedly not.[71]

Little is needed in terms of commonalities to build a group, as shown by two famous behavioural science experiments. In the 'Robbers Cave Experiment'[72] 22 boys from homogenous white, protestant, middle-class backgrounds were split into two groups for summer camp. Separated for the first week, the groups formed group identities as 'Rattlers' and 'Eagles' and when they met again, they seized on minute differences between the customs of the groups that had developed to strengthen their identity – going so far as to enforce these customs on members of the respective groups. The experiment was repeated in Beirut with two groups composed of both Christian and Muslim children.[73] The experiment had to be broken off because fights broke out between the groups, but not – as one might have expected – between members of the religious groups, but between members of the same religion of the different (and artificially created) groups.

While these experiments illustrate that groups seize on their differences to self-identify, using whatever differences they may find, a second type of experiment shows that even entirely artificial groups trigger group self-identification mechanisms.[74] In that experiment, schoolmates were assigned randomly into two groups and told they had been put into the groups according to preferences for painters, whose paintings they had been shown before. They then had to divide payments for participating in the experiment among all the participants. As group identification along the lines of preferences for certain painters is an evidently artificial criterion one might have expected an equal division between the groups or maximization of ones own profits as the outcome, but instead participants chose payments that maximized the difference between the groups.

It would be a misreading to deduce from these experiments that homogeneity is not relevant or existent in nation-states. In generation after generation, processes of self-identification and socialization in nation-states have strengthened common features.[75] Even though individuals in a nation-state are of flabbergasting diversity, we all read guide-books to tell us about customs in a nation we visit. We are not mistaken to assume that a person we encounter in Italy is more likely to speak Italian than one we encounter in France, or a person we meet in Mexico is more likely to get emotional about the *Grito de Dolores* celebrating Mexican independence than a

Frenchman. What is striking, however, is that these points of self-identifications are malleable, and under the right circumstances other group identifications might become relevant and take precedence, e.g. religious identification over national identification. To say that a *Staatsvolk* is relatively homogenous is both true[76] and empty; human groups can be formed along any given number of commonalities. Other commonalities can become relevant under different circumstances. One might hence study what it is that binds the US people together or the German people. However, this study is neither a convincing predictor for the future nor should it be misunderstood as a normative statement about what should, or must be, common to persons for them to form a people. An exception has to be made, however, for human rights: social order relies on the recognition by individuals of the rights of other individuals. With homogeneity thus being a poor descriptor of what constitutes a people, one is enticed to fall back on citizenship as the relevant criterion for defining a people.[77]

Epilogue

Roughly 15 years after its *Maastricht* decision, the Federal Constitutional Court confirmed in its *Lisbon* judgment that it regards the *Völker* as the basis of the legitimization of the EU:

> It is true that the Basic Law grants the legislature powers to engage in a far-reaching transfer of sovereign powers to the European Union. However, the powers are granted under the condition that the sovereign statehood of a constitutional state is maintained on the basis of an integration program according to the principal of conferral and respecting the Member States' constitutional identity, and that at the same time the Member States do not lose their ability to politically and socially shape living conditions on their own responsibility.[78]

The concept of identity clearly is close to the heart of the Court; it repeats the term over 30 times. Its constitutional foundation is Article 23(1) of the Basic Law that subjects changes in the EU's treaty foundations to Article 79(3) – prohibiting certain amendments to the Basic Law.[79] The decision, which bears the hallmarks of a tough political compromise, namely an often incomprehensible methodology of the Court, has been the subject of much discussion and criticism.[80] One aspect of it does, however, deserve praise: it refrains from any reference to an alleged homogeneity of the *Volk*.

Notes

1 The author thanks the participants of the conference on Citizenship and Democracy at the Università di Ferrara, Dominik Remmert and Victoria Reuter for helpful discussions.

2 W. Reinhard, *Geschichte des modernen Staates*, München: Beck, 2007, p. 90; H. Schulze, *Staat und Nation in der europäischen Geschichte*, 2nd edn, München: Beck, 2004, pp. 108ff.
3 On the history of Italian Unification see P. Milza, *Storia d'Italia: dalla preistoria ai giorni nostri* (transl. to Italian Studio Oltremare), Milano: Corbaccio, 2006, pp. 644ff.
4 Article 1 TEU.
5 G. Jellinek, *Allgemeine Staatslehre*, 3rd edn, Berlin: Häring, pp. 394ff.
6 See only J. Delbrück and R. Wolfrum, *Völkerrecht: Band I: Die Grundlagen. Die Völkerrechtssubjekte*, 2nd edn, Berlin: de Gruyter, 1989, pp. 126ff.
7 D. Anzilotti, *Lehrbuch des Völkerrechts* (transl. to German C. Bruns and K. Schmid), Berlin: de Gruyter, 1929, p. 32.
8 *Supplement to the American Journal of International Law* 28, 1934, 75–8.
9 Jellinek, *Allgemeine Staatslehre*, pp. 406ff.
10 Criticized by K. Popper, *Die offene Gesellschaft und ihre Feinde, Der Zauber Platons*, 8th edn, München: Francke, 2003.
11 Platon, *Der Staat* (transl. to German F. Schleiermacher), Darmstadt: Wissenschaftliche Buchgesellschaft, 1971, 462a–464b.
12 Aristotle, *Politics*, III.9, cited from Aristotles *Politik* (transl. to German E. Schütrumpf), Berlin: Akademie-Verlag, 1991, translation by author.
13 H. Kitto, *The Greeks*, Baltimore: Penguin, 1951, p. 66.
14 R. Dunbar, *Grooming, Gossip, and the Evolution of Language*, Harvard: Harvard University Press, 1996, pp. 69–79.
15 Case BvR 2134, 2159/92, judgment of 12 October 1993, *Entscheidungen des Bundesverfassungsgerichts* 89, pp. 155ff. at 186.
16 H. Heller, 'Politische Demokratie und soziale Homogenität', in Drath *et al.* (eds) *Gesammelte Schriften*, vol. II, Leiden: Sijthoff, 1971, pp. 421–33.
17 H. Heller, *Staatslehre*, 6th edn, Tübingen: Mohr, 1983, p. 185.
18 J. Weiler, 'Der Staat "über alles"', Demos, Telos und die Maastricht-Entscheidung des Bundesverfassungsgerichts', *Jahrbuch des öffentlichen Rechts der Gegenwart* 44, 1996, 91ff. at 95.
19 Infamous: C. Schmitt, 'Der Führer schützt das Recht', *Deutsche Juristen-Zeitung* 39, 1934, 945ff. On Schmitt: R. Mehring, *Carl Schmitt: Aufstieg und Fall: Eine Biographie*, München: Beck, 2009.
20 Transl. C. Tomuschat *et al.* Online. Available at: www.gesetze-im-internet.de/englisch_gg/index.html (accessed 26 August 2012). This translation will be used also for further references to the Basic Law. I discuss this principle and its historical roots in H. Hestermeyer, 'Un análisis sincrónico del principio de la homogeneidad: Un principio clave de sistemas federales y sistemas de integración', in J.I. Núñez Leiva (ed.) *Nuevas Perspectivas en Derecho Público*, Santiago: Librotecnia, 2011, pp. 559–90.
21 See M. Vogt, 'Die Weimarer Republik (1918–1933)', in M. Vogt (ed.) *Deutsche Geschichte. Von den Anfängen bis zur Gegenwart*, 3rd edn, Frankfurt am Main: Fischer, 2006, pp. 616ff.
22 H. Kelsen, *Reine Rechtslehre. Studienausgabe der 1. Auflage 1934*, Tübingen: Mohr Siebeck, 2008.
23 H. Kelsen, *Allgemeine Staatslehre*, Wien: Österreichische Staatsdruckerei (reprint) 1993, p. 16; see also H. Dreier, *Rechtslehre, Staatssoziologie und Demokratietheorie bei Hans Kelsen*, 2nd edn, Baden-Baden: Nomos, 1990, p. 209.

24 T. Litt, *Individuum und Gemeinschaft*, 3rd edn, Leipzig: Teubner, 1926. See also M. Stolleis, *Geschichte des öffentlichen Rechts in Deutschland: Band III: 1914–1945*, München: Beck, 1999, pp. 174ff.; Kelsen pointed out discrepancies in Smend's treatment of Litt in H. Kelsen, *Der Staat als Integration: Eine prinzipielle Auseinandersetzung*, Wien: Springer, 1930, pp. 6–8.

25 R. Smend, *Verfassung und Verfassungsrecht*, München: Duncker & Humblot, 1928, pp. 2, 6–9, 18, 25–65, 72. For criticism from the point of view of the *Reine Rechtslehre* see H. Kelsen, *Der Staat als Integration: Eine prinzipielle Auseinandersetzung*, Wien: Springer, 1930. Heller irreverently quipped that integration could hardly be regarded as the core of the state as it was just as important for a bowling club. Heller, *Staatslehre*, p. 187.

26 C. Schmitt, *Politische Theologie: Vier Kapitel zur Lehre von der Souveränität*, 9th edn, Berlin: Duncker & Humblot, 2009, p. 19.

27 C. Schmitt, *Über die drei Arten des rechtswissenschaftlichen Denkens*, Hamburg: Hanseatische, 1934, pp. 24ff.

28 C. Schmitt, *Verfassungslehre*, 9th edn, Berlin: Duncker & Humblot, 2003, pp. 223ff.

29 Ibid., p. 232 (translation by the author).

30 Kelsen, *Allgemeine Staatslehre*, pp. 7–9, 149–50.

31 K. Doehring, *Allgemeine Staatslehre: Eine systematische Darstellung*, 3rd edn, Heidelberg: Müller, 2004, p. 24.

32 Heller, *Staatslehre*, pp. 38, 43–4.

33 Ibid., p. 268.

34 E. Renan, *Qu'est-ce qu'une nation?*, 1882. Online. Available at: www.bmlisieux.com/archives/nation01.htm (accessed 18 March 2011), chapter 3.

35 Heller, *Staatslehre*, pp. 181–2, 185–6.

36 Heller, 'Politische Demokratie und soziale Homogenität', pp. 427ff.

37 Schmitt lost his political status in 1936/1937 through a conspiracy of his enemies – not because of a realization of the nature of the Nazi regime. Mehring, *Carl Schmitt: Aufstieg und Fall: Eine Biographie*, pp. 378ff.

38 Stolleis, *Geschichte des öffentlichen Rechts in Deutschland*, p. 323.

39 C. Schmitt, *Staat, Bewegung, Volk: Die Dreigliederung der politischen Einheit*, Hamburg: Hanseatische, 1933. On the development of the term *Volk* during the Weimar Republic and the Third Reich see also O. Lepsius, *Die gegensatzaufhebende Begriffsbildung: Methodenentwicklungen in der Weimarer Republik und ihr Verhältnis zur Ideologisierung der Rechtswissenschaft unter dem Nationalsozialismus*, München: Beck, 1994, pp. 13–49.

40 Mehring, *Carl Schmitt: Aufstieg und Fall: Eine Biographie*, pp. 374ff.; Stolleis, *Geschichte des öffentlichen Rechts in Deutschland*, p. 252.

41 Sources for the figures are: Statistisches Bundesamt, *Bevölkerung und Erwerbstätigkeit: Bevölkerung mit Migrationshintergrund – Ergebnisse des Mikorzensus*, Wiesbaden, 2009 (2010) as well as Bundeszentrale für politische Bildung *et al.*, *Focus Migration, Länderprofil Nr. 1 Deutschland*, May 2007. Online. Available at: www.destatis.de (accessed 18 March 2011).

42 Unlike Article 146 or the preamble Article 20(2) fails to modify the word 'people' with 'German'. Some authors have argued that the provision hence refers to a larger subset of mankind. However, Isensee convincingly argues that the German constitution assumes the *demos* to be, by default, the German people, rendering the constant repetition of the word 'German' superfluous (J. Isensee,

'Abschied der Demokratie vom Demos: Ausländerwahlrecht als Identitätsfrage für Volk, Demokratie und Verfassung', in D. Schwab *et al.* (eds) *Staat, Kirche, Wissenschaft in einer pluralistischen Gesellschaft: Festschrift zum 65. Geburtstag von Paul Mikat*, Berlin: Duncker & Humblot, 1990, pp. 705ff. at 720–2); see also: M. Zuleeg, 'Zur Verfassungsmäßigkeit der Einführung des Kommunalwahlrechts in Nordrhein-Westfalen', *Kritische Vierteljahresschrift für Gesetzgebung und Rechtswissenschaft* 70, 1987, 322–30.

43 See, e.g. F. Wittreck, 'Art. 116', in H. Dreier (ed.) *Grundgesetz Kommentar*, 2nd edn, Tübingen: Mohr Siebeck, 2008, paras 1–105; J. Kokott, 'Art. 116', in M. Sachs (ed.) *Grundgesetz Kommentar*, 5th edn, München: Beck, 2009, paras 1–34; H. Jarass, 'Art. 116', in H. Jarass and B. Pieroth (eds) *GG Grundgesetz für die Bundesrepublik Deutschland Kommentar*, 10th edn, München: Beck, 2009, paras 1–17.

44 See, e.g. Wittreck, 'Art. 116', para. 3.

45 Gesetz über die Angelegenheiten der Vertriebenen und Flüchtlinge of 19 May 1953 as publicized on 10 August 2007, *Bundesgesetzblatt* I, 1902, last amended on 7 July 2009, *Bundesgesetzblatt* I, 1694.

46 The provision goes back to a 1939 definition that in a second part withheld German *Volkszugehörigkeit* from people of other races. See A. Makarov and H. von Mangoldt, *Deutsches Staatsangehörigkeitsrecht: Kommentar*, Abschnitt 11, 10th edn, Frankfurt am Main: Metzner, 1993, para. 5.

47 T. Gnatzy, 'Art. 116', in B. Schmidt Bleibtreu (ed.) *GG Kommentar zum Grundgesetz*, Köln: Heymanns, 2011, para. 9.

48 Jarass, 'Art. 116', para. 3.

49 I. von Münch, *Die deutsche Staatsangehörigkeit: Vergangenheit – Gegenwart – Zukunft*, Berlin: De Gruyter Recht, 2007, pp. 152ff.; K. Hailbronner, 'Grundlagen', in K. Hailbronner *et al.* (eds) *Staatsangehörigkeitsrecht*, 5th edn, München: Beck, 2010, paras 1–67.

50 Adopted on 16 December 1966, UNTS, vol. 999, No. 14668.

51 Adopted on 16 December 1966, UNTS, vol. 993, No. 14531.

52 UN General Assembly, Resolution No. 2625 (XXV), 'Declaration on Principles of International Law concerning Friendly Relations and Co-operation among States in accordance with the Charter of the United Nations', 24 October 1970.

53 ICJ, *Western Sahara*, advisory opinion of 16 October 1975, *ICJ Reports 1975*, p. 12, para. 70; *East Timor (Portugal v Australia)*, judgment of 30 June 1995, *ICJ Reports 1995*, p. 90, paras 31 and 37; *Legal Consequences of the Construction of a Wall in the Occupied Palestinian Territory*, advisory opinion of 9 July 2004, *ICJ Reports 2004*, p. 136, para. 118.

54 See only D. Thürer and T. Burri, 'Self-Determination', in R. Wolfrum (ed.) *Max Planck Encyclopedia of Public International Law*, Oxford: Oxford University Press, 2011; E. McWhinney, *Self-Determination of Peoples and Plural-Ethnic States in Contemporary International Law: Failed States, Nation-Building, and the Alternative, Federal Option*, Leiden: M. Nijhoff, 2007; J. Klabbers, 'The Right to be Taken Seriously: Self-Determination in International Law', *Human Rights Quarterly* 28, 2006, 186–206; C. Tomuschat (ed.) *Modern Law of Self-Determination*, Dordrecht: M. Nijhoff, 1993; S. Oeter, 'Selbstbestimmungsrecht im Wandel, Überlegungen zur Debatte um Selbstbestimmung, Sezessionsrecht und "vorzeitige" Anerkennung', *Zeitschrift für ausländisches öffentliches Recht und Völkerrecht* 52, 1992, 741–80.

55 ICJ, *Accordance with International Law of the Unilateral Declaration of Independence in Respect of Kosovo*, advisory opinion of 22 July 2010, *ICJ Reports 2010*, p. 1; see also: C. Pippan, 'The International Court of Justice's advisory opinion on Kosovo's declaration of independence', *Europäisches Journal für Minderheitenfragen* 3, 2010, 145–66; C. Ryngaert, 'The ICJ's advisory opinion on Kosovo's declaration of independence: A missed opportunity?', *Netherlands International Law Review* 57, 2010, 481–94.

56 Tribunal Constitucional de España, No. 31/2010, judgment of 28 June 2010, *Boletin oficial del Estado* No. 172, 16 July 2010. Online. Available at: www.tribunalconstitucional.es/es/jurisprudencia/Paginas/Sentencia.aspx?cod=9873 (accessed 18 March 2011).

57 P. Kirchhof, 'Der demokratische Rechtsstaat – die Staatsform der Zugehörigen', in J. Isensee and P. Kirchhof (eds) *Handbuch des Staatsrechts*, vol. IX, section 221, Heidelberg: Müller, 1997, para. 16. Similar: F. Ossenbühl, 'Maastricht und das Grundgesetz – eine verfassungsrechtliche Wende?', *Deutsches Verwaltungsblatt*, 1993, pp. 629–37 at 634; P. Kirchhof, 'Verfaßter Staat ohne verfaßte Gesellschaft?', in G. Pfeiffer *et al.* (eds) *Der verfaßte Rechtsstaat. Festgabe für Karin Graßhof*, Heidelberg: Müller, 1998, pp. 17–18.

58 J. Isensee, 'Abschied der Demokratie vom Demos: Ausländerwahlrecht als Identitätsfrage für Volk, Demokratie und Verfassung', in D. Schwab *et al.* (eds) *Staat, Kirche, Wissenschaft in einer pluralistischen Gesellschaft: Festschrift zum 65. Geburtstag von Paul Mikat*, Berlin: Duncker & Humblot, 1990, pp. 705–40 at 708.

59 Explicitly relying on Schmitt, E. Böckenförde, 'Demokratie als Verfassungsprinzip', in J. Isensee and P. Kirchhof, *Handbuch des Staatsrechts*, vol. I, section 22, Heidelberg: Müller, 1987, paras 46ff.

60 P. Kirchhof, 'Der deutsche Staat im Prozeß der europäischen Integration', in J. Isensee and P. Kirchhof (eds) *Handbuch des Staatsrechts*, vol. VII, section 183, Heidelberg: Müller, 1992, paras 12 and 25; Ossenbühl, 'Maastricht und das Grundgesetz', p. 634.

61 B.-O. Bryde, 'Die bundesrepublikanische Volksdemokratie als Irrweg der Demokratietheorie', *Staatswissenschaft und Staatspraxis* 5, 1994, 305ff. at 311–13, 322.

62 I. Pernice, 'Carl Schmitt, Rudolf Smend und die europäische Integration', *Archiv des öffentlichen Rechts* 120, 1995, 100–20 at 107.

63 F. Hanschmann, *Der Begriff der Homogenität in der Verfassungslehre und Europarechtswissenschaft. Zur These von der Notwendigkeit homogener Kollektive unter besonderer Berücksichtigung der Homogenitätskriterien 'Geschichte' und 'Sprache'*, Berlin: Springer, 2008, pp. 179, 236, 302.

64 A. von Bogdandy, 'Europäische und nationale Identität: Integration durch Verfassungsrecht?', *Veröffentlichungen der Vereinigung der Deutschen Staatsrechtslehrer* 62, 2003, 156–93 at 173.

65 Weiler, 'Der Staat "über alles" ', p. 118.

66 C. Tomuschat, 'Die Europäische Union unter der Aufsicht des Bundesverfassungsgerichts', *Europäische Grundrechte Zeitschrift* 20, 1993, 489–96 at 494; see also Weiler, 'Der Staat "über alles" ', p. 111 (stating that the Court could have acted constructively by pointing out where the EU suffers from a democracy deficit).

67 D. König, 'Das Urteil des Bundesverfassungsgerichts zum Vertrag von Maastricht – ein Stolperstein auf dem Weg in die europäische Integration?', *Zeitschrift*

für ausländisches öffentliches Recht und Völkerrecht 54, 1994, 17–49 at 38. See also J.A. Frowein, 'Das Maastricht-Urteil und die Grenzen der Verfassungsgerichtsbarkeit', *Zeitschrift für ausländisches öffentliches Recht und Völkerrecht* 54, 1994, 1ff. at 8–10.

68 A. von Bogdandy, 'Europäische Verfassung und europäische Identität', in G. Folke Schuppert *et al.* (eds) *Europawissenschaft*, Baden-Baden: Nomos, 2005, pp. 331–71 at 362; A. von Bogdandy, 'Zur Übertragbarkeit staatsrechtlicher Figuren auf die Europäische Union: Vom Nutzen der Gestaltidee supranationaler Föderalismus anhand des Demokratieprinzips', in M. Brenner *et al.* (eds) *Der Staat des Grundgesetzes – Kontinuität und Wandel: Festschrift für Peter Badura zum siebzigsten Geburtstag*, Tübingen: Mohr Siebeck, 2004, pp. 1033–52 at 1045; P. Huber, 'Demokratie ohne Volk oder Demokratie der Völker? Zur Demokratiefähigkeit der Europäischen Union', in J. Drexl *et al.* (eds) *Europäische Demokratie*, Baden-Baden: Nomos, 1999, pp. 27ff. at 57.

69 Weiler, 'Der Staat "über alles"', pp. 119 and 127; J. Weiler, 'To Be a European Citizen: Eros and Civilization', in J. Weiler, *The Constitution of Europe: Do the New Clothes Have an Emperor? and Other Essays on European Integration*, Cambridge: Cambridge University Press, 2007, pp. 324–57 at 346–7.

70 The following section is largely based on D. Berreby, *Us and Them: Understanding Your Tribal Mind*, New York: Little, Brown and Company, 2005.

71 M. Shih *et al.*, 'Stereotype Susceptibility: Identity Salience and Shifts in Quantitative Performance', *Psychological Science* 10, 1999, 80–3.

72 M. Sherif *et al.*, *The Robbers Cave Experiment: Intergroup Conflict and Cooperation*, Middletown: Wesleyan University Press, 1988.

73 L. Diab, 'A Study of Intragroup and Intergroup Relations among Experimentally Produced Small Groups', *Genetic Psychology Monographs* 82, 1970, 49–82.

74 H. Tajfel, 'Experiments in Intergroup Discrimination', *Scientific American* 223, 1970, 96–102.

75 Vgl. G. Roellecke, 'Zum Problem der Nation', in O. Depenheuer *et al.* (eds) *Staat im Wort: Festschrift für Josef Isensee*, Heidelberg: Müller, 2007, pp. 29–42 at 33.

76 Grawert points out that part of what makes them true and relevant is that they are used in the process of self-identification of a people. R. Grawert, 'Staatsvolk und Staatsangehörigkeit', in J. Isensee and P. Kirchhof (eds) *Handbuch des Staatsrechts*, vol. II, section 16, 3rd edn, 2004, para. 14.

77 The author is acutely aware that this fallback position is open to charges of circularity: the state is defined by three elements, including its people; the people in turn are defined by the state.

78 Bundesverfassungsgericht, 2 BvE 2/08, judgment of 30 June 2009, para. 226. Online. Available at: www.bundesverfassungsgericht.de/en/decisions/es20090630_2bve000208en.html (accessed 18 March 2011).

79 A reverse obligation of the EU to respect the national identities of Member States is contained in Article 4(2) TEU.

80 A. von Bogdandy, 'Prinzipien der Rechtsfortbildung im europäischen Rechtsraum: Überlegungen zum Lissabon-Urteil des BVerfG', *Neue Juristische Wochenschrift* 63, 2010, 1–5; C. Calliess, 'Nach dem Lissabon-Urteil des Bundesverfassungsgerichts: Parlamentarische Integrationsverantwortung auf europäischer und nationaler Ebene', *Zeitschrift für Gesetzgebung* 25, 2010, 1–34; D. Grimm, 'Das Grundgesetz als Riegel vor einer Verstaatlichung der Europäischen Union: Zum Lissabon-Urteil des Bundesverfassungsgerichts', *Der Staat* 48, 2009, 475–95; P. Häberle, 'Das

retrospektive Lissabon-Urteil als versteinernde Maastricht II-Entscheidung', *Jahrbuch des öffentlichen Rechts der Gegenwart* 58, 2010, 317–36; M. Jestaedt, 'Warum in die Ferne schweifen, wenn der Maßstab liegt so nah? Verfassungshandwerkliche Anfragen an das Lissabon-Urteil des BVerfG', *Der Staat* 48, 2009, 497–516; J. Khushal Murkens, 'Identity Trumps Integration: The Lisbon Treaty in the German Federal Constitutional Court', *Der Staat* 48, 2009, 517–34; M. Nettesheim, 'Die Lissabon-Entscheidung des Bundesverfassungsgerichts: grundgesetzliche Grenzen der Integration', *Jahrbuch des Föderalismus* 11, 2010, 403–13; C. Schönberger, 'Die Europäische Union zwischen "Demokratiedefizit" und Bundesstaatsverbot: Anmerkungen zum Lissabon-Urteil des Bundesverfassungsgerichts', *Der Staat* 48, 2009, 535–58; D. Thym, 'Europäische Integration im Schaaten souveränder Staatlichkeit: Anmerkungen zum Lissabon-Urteil des Bundesverfassungsgerichts', *Der Staat* 48, 2009, 559–86; C. Tomuschat, 'Lisbon, Terminal of the European Integration Process? The Jugement of the German Constitutional Court of 30 June 2009', *Zeitschrift für ausländisches öffentliches Recht und Völkerrecht* 70, 2010, 251–82; R. Wahl, 'Die Schwebelage im Verhältnis von Europäischer Union und Mitgliedstaaten: Zum Lissabon-Urteil des Bundesverfassungsgerichts', *Der Staat* 48, 2009, 587–614.

2 Nationality as a human right

Serena Forlati

Introduction

The aim of this chapter is to assess whether an individual right to a nationality can be established in contemporary international law. As is well known, under 'classical' international law states enjoyed unfettered discretion in regulating nationality issues. In its 1923 advisory opinion on the *Nationality Decrees in Tunis and Morocco* the Permanent Court of International Justice held that, 'in the present state of international law, questions of nationality are [. . .] in principle within [each State's] reserved domain' in the absence of any 'obligations which it may have undertaken towards other States';[1] a similar stance was taken by the International Court of Justice in the *Nottebohm Case*, of 1955.[2]

The disputes underlying those two pronouncements clearly show that the existence of any limitations in this regard was discussed essentially from the perspective of inter-state relations. On one hand, attribution of nationality by one state could be deemed an unlawful interference with the bond of allegiance between other states and the concerned individual, thus infringing the formers' sovereignty (this was the thrust of the UK's objections to the nationality decrees relating to Tunisia and Morocco);[3] on the other hand, attribution of nationality in the absence of significant factual ties between the individual and the attributing state could lead to non-recognition of the nationality bond on the international plane (as in *Nottebohm*). Also, the early efforts to regulate and eradicate statelessness, through the Hague Convention on Certain Questions relating to the Conflict of Nationality Laws[4] and the Protocol relating to Certain Cases of Statelessness,[5] can be read from this perspective; this is made clear by the preamble of the Convention, expressing the belief 'that it is in the general interest of the *international community* to secure that all its members should recognize that every person should have a nationality and should have one nationality only', while there is no mention of the existence of individuals' (and possibly competing) interests in this context.[6]

The developments in the field of international human rights protection since 1945, alongside with the gradual recognition of the international legal personality of individuals,[7] have significantly modified this legal picture. While the need to respect the sovereignty of other states is still a relevant factor in assessing whether domestic choices concerning nationality are lawful under international law,[8] further limitations in this regard may now stem from rights accruing to individuals, specifically from the right to a nationality. In the following paragraphs, the elements of international practice pointing at the existence of such a human right will be analysed in an attempt to assess where the balance between states' discretion and individual entitlements is struck today.

The right to a nationality in international human rights instruments

The existence of a human right to nationality was set out for the first time by the Universal Declaration of Human Rights (UDHR), whose Article 15(1) stipulates: 'Everyone has the right to a nationality. No one shall be arbitrarily deprived of his nationality nor denied the right to change his nationality.' The right to *acquire* a nationality was subsequently included in a number of international treaties. Some of them, such as the International Covenant on Civil and Political Rights (ICCPR),[9] the Convention on the Rights of the Child (CRC),[10] the International Convention on the Protection of the Rights of All Migrant Workers and Members of Their Families,[11] the Covenant on the Rights of the Child in Islam[12] and the African Charter on the Rights and Welfare of the Child (ACRWC),[13] establish this right only in favour of children, whereas the Convention on the Rights of Persons with Disabilities (CRPD) includes a provision concerning specifically this group of persons.[14] Other instruments, notably the American Convention on Human Rights (ACHR),[15] the Commonwealth of Independent States Convention on Human Rights and Fundamental Freedoms (CIS Convention),[16] and the Arab Charter on Human Rights (ArCHR)[17] use a broader language, encompassing all human beings. The European Convention on Nationality (ECN) qualifies the right to a nationality and the need to avoid statelessness as 'principles' on which 'rules on nationality of each State Party shall be based'.[18] Various other instruments, adopted at universal and regional level, aim at reducing statelessness both in general[19] and in relation to specific circumstances, such as state succession.[20] Furthermore, according to the Inter-American Court of Human Rights (IACHR) 'it is generally accepted today that nationality is an inherent human right of all human beings';[21] the Human Rights Council stated that 'the right to a nationality of every human person is a fundamental human right';[22] also according to the Human Rights Committee (HRC) there is a 'right of all persons to receive a nationality'.[23]

Nevertheless, the reluctance shown by states in giving up their discretion in these matters hinders full implementation of the relevant treaty provisions. The absence of universally accepted standards on attribution of nationality was the main reason for perplexity in the negotiations on the right to a nationality concerning, for instance, the UDHR,[24] the ICCPR,[25] and, to a lesser extent, the CRC.[26] It is still difficult to identify in all situations the state against which affected individuals are entitled to invoke their right to *acquire* a nationality; in the words of Emmanuel Decaux, 'Le droit à la nationalité a un sujet et un objet, mais non un débiteur'.[27] This, in turn, gives rise to doubts as regards the customary nature of the right to a nationality. Nonetheless, it would seem that the almost 65 years since the adoption of the UDHR have not passed in vain. Some trends towards the identification of the duty bearers can be clearly assessed: it remains to be seen whether those trends reflect, at least in part, binding rules – possibly of customary law.

While the right to *retain* and to *change* one's nationality are less problematic in this regard, they raise other difficulties. They are specifically encompassed by UDHR, but are the object of binding obligations only in the context of a limited number of treaties – namely, the ACHR,[28] the CIS Convention,[29] the ECN,[30] and the ArCHR[31] – that, moreover, do not adopt a uniform formulation of these rights. However, the rationale underlying the prohibition of arbitrary deprivation of nationality is reflected by the 1961 Convention on the Reduction of Statelessness (1961 Convention)[32] and Article 8 CRC; as we shall see, this principle is by now part of customary international law.

The right to acquire a nationality

The tension between states' discretion and acknowledgement of a fully fledged human right to a nationality emerges very clearly as regards the acquisition of nationality. Even when a treaty stipulates such a right, the criteria identifying the addressee of the obligation to grant nationality are often not specified. When the relevant criteria are actually set out, 'original' acquisition of nationality by birth (or at birth[33]) is usually distinguished from subsequent, 'derivative', naturalization. The two situations will be examined separately, and the developments in the context of state succession are the object of a specific chapter in this volume.

Acquisition of nationality by birth

A general consensus has gradually emerged as to the right of children to acquire a nationality: evidence of such a consensus comes from the high ratification rate of the ICCPR, which is now in force for 167 states,[34] and especially from the virtually universal ratification of the CRC, now counting 193 parties.[35] In this regard, it is noteworthy that a number of parties appended reservations affecting the right to acquire a nationality when ratifying the CRC; however, several reservations were withdrawn in recent years.[36] Reservations or declarations which are still operating concern seven parties: Oman and Monaco appended declarations directed at avoiding changes to this aspect of their domestic legislation;[37] whereas the Bahamas, the Cook Islands, the Holy See and Singapore formally reserved the right to apply their national legislation;[38] only the United Arab Emirates (UAE) assume that 'the acquisition of nationality is an internal matter and one that is regulated and whose terms and conditions are established by national legislation.'[39] This single objection of principle would not seem to be enough to exclude the emergence of a right for any child to acquire a nationality also under customary international law. Such a customary rule would bind also the states whose reservations under the CRC are still operating, possibly with the exception of UAE, which might claim to be a persistent objector.

Nonetheless, it is at times still problematic to identify the state that is bound to grant nationality by birth in a specific case. Neither the ICCPR nor the CRC specify the relevant criteria. While other instruments do set forth such criteria, those adopted at universal level do not enjoy wide participation. The most prominent example in this regard is the 1961 Convention,[40] which combines rules based on the principles of both *jus soli* and *jus sanguinis*. On one hand, according to Article 1(1) each 'Contracting State shall grant its nationality to a person born in its territory who would otherwise be stateless';[41] on the other hand, Article 4(1) stipulates:

> A Contracting State shall grant its nationality to a person, not born in the territory of a Contracting State, who would otherwise be stateless, if the nationality of one of his parents at the time of the person's birth was that of that State.

Notwithstanding its low ratification rate, the United Nations High Commissioner for Refugees (UNHCR) uses the 1961 Convention as a yardstick to assess domestic legislation on nationality issues.[42] It is also significant that the rules it stipulates are reflected in some regional instruments: more specifically, the *jus soli* principle, as set forth by Article 1, is accepted also by the ECN,[43] the ACHR,[44] and the ACRWC.[45] According to the UNHCR, however, in 2010 only 100 states were party to either the 1961 Convention or a regional treaty that contains a safeguard for children born in the territory who would otherwise be stateless.[46]

These developments offer some useful elements for the interpretation of Article 24(3) ICCPR and Article 7 CRC; as provided by Article 7(2) CRC, implementation of the right to a nationality must be ensured by the parties 'in accordance with their national law and *their obligations under the relevant international instruments in this field*, in particular where the child would otherwise be stateless', whereas the same conclusion could be drawn for the ICCPR in the light of the principle of systemic integration.[47]

Nonetheless, almost half the states of the world did not accept the *jus soli* principle, even in the restrictive formulation accepted by the 1961 Convention;[48] furthermore, acquisition of nationality may be subject to conditions under both that text and ECN, whereas national legislations adopt a variety of solutions on this point.[49] A more uniform approach has emerged as regards foundlings, who are entitled to the nationality of the state where they are born under both the 1961 Convention and the regional conventions mentioned above. The principle is accepted even by countries which are not parties to those conventions and that otherwise adhere to the *jus sanguinis* principle, e.g. Japan,[50] Oman,[51] or Italy.[52] Still, Bhutan, which did not include a similar provision in its nationality law, was not the object of specific criticism in this regard by the Committee on the Rights of the Child (CtRC): when assessing the country's respect for Article 7, the CtRC expressed its concern only in general terms, urging Bhutan to take 'the necessary measures to ensure that no child is or risks being stateless, in accordance of article 7 of the Convention'.[53] It is thus not possible to conclude that every child who would otherwise be stateless is automatically entitled to the nationality of her or his country of birth under the ICCPR, the CRC, or general international law.[54]

This does not mean, however, that the state under whose jurisdiction a child is born is free from any obligation as regards her or his acquisition of a nationality.[55]

As the HRC pointed out, 'States are required to adopt every appropriate measure, both internally and in cooperation with other States, to ensure that every child has a nationality when he is born'.[56] The African Committee of Experts on the Rights and Welfare of the Child (ACERWC) took a similar approach in its landmark decision on the *Nubian Children* case, stressing that all ACRWC rights 'generate obligations to respect, protect, promote and fulfil. This is no less so in respect of the rights implicated when nationality and identity rights are violated'.[57]

The test that should be applied in assessing states' behaviour in the field of nationality would appear to be one of fairness, as with all positive obligations in the field of human rights. A parallel may be made, in this regard, with the positive obligations concerning admission of aliens into a state's territory under Article 8 of the European Convention on Human Rights (ECHR). The European Court of Human Rights (ECtHR) acknowledged that states are, in principle, entitled under international law to establish autonomously the criteria for such admission. Nonetheless, according to its case law a 'fair balance [...] has to be struck between the competing interests of the individual and of the community as a whole'.[58]

Whereas the position of the state where a child is born is indeed distinguishable from that of the generality of states, this implies the obligation to take all reasonable steps, in the light of the circumstances of every specific case, to ensure that she or he obtains a nationality. That state should, in particular, ensure that the birth is properly registered (although this is often very problematic in practice, as shown for instance by the *Yean and Bosico* case[59]). Furthermore, if the state does not intend to grant nationality, it should take action in order to verify if and under which conditions the child could acquire the nationality of another state; the state should further inform the child or the guardian of such an option and assist them so that they may apply successfully for an alternative nationality.[60] An actual obligation to grant nationality would seem to arise if no other state is ready to confer it,[61] or if it is unreasonable, under the specific circumstances, to expect the child to seek it.[62] If, however, the refusal to take such a step is a form of 'nationality shopping', the situation could be treated as one of voluntary renunciation and, absent any more specific treaty engagement, requiring attribution of nationality by the state of birth would appear to go beyond the fair balance threshold mentioned above.

Naturalization

The picture is quite different as regards naturalization. With the possible exception of the area of state succession, international obligations in this field are much more flexible than the ones concerning acquisition of nationality by birth. This applies also in cases of de jure or de facto statelessness: Article 32 of the 1954 Convention relating to the Status of Stateless Persons[63] and Article 34 of the 1951 Convention relating to the Status of Refugees[64] only impose an obligation to *facilitate* access to the nationality of the state of habitual residence, without setting forth any entitlement to it for the individual concerned. Article 6(4) ECN uses similar wording, and treats stateless persons and refugees on the same footing as other groups of individuals (e.g. spouses or children of nationals).[65] At domestic level, states show a clear tendency to keep their discretion in deciding who should acquire citizenship through naturalization; this is well exemplified by the stance of the US Court of Appeal (6th Circuit) to the effect that 'naturalization [is] a privilege to be given or withheld on such conditions as Congress sees fit'.[66]

Still, some limitations to a state's discretion come, on one hand, from the need to respect both the will of the individual concerned and the sovereignty of other states. Thus, naturalization without the addressee's consent would appear to be unlawful,[67] whereas consent may not be enough for some extreme 'passportization' practices to be deemed lawful.[68] Beyond these specific situations, the requirement to show an effective link between individuals and states is not a condition for the lawfulness of naturalization. Even as regards attribution of effects to such naturalization on the international plane, the *Nottebohm* precedent seems to have lost, at least in part, its relevance.[69] On the other hand, further requirements stem from some principles of more general scope, such as those relating to procedural safeguards against arbitrariness[70] and to the prohibition of discrimination, which is by now a customary rule of international law, and has a peremptory nature. Moreover, the right to a nationality is a principle that influences (or should influence) the interpretation both of other international legal rules and of national legislation on the issue.

Prohibition of discrimination

A prohibition of discrimination in the field of nationality is set forth by instruments such as Convention on the Elimination of All Forms of Racial Discrimination, which binds states parties to 'guarantee the right of everyone, without distinction as to race, colour, or national or ethnic origin, to equality before the law, notably in the enjoyment of the [...] right to nationality';[71] the 1961 Convention, setting forth that '[a] Contracting State may not deprive any person or group of persons of their nationality on racial, ethnic, religious or political grounds';[72] the Convention on the Elimination of All Forms of Discrimination against Women, which imposes the obligation to 'grant women equal rights with men to acquire, change or retain their nationality',[73] as well as 'with respect to the nationality of their children';[74] CRPD, to the effect that 'States parties should recognize, inter alia, the right of persons with disabilities to a nationality, on an equal basis with others';[75] and ECN, stipulating that the 'rules of a State Party on nationality shall not contain distinctions or include any practice which amount to discrimination on the grounds of sex, religion, race, colour or national or ethnic origin.'[76]

Moreover, the general prohibition of discrimination included in human rights treaties applies to the acquisition of nationality. This prohibition is stressed by a number of monitoring bodies, such as the HRC in its General Comment No. 17,[77] the IACHR in *Yean and Bosico*,[78] and, more recently, by the ACERWC in the *Nubian Children* case.[79] Even when the right to a nationality is not enshrined in a given treaty, denial of this right on a discriminatory basis may infringe other human rights. In *Modise v Botswana*, for instance, the African Commission on Human and Peoples' Rights found that denial of nationality by birth to the author of the communication, essentially because of his political opinions and activity, amounted to a breach of 3(2), 5, 12(1) and (2), 13(1) and (2), 14, and 18(1) of the African Charter of Human and Peoples' Rights.[80] A similar approach was taken by the ECtHR with regard to discrimination against children born out of wedlock; in *Genovese v Malta*, the Court held:

> [T]he denial of citizenship may raise an issue under Article 8 because of its impact on the private life of an individual, which concept is wide enough to embrace aspects of a person's social identity. [...] Maltese legislation expressly granted the right to citizenship by descent and established a procedure to that end. Consequently, the State, which has gone beyond its obligations under Article 8 in creating such a right – a possibility open to it under Article 53 of the Convention – must ensure that the right is secured without discrimination within the meaning of Article 14.[81]

The customary (and peremptory) nature of the principle of non-discrimination[82] implies that similar conclusions should be drawn also under customary international law.

The right to acquire a nationality as a principle influencing the interpretation of international legal rules and of national legislation

Even when no specific obligation to grant nationality exists at the international level, the right to acquire a nationality should influence the interpretation of other international rules in the field of human rights, as well as domestic legislation relating to attribution of nationality. As regards the interpretation of international rules, some significant developments come from the ECtHR case law. Although the right to a nationality is not specifically protected by the ECHR,[83] and ratification of the ECN and the Council of Europe Convention on the Avoidance of Statelessness in Relation to State Succession is not widespread, denial of citizenship may raise an issue under Article 8 ECHR, in that it may amount to an unlawful interference in the right to private or family life.[84] In *Kuric and others v Slovenia* the Court has dealt with the allegation that the applicants had been arbitrarily deprived of the possibility of acquiring Slovenian citizenship after Slovenia declared its independence in 1991, because they were not in a position to submit a formal request for citizenship within the short period set out in the relevant domestic legislation. Furthermore, after the deadline for applying for citizenship had expired, some applicants had become stateless.[85] While the Chamber held the issue inadmissible *ratione temporis*,[86] it did take care to stress that:

> [P]rior to 1991 the applicants did not enter Slovenia as aliens but settled there as SFRY citizens and registered their permanent residence in the same way as citizens of the then Socialist Republic of Slovenia [...]. At the moment of the "erasure" on 26 February 1992, the applicants therefore had a stronger residence status than long-term migrants.[87]

This would appear to imply that they were entitled to acquire citizenship on a non-discriminatory basis. The Chamber concluded that Article 8 had been infringed also 'in the light of relevant international-law standards aimed at the avoidance of statelessness, especially in situations of state succession'.[88]

In the Grand Chamber proceedings that took place upon referral under Article 43 ECHR, this systemic interpretation of the Convention, a rather common feature in the Court's case law, was criticized by the respondent government in that the 'erasure', the only measure that fell under the Court's jurisdiction *ratione temporis*, did not per se have an impact on citizenship;[89] but the soundness of that approach was not specifically challenged on the merits. While the Grand Chamber did not rely on the same kind of argument, it did not contradict the merits of the Chamber's findings. The same approach should be followed not only as regards situations of state succession, but also as regards other instances (notably, those concerning acquisition of nationality by birth) in which rules concerning the identification of the duty-bearer have emerged at international level.

Furthermore, it is submitted that national legislation should be interpreted, in doubtful cases, in a manner favouring acquisition of a nationality; specifically as regards children, the right to acquire a nationality is one of the elements that should be taken into account in assessing the 'best interest of the child', e.g. in the context of highly controversial situations such as those involving subrogate motherhood.[90]

The right to retain and change one's nationality

Deprivation of nationality on political, religious, or ethnic grounds, while far from uncommon,[91] is specifically prohibited by a number of treaty provisions, some of which are quoted above. If deprivation is pursued on grounds such as religion or ethnicity, denationalization may also amount to persecution for the purposes of recognition of refugee status.[92]

Whereas prohibition of discrimination has certainly acquired customary nature also as regards the right to retain one's nationality, it is not the only limitation to states' discretion in this regard under international law. The notion of 'arbitrary deprivation of nationality', which is held to be a 'general principle of international law',[93] has a broader meaning. It should be stressed, in this regard, that human rights standards do not absolutely prohibit denationalization, even if it causes statelessness: both the 1961 Convention and the ECN allow for it under specific circumstances.[94] However, such exceptions should be interpreted narrowly.[95] When no specific treaty obligations apply, the prohibition of arbitrariness would still be of relevance: as stated by the UN secretary general, deprivation of nationality 'must be in conformity with domestic law and comply with specific procedural and substantive standards, in particular the principle of proportionality';[96] it would not be arbitrary if it serves 'a legitimate purpose that is consistent with international law and, in particular, the objectives of international human rights law.'[97]

The European Court of Justice applied those standards in *Rottman*:

> A decision withdrawing naturalisation because of deception corresponds to a reason relating to the public interest. In this regard, it is legitimate for a Member State to wish to protect the special relationship of solidarity and good faith between it and its nationals and also the reciprocity of rights and duties, which form the bedrock of the bond of nationality. [...] In such a case it is, however, for the national court to ascertain whether the withdrawal decision [...] observes the principle of proportionality so far as concerns the consequences it entails for the situation of the person concerned in the light of European Union Law [...]. In this respect it is necessary to establish, in particular, whether that loss is justified in relation to the gravity of the offence committed by that person, to the lapse of time between the naturalisation decision and the withdrawal decision and to whether it is possible for that person to recover his original nationality.[98]

While these principles apply to any case of withdrawal of nationality, the test of proportionality, as formulated above, clearly implies that heavy weight should be given to the individual's interest not to be rendered stateless. This was made clear by the Eritrea-Ethiopia Claims Commission in the *Civilian claims cases 15, 16, 23 27–32*:

> [I]nternational law limits States' power to deprive persons of their nationality. In this regard, the Commission attaches particular importance to the principle expressed in Article 15, paragraph 2, of the Universal Declaration of Human Rights, that 'no one shall be arbitrarily deprived of his nationality.' In assessing whether deprivation of nationality was arbitrary, the Commission considered several factors, including whether the action had a basis in law; *whether it resulted in persons being rendered stateless*; and whether there were legitimate reasons for it to be taken given the totality of the circumstances.[99]

Also the right to change one's nationality is not absolute: the role of the individual's choices needs to be balanced against the possibly competing interests of the state whose nationality would be renounced, and against the general interest of reducing statelessness. Only arbitrary interferences in the exercise of this right should thus be deemed unlawful.[100] A state would not be bound by customary international law to allow renunciation of one nationality in favour of another one if the former is based on an effective link (e.g. residence),[101] and the renunciation aims, for instance, at avoiding taxes[102] or military service; on the other hand, seeking naturalization by a foreign state should not result in loss of the former nationality, unless the person concerned actually possesses or acquires another nationality.[103]

Furthermore, customary international law does not prohibit renunciation when this causes statelessness of the affected person. Evidence of this may be drawn from the circumstances originating cases such as *Okonkwo against Austria* or *Mogos v Romania*,[104] in which this kind of practice was the source of difficulties at international level, but was not the object of specific criticisms or protests; states rather seek to solve the practical problems caused by renunciation through specific agreements, e.g. as to the readmission of former citizens in case of expulsion.[105] On the other hand, treaty engagements such as Article 8(1) ECN confirm that states of nationality may refuse to allow renunciation in such a situation without being arbitrary, in keeping with the general aim of avoiding statelessness.[106]

Conclusion

The persisting reluctance of states to accept general limitations on their discretion to identify the criteria for attribution of citizenship, and the possibility to withdraw nationality, under specific circumstances, even if this causes statelessness, make it difficult to construe the human right to a nationality as a rule of *jus cogens*.[107] However, this right seems by now to be part of customary international law.

Specifically as regards its most problematic aspect, i.e. the right to *acquire* a nationality, a distinction needs to be made between acquisition of nationality by birth and naturalization. Recent practice shows almost universal acceptance of the principle according to which children are entitled to a nationality by reason of their birth, even if full implementation of this right is often hindered. In the absence of specific treaty obligations, the addressee of the obligation to confer nationality in this context may be identified through a test of fair balance between the interests of the states (and, specifically, of the state where a child is born) and the concerned individual, as is the case with all positive obligations. On the other hand, no obligation to grant nationality through naturalization has arisen so far, even when the concerned individuals are stateless de jure or de facto. The prohibition of discrimination applies also in these cases, whereas the right to acquire a nationality is a principle in the light of which both international and national legal rules should be interpreted.

The right to retain and change one's nationality are not framed as absolute rights, but the prohibition of arbitrariness in this field is by now part of international customary law. While a fair balance must be struck between states' and individuals' interests, the need to avoid statelessness is a key element in assessing the proportionality of any measure affecting such rights.

Notes

1 PCIJ, *Nationality Decrees in Tunisia and Morocco*, advisory opinion of 7 February 1923, PCIJ *Series B*, No. 4, p. 24.
2 ICJ, *Nottebohm Case (Second Phase) (Lichtenstein v Guatemala)*, judgment of 6 April 1955, *ICJ Reports 1955*, p. 20.
3 See I. Brownlie, 'The Relations of Nationality in Public International Law', *British Year Book of International Law* 39, 1963, pp. 284–364 at 294ff.
4 Adopted on 12 April 1930, LNTS, vol. 179, No. 4137.
5 Adopted on 12 April 1930, LNTS, vol. 179, No. 4138.
6 Emphasis added. Cf. the different wording used, e.g. in the preamble of the ECN (Strasbourg, 6 November 1997, CETS 166). See also the preamble to the ILC Draft Articles on Nationality of Natural Persons in relation to the Succession of States, adopted in 1999, *UNGAOR, Fifty-fourth Session, Supplement No. 10*, UN Doc. A/54/10 (1999 Draft Articles).
7 The fact that international legal rules may directly affect individuals was confirmed by the ICJ in *LaGrand (Germany v United States)*, judgment of 27 June 2001, *ICJ Reports 2001*, p. 492, para. 74.
8 See J.M.M. Chan, 'The Right to a Nationality as a Human Right: The Current Trend Towards Recognition', *Human Rights Law Journal* 12, 1991, 1–14 at 1; A. Peters, 'Extraterritorial Naturalizations: Between the Human Right to Nationality, State Sovereignty and Fair Principles of Jurisdiction', *German Yearbook of International Law* 53, 2010, pp. 623–725 at 624. In specific situations other international rules may also be at stake: e.g. the inclusion of

provisions on the acquisition of nationality in the Transitional Administration Law, adopted by the Iraqi Governing Council in 2004, was deemed incompatible with the law of belligerent occupation (EWCA, *Hilal Abdul-Razzaq Ali Al-Jedda v Secretary of State for the Home Department*, 29 March 2012, *per* Lord Richards, para. 98).

9 Adopted on 16 December 1966, UNTS, vol. 999, No. 14668, Article 24(3).

10 Adopted on 20 November 1989, UNTS, vol. 1577, No. 27531, Article 7.

11 Adopted on 18 December 1990, UNTS, vol. 2220, No. 39481.

12 Organization of the Islamic Conference, *Covenant on the Rights of the Child in Islam*, June 2005, OIC/9-IGGE/HRI/2004/Rep.Final, Articles 7(2)-7(3).

13 Adopted on 1 July 1990, OAU Doc. CAB/LEG/24.9/49 (1990), Article 6(3).

14 Adopted on 13 December 2006, UNTS, vol. 2515, No. 44910, Article 18. The Convention is currently in force for 126 states (Online. Available at: http://treaties.un.org (accessed 10 November 2012)).

15 Adopted on 22 November 1969, OAS Treaty Series, No. 36, Article 20. The right to a nationality is non-derogable under Article 27 of the Convention.

16 Adopted on 26 May 1995. Online. Available at: www.unhcr.org/refworld/docid/49997ae32c.html (accessed 27 June 2012), Article 24(1).

17 Adopted by the League of Arab States on 22 May 2004, reprinted in *Boston University International Law Journal* 24, 2006, 147–64, Article 29(1). The Charter, which is in force since 15 March 15 2008, provides for the non-derogability of the right to a nationality (Article 4(2)).

18 Article 4. The ECN is currently in force for 20 states (Online. Available at: www.conventions.coe.int (accessed 13 June 2012)).

19 This is the aim of the 1961 Convention, UNTS, vol. 989, No. 14458, and of the Convention on the Nationality of Married Women, 29 January 1957, UNTS, vol. 309, No. 4468.

20 See notably the 1999 Draft Articles and the 2006 Convention (Strasbourg, 19 May 2006, ECTS 200), which was ratified only by six states so far (Online. Available at: www.conventions.coe.int (accessed 13 June 2012)). On this topic see further F. Costamagna, 'Statelessness in the context of state succession: an appraisal under international law', *infra*, at 42ff.

21 IACHR, *Proposed Amendments to the Naturalization Provisions of the Constitution of Costa Rica*, advisory opinion OC-4/84 of 19 January 1984, *Series A*, No. 4, para. 32.

22 Human Rights Council, Resolution No. 20/5, 'Arbitrary Deprivation of Nationality', 16 July 2012, UN Doc. A/HRC/RES/20/5, para. 1; see already Human Rights Council Resolutions Nos. 13/2, 24 March 2010, UN Doc. A/HRC/RES/13/2; 10/13, 26 March 2009, UN Doc. A/HRC/RES/10/13; 7/10, 27 March 2008, UN Doc. A/HRC/RES/7/10; as well as UN Commission on Human Rights Resolutions Nos. 2005/45, 19 April 2005, UN Doc. E/CN.4/RES/2005/45, and 1999/28, 26 April 1999, UN Doc. E/CN.4/RES/1999/28. Cf. also the conclusions of the secretary general's report to the Human Rights Council, 'Human Rights and Arbitrary Deprivation of Nationality', 14 December 2009, A/HRC/13/34, para. 56:

> The right of every individual to a nationality is clearly regulated in international human rights law, which provides for the explicit recognition of that right. International human rights law also explicitly provides for the prohibition of arbitrary deprivation of nationality.

23 HRC, 'Concluding Observations: Mongolia', 30 March 2011, CCPR/C/MNG/CO/5, para. 26.

24 I. Ziemele and G.C. Schram, 'Article 15', in G. Alfredsson and A. Eide (eds) *The Universal Declaration of Human Rights – A Common Standard of Achievement*, The Hague–Boston–London: M. Nijhoff, 1999, pp. 297–323 at 301.

25 M. Nowak, *U.N. Covenant on Civil and Political Rights – CCPR Commentary*, 2nd edn, Kehl: N.P. Engel, 2005, p. 561.

26 I. Ziemele, *Article 7 – The Right to Birth Registration, Name and Nationality, and the Right to Know and be Cared for by Parents*, part of A. Alen and others (eds) *A Commentary on the United Nations Convention on the Rights of the Child*, Leiden-Boston: M. Nijhoff, 2007, pp. 23ff.

27 E. Decaux, 'Le droit à une nationalité, en tant que droit de l'homme', *Revue trimestrielle des droits de l'homme* 86, 2011, 237–60 at 242. See further J.F. Rezek, 'Le droit international et la nationalité', *Collected Courses of the Hague Academy of International Law* 198, 1986-III, 336–400 at 354; J.P. Puissochet, 'Article 15', in M. Bettati, O. Duhamel, L. Greisalmer, *Déclaration universelle des droits de l'homme*, 2nd edn, Paris: Folio-Le Monde, 2008. Cf. however the ILC Commentary to Article 1 of the 1999 Draft Articles, para. 2.

28 ACHR, Article 20(3).

29 CIS Convention, Article 24(2).

30 ECN, respectively Article 4(c) and Article 8, which does not set forth a right to *change* nationality but rather a right to *renounce* one's nationality, 'provided the persons concerned do not thereby become stateless'.

31 ArCHR, respectively Article 29(1) ('no citizen shall be deprived of his nationality without a legally valid reason') and 29(3) ('No one shall be denied the right to acquire another nationality in accordance with the applicable legal procedures of his country').

32 1961 Convention, Articles 5ff.

33 Article 24(3) ICCPR and Article 7 CRC do not set forth a right to a nationality *from birth*, which is, on the contrary, proclaimed by Principle 3 of the Declaration on the Rights of the Child, UN General Assembly Resolution No. 1386 (XIV) of 10 December 1959. On the preparatory work on this issue see S.S. Detrick, *A Commentary on the United Nations Convention on The Rights of the Child*, The Hague–Boston–London: M. Nijhoff, 1999, p. 149. However, according to HRC General Comment No. 17, 'Rights of the Child (Article 24)', 7 April 1989, para. 8, states parties to the ICCPR are bound 'to ensure that every child has a nationality *when he is born*' (emphasis added). See further ACERWC, *Decision on the communication submitted by the Institute for Human Rights and Development in Africa and the Open Society Justice Initiative (on behalf of children of Nubian descent in Kenya) against the Government of Kenya*, Communication: No. Com/002/2009, 22 March 2011, para. 42.

34 Online. Available at: http://treaties.un.org (accessed 1 June 2012). Only the United Kingdom appended a reservation concerning Article 24, in the following terms:

> The Government of the United Kingdom reserve the right to enact such nationality legislation as they may deem necessary from time to time to reserve the acquisition and possession of citizenship under such legislation to those having sufficient connection with the United Kingdom or any of its

dependent territories and accordingly their acceptance of Article 24 (3) and of the other provisions of the Covenant is subject to the provisions of any such legislation.

(ibid.)

35 Online. Available at: http://treaties.un.org (accessed 13 June 2012). The United States of America have not ratified the CRC yet. They did, however, ratify the ICCPR on 8 June 1992 (ibid.).
36 Namely by Andorra on 1 March 2006; Switzerland on 1 May 2007; Tunisia on 23 September 2008; Liechtenstein on 1 October 2009; Thailand on 13 December 2010: Online. Available at: http://treaties.un.org (accessed 12 June 2012).
37 Oman declared:

> The Sultanate considers that article 7 of the Convention as it relates to the nationality of a child shall be understood to mean that a child born in the Sultanate of unknown parents shall acquire Oman nationality, as stipulated in the Sultanate's Nationality Law.

Monaco declared that the 'Convention, especially article 7, shall not affect the rules laid down in Monegasque legislation regarding nationality' (ibid.); while Monaco expressed its intention to withdraw the declaration (CRC, 'Concluding Observations: Monaco', 8 June 2001, CRC/C/15/Add.158, para. 11), it did not actually do it so far.
38 Online. Available at: http://treaties.un.org (accessed 12 June 2012).
39 Ibid.
40 There are currently only 48 parties to the Convention: Online. Available at: http://treaties.un.org (accessed 10 November 2012). As UN High Commissioner for Refugees Antonio Gutierrez recently noted, 'The number of countries that have ratified the statelessness conventions is out of proportion to the number of countries that have ratified the 1951 [Refugee] Convention and its [1967] Protocol' (cf. 'UNHCR Chief hails landmark conference for making "quantum leap" on statelessness', 8 November 2011. Online. Available at: www.unhcr.org/4ee0ba009.html (accessed 13 June 2012)).
41 The 1930 Hague Protocol Relating to Certain Cases of Statelessness, prescribing (Article 1) that in

> a State whose nationality is not conferred by the mere fact of birth in its territory, a person born in its territory of a mother possessing the nationality of that State and of a father without nationality or of unknown nationality shall have the nationality of the said State,

was ratified by 11 states. Online. Available at: http://treaties.un.org.
42 See UNHCR, *UNHCR Action to Address Statelessness – A Strategy Note*, 2010. Online. Available at: www.unhcr.org/refworld (accessed on 3 September 2012), p. 5, para. 8. On the mandate of the UNCHR on statelessness see General Assembly Resolutions Nos. 3274 (XXIX) of 10 December 1974; 31/36 of 30 November 1976; 49/169 of 23 December 1994; 50/152 of 21 December 1995; 61/137 of 19 December 2006.
43 Article 6.2. The ECN also stipulates (Article 6.1(a)) that nationality shall be granted *ex lege* to 'children one of whose parents possesses, at the time of the birth of these children, the nationality of that State Party, subject to any

exceptions which may be provided for by its internal law as regards children born abroad.' The ArCHR includes only a rule aimed at avoiding discriminations based on the sex of the parents, in Article 29(2): 'The State Parties shall undertake, in accordance with their legislation, all appropriate measures to allow a child to acquire the nationality of his mother with regard to the interest of the child'.

44 ACHR, Article 20(2) stipulates that every person 'has the right to the nationality of the state in whose territory he was born if he does not have the right to any other nationality'. There are currently 23 states parties to the ACHR: Online. Available at: http://www.oas.org/dil/treaties.htm (accessed 10 November 2012). However, Venezuala denounced the convention on 10 September 2012 (ibid.), with effect from 10 September 2013.

45 Article 6.4 ACRWC reads:

> States Parties to the present Charter shall undertake to ensure that their Constitutional legislation recognize the principles according to which a child shall acquire the nationality of the State in the territory of which he has been born if, at the time of the child's birth, he is not granted nationality by any other State in accordance with its laws.

46 UNHCR, *UNHCR Action*, Annex V.

47 See C. McLachlan, 'The Principle of Systemic Integration and Article 31(3)(c) of the Vienna Convention', *International and Comparative Law Quarterly* 54, 2005, 279–320.

48 The HRC expressly rejected the idea that the *jus soli* principle could apply in broader terms in the context of Article 24(3) ICCPR, when stating that the latter 'does not necessarily make it an obligation for States to give their nationality to every child born in their territory.' (General Comment No. 17, para. 8).

49 Cf., e.g. the various solutions adopted by the countries under review in the EUDO citizenship database. Online. Available at: http://eudo-citizenship.eu (accessed 13 August 2012).

50 Cf. Article 2(3) of the Nationality Law: 'A child shall, in any of the following cases, be a Japanese national: [...] When both parents are unknown or have no nationality in a case where the child is born in Japan' (Law No. 147 of 1950, as amended by Law No. 268 of 1952, Law No. 45 of 1984, Law No. 89 of 1993 and Law No. 147 of 2004, Law No. 88 of 2008. Online. Available at: www.moj.go.jp/ENGLISH/information/tnl-01.html (accessed 15 June 2012)).

51 Cf. the declaration quoted above.

52 Italy has signed the ECN but did not ratify it yet. According to Article 1(b) of the Nationality Law (Law No. 91 of 5 February 1992, *Gazzetta Ufficiale della Repubblica Italiana* No. 38 of 15 February 1992, as amended), Italian nationality is acquired by birth in case of birth on Italian soil if both parents are unknown or stateless, or if the child does not acquire their nationality. A child whose parents are unknown who is found on Italian soil is deemed a citizen by birth unless possession of another nationality is proven (Article 1 (c)). In Europe, all the states under review in the framework of the EUDO citizenship database provide for automatic acquisition of nationality for foundlings born on their soil (Online. Available at: http://eudo-citizenship.eu (accessed 11 June 2012)). On the situation at global level cf. 'Human Rights and Arbitrary Deprivation of Nationality', p. 10, para. 39.

53 CtRC, 'Concluding Observations: Bhutan', 8 October 2008, CRC/C/BTN/CO/2, para. 34.

54 In its Concluding Observations on Kuwait, 1–2 November 2011, the HRC expressed concern 'that children who are born in Kuwait to stateless parents may not acquire *any* nationality', without further specification (CCPR/C/KWT/CO/2, para. 12, emphasis added); cf. also 'Concluding Observations: Mongolia'. The CtRC took a similar approach in its Concluding Observations on Japan (30 January 2004, CRC/C/15/Add.231, para. 32, and 11 June 2010, CRC/C/JPN/CO/3, paras 45–6) Thailand (27 January 2006, CRC/C/THA/CO/2, para. 34), Belarus (4 February 2011, CRC/C/BLR/CO/3–4, paras 33–4), and the Czech Republic (17 June 2011, CRC/C/CZE/CO/3–4, para. 38). Cf. however, also for further references to the practice of the CtRC, I. Ziemele, *Article* 7, p. 25.

55 Cf. Nowak, *The UN Covenant*, pp. 561–2. As regards the position of the state of nationality of the parents and of the state of residence of the child, see CtRC, respectively 'Concluding Observations: Cuba', 17 June 2011, CRC/C/CUB/CO/2, paras 30–31; and 'Concluding Observations: India', 30 January 2004, CRC/C/15/Add.228, paras 40–1.

56 HRC, General Comment No. 17, para. 8.

57 ACERWC, *Nubian Children*, para. 58. Cf. also ECtHR, *Kuric and others v Slovenia*, No. 26828/06, judgment of 13 July 2010, para. 354.

58 ECtHR, *Tukabo-Tekle v the Netherlands*, No. 60665/00, judgment of 1 December 2005, para. 42; cf. also *Sen v the Netherlands*, No. 31465/96, judgment of 21 December 2001, p. 5, and, generally on positive obligations, *Ilaşcu and Others v Moldova and Russia*, No. 48787/99, judgment (GC) of 8 July 2004, para. 332. On the developments concerning the 'obligation to fulfil' human rights see, also for further references, O. De Schutter, *International Human Rights Law*, Cambridge: Cambridge University Press, 2010, pp. 242ff.

59 IACHR, *Case of the Girls Yean and Bosico v Dominican Republic*, judgment of 8 September 2005, *Series C*, No. 130. Cf. also CRC, General Comment No. 7, 'Implementing Child Rights in Early Childhood', CRC/C/GC/7/Rev 1, 20 September 2006, para. 25.

60 See, in this regard, Committee of Ministers of the CoE, Recommendation on the nationality of children, 9 December 2009, CM/Rec(2009)13, para. 3.

61 Cf. CMW, 'Concluding Observations: Chile', 21 September 2011: 'The Committee encourages the State party to grant nationality to children who are born in Chile and whose parents are in an irregular situation, *whenever parents are unable to transfer their nationality to the children*.' (UN Doc. CMW/C/CHL/CO/1, para. 33, emphasis added).

62 Ibid., para. 4. In a different context, the Federal Court of Switzerland deemed the refusal of former refugees to seek re-acquisition of Czech nationality not to be an abuse of right: *i.S. V. gegen Einwohnergemeinde X. und Regierungsrat des Kantons Bern (staatsrechtliche Beschwerde)*, judgment of 27 October 1995, BGE 121 I 367, para. 3(c).

63 UNTS, vol. 360, No. 5158, Article 32.

64 UNTS, vol. 189, No. 2545, Article 34.

65 ECN, Article 6(4).

66 *United States v Mandycz*, 447 F.3d 951, 956–57 (6th Cir.). 'Ordinary' naturalization is mostly issued on a discretionary basis by the 15 European countries

reviewed in the EUDO citizenship database, but the same applies for recognized refugees or persons who are stateless or of unclear citizenship: Online. Available at: http://eudo-citizenship.eu (accessed 21 June 2012). Specifically on Italy see F. Salerno, *Diritto internazionale – Principi e norme*, 2nd edn, Padova: Cedam, 2011, p. 314.

67 Cf EWCA, *Hilal Abdul-Razzaq Ali Al-Jedda*, para. 81:

> For a State to confer nationality automatically and irrespective of their wishes on some 1.5 million foreign nationals (albeit former Iraqi nationals) spread around the world would be a very surprising step even in the absence of the constraint imposed by the international law of occupation and even in the special circumstances of Iraq in the post-Saddam era.

Cf. H. Lauterpacht, 'The Nationality of Denationalized Persons', *Jewish Yearbook of International Law* 1, 1948, pp. 164–85 at 172; Peters, 'Extraterritorial Naturalizations', p. 666, and the authorities quoted therein.

68 See Peters, 'Extraterritorial Naturalizations', pp. 634ff.

69 Cf. R.D. Sloane, 'Breaking the Genuine Link: The Contemporary Legal Regulation of Nationality', *Harvard International Law Journal* 50, 2009, 1–60; A. Vermeer-Künzli, 'Nationality and diplomatic protection: a reappraisal', *infra*. pp. 76–95.

70 Cf. UN secretary general, 'Human Rights and Arbitrary Deprivation of Nationality', p. 11, para. 43; J.-F. Flauss, 'Naturalisation et droit international des droits de l'homme', in *Chemins d'Europe – Mélanges en l'honneur de Jean Paul Jaqué*, Paris: Dalloz, 2010, pp. 279–303 at 285ff. This topic will not be analysed in detail here.

71 CERD, 7 March 1966, UNTS, vol. 660, No. 9464, Article 5(c)(iii).

72 1961 Convention, Article 9. The notion of 'arbitrary deprivation' applies primarily to the loss of nationality, and will be discussed here mainly in that perspective. However, it encompasses also situations in which an individual is arbitrarily precluded from obtaining a nationality: see UN secretary general, 'Human Rights and Arbitrary Deprivation of Nationality', para. 23.

73 CEDAW, 18 December 1979, UNTS, vol. 1249, No. 20378, Article 9(1).

74 CEDAW, Article 9(2). On this aspect see CEDW, *Ragan Salgado v United Kingdom*, decision of 22 January 2007, CEDAW/C/37/D/11/2006, which was, however, declared inadmissible.

75 CRPD, Article 18.

76 ECN, Article 5(1).

77 Para. 8, with specific reference to the distinction between legitimate children and children born out of wedlock. As regards discrimination on grounds of ethnicity see, e.g. CtRC, 'Concluding Observations: Kuwait', para. 13.

78 IACHR, *Yean and Bosico*, para. 141.

79 ACERWC, *Nubian Children*, paras 55ff.

80 AComHPR, Communication 97/93, decided at the 28th ordinary session, Oct./Nov. 2000, *African Human Rights Law Reports*, 2000, p. 30. Cf. ECtHR, *Petropavlovskis v Latvia*, No. 44230/06, decision of 3 June 2008, on denial of naturalization because of the political activities of the applicant; HRC, *Gonzales v Guyana*, views of 25 March 2010, CCPR/C/98/D/1246/2004.

81 ECtHR, *Genovese v Malta*, No. 53124/09, judgment of 11 October 2011, paras 33–4. This case did not concern, however, a person who would otherwise be stateless. Article 14 ECHR, read in conjunction with Article 8, may apply also

to involuntary loss of nationality under circumstances such as those of *Zeïbek v Greece*, No. 46368/06, judgment of 9 July 2010. The application concerned a discrimination on allocation of pension rights, but led the Court to touch upon a widespread policy of denationalization on ethnic grounds pursued by Greece: cf. especially para. 48 of the judgment.

82 Cf. IACHR, *Yean and Bosico*, para. 141; ACERWC, *Nubian Children*, para. 56, with specific reference to racial or ethnic discrimination; Cf. Ziemele and Schram, 'Article 15', p. 308.

83 The conclusion of an optional protocol on the issue was discussed in the past (see Chan, 'The Right to a Nationality', p. 7) and suggested also by the 4th CoE Conference on Nationality: see 'Concepts of Nationality in a Globalised World', 17 November 2010, CONF-NAT (2010) CONCL. E of 21 January 2011.

84 ECtHR, *Karassev and Others v Finland*, No. 31414/96, decision of 12 January 1999; *Slivenko v Latvia*, No. 48321/99, decision of 23 January 2002; *Kuduzović v Slovenia*, No. 60723/00, decision of 17 March 2005; *Genovese v Malta*.

85 ECtHR, *Kuric and others*, paras 316 and 330. Cf. also the Grand Chamber judgment of 26 June 2012, para. 236.

86 Cf. also ECtHR, *Makuc and Others v Slovenia*, No. 26828/06, decision of 31 May 2007.

87 Para. 357.

88 Ibid., para. 376.

89 ECtHR, *Kuric and others*, Grand Chamber judgment, para. 329.

90 On the legal effects of subrogate motherhood in countries where it is not admitted cf. Austrian Constitutional Court, case B 13/11–10, judgment of 14 December 2011, para. 4.1, to the effect that the protection of the welfare of the child is part of Austria's public order (the case did not involve an issue of statelessness). A different stance is taken by the French Cassation Court: see the judgments of the First Civil Section of 6 April 2011, Nos. 369, 370 and 371. Cf. however Rennes Court of Appeals, judgment of 21 February 2012, No. 434 (case 11/02758). Online. Available at: http://avocats.fr/space/caroline.mecary/content/_06037211–521E-45BF-8F57–0E17CED85156 (accessed 15 June 2012).

91 Ziemele and Schram, 'Article 15', p. 308; Peters, 'Extraterritorial Naturalizations', p. 631.

92 United States Court of Appeals for the Seventh Circuit, *Haile v Holder*, 591 F.3d 572, 6 January 2010, pp. 4–5.

93 ECJ, C-135/08, *Rottmann v Freistaat Beyern*, judgment (GC) of 2 March 2010, para. 53.

94 1961 Convention, Article 8; ECN, Article 7(3). Furthermore, a number of reservations were appended to the provisions concerning deprivation of nationality in both conventions: Online. Available at: http://treaties.un.org (accessed 10 June 2012) and www.conventions.coe.int (accessed 10 June 2012). In *Keshva Rajan and Sashi Kantra Rajan v New Zealand*, the scope of the obligation stemming from Article 24(3) ICCPR in this regard was discussed, but not decided, by the HRC since the affected child was deemed to hold another nationality (views of 6 August 2003, CCPR/C/78/D/820/1998, para. 7.5).

95 UN secretary general, 'Human Rights and arbitrary deprivation of nationality', p. 14, para. 58. For the contention that customary international law prohibits deprivation of nationality if it causes statelessness see, however, M. Bennouna,

'De la reconnaissance d'un "droit à la nationalité" en droit international', in SFDI, *Droit international et nationalité – Colloque de Poitiers*, Paris: Pedone, 2012, pp. 119–26 at 123.

96 UN secretary general, 'Human Rights and arbitrary deprivation of nationality', p. 7, para. 25.

97 Ibid.

98 ECJ, *Rottmann*, paras 51, 55–6. While the issue is discussed only with reference to EU law, the latter must respect customary international law (cf. ECJ, C-162/86, *Racke*, judgment of 16 June 1998). According to the United States Court of Appeals for the Sixth Circuit there is a 'fundamental distinction between denying someone citizenship and divesting someone of citizenship' (*Tserba v Holder*, No. 09–4312, 20 May 2011. Online. Available at: www.unhcr.org/refworld/docid/4e04890a2.html (accessed 20 June 2012), p. 8) and the government 'faces a rigorous burden of proof' in denaturalization proceedings (*United States v Mandycz*, judgment of 22 May 2006, F.3d 951, 956–57 (6th Cir.), cert. denied, 549 U.S. 956 (2006), para. II.A).

99 *Civilian Claims – Eritrea's Claims 15, 16, 23 & 27–32*, partial award of 17 December 2004. Online. Available at: www.pca-cpa.org (accessed 14 August 2012), para. 60. Emphasis added.

100 Peters, 'Extraterritorial Naturalizations', pp. 662ff.

101 Cf. Article 8(2) ECN.

102 The issue is discussed in ECtHR, *Riener v Bulgaria*, No. 46343/99, judgment of 23 May 2006, where the Court did not 'exclude that an arbitrary refusal of a request to renounce citizenship might in certain very exceptional circumstances raise an issue under Article 8 of the Convention if such a refusal has an impact on the individual's private life'.

103 Cf. Article 7 of the 1961 Convention.

104 ECtHR, *Okonkwo against Austria*, No. 35117/97, decision of 22 May 2001; ECtHR, *Mogos v Romania*, No. 20420/02, judgment of 13 October 2005.

105 Cf. ECtHR, *Mogos*, para. 10.

106 Cf. also Appeals Administrative Court of Ukraine, Decision No. 2a-2952/09/0870 of 15 June 2010, English summary. Online. Available at: http://eudo-citizenship.eu/citizenship-case-law/?search=1&name=statelessness&year=&country=&national=1 (accessed 13 August 2012), to the effect that the renunciation of citizenship can be refused if it results in statelessness.

107 This is suggested by Decaux, 'Le droit à une nationalité', p. 260, since the right to a nationality would prevail over treaties in the field of state succession; however, the fact that states may not agree *inter se* on a waiver of the right to a nationality would seem to depend not so much on its peremptory nature but rather on the circumstance that they are not the holders of such a right, which accrues to individuals.

3 Statelessness in the context of state succession

An appraisal under international law

Francesco Costamagna

Introduction

The number of stateless individuals stands, according to the United Nations High Commissioner for Refugees,[1] at some 3.5 million persons. However, this is a partial figure, as only a minority of states have procedures in place for identifying statelessness. Therefore, it is safe to assume that the number of stateless persons is much higher, as it has been estimated at up to 12 million people.[2] The uncertainty surrounding the magnitude of the problem is proof of the scant attention traditionally paid by states to the phenomenon, or of the 'decision by statesmen to solve the problem of statelessness by ignoring it'.[3]

Hannah Arendt equated the condition of being without a nationality to one of rightlessness.[4] This equation rested on the assumption that the sovereign state is the sole meaningful guarantor of rights. Therefore, citizenship, poignantly described as 'the right to have rights',[5] is considered as an essential prerequisite to enjoy these rights. International efforts to go beyond this state of affairs were seen as meaningless, being unable to offer proper enforcement mechanisms. This assumption should be revised in the light of the evolution that affected the international system for the protection of human rights since then and that led to the creation of more effective mechanisms[6] to enforce rights that belong to all individuals, irrespective of their nationality and even in the case they have no nationality at all.

At the same time, it is true that this evolution has taken place only in some regions of the world and, even there, only with regard to certain categories of rights. For instance, the enjoyment of most political[7] and social rights[8] is still restricted to those belonging to the national community. The process of marginalization that follows the deprivation of these rights has a profound negative impact on the life of stateless persons,[9] forcing them 'to live in a precarious situation at the margin of society'.[10] Statelessness may indeed become a major driver for economic insecurity, as stateless persons are denied land rights,[11] or have a reduced capacity to access health and educational services;[12] furthermore, statelessness can make affected individuals voiceless on the political stage.

State succession[13] represents one of the possible paths to statelessness[14] and, in particular, it may lead to *collective* statelessness, which results when mass denationalization is used as a weapon by states seeking to assert their power over a territory and a population. This is the reason why, especially since the 1990s, the matter has attracted considerable attention at the international level. This chapter examines the outcomes of this increased attention, and whether it can have any meaningful impact on the avoidance of statelessness in the context of state succession. Preliminarily, the chapter gives an overview of the international legal framework on statelessness and its evolution. Subsequently, it focuses on statelessness in the context of state succession and takes into account some attempts to codify international law rules on the matter. The analysis pays particular attention to the emergence of a set of principles that represents the backbone of these codification attempts, going beyond the traditional idea according to which these matters are within states' exclusive competence and imposing greater respect for individual rights. Furthermore, this chapter looks at the attempts to better define the responsibilities of concerned states in ensuring full adherence to these principles. Lastly, as a way of conclusion, the chapter seeks to assess the impact of these instruments.

Combating statelessness under international law

A stateless person is, according to Article 1 of the Convention relating to the Status of Stateless Persons (1954 Convention), someone 'who is not considered as a national by any State under the operation of its law'.[15] This definition, widely regarded as having a customary nature,[16] only covers de jure statelessness, as it points to the lack of a formal bond between the individual and the state. Beside this, there are cases where persons, despite not having been formally deprived of their nationality, are unable to enjoy the protection of their national authorities or to establish their nationality. However, this type of statelessness, generally known as de facto statelessness,[17] is not covered by any of the international legal instruments dealing with statelessness.

Statelessness has long been recognized as a reason for concern by the international community. The initiatives taken to regulate the matter have gradually led to the emergence of a multi-layered legal regime. This notwithstanding, there is still considerable uncertainty as to whether statelessness as such can be considered unlawful under international law, or simply 'undesirable'.[18] Conversely, there is no doubt that certain forms of denationalization, such as those carried out in a discriminatory or arbitrary fashion, are to be regarded as a violation of international rules.

The first attempts to combat statelessness at the international level were made between the First and Second World Wars. The Convention on Certain Questions relating to the Conflict of Nationality Laws[19] represents the first major example in this regard. The Convention, although not addressing the issue in a comprehensive way, contains several provisions dealing with aspects related to statelessness.[20] These provisions were supplemented by the Protocol relating to Certain Cases of Statelessness,[21] adopted on the same day.

In the 1930s, the rise of totalitarian regimes made denationalization of minority groups a sadly recurring event.[22] However, it was only after the Second World War, and the establishment of the United Nations (UN), that these concerns were addressed at the normative level. The first instrument dealing with this matter was the Universal Declaration of Human Rights (UDHR),[23] whose Article 15 proclaims that any individual has the right to have a nationality and that 'no one shall be arbitrarily deprived of his nationality'.

In the following years, the international efforts to combat statelessness took two different, albeit closely related, paths. The first path aimed at regulating the status of stateless persons, addressing some of the worst effects deriving from such a condition. This course of action has traditionally been considered as a second-best option,[24] finding its *raison d'être* in the absence of effective measures for the abolition of statelessness. Nonetheless, this approach was the first to meet with some success, with the adoption of the 1954 Convention.

The second path pointed towards the reduction and the progressive elimination of statelessness, by addressing some of its root causes. These efforts culminated in the adoption, in 1961, of the Convention on the Reduction of Statelessness (1961 Convention).[25] Article 1 of the Convention obliges contracting states to grant their nationality to a person born in their territory who would otherwise be stateless. Article 8 deals with the issue of subsequent statelessness by preventing contracting states from depriving individuals of their nationality if this would make them stateless. Article 9 forbids individual or collective deprivations of nationality if grounded on a racial, ethnic, political, or religious basis.[26]

The 1954 and 1961 Conventions represent the two main pillars of what can be loosely defined as the international legal regime on statelessness. However, their impact is still rather limited, due to two main reasons.[27] The first reason is the low ratification rate of these Conventions.[28] The second reason is the absence of a proper monitoring system, so to ensure the enforcement of states' obligations.[29]

Beside these Conventions, there are other international provisions that deal with statelessness by focusing on the situation of certain vulnerable groups. This is the case, for instance, of Article 9 of the Convention on the Elimination of All Forms of Discrimination against Women of 1979[30] and Article 7 of the Convention on the Rights of the Child of 1989.[31]

The international regime also comprises some instruments adopted at the regional level. Among the others, it is worth mentioning the European Convention on Nationality (ECN),[32] adopted under the auspices of the Council of Europe (CoE). The ECN deals with a number of nationality-related matters, not just statelessness. Its provisions focus on the prevention of statelessness and refer to many of the solutions already codified in the 1961 Convention. Unfortunately, also the ECN has been ratified by a relatively low number of states[33] and it lacks a proper monitoring mechanism.

Statelessness and state succession under international law: between state sovereignty and individual rights

A difficult path towards a comprehensive legal framework

A change of sovereignty can affect nationality and it represents a potential source of statelessness. However, being it 'one of the most difficult problems in the law of state succession',[34] it is hardly surprising that the law addressing the problem is yet to be codified. The existence and the content of customary norms on this matter are still controversial, due to a fragmented state practice largely motivated by political considerations. On the other hand, this issue has traditionally received scant attention in the multilateral treaties on statelessness.[35] In the 1961 Convention, for instance, there is just one provision dealing with the matter.[36]

The situation changed in the 1990s, when the break up of countries, such as the Soviet Union, Czechoslovakia, and Yugoslavia, showed the dramatic impact that state succession can have on the nationality of large numbers of people. In a context of heated political, and even military, confrontation, many of the concerned states made use of newly enacted citizenship laws as tools for ethnic engineering – or even ethnic cleansing[37] – to exclude those groups that were perceived as having some form of bond with the enemy. Ethnic engineering has been defined as 'an intentional policy on behalf of governments and lawmakers to influence, by legal means and related administrative practices, the ethnic composition of their population in favour of their core ethnic group'.[38]

A well-known example was the dissolution of the Socialist Federal Republic of Yugoslavia (SFRY), as all its successor states sought to define their population along ethnic lines. Croatia, for instance, passed a law in 1991 automatically granting citizenship only to those holding former Croatian republican citizenship and forcing all the others, even those that had been living in its territory for generations, to go through a difficult process of naturalization.[39] Furthermore, this law even issued an invitation for nationality to all those of Croat ethnicity.[40] A similar path was followed by Slovenia with the erasure from the Registry of Permanent Residents of more than 25,000 SFRY nationals that failed to apply for Slovenian citizenship before the deadline of 25 December 1991. Although formally determining only the cessation of registered permanent residence, the measure had an impact on the nationality of many of the affected individuals and a number of them became stateless.[41]

Equally concerning was the situation in the Baltic States and, more precisely, Latvia and Estonia.[42] After having gained independence from the Soviet Union, both these countries decided to reinstate their pre-soviet era citizenship laws,[43] which granted automatic nationality only to those that already enjoyed it prior to the annexation by the Soviet Union and to their descendants. This was meant to exclude all the Soviet-era migrants and their descendants,[44] in an attempt to take revenge for the 'russification' process carried out by Soviet authorities for decades.[45] The result of this policy was dramatic, leaving thousands of residents in the Latvian and Estonian territories stateless and, thus, making them voiceless on the political stage.[46] A similar path was followed also in other regions of the world. An illustrative example is that of Ethiopia, where in 1998, after the eruption of the war with Eritrea, 75,000 individuals were deported and denationalized[47] only because they had some links with Eritrea[48] or because they voted in the 1993 referendum on the independence of Eritrea.

The response by the international community, quite elusive to many extents, was mainly directed towards the codification of the international rules on the matter and to better define the responsibilities of the concerned states. Two bodies have been particularly active to this end, namely the International Law Commission (ILC) and, at the regional level, the European Commission for Democracy through Law (Venice Commission). The former decided to include in its agenda[49] the question of state succession and its impact on nationality of natural and juridical persons in 1993. This proposal, immediately endorsed by the UN General Assembly,[50] aimed at completing the work already carried out by the same body on other aspects of state succession.[51] In 1999 the ILC adopted the Draft Articles on Nationality of Natural Persons in Relation to the Succession of States (1999 Draft Articles).[52] The Draft, which is still to be transposed into a legally binding instrument,[53] aims at the codification and the progressive development of international law rules concerning the conferral and withdrawal of nationality in the context of state succession, in order to ensure greater legal certainty to states and individuals. To do so, the ILC sought to work out a comprehensive legal framework dealing in great detail with the main aspects of this multifarious issue. The outcome is a rather complex document articulated into two main parts. The first part contains general provisions codifying some fundamental principles that apply to all categories of state succession. The second part addresses the issues of conferral and withdrawal of nationality, by establishing specific rules concerning each of the four different types of succession.

An important contribution to the codification of this set of rules has been given by the Venice Commission, which in 1996 elaborated the Declaration on the Consequences of State Succession for Nationality of Natural Persons.[54] This soft-law document contains a number of principles that have been subsequently transposed into two different conventions adopted under the auspices of the CoE. The first is the ECN and, in particular, its chapter VII, which sets out a number of principles that both predecessor and successor states are bound to respect in dealing with nationality matters. The other, more relevant from this chapter's perspective, is the CoE Convention on the Avoidance of Statelessness in Relation to State Succession of 2006 (2006 Convention).[55] This instrument has a narrower focus than both the 1999 Draft Articles and the ECN, as it only deals with the issue of statelessness, having identified it as 'one of the main concerns for the international community in the field of nationality'.[56] Unlike the 1999 Draft Articles, the 2006 Convention does not dwell on details, seeking instead to elaborate a comprehensive set of principles that can apply to all the different types of succession.

Protecting individuals' rights: emerging principles

All these instruments rest on a common set of principles that have a foundational value, informing the content of their substantive provisions.[57] These are the right to a nationality, the duty to avoid statelessness, and the principle of non-discrimination. The emphasis put on these principles is a sign of a new approach toward the matter, which is more attentive to the position of the individual, even at the expenses of the sovereign. This evolution challenges the conventional wisdom, according to which conferral and withdrawal of nationality fall within the exclusive domestic jurisdiction of each state. This is not to say that states have lost their sovereign power to determine the criteria for the acquisition and loss of their nationality. Rather this power has to be exercised while respecting competing values and interests that are perceived as fundamental by the international community as a whole.

The first fundamental principle is the right to a nationality.[58] This right has been proclaimed by several international instruments, starting from Article 15 UDHR. Article 1 of the 1999 Draft Articles and Article 2 of the 2006 Convention codify this right, with particular regard to the context of state succession. Beneficiaries of this version of the right are only the so-called 'persons concerned', that is those individuals that, at the time of the succession, had the nationality of the predecessor state and that can become statelessness due to the succession.[59] Indeed, the main concern of these documents is not to reassert the existence of a universal right to have a nationality, but simply to avoid that individuals might end up losing their nationality because of a change of sovereignty.[60]

A similar pattern can also be observed with regard to the identification of the addressee of the obligation corresponding to the right, as these provisions only refer to the states concerned, i.e. the predecessor state and the successor state. In this regard, Article 1 of the 1999 Draft Articles speaks of 'the right to a nationality of *at least one* of the States concerned'.[61] The provision intends to cover those cases where persons have links with more than one of these states and, thus, they may end up with the nationality of two or more states. However, this choice has been criticized by some states, such as Greece, and scholars[62] for conveying the idea that there exists a right to multiple nationality under international law. State practice does not support the existence of such a right, as many states do not allow individuals to have more than one nationality at the same time.

The second principle is the duty for all the concerned states to avoid state succession giving origin to cases of statelessness. A light version[63] of this obligation was already contained in Article 10 of the 1961 Convention, which requires contracting parties to 'use [their] best endeavour to include in their treaties regulating the transfer of territory provisions to secure that no one could become stateless' because of this event. Alternatively, it asks the party that acquires the territory to grant its nationality to all those that may loose their nationality because of the transfer. A bolder approach has been taken by the drafters of Article 18 ECN, where avoiding statelessness is seen as an objective to be pursued through the respect of other principles and rules.

The obligation has been codified in Article 4 of the 1999 Draft Articles and Article 3 of the 2006 Convention. Both provisions require the concerned states to take all the appropriate measures to prevent persons that had the nationality of the predecessor state from becoming stateless. In this context, the duty to avoid statelessness, just as it is the case for the right to nationality seen above, is limited in scope. Indeed, the duty does not aim to reduce statelessness in all its forms; rather, it applies only to cases where a person has a nationality and risks loosing it because of state succession. The wording used by both these articles suggests, and this is supported by the Commentary to Article 4 of the 1999 Draft Articles, that they set out an obligation of means, rather than one of result. According to some commentators, this obligation jointly weights on all the concerned states, as none of them can be held responsible *uti singuli*.[64] Conversely, there are other authors that argue that this duty can be broken down into individual obligations, by identifying, on a case-by-case basis, which state has the primary duty to confer its nationality.[65] This can be done through the use of different criteria to identify the state that has the strongest linkage with the individual.

The last fundamental principle upon which the whole system is based is that of non-discrimination. This principle, a cornerstone of the international regime for the protection of human rights, plays a pivotal role also in the field of nationality. The prohibition of discrimination limits states' discretion in setting the conditions for the acquisition and loss of their citizenship. The ban has been codified in Articles 1(3) and 5 of the Convention on the Elimination of All Forms of Racial Discrimination[66] and, although only with regard to the deprivation of nationality, in Article 9 of the 1961 Convention. The same happened at the regional level, where Article 5 ECN forbids states parties from adopting discriminatory rules and practices.

The prohibition of discrimination has an even more important role to play in the field of state succession,[67] where it goes to the core of the problem, by outlawing the use of nationality laws as a tool for ethnic engineering. As seen above, these practices rest upon the use of discriminatory criteria aimed at excluding some minority groups from nationality, so to push these groups to the margin of the society or, in some extreme circumstances, to force them out of the national territory. The prohibition has to be intended in its widest sense to cover situations of indirect or disguised discrimination. Indeed, there may be cases where the conditions appear to be neutral if taken at their face value, but may have discriminatory effects with regard to specific groups. The issue has been thoroughly discussed in connection to the clean criminal record requirement set out by the Czech citizenship law of 1993. This criterion is used by many states, but in this particular context it had the effect of excluding vast numbers of Roma from applying for Czech citizenship, even though they had been living in that territory for generations.[68] Also, the point has been raised in a study conducted by a group of experts nominated by the CoE. In particular, they noted that:

> [While a] clean criminal record requirement in the context of naturalization is a usual and normal condition [...] the problem is different in the context of state succession [where] it is doubtful whether [...] under international law citizens that have lived for decades in the territory, perhaps [were] even born there, can be excluded from citizenship just because they have a criminal record.[69]

In the light of the above, it is hardly surprising that both the 1999 Draft Articles and the 2006 Convention contain a broad version of the principle. In particular, Article 15 of the 1999 Draft Articles prohibits discrimination 'on any ground', omitting any illustrative list to avoid the risk of *a contrario* interpretation. Article 4 of the 2006 Convention goes in the same direction, although along a different path, as it contains a long list of proscribed grounds.

Towards a clearer definition of concerned states' responsibilities

One of the main obstacles to the effective implementation of the abovementioned principles is the uncertainty surrounding the allocation of responsibilities among the states concerned. The only obvious exception is represented by the case of unification of states, as there is just one state – the unified one – that has the obligation to confer nationality. In particular, the successor state is to consider as its nationals all those persons having the nationality of one of the predecessor states. This is a rule that, as demonstrated by the cases of Germany[70] and Yemen,[71] finds support in state practice and can be considered to have a customary nature.[72]

The situation is far more complex in those cases where there are more than one successor states or when there is a continuing presence of the predecessor state. The ILC chose to address the matter by defining states' responsibilities in relation to four different types of state succession: transfer of territory, unification of states, dissolution, and separation of a part of territory.[73] The outcome is an intricate web of detailed rules that, in many cases, are clear examples of progressive development, rather than mere codification. A different approach has been followed by the 2006 Convention. This instrument does not distinguish between different types of succession, addressing the responsibilities of successor and predecessor states in two provisions that apply in all circumstances.[74]

Despite these differences, the criteria used to identify which state is under the obligation to confer nationality shows a high degree of similarity. This is due to the fact that the criteria are based upon the same assumption: the primary responsibility to ensure the respect of the right to a nationality and of the duty to avoid statelessness falls upon the state with which the concerned individual holds the strongest connection. The solution appears to be fully in line with the doctrine of effective nationality within the meaning of the *Nottebohm* case decided by the International Court of Justice.[75] This doctrine has been traditionally considered as a general principle limiting a state's capacity to confer its nationality to persons that do not have any relevant bond with it.[76] However, in this context, the doctrine performs also a different function – a positive one – as it serves to identify which state has the duty to grant its nationality to the persons concerned.

The main criterion used to determine the existence of such a link is that of habitual residence. The notion is to be defined by looking to the factual situation or, as clarified by Article 1(d) of the 2006 Convention, the 'stable factual residence'. The importance of the criterion is apparent in each of the legal instruments dealing with the matter.[77] Article 5 of the 1999 Draft Articles goes as far as to establish a presumption of nationality for all the habitual residents, introducing, thus, the possibility of an automatic acquisition of nationality by this group of persons. However, this provision has a limited temporal scope as it applies, as stated in the ILC Commentary, only in the time lag between state succession and the adoption of legislation on the question of nationality.

The existence of a stable link with the territory of the state is seen as a compelling evidence of the existence of a 'real connection between the individual and the state'[78] and, thus, a valuable criterion to establish the existence of a legal obligation upon the successor state to confer its nationality. The solution is fully consistent with the traditional rule: when a change of sovereignty occurs, the population goes with the territory in matters of nationality.[79] A rule that reflects 'le lien très étroit existant entre la souveraineté, le territoire et la nationalité des personnes'.[80] Furthermore, imposing on the successor state the duty to confer its nationality to all the concerned persons habitually residing on its territory is instrumental in avoiding statelessness in the context of state succession and fills any possible gap in the transition from a sovereign to another.

This notwithstanding, doubts have been raised as to whether this rule can be regarded as having a customary nature.[81] Indeed, it is true that habitual residence has been used as the key criterion for the conferral of nationality by many successor states, such as Bangladesh when it gained independence in 1971, Russia, Belarus, Georgia, and other countries that emerged from the collapse of the Soviet Union, as wells as Kosovo. At the same time, there have been many cases where habitual residence was not the sole criterion or it was not used at all. For instance, in the break up of a number of federal states, successor states tended to rely upon the criterion of secondary, or republican, citizenship as the starting point for the conferral of their nationality. This was the case in Slovenia, Croatia, Bosnia-Herzegovina, the Former Yugoslav Republic of Macedonia, the Czech Republic, and Slovakia. The same had happened after the dismemberment of the Austro-Hungarian Empire, as the Treaties of Saint-Germain-en-Laye and Trianon provided that 'every person possessing rights of citizenship (*pertinenza*) in territory which formed part of the former Austro-Hungarian Monarchy shall obtain *ipso facto* [...] the nationality of the state exercising sovereignty over such territory'.[82]

The possibility to resort to criteria other than habitual residence is sanctioned by both the 1999 Draft Articles and the 2006 Convention. However, these documents see it as a residual option that cannot be used by a successor state to deny nationality to persons habitually residing in its territory. Such a restrictive stance reflects a legitimate concern with the use of criteria that, albeit apparently neutral, are often used to exclude individuals or groups of persons from receiving nationality, despite their strong territorial connection with the state. The lawfulness of these criteria is to be assessed *in concreto*, looking at their effects, rather than at their abstract features. Indeed, even assuming that there is not a general obligation for the successor state to grant its nationality to all the *resortissants* of the predecessor state habitually residing on its territory, it can be hardly denied that alternative criteria can be used only in so far as they do not contribute to creating statelessness by discriminating against groups of people.

The quest for a solution to the problem of statelessness in the context of state succession requires to look also at the position of the predecessor state. The key issue in this regard is the regulation of a state's right to withdraw its nationality from persons qualified to become nationals of the successor state. In the past, this issue has been mainly dealt with from another perspective, seeking to establish whether the predecessor state was under a general obligation to withdraw its nationality from these individuals. The existence of this obligation has been seen as a corollary of the effective link doctrine and of the duty to avoid undue interferences into successor state's sovereignty on nationality matters.[83]

The growing influence of the principles imposing that statelessness be avoided leads us to look at the issue from another angle, in order to establish whether the predecessor state has a right to withdraw its nationality and, more importantly, whether this right suffers any limitation under international law. Indeed, there have been cases where individuals were stripped of their nationality only because they were entitled to acquire the one of the successor state, even though there was no guarantee for that to happen. One of the most recent examples is that of Sudan, after the secession of South Sudan in July 2011.[84] In August 2011, in response to the South Sudanese Nationality Act,[85] adopted just one month earlier, Sudan amended its Citizenship Act of 1994, by setting forth that individuals that are entitled to acquire South Sudan's nationality de jure or de facto would lose their Sudanese nationality.[86] The problem is that Sudan's revocation of nationality was automatic and it began to operate in a moment[87] in which South Sudan had still to establish the procedures to issue nationality documents, especially with regard to people living abroad. This meant that many individuals[88] of South Sudanese origin that had been living in Sudan for generations found themselves in a desperate situation, having lost all their rights deriving from the Sudanese nationality[89] and with no means to prove their new status.

Both the 1999 Draft Articles and the 2006 Convention deal with the matter and forbid predecessor states from withdrawing nationality from individuals that are yet to acquire the nationality of the successor state, even though they may be qualified to do so. Article 25 of the 1999 Draft Articles identifies certain categories of nationals of the predecessor state that, unless they opt otherwise, cannot be deprived of their nationality. The criteria that are used to identify the beneficiaries of this treatment are the same as those seen above, as the provision covers persons habitually residing in its territory or at least having an appropriate legal connection to a constituent part of the predecessor state that has remained part of it. As demonstrated by the Sudanese case, these categories of persons find themselves in a particularly vulnerable position as they risk losing the nationality of the state that they live in and to which they have the strongest ties.

Conclusions

Statelessness has been considered to be a reason for concern by the international community for a long time, due to the dire consequences that this phenomenon can have on individuals' rights and their living conditions. However, the normative response to these concerns has been slow and far from satisfactory. This situation is particularly evident with regard to state succession, despite the fact that there is now widespread awareness of its potential for creating cases of collective statelessness. In this context, denationalization of minority groups has often been used to push their members to the margins of society, or even outside the national borders. Since the 1990s, many initiatives have been started to work out a comprehensive set of rules that could avoid, or at least reduce, statelessness. The ILC and, at the European level, the Venice Commission have been particularly active to this end. These activities have led to the adoption of instruments that go to great lengths to better clarify states' responsibilities and individuals' rights in this field. These instruments seek to go beyond the traditional assumption according to which this is a matter within the exclusive competence of states and attempt to give greater substance to principles that aim to strengthen the position of individuals, such as the duty to avoid statelessness.

Unfortunately, the impact of these instruments is still limited. On one hand, the 1999 Draft Articles are yet to be transposed into a legally binding instrument, despite repeated urging by the UN General Assembly for states to consider its adoption. On the other hand, the 2006 Convention has been ratified by an extremely low number of states. Furthermore, neither of these instruments, not even the European one, envisages proper enforcement mechanisms that could allow individuals to have recourse to judicial or quasi-judicial bodies. Indeed, the 2006 Convention only deals with disputes concerning its interpretation, and establishes that disputes must be settled through negotiation.[90] The choice, which represents a step back even with regard to the 1961 Convention, is reminiscent of a state-centric attitude toward the matter that is hardly compatible with the approach adopted in drafting the substantive part of these instruments. Ultimately, this approach could defeat any attempt to elaborate a credible response to statelessness in the context of state succession. In some cases, human rights enforcement mechanisms could step in to partially fill this gap, as demonstrated by the European Court of Human Rights (ECtHR) Chamber' decision in the *Kuric* case, where the violation of international law standards aimed at the avoidance of statelessness was considered as an unlawful interference in the right to private or family life under Article 8 of the European Convention on Human Rights. Albeit promising, this approach needs to be further developed, even within the ECtHR case law, in order to represent a meaningful response to statelessness.

Notes

1 UNHCR, *Global Trends Report 2010*, New York, 2010. Online. Available at: www.unhcr.org/4dfa11499.html (accessed 3 September 2012), p. 29.
2 I. Shearer and B. Opeskin, 'Nationality and Statelessness', in B. Opeskin, R. Perruchod and J. Redpath-Cross (eds) *Foundations of International Migration Law*, Cambridge: Cambridge University Press, 2012. Online. Available at: http://papers.ssrn.com/sol3/papers.cfm?abstract_id=1863587 (accessed 3 September 2012), p. 9.
3 H. Arendt, *The Origins of Totalitarianism*, 2nd edn, London: Ruskin House, 1958, p. 279.
4 Ibid., pp. 293–7.
5 Ibid., p. 296.
6 The main example being the ECHR, 4 November 1950, CETS 5.
7 On the relationship between nationality and the exercise of political rights see D. Rudan, 'Nationality and political rights', *infra*, pp. 117–34.
8 On access to social rights by non-nationals see A. Annoni, 'Nationality and social rights', *infra*, pp. 135–52.
9 D. Weissbrodt and C. Collins, 'The Human Rights of Stateless Persons', *Human Rights Quarterly* 28, 2006, 264–70.
10 UNCHR, *Global Trends Report*, p. 28.
11 For instance, the denationalization of some 1.5 millions Banyarwanda in the Democratic Republic of Congo that followed the adoption, in 1981, of a citizenship law by the then President Mobutu was aimed, *inter alia*, to deprive this group of their land rights.
12 This is what happened, for instance, in the case of Dilicia Yean and Violeta Bosico that, after being denied Dominican citizenship, despite the fact they had

the right to obtain it, were unable to enrol in school. The IACHR issued a landmark decision against the Dominican Republic, finding that these discriminatory policies rendered these children unable to access fundamental rights, such as that to education (IACHR, *Yean and Bosico v Dominican Republic*, judgment of 8 September 2005, *Series C*, No. 130).

13 State succession is to be defined as the replacement of one state by another in the responsibility for the international relations of territory.

14 The paths to statelessness can be broadly divided into two main categories, as a person can be either denied a nationality at birth or be subsequently deprived of it, without acquiring a new one. On this point see Shearer and Opeskin, 'Nationality and Statelessness', pp. 9–11.

15 Adopted on 28 September 1954, UNTS, vol. 360, p. 117.

16 ILC, 'Report on the work of its fifty-eighth session', 1 May–9 June and 3 July–11 August 2006, UN Doc. A/61/10, p. 49.

17 For a detailed survey on the scope and the meaning of the concept see H. Massey, *UNHCR and* De Facto *Statelessness*, UNHCR Legal and Protection Policy Research Series, LPPR/2010/01, April 2010, pp. 27–60.

18 P. Weis, *Nationality and Statelessness in International Law*, 2nd edn, Alphen aan den Rijn and Germantown, Maryland: Sijthoff & Noordhoff, 1979, p. 162.

19 Adopted on 12 April 1930, LNTS, vol. 179, No. 4137.

20 Article 7 on expatriating permits, Articles 8–9 on the nationality of married women, Articles 13–15 on the nationality of children and Article 17 on adoption.

21 Adopted on 12 April 1930, LNTS, vol. 179, No. 4137.

22 For an historical overview of mass nationalizations see M.O. Hudson, 'Report on Nationality, Including Statelessness', 21 February 1952, UN Doc. A/CN.4/50.

23 Adopted on 10 December 1948, UN Doc. A/810, p. 71.

24 L.V. Oppenheim, *International Law*, vol. I, 8th edn (edited by H. Lauterpacht), London: Longmans Green, 1955, p. 669.

25 Adopted on 30 August 1961, UNTS, vol. 989, No. 14458.

26 Further on this issue S. Forlati, 'Nationality as a human right', *supra*, pp. 18–36.

27 Weissbrodt and Collins, 'The Human Rights', pp. 272–3.

28 As of 20 November 2012, the 1954 Convention has been ratified by 76 states, while the 1961 Convention by 48 states. Online. Available at: http://treaties.un.org.

29 Article 11 foresaw the creation of a body within the UN to which individuals claiming the benefit of the Convention may apply for the examination of their claims. However, the body has not been created so far.

30 Adopted on 18 December 1979, UNTS, vol. 1249, No. 20378.

31 Adopted on 20 November 1989, UNTS, vol. 1577, No. 27531.

32 Adopted on 6 November 1997, CETS 166.

33 As of 26 April 2012, the ECN has been ratified by 20 states. Online: Available at: http://www.conventions.coe.int.

34 D. O'Connell, *The Law of State Succession*, Cambridge: Cambridge University Press, 1956, p. 245.

35 A. Zimmermann, 'State Succession and Nationality of Natural Persons. Facts and Possible Codification', in P. Eisemann and M. Koskenniemi (eds) *La succession d'Etats: la codification à l'épreuve des faits. State Succession: Codification Tested against the Facts*, The Hague–London–Boston: M. Nijhoff, 2000, pp. 611–12.

36 1961 Convention, Article 10.

37 The concept has been expressly used by Judge Vučinić in his partly concurring, partly dissenting opinion to the judgment of the ECtHR in the *Case of Kurić and Others v Slovenia*, No. 26838/06, judgment (GC) of 26 June 2012, to define the 'erasure' of more than 25,000 persons from the Slovenian legal system.

38 I. Štiks, 'A Laboratory of Citizenship: Shifting Conceptions of Citizenship in Yugoslavia and its Successor States', *CITSEE Working Paper Series*, WP 2010/02, p. 11.

39 One of the conditions was that applicants had to provide a certificate demonstrating that they had been released from foreign citizenship, such as the republican citizenship of another of the republics composing the Yugoslav federation. However, because of the war, several persons were unable to obtain this evidence.

40 F. Ragazzi and I. Štiks, 'Croatian Citizenship: From Ethnic Engineering to Inclusiveness', in R. Bauböck, B. Perchinig and W. Sievers (eds) *Citizenship Policies in the New Europe*, Amsterdam: Amsterdam University Press, 2009, pp. 343–7.

41 On 26 June 2012 the ECtHR (GC) issued an important decision on this matter (*Kurić*), holding that Slovenian measures constituted a violation of Articles 8, 13 and 14 ECHR. The judgment did not specifically deal with the issue of statelessness, nor, more generally, with the impact of the erasure on the nationality of the affected individuals, as these complaints were declared incompatible *ratione temporis* with the provisions of the ECHR. This notwithstanding, it is worth highlighting that the Grand Chamber did not challenge the finding of the Chamber (judgment of 13 July 2010) according to which there has been a violation of Article 8 ECHR also 'in the light of relevant international law standards aimed at the avoidance of statelessness, especially in situations of State succession' (para. 376).

42 The situation was different in Lithuania, as the latter decided to grant its nationality to all permanent residents, thus accepting also Soviet-era migrants. On this see N. Gelazis, 'The European Union and the Statelessness Problem in the Baltic States', *European Journal of Migration and Law* 6, 2004, 227–8.

43 Baltic States claim that they never ceased to exist, despite 50 years of Soviet rule. This claim, grounded on the illegal nature of the Soviet incorporation, was backed by many states, although it was clearly inconsistent with international rules on statehood.

44 For a rightly critical account of these policies see Gelazis, 'The European Union', pp. 232–8.

45 The Latvian and Estonian governments maintained that their policies were not discriminatory, as they simply tried to undo forced cultural and demographic transformations that took place during the Soviet era. On this see A. Lottmann, 'No Direction Home: Nationalism and Statelessness in the Baltics', *Texas International Law Journal* 43, 2008, 515–16.

46 As a result of these policies, only 64 per cent of the resident population was eligible to participate to the 1993 elections in Latvia and around 60 per cent to the 1992 constitutional referendum in Estonia. Since then, the situation has slightly improved, but it is still far from having found a solution. According to UNHCR, as of January 2011 there were still 326,906 stateless persons in Latvia and 100,983 in Estonia.

47 Eritrea retaliated by deporting around 70,000 Ethiopians during the war. Although this represented a grave violation of the rights of the expelled

individuals, it did not put their nationality status in jeopardy, as they were Ethiopians nationals.

48 Such as being considered a supporter of the Eritrean government, being born in Eritrea, being born in Ethiopia but from at least one parent (or even grandparent) that was born in Eritrea. See J.R. Campbell, 'The Enduring Problem of Statelessness in the Horn of Africa: How Nation-States and Western Courts (Re) Define Nationality', *International Journal of Refugee Law* 23, 2011, 657–67.

49 *Yearbook of the International Law Commission*, 1993, vol. II, Part Two, p. 97, para. 440.

50 General Assembly, Resolution No. 48/31, 'Report of the International Law Commission on the work of its forty-fifth session', 9 December 1993.

51 Vienna Convention on Succession of States in Respect of Treaties, 23 August 1978, UNTS, vol. 1946, No. 33356, and Vienna Convention on Succession of States in Respect of State Property, Archives and Debts, 8 April 1983, UN Doc. A/CONF.11/14.

52 *Yearbook of the International Law Commission*, 1999, vol. II, Part Two, pp. 20–47.

53 The final form of the 1999 Draft Articles is still an issue for debate within the General Assembly. See General Assembly, Resolution No. 63/118, 'Nationality of natural persons in relation to the succession of states', 11 December 2008.

54 Adopted on 13–14 September 1997, *CDL-NAT*, vol. 7, 1996.

55 Adopted on 19 May 2006, CETS 200.

56 Preamble of the 2006 Convention.

57 C.P. Economidès, 'Les effets de la succession d'États sur la nationalité des personnes physiques', *Revue générale de droit international public* 103, 1999, p. 583.

58 A detailed analysis of this right and its legal status can be found in Forlati, 'Nationality as a human right', pp. 18–36.

59 This definition can be found in Article 1 of the 2006 Convention and Article 2 of the 1999 Draft Articles.

60 Explanatory Report to the 2006 Convention, para. 12.

61 Emphasis added.

62 Economidès, 'Les effets', p. 584.

63 Zimmermann, 'State Succession and Nationality', p. 643.

64 Ibid., pp. 644–5.

65 R. Schärer, 'The Council of Europe and the Reduction of Statelessness', *Refugee Survey Quarterly* 25, 2006, p. 35.

66 Adopted on 7 March 1966, UNTS, vol. 660, No. 9464.

67 Zimmermann, 'State Succession and Nationality', pp. 647–51.

68 D. Kochenov, 'EU Influence on the Citizenship Policies of the Candidate Countries: The Case of the Roma Exclusion in the Czech Republic', *Journal of Contemporary European Research* 3, 2007, 135–6.

69 'Report of the experts of the Council of Europe on the citizenship laws of the Czech Republic and Slovakia and their implementation', Strasbourg, 2 April 1996, DIR/JUR(96)4, paras 73–6.

70 This was not a case of unification in the proper sense, but one of annexation, as on 3 October 1990 the German Democratic Republic ceased to exist, becoming part of the Federal Republic of Germany.

71 North Yemen and South Yemen formed the Republic of Yemen on 22 May 1990.

72 Zimmermann, 'State Succession and Nationality', p. 616.

73 Part II of the 1999 Draft Articles.

74 Article 5 reads as follows:

> 1. A successor State shall grant its nationality to persons who, at the time of the State succession, had the nationality of the predecessor State, and who have or would become stateless as a result of the State succession if at that time: a. they were habitually resident in the territory which has become territory of the successor State, or b. they were not habitually resident in any State concerned but had an appropriate connection with the successor State. 2. For the purpose of paragraph 1, sub-paragraph b, an appropriate connection includes *inter alia:* a. a legal bond to a territorial unit of a predecessor State which has become territory of the successor State; b. birth on the territory which has become territory of the successor State; c. last habitual residence on the territory of the predecessor State which has become territory of the successor State.

Article 6 establishes that 'A predecessor State shall not withdraw its nationality from its nationals who have not acquired the nationality of a successor State and who would otherwise become stateless as a result of the State succession.'

75 See ICJ, *Nottebohm Case (Second Phase)(Liechtenstein v Guatemala)*, judgement of 6 April 1955, *ICJ Reports 1955*, pp. 16–17 and 20–1.

76 Weis, *Nationality and Statelessness*, pp. 196–7.

77 Article 20 (transfer of part of the territory), Article 22 (dissolution of a state) and Article 24 (separation of part of the territory) of the 1999 Draft Articles. See also Article 5 of the 2006 Convention.

78 J.F. Rezek, 'Le droit international de la nationalité', *Collected Courses of the Hague Academy of International Law* 198, 1987, 357.

79 I. Brownlie, *Principles of Public International Law*, 7th edn, Oxford: Oxford University Press, 2008, p. 656. *Contra* Weis, *Nationality and Statelessness*, pp. 143–4.

80 Economidès, 'Les effets', p. 584.

81 A. Zimmermann, 'State Succession in Other Matters than Treaties', *Max Planck Encyclopedia of Public International Law*, Oxford: Oxford University Press. Online. Available at: www.mpepil.com (accessed 22 May 2012), p. 6.

82 Treaty of Peace between the Allied and Associated Powers and Austria, Saint-Germain-en-Laye, 10 September 1919. Online. Available at: www.austlii.edu.au (accessed 3 September 2012), Article 70; Treaty of Peace between the Allied and Associated Powers and Hungary, Trianon, 4 June 1920. Online. Available at: www.austlii.edu.au (accessed 3 September 2012), Article 61.

83 Weis, *Nationality and Statelessness*, p. 147.

84 The Republic of South Sudan declared its independence after a referendum that was held from 9 to 15 January 2011 and that saw 98 per cent of the population voting in favour of independence.

85 This Act grants South Sudanese nationality to individuals with one parent, grand parent or great-grand parent born in South Sudan, to those belonging to one of the 'indigenous ethnic communities of South Sudan', and to those who (or whose parents or grandparents) had been habitual residents since 1956.

86 The situation is compounded by the fact that the new Sudanese Act does not allow dual nationality with South Sudan – while it does with all other countries – nor it gives to South Sudanese citizens any mean to renounce to their newly acquired nationality in order to retain their Sudanese one. On this point, and for a broad overview of both laws, see B. Manby, *The Right to a Nationality and the Secession of*

South Sudan: A Commentary on the Impact of the New Laws, Open Society Initiative for Eastern Africa, 2012. Online. Available at: www.soros.org/sites/default/files/right-nationality-and-secession-south-sudan-commentary-20120618.pdf (accessed 3 September 2012), pp. 26–32.

87 The law began to operate after the expiry of the 8 April 2012 deadline.

88 Estimates of the number of potentially affected individuals ranges between 500,000 to 700,000 individuals.

89 For instance, the Interim National Constitution of Sudan provides that the right to property is protected only for citizens.

90 2006 Convention, Article 17.

4 Nationality of individuals in public international law

A functional approach

Alice Sironi[1]

Introduction

Unity and fragmentation in nationality regulation

In today's international law, nationality regulation is torn between unity and fragmentation. Granting nationality status is still a prerogative that falls within states' sovereignty. States have the power to determine who their nationals are by establishing their domestic rules on the granting and withdrawal of nationality. Such a prerogative is the clear reflection of the close linkage between a state and its permanent population, generally considered as one of the elements of statehood.[2] In this respect, the current international discourse on nationality tends to over-emphasize the loss of states' prerogatives in this area. States' exclusive competence to establish domestic rules on nationality has remained almost unchanged for many years. Every attempt to identify a general rule binding states in this domain and applying in all circumstances has failed. The principle of the 'genuine link', so peremptorily reaffirmed by the International Court of Justice (ICJ) in 1955,[3] has little basis in international practice, at least beyond the specific field of multiple nationality.[4]

A number of scholars purported the application of the principle of the abuse of right to limit states' discretion to confer their nationality.[5] According to Leibholz, for example, an abuse of right is perpetrated when 'les causes d'acquisition de la nationalité n'étaient pas choisies par le législateur parmi les principes élaborés dans la pratique internationale et fondés dans la conscience juridique (Rechtsbewusstsein) des peuples'.[6] Oppenheim affirms that 'the conferment and deprivation of nationality is a right that International Law recognises as being within the exclusive competence of States; but it is a right the abuse of which may be a ground for an international claim'.[7] However, neither these nor other authors identify the exact scope of the principle of the abuse of right in the context of nationality, nor has the case law of international jurisdictions, so far, shed light on this issue.[8]

Few more specific rules could, instead, be considered as corresponding to international customary law: for instance, the prohibition of impinging on the rules on nationality of other states,[9] the prohibition of forced conferral of nationality upon individuals who have another nationality,[10] the prohibition of discrimination in the granting or withdrawal of nationality,[11] the right to change nationality or to renounce to a nationality,[12] and the obligation to prevent statelessness at birth and in the context of state succession.[13] In our view, these are the only international norms directly limiting the exclusive competence of states to design their internal rules on nationality. Beyond such norms, as far as the determination of nationality is concerned, the competence of a state remains unchanged.

International law takes into consideration the formal rules on nationality designed by each state in its domestic legislation. Except for the very specific limitations imposed by international law mentioned above, the rules established at the national level are fully valid also from an international perspective. In this domain international law does not attempt to define a model to be followed by domestic legislation in order to comply with international obligations. International law simply takes the formal, internal rules as they are. It is only when such rules are removed from the realm of the domestic jurisdiction and are inserted into one of the fields of international law in which they apply, that they are moulded and reinterpreted in order to make them better serve the function that they are called to fulfil in each specific international regime.

The theory of the functional approach to nationality is not a new one. Van Panhuys, among the first scholars to refer to this theory in the specific context of nationality, affirmed that 'restrictions imposed by international law on the competence of States to issue nationality rules are, of course, closely connected with the function of nationality in substantive law.'[14] More recently, the same approach has been adopted by Brownlie and Sloane.[15] Brownlie goes so far as to affirm that 'there seems to be general acquiescence in this splitting up of the legal content of nationality for particular purposes.'[16] Nevertheless, one must recognize that this fragmented approach has been repeatedly criticized by a number of scholars,[17] due to the risk of excessive relativization, which may lead to the unacceptable consequence of considering the same person as a national of a state, according to the interpretation imposed in pursuing one function, and as an alien, according to another function.

The theory of the functional approach to nationality in international law is only acceptable if interpreted in a way that does not exclude its coexistence with a unitary and necessarily formal concept of nationality. In this respect, Van Panhuys affirmed that

> the fact that within certain limits such concepts of nationality qualified for a special purpose, are permissible, does not mean, however, that, for the purpose of general international law, there does not exist a *general* concept of nationality (as a formal status) but only different status corresponding to different "functions" of nationality.[18]

In our view, this uniform status is the one established through the determination of the internal rules of each state relating to nationality.

International law still refers to national law for the determination of the nationality of individuals. The existence of this unitary and formal concept of nationality as established in national legislation tempers, to some extent, the centrifugal tendency of the functional theory. As a matter of fact, national rules, even when looked at through the lens of international law, are disregarded or considered devoid of any effect only in very rare and extreme cases. Examples include: the case of the withdrawal of the nationality of an international official by a state, with respect to which the organization employing the official refused to recognize such withdrawal and continued to consider the official as having his or her previous nationality for the application of its staff rules and regulations;[19] the same situation also arose in the case of a change of nationality made in view of eluding the organization's internal rules;[20] or, lastly, when the national law is clearly discriminatory.[21]

The functional approach to the rules on nationality comes as no surprise if it is framed within the general trend of fragmentation and progressive specialization of international law.[22] In each international regime, characterized by the application of some rules which are specific to that regime, the rules on nationality are also interpreted following the values and purposes that are pursued within the relevant framework.

The tension existing between unity and fragmentation in international law[23] is, therefore, also reflected in the regulation of nationality at the international level, where the unitary concept derived from the recognition of the validity of the internal rules on nationality is coupled with an atomization of the interpretation of such rules when inserted into each specific international regime. Nonetheless, one should not lose sight of the fact that, despite such a fragmented approach to nationality rules, general principles of international law still apply to matters of nationality.[24]

Functions of the rules on nationality in international law

The functions pursued in the interpretation of the rules on nationality in international law can be grouped in two broad categories. In some instances, the function is exogenous. This means that the function lies outside the general objectives of the specific legal domain in which it is inserted and responds instead to the purpose of protecting human rights. In other instances, the function is endogenous. In other words, it clearly reflects the purposes and values pursued in the specific legal regime in which the rules are inserted.

Clear signs of the first function can be found in the recent developments concerning the requirement of possession of the nationality of a given state in order to benefit from the latter's diplomatic protection. Such a requirement is interpreted and applied with increasing flexibility in consideration of the greater attention accorded to individuals' rights in comparison to state interests. The same pattern emerges from the case law of human rights bodies concerning the scope of states' obligations under international human rights law with respect to the conferral or withdrawal of nationality. Lastly, this first function finds further confirmation in the context of state succession, where great importance is accorded to the prevention of statelessness, as well as to the respect of the individual's will.

With regard to the second function, three main examples require attention. First, the International Centre for Settlement of Investment Disputes (ICSID) and its dispute tribunals in the domain of foreign investments have disavowed the principle of the genuine link with a view to recognizing the primacy of the domestic rules on nationality. The final aim of this approach is to encourage the participation of states in the arbitral system and, more generally, to promote a favourable environment for foreign investments.

A second example can be found in the practice of international organizations regarding the determination of the nationality of staff members. In case of inconsistencies in the interpretation given to the rules on nationality by the state of which the official is a national and by the organization, the position of the organization prevails, at least so far as the application of the internal rules of the organization is concerned.

Lastly, the recent developments in the restrictions imposed on national decisions regarding nationality by the European Court of Justice in order to protect European citizenship follow the direction of this second endogenous function as well.[25]

Interpretation of the rules on nationality in view of the protection of individuals' rights and interests

Nationality rules and diplomatic protection

The recent developments in the regulation of diplomatic protection towards an increased attention accorded to the rights and interests of individuals are clearly reflected in the Draft Articles adopted on second reading by the International Law Commission (ILC) in 2006 (2006 Draft Articles).[26] Such developments are particularly striking in the field of diplomatic protection, which was for a long time interpreted as a means to protect states' interests regarding the treatment of their nationals abroad.[27]

In its 2006 Draft Articles, the ILC begins by reiterating the traditional thesis according to which it is for each state to determine its rules on nationality. Article 4 provides that:

> For the purpose of nationality of natural persons, a State of nationality means a State whose nationality that person has acquired, in accordance with the law of that State, by birth, descent, naturalization, succession of States, or any other manner not inconsistent with international law.

The pertinence of the genuine link principle, in this domain, is expressly excluded in the Commentary to Article 4.[28] This exclusion could be interpreted as the first sign of an approach favourable to the interests of individuals. This is because such a strict condition for the validity of nationality would have the effect of making the nationality of a high number of persons who do not possess sufficient ties to their state of nationality, for instance if they have lived abroad for a long period, non-opposable to third states.

Moreover the ILC, in its analysis of the choice of cases in which the conferral of nationality would be inconsistent with international law, recognizes that, if a person acquires a nationality involuntarily in a manner inconsistent with international law, such person should in principle still enjoy the protection of his or her state of former nationality. Conversely, if the person lost his or her former nationality, equitable considerations require that the new state be entitled to exercise its diplomatic protection.[29]

A further development reflected in the 2006 Draft Articles concerns the traditional nationality-of-claims rule.[30] According to this rule, in order to identify the state having the right to file a claim for diplomatic protection for one of its nationals, the person concerned should have the nationality of that state both at the moment of the breach of international law on which the claim is based and at the moment the claim is filed. The ILC, adopting a view which is clearly oriented towards increasing the chances for individuals to be protected by their state of nationality, considers that an exception to the nationality-of-claims rule should be applied when the individual loses, either voluntarily or involuntary, his or her previous nationality and acquires a new nationality for reasons not related to the submission of the claim.

With respect to the question of multiple nationality, the ILC puts forward, yet again, a position favourable to individuals' interests. By going against a well-established rule of international law (i.e. the principle of equality),[31] in Article 7 of the 2006 Draft Articles, the ILC adopts the rule of the dominant nationality. According to this rule, a state can exercise its diplomatic protection even against a state of which the individual is also a national if the nationality of the claiming state can be considered as predominant. This position increases the chances of an individual to be protected by his or her state of nationality even when the claim is against a state of which the individual also possesses the nationality.[32]

In concluding on this first example of the interpretation of the rules on nationality in observing the specific function of the protection of the individuals' interests, it is worth noting that such a function is not exclusively pursued in the interpretation of questions relating to nationality status, but permeates the entire 2006 Draft Articles, including provisions relating to the diplomatic protection of refugees and stateless persons, legally resident in the territory of the state,[33] as well as of ships' crews.[34]

The right to a nationality

The approach serving the specific function of protecting the rights of individuals is, undoubtedly, at the core of designing the exact meaning and scope of the right to a nationality.[35] Such right is explicitly recognized in a number of international instruments.[36] The two main components of the right that one can find in the majority of relevant international texts are: the right to a nationality and the right not to be arbitrarily deprived of one's nationality.

The Inter-American Court of Human Rights (IACHR) explained the meaning of such two components as follows:

> [F]irst, the right to a nationality [...] provides the individual with a minimum measure of legal protection in international relations, through the link his nationality establishes between him and the State in question; and, second, the protection therein accorded [to] the individual against the arbitrary deprivation of his nationality, without which he would be deprived for all practical purposes of his political rights as well as of those civil rights that are tied to the nationality of the individual.[37]

The two components are often applied in conjunction in order to offer the broadest protection possible. In particular, these components applied together cover not only cases of arbitrary deprivation, but also of arbitrary denial of the nationality that one should be entitled to acquire in compliance with the legal provisions of a particular state. A brief study of the case law of different international and regional human rights monitoring bodies may help to shed some light on the meaning of the term 'arbitrary' in this context. The Human Rights Committee (HRC) has relied on some interesting elements in the interpretation of the term. In its General Comment No. 16 on the right to respect for private and family life, the HRC clarified that, for a measure not to be considered arbitrary, it is not sufficient that it complies with the law, but it should also be 'in accordance with the provisions, aims and objectives of the Covenant and should be, in any event, reasonable in the particular circumstances'.[38] In its General Comment No. 27, the HRC also specified that the interference can derive from any state action, legislative, administrative, or judicial.[39]

The judicial interpretation of the right to nationality, both with respect to the international legal texts which expressly recognize it[40] and to those texts for which the monitoring bodies need to refer to the extensive interpretation of a different provision,[41] is not well developed yet. In most cases, the concept of arbitrariness in the context of the right to nationality is interpreted as implying an infringement of the internal law.

This was the case, for example, of the IACHR's judgment in the *Bronstein v Peru* case, recognizing the violation of Articles 20(1) and 20(3) of the American Convention on Human Rights (ACHR) for the deprivation of nationality of a Peruvian, who was a former Israeli national, and had renounced his Israeli nationality to be naturalized in Peru. Peru withdrew his Peruvian nationality in violation of domestic law that did not provide for any possibility of withdrawal of nationality from a Peruvian citizen.[42]

In the more recent *Serrano Saenz v Ecuador* case, concerning a double national of Ecuador and United States, the Inter-American Commission on Human Rights considered that the deprivation of nationality suffered by the applicant was devoid of legal basis in internal law and, thus, carried out in breach of the ACHR.[43]

The HRC adopted the same approach in the *Gonzales v Guyana* case, concerning an arbitral denial of access to Guyanese nationality of a Cuban citizen, who regularly entered into Guyana and was married to a Guyanese national.[44] In this case too, the denial was considered arbitrary because it was carried out in violation of the internal law conferring the Guyanese nationality to persons married to a Guyanese citizen.

Although in the context of a judgment that did not find a violation of the Convention, the European Court of Human Rights (ECtHR) also recognized that the rejection of a demand to renounce one's nationality can, in some instances, entail a violation of Article 8 on the right to respect of private and family life.[45] Such a provision is the most frequently utilized by the ECtHR to deal with cases concerning nationality issues.

In other instances, international monitoring bodies still respect domestic law regulating nationality, but offer a different interpretation compared to the one followed by national authorities. This was the case, for example, in the very well-known judgment *Yean and Bosico v Dominican Republic*, rendered by the IACHR. The Court rejected the interpretation of the national authorities of the law applying the exception to the rule of *jus soli*, applicable to the children of foreigners in transit under the Dominican Constitution, to the children of Haitian migrant workers.[46]

The interpretation given to the domestic regulation by national authorities was disregarded also in a case lodged before the African Commission on Human and Peoples' Rights (AComHPR). In this case, the AComHPR, while respecting the principle that the rules on the granting and withdrawal of nationality were established by each state, reinterpreted autonomously the provisions of the Botswanian Constitution on the conferral of nationality. The AComHPR established that the applicant should have been considered as a national by birth in application of such provisions.[47]

To our knowledge, to date there is only one case in which the relevant national legislation was deemed by an international judicial body to be in breach of international law. In the recent case *Genovese v Malta*, the ECtHR found that the legislation of Malta, which discriminated among legitimate children and children born out of wedlock for the acquisition of the nationality of their father, violated Article 14 read in conjunction with Article 8 of the European Convention on Human Rights.[48] The case represents a possible development in the sense of a stricter control by the monitoring bodies of the content of domestic laws on nationality. However, it should be noted that this can easily be justified in light of the strong support existing at the international level of the prohibition of discrimination. Such prohibition can even be considered as corresponding to a customary norm of a peremptory nature.[49]

In conclusion, it is interesting to note that, even if the protection of the interests of individuals represents the *raison d'être* of human rights, i.e. the primary function pursued in this field, international monitoring bodies do not go so far as to put into question the lawfulness of national law, except in extreme cases, as in the ECtHR's case *Genovese* mentioned above. Nonetheless, international bodies clearly tend to autonomously reinterpret the relevant internal regulation in order to put it in line with the primary function pursued in this specific legal regime.

Nationality in the context of state succession

The regulation of nationality in the context of the succession of states is also clearly influenced by the development of the protection of human rights. The ILC expressly recognized that 'work on the topic should aim at the protection of the individual against any detrimental effects in the area of nationality resulting from State succession'.[50] In this specific context the principle of the effective link acquires renewed relevance.[51] Such a principle is however utilized to serve the specific function of finding the best solution for the situation of the individuals involved in the state succession. This means that the effective link is used as a parameter to identify the state responsible to grant its nationality to the individual. It is, then, clear that, in this context, the principle is not conceived as a limit to a state's competence to confer its nationality as it was in the *Nottebohm* judgment, but is rather aimed at identifying the state with which the individual is most closely connected, which is also responsible for attributing nationality to the individual.[52]

The function of protecting individuals' interests is particularly evident in two classes of provisions contained in the ILC Draft Articles on Nationality of Natural Persons in Relation to the Succession of States of 1999 (1999 Draft Articles),[53] as well as in other relevant international instruments. These include the provisions regulating the acquisition of nationality, which serve the objective of preventing statelessness, and the provisions that accord a particular importance to the individual's will, through the attribution to the same of a right of option.

The 1999 Draft Articles recall, at the outset, the applicability in this specific context of the right to a nationality, which is already recognized in a number of other international instruments.[54] The wording of Article 1 is of a particular interest because of the explicit reference contained therein to the irrelevance of the mode of acquisition of the nationality that the person concerned had before the state succession.[55] This is in line with the general tendency at international level to avoid any unjustified distinction based on the fact that the nationality has been obtained at birth or through subsequent naturalization.[56] Article 4 also reiterates the obligation for the states involved in the succession to prevent the persons who had the nationality of one of those states before the succession from becoming stateless. Nonetheless, identifying the state responsible for the conferral of nationality is not an easy task. The presumption of acquisition of nationality by all the persons having their habitual residence in the territory affected by the succession of states, contained in Article 5, is particularly interesting in this respect. However, such a presumption can be rebutted if the application of the provisions of the following draft articles leads to a different result.[57] The corresponding provision of the 2006 Council of Europe Convention on the Avoidance of Statelessness in Relation to State Succession (2006 Convention) is stricter, quite rightly, since its application is limited to those who had the nationality of the predecessor state, with the exclusion of stateless persons and of other permanent residents.[58] Stateless persons are still protected under Article 6(4) of the 2006 Convention, which obliges states to facilitate the acquisition of nationality by any stateless persons residing permanently on their territory.[59]

The particular attention accorded to the protection of the rights of the persons affected by a states succession is also clearly reflected in the provisions regarding the protection of the unity of the family,[60] the prohibition of discrimination on any ground,[61] the prohibition of arbitrary decisions,[62] and the protection of procedural rights relating to nationality issues.[63]

The influence of the human rights doctrine in this domain is further confirmed by the inclusion of a right of option in the 1999 Draft Articles,[64] as well as in the 2006 Convention.[65] The right of option is accorded to the individuals who have an appropriate connection with one of the successor states.[66] In this context, even the genuine or effective link principle is interpreted in a functional manner, and is reformulated to become an 'appropriate connection'. The ILC in the Commentary to Article 11 recognizes that such a term has a broader meaning to ensure that the highest possible number of persons be entitled to opt for the nationality of the successor state.[67] The same term is used also in the 2006 Convention in the context of state succession.[68]

The Commentary to the 1999 Draft Articles further specifies that the right of option, not only concerns the possibility to choose which nationality one wants to acquire (opting in), but also the right to renounce a nationality acquired *ex lege* (opting out).[69] Doctrinal views considerably diverge on the correspondence of the right of option to customary law. O'Connell refers to a conspicuous number of opinions by authors recognizing the right of the successor state to extend its nationality to persons by application of its law, without taking into consideration the will of such persons.[70] Opposing views also exist.[71] Many of them, however, consider that the rule can only be derived from a treaty provision. Indeed, there are many examples of the recognition of such a right in international treaties.[72] Other authors derive the principle and its customary nature from an extensive interpretation of the principle of self-determination.[73] The Badinter Arbitration Committee, dealing with the new republics created after the break-up of former Yugoslavia, in its opinion No. 2, referred to the principle of self-determination to conclude that the members of the Serbian population in Bosnia-Herzegovina and Croatia may be recognized under agreements between the republics 'as having the nationality of their choice'.[74] The importance attributed to the individual's will is also confirmed in the above-mentioned 2006 Convention as well as in the European Convention on Nationality (ECN).[75]

Interpretation of the rules on nationality in view of the broader objectives pursued in a specific legal regime

Nationality and international investments in the ICSID dispute tribunals' case law

The second category of function – i.e. the one in which the rules on nationality are interpreted in view of the objectives and values of the specific legal regime in which they are inserted – appears clearly in the regulation of international investments. This chapter will look in particular into the case law of the arbitration panels of the ICSID. In this context the investor should not be a national of the defendant state. This condition preserves the international character of the dispute. Article 25 of the Convention on the Settlement of Investment Disputes between States and Nationals of Other States (ICSID Convention)[76] clearly establishes this rule and defines a national of another contracting state as:

> [A]ny natural person who had the nationality of a Contracting State other than the State party to the dispute on the date on which the Parties consented to submit such dispute to conciliation or arbitration, as well as on the date on which the request was registered pursuant to paragraph (3) of Article 28 or paragraph (3) of Article 36, but does not include any person who on either date also had the nationality of the Contracting State to the dispute.[77]

The ICSID Convention, however, does not define the term 'nationality'. This gap is voluntary[78] and reflects the will of the drafters of the Convention to refer to the internal definition of nationality by each state.[79]

A short outline of the relevant case law will allow identifying the specific function pursued in this context. In the case *Champion Trading Company v Egypt*,[80] for instance, the Tribunal had to rule on the admissibility of a request for arbitration filed by three claimants, all with dual nationality of the USA and Egypt. They acquired the Egyptian nationality automatically at birth, *jure sanguinis*, from their father who was an Egyptian national. However, they did not have any significant tie to this country. The applicants maintained that their Egyptian nationality should not be considered valid in the absence of a genuine link between them and Egypt, as defined in the *Nottebohm* judgment and restated by the Iran–United States Claim Tribunal in case No. A/18. The Tribunal recalled the clear provision of Article 25(2)(A) of the ICSID Convention, which should be interpreted following their ordinary meaning, in compliance with Article 31 of the Vienna Convention on the Law of Treaties. It further evoked the possibility that it might 'be questionable if the third or fourth foreign born generation, which has no ties whatsoever with the country of its forefathers, could still be considered to have, for the purpose of the Convention, the nationality of this state.'[81] Nonetheless, having considered that such situation did not arise in the case under consideration, it concluded that the question need not be answered.[82]

In the case *Siag v Egypt*,[83] the Tribunal refused to consider any reference to the factual ties of the claimants to a specific state as relevant. The case was brought to the Tribunal by three Italian nationals. Egypt argued that they had retained their Egyptian nationality and that, consequently, the claim should be declared inadmissible. Although the claimants had very close ties to Egypt and much weaker ties to Italy, the Tribunal preferred to rely on the textual provision of the Italian law to recognize that they had acquired the Italian nationality and contextually lost the Egyptian citizenship. Consequently, the case was declared admissible, under Article 25(2)(a) of the ICSID Convention.

In the case *Soufraki v the United Arab Emirates*,[84] Mr Soufraki, a Canadian national, contended that he could benefit from the protection afforded to Italian citizens by the Bilateral Investment Treaty (BIT), which was concluded between Italy and the United Arab Emirates. Notwithstanding his submission to the Tribunal of two Italian passports, five birth certificates and a letter from the Italian ministry of foreign affairs recognizing that Mr Soufraki had Italian nationality, the Tribunal rejected his contention. The decision of the ICSID panel was based on the application of the Italian law providing that a formal request to keep the Italian nationality is required in case of acquisition of another nationality. Mr Soufraki did not submit this request to the Italian authorities when he acquired the Canadian nationality and, thus, could not be considered an Italian citizen anymore.

In the case *Micula v Romania*, involving two former Romanian nationals who had acquired Swedish nationality, the Tribunal refused to apply the effective link principle and explicitly recognized, not only the application of national law for the determination of nationality of the claimant, but also the wide margin of appreciation which states have in applying their internal law.[85]

The case law of the ICSID tribunals on the issue of nationality of natural persons clearly reflects the function pursued according to the object and purpose of the relevant Convention. The World Bank, in creating the ICSID system aimed to promote the flow of capital from developed to underdeveloped countries, by establishing a dispute settlement system to diminish the political risks, which may deter international investments.[86]

Instead of following the uneven path of the application of the effective nationality principle, the ICSID tribunals prefer to interpret the rules on nationality in a formal way. Thus, they simply apply the rules established internally by the state the nationality of which is concerned. In this way, states' sovereignty to determine nationality is fully respected and the outcome of the determination of jurisdiction is more foreseeable. This approach serves the primary purpose of the ICSID Convention to favour an atmosphere of mutual confidence, thus stimulating international capital flows.

Nationality of international civil servants

One of the fields in which the functional approach to nationality is most evident is the nationality of international organizations' officials. Nationality plays a fundamental role both at the recruitment stage and in the following service of the official with the organization. The two main rules applicable in these two stages are: the rule of the equitable geographical distribution[87] and the rule of the independence of international officials from states, which requires commitment to pursue exclusively the interests of the organization in the discharge of their duties.[88]

In this domain, the organization goes so far as to interfere with the states' prerogative to determine the nationality of natural persons. In some cases, the organization refuses to accept a change of nationality for the purpose of the application of its internal rules. This happened in a number of cases during the last century, particularly before the outbreak of the Second World War, with the establishment of totalitarian regimes. Certain states adopted the practice to revoke the nationality of individuals who had become *personae non gratae*. However, in some instances, the international organizations, in order to safeguard their independence, refused to recognize such loss of nationality and continued to consider the person as a national of their former state of nationality.[89]

This practice clearly shows that in case of inconsistencies in the determination of nationality made by the state and by the organization employing the national of the said state, the opinion of the organization expressed by its secretary or director general should prevail, at least as far as the application of the internal rules of the organization is concerned.[90]

Such a position is confirmed also by the case law of the international organizations' administrative tribunals. In one case, a change in nationality made with the exclusive purpose of obtaining an economical advantage within the UN – in particular, a repatriation grant – was considered by the United Nations Administrative Tribunal (UNAT) as abusive and was not recognized for the purpose of the application of the Staff Rules and Regulations.[91]

The second domain in which the interpretation of the rules on nationality in view of the specific purposes of international organizations is clearly visible is the determination of the dominant nationality in the case of officials with multiple nationality. Rule 4.3 of the United Nations Staff Rules, for instance, regulates this matter as follows:

> (a) In the application of the Staff Regulations and Staff Rules, the United Nations shall not recognize more than one nationality for each Staff member; (b) When a Staff member has been legally accorded nationality status by more than one state, the staff member's nationality for the purposes of Staff Regulations and Staff Rules shall be the nationality of the state with which the staff member is, in the opinion of the Secretary-General, most closely associated.[92]

The secretary general has the power to determine the nationality that should be considered to be the dominant nationality for purposes of the organization. The international administrative tribunals respect the discretionary power of the secretary or director general, and limit their control to the cases of error of law or of fact.[93]

Lastly, it is interesting to note the actual rejection of the rationale underpinning the principle of genuine link by international organizations, which tend to separate the notion of nationality from the notion of *home country* for the purposes of the determination of some entitlements, such as the repatriation grant. Rule 5.2(d)(iii) of the UN Staff Rules and Regulations, for example, provides that 'The Secretary general may authorize: a. A country other than the country of nationality as the home country, for the purpose of this rule, in exceptional and compelling circumstances.'

Conclusion

From the brief analysis of the interpretation given to the rules on nationality in different domains, it is clear that the traditional view of the states' exclusive competence to legislate their own rules on the conferral and withdrawal of nationality in most cases is still valid. Recent exceptions to the exclusive competence of states in this domain have only involved extreme cases, such as rules patently in breach of the prohibition of discrimination,[94] or changes of nationality carried out with the exclusive view to eluding the internal rules of an international organization by one of its staff members.[95]

Notwithstanding states' competence to determine who their nationals are, the rules relating to nationality are interpreted at the international level with a view to serving the specific function of the protection of individuals' rights or of the broad objectives underlying a particular legal regime. This functional interpretation generally refers to national law to determine the nationality status of a natural person. However, in some cases, international bodies interpret national law differently than the interpretation adopted by national authorities.[96] This is an evolution worth noting and comparing to the traditional position, according to which 'From the standpoint of International Law [...], municipal laws are merely facts'.[97] This evolution is especially noteworthy, considering that the traditional position implies that international jurisdictions have to defer to national authorities as far as the interpretation of national law is concerned, and cannot interpret it autonomously.[98]

The competence to reinterpret national law is generally accepted at the international level in cases where it is necessary to determine whether an international tribunal has jurisdiction over a specific case.[99] This is true also when jurisdiction is based on the determination of the nationality of one of the parties, as in the ICSID system. The ICSID ad hoc Committee, called to decide on the application for annulment of Mr Soufraki, recognized that:

> [I]t is a general principle that a State does not have the last word when a question is raised before an international tribunal concerning the interpretation of its national law, when it comes to a question on which the jurisdiction of the Tribunal depends.[100]

Specifically concerning the determination of nationality of one of the parties the ad hoc Committee stated that:

> [I]nternational tribunals are empowered to determine whether a party has the alleged nationality in order to ascertain their own jurisdiction, and are not bound by national certificates of nationality or passports or other documentation in making that determination and ascertainment.[101]

Conversely, when the determination of nationality is not related to the determination of the jurisdiction of a judicial authority, but rather to the decision on the merit of the case, international tribunals are generally inclined to recognize the exclusive competence of states' authorities to interpret their internal law.[102] In the human rights domain, for example, the judicial and semi-judicial bodies, which control the application of the human rights instruments, constantly reiterate that 'it falls to the national authorities to apply and to interpret domestic law'.[103]

However, in the field of nationality, there are now visible signs of a tendency to reinterpret national law independently in case the interpretation provided by national authorities of their law would be in breach of the function pursued in this domain. This approach was adopted at least in two cases mentioned above: in the judgment *Yean and Bosico v Dominican Republic* of the IACHR and in the decision *John Modise v Botswana* of the AComHPR. Such a development is particularly striking in the field of nationality, which is generally considered to be reserved to the domain of domestic jurisdiction.[104]

To complete the outline of the current approach to nationality issues in international law, it is interesting to look at the role left to the genuine link principle. Such a principle and its underlying rationale, while they do not have a general validity as a limitation to states' competence in this field, still re-emerge intermittently solely when they serve the function pursued in the context of a specific legal regime. For example, when the identification of the nationality is taken into account by an international organization with respect to a staff member with multiple nationality – or when it allows for a better protection of the rights of individuals. Another example is in the context of state succession for the identification of the state responsible for granting its nationality.

Therefore, the study of the contemporary practice in the field of nationality at international level shows that the genuine link principle should not be considered as a general principle of international law limiting the competence of states to grant or withdraw their nationality. However, its underlying rationale is still used as a parameter that allows for more concreteness to the application of the rules on nationality, when the specific function pursued in the relevant context so requires. The scope of the genuine link principle, which for a long time has been overemphasized, should then be put back in its correct perspective.

Notes

1 The author wishes to warmly thank Aliya, Niccolò and Laura for their very useful linguistic comments on the text.

2 H.J. Sonnenberg and H. von Mangoldt, 'Anerkennung der Staatsangehörigkeit und effektive Staatsangehörigkeit natürlicher Personen im Völkerrecht und im internationalen Privatrecht', *Berichte der Deutschen Gesellschaft für Völkerrecht* 29, 1988, 63, and J.F. Rezek, 'Le droit international et la nationalité', *Collected Courses of the Hague Academy of International Law* 198, 1986-III, 336ff. at 341, where the author states that nationality is 'la dimension personnelle de l'Etat'.

3 *Nottebohm Case (Guatemala v Liechtenstein)*, judgment of 6 April 1955, *ICJ Reports 1955*, p. 4.

4 The ICJ itself, when it outlines the previous relevant practice, refers to cases concerning double or multiple nationality. In these cases, the use of the principle has a completely different meaning since its purpose is not to define a limit for states relating to the conferral of nationality but to compare the positions of two states with regard to an individual in order to determine which one of the two states has the right to exercise its diplomatic protection in respect of the individual. Ibid., pp. 22–3. For a critical appraisal of the *Nottebohm* judgment see R.D. Sloane, 'Breaking the Genuine Link: The Contemporary Legal Regulation of Nationality', *Harvard International Law Journal* 50, 2009, 1–60.

5 Ibid., pp. 19ff.; A. Kiss, *L'abus de droit en droit international*, Paris: Librairie générale de droit et de jurisprudence, 1953, pp. 147–61; G. Leibholz, 'Staatsangehörigkeit und Naturalisation', in J. Hatschek and K. Strupp (eds) *Wörterbuch des Völkerrechts und der Diplomatie*, vol. II, 1925, p. 589; G. Scelle, *Manuel de droit international public*, Paris: Domat-Monchrestien, 1948, pp. 110–11.

6 Leibholz, 'Staatsangehörigkeit und Naturalisation', p. 589, as quoted by A.N. Makarov, 'Règles générales du droit de la nationalité', *Collected Courses of the Hague Academy of International Law* 74, 1949, 273–375 at 300.

7 L. Oppenheim, *International Law: A Treatise*, London–New York–Toronto: Longmans, Green and Co., 1937, vol. 1, p. 280.

8 To our knowledge, to date, the principle has only been expressly recognised as applicable to the conducts of individuals whose acquisition of nationality was allegedly obtained in a fraudulent manner or in breach of the obligation of *bona fide*. In these cases, it was recognized that the state, that had conferred

its nationality, could not invoke it to justify its claim. See, for example, *Salem Case (Egypt v USA)*, 8 June 1932, *UNRIAA*, vol. II, pp. 1161–237 at 1186. More recently, the United Nations Compensation Commission created to redress injuries suffered by Kuwaitis and others after the Gulf War of 1991 decided that only the Iraqi nationals who had acquired a second nationality *bona fide* were eligible for claiming compensation before the Commission (United Nations Compensation Commission, Governing Council, 'Report and Recommendations Made by the Panel of Commissioners Concerning the Sixth Instalment of Claims for Departure from Iraq or Kuwait (Category "A" Claims)', 16 October 2006, UN Doc. S/AC.26/1996/3, paras 29–31). Judges Kleastad and Read referred to the applicability of the concept of fraud and abuse of right in their dissenting opinions to the ICJ *Nottebohm* judgement (pp. 28 and 34 respectively). However, only Judge Read recognized the applicability of the abuse of right to the conduct of the government of Liechtenstein (ibid., p. 49). The Iran–United States Claims Tribunal considered the concept of effectiveness set forth in the *Nottebohm* judgement as an application of the principle of the abuse of the competence of states to grant their nationality (Case A/18, 6 April 1984, *International Law Reports* 75, 1987, 176–268 at 254). On the application of the principle of the abuse of right in the context of the determination of nationality of companies see G. D'Agnone, 'Determining the nationality of companies in ICSID arbitration', *infra*, pp. 153–68.

9 A number of authors referred to this limit: J.P. Niboyet, *Traité de droit international privé*, Paris: Sirey, 1943, vol. 1, p. 83; Makarov, 'Règles générales du droit de la nationalité', p. 296; A.F. Panzera, *I limiti internazionali in materia di cittadinanza*, Napoli: Jovene, 1984, p. 63.

10 See the practice mentioned in P. Weis, *Nationality and Statelessness in International Law*, Alphen aan den Rijn: Sijthoff & Noordhoff, 1979, pp. 103–13.

11 See S. Forlati, 'Nationality as a human right', *supra*, pp. 18–36 at 23.

12 However, it has to be noted that this right does not have an absolute character and states can impose some restrictions to its enjoyment, for example in order to oblige the individual to comply with tax obligations or with military service duties. In addition, the right can be limited if, as a result of its exercise, the person becomes stateless. On the right to renounce to one's nationality, see, for instance, ECtHR, *Riener v Bulgaria*, No. 46343/99, judgment of 23 May 2006, paras 151–9. On the relevant legislation of the states parties to the Convention, see paras 85–8. However, the Explanatory Report of the ECN states that military obligations in the country of origin or pending civil or penal proceedings are not sufficient justifications to refuse renunciation of a nationality (Online. Available at: http://conventions.coe.int/Treaty/EN/Reports/Html/166.htm (accessed 3 September 2012), para. 78). See also A. Peters, 'Extraterritorial Naturalizations: Between the Human Right to Nationality, State Sovereignty and Fair Principles of Jurisdiction', *German Yearbook of International Law* 53, 2010, pp. 623–725 at 659–77, and Forlati, 'Nationality as a human right', p. 27.

13 See F. Costamagna, 'Statelessness in the context of state succession', *supra*, pp. 37–53.

14 H.F. Van Panhuys, *The Role of Nationality in International Law. An Outline*, Leiden: Sijthoff, 1959, p. 165.

15 Sloane, 'Breaking the Genuine Link', pp. 23–7.

16 I. Brownlie, *International Public Law*, Oxford: Oxford University Press, 2008, p. 406.

17 For example, F. De Castro y Bravo, 'La nationalité, la double-nationalité et la supra-nationalité', *Collected Courses of the Hague Academy of International Law* 102, 1961-I, 515–634 at 555 and Panzera, *I limiti internazionali in materia di cittadinanza*, p. 24.

18 Van Panhuys, *The Role of Nationality in International Law*, p. 167.

19 See notes 89 and 90 below.

20 See note 90 below.

21 See note 47 below.

22 See the work of the ILC, 'Conclusions of the work of the Study Group on Fragmentation of International Law: Difficulties arising from the Diversification and Expansion of International Law', *Yearbook of the International Law Commission*, 2006, vol. II, pp. 407–23; J. Crawford, A. Pellet and S. Wittich (eds) *International Law Between Universalism and Fragmentation*, Leiden: M. Nijhoff, 2009.

23 C. Tomuschat, 'International Law as a Coherent System: Unity or Fragmentation?', in M.H. Arsanjani, *Looking to the Future: Essays on International Law in Honor of W. Micheal Reisman*, The Hague: M. Nijhoff, 2011, p. 323.

24 In 2008, for example, with respect to the 'passaportization' policy of Russia in South Ossetia and Abkhazia, the EU fact-finding mission on the conflict between Georgia and Russia recognized the applicability of the general principles of the prohibition of violation of another state's personal jurisdiction, the prohibition of violation of territorial sovereignty, the principle of non-interference in the internal affairs of another state and the principle of good neighborliness: International Independent Fact-finding Mission on the Conflict in Georgia, *Report*. Online. Available at: www.ceiig.ch/Report.html (accessed 12 April 2012), vol. II, pp. 171, 172 and 174.

25 See, in particular, ECJ, C-135/08, *Rottman*, judgment (GC) of 2 March 2010. Due to space limitation, this particular domain will not be covered in this chapter. For a discussion on the recent developments in the EU law on matters related to member states nationality and European citizenship please refer to the chapter of P. Simone, 'Nationality and regional integration: the case of the European Union', *infra*, pp. 169–92.

26 The text of the 2006 Draft Articles, together with the Commentaries, are contained in ILC, 'Report on the work of the fifty-eighth session', *UNGAOR, Sixty-first Session, Supplement No. 10*, UN Doc. A/61/10.

27 On the traditional approach to diplomatic protection see E. de Vattel, *Le droit des gens, ou principes de la loi naturelle appliqués à la conduite et aux affaires des nations et des souverains*, 1758, book I, pp. 309–10, paras 71–2; J. Brown Scott (ed.) *Classics of International Law*, vol. II, Washington D.C.: Carnegie Institution of Washington, 1916; H.W. Briggs, 'The Diplomatic Protection of Individuals in International Law. The Nationality of Claims', *Yearbook of the Institute of International Law* 51, 1965-I, pp. 9ff.; G. Berlia, 'Contribution à l'étude de la nature de la protection diplomatique', *Annuaire français de droit international* 3, 1957, pp. 63–72; J. Cuthbert, *Nationality and Diplomatic Protection: The Commonwealth of Nations*, Leiden: Sijthoff, 1969. C.F. Amerasinghe, *Diplomatic Protection*, Oxford: Oxford University Press, 2008.

28 See, in particular, Commentary to Article 4, para. 5.

29 Ibid., pp. 34–5. To support its thesis the ILC makes reference to the ICJ advisory opinion on Namibia, in which the Court recognized that: 'individual rights should not be affected by an illegal act on the part of the State with which the individual is associated', *Legal Consequences for States of the Continued Presence of South Africa in Namibia (South West Africa) Notwithstanding Security Council resolution 276 (1970)*, advisory opinion of 21 June 1971, *ICJ Reports 1971*, p. 16 at 56, para. 125.

30 On the decreasing importance of such rule, see Vermeer-Künzli, 'Nationality and diplomatic protection: a reappraisal', *infra*, pp. 76–95.

31 Such principle was characterised as 'ordinary practice' in ICJ, *Reparation for Injuries Suffered in the Service of the United Nations*, advisory opinion of 11 April 1949, *ICJ Reports 1949*, p. 174. The principle was also adopted in the 1930 Convention. Article 4 provides that: '[a] State may not afford diplomatic protection to one of its nationals against a State whose nationality such person also possess'. On the two principles of dominant nationality and of equality see A.M. Boll, *Multiple Nationality and International Law*, Leiden: M. Nijhoff, 2007, pp. 116–21.

32 The described developments concerning diplomatic protection can easily be framed within the general increasing tendency of states to take action with a view to protecting the rights of their nationals. See, in particular, the increasing number of cases brought before the ICJ with a view to ensuring the respect of individuals rights, such as *Amadou Sadio Diallo (Republic of Guinea v Democratic Republic of the Congo*, judgment of 24 May 2007, *ICJ Reports 2007*, p. 582; *Avena and Other Mexican Nationals (Mexico v United States of America)*, judgment of 31 March 2004, *ICJ Reports 2004*, p. 12; *LaGrand (Germany v United States of America)*, judgment of 27 June 2001, *ICJ Reports 2001*, p. 466; *Breard (Paraguay v United States of America)*, order of 9 April 1998, *ICJ Reports 1998*, p. 248. See also E. Milano, 'Diplomatic protection and human rights before the International Court of Justice: refashioning tradition?', *Netherlands Yearbook of International Law* 35, 2004, pp. 85–142.

33 2006 Draft Articles, Article 8.

34 Ibid., Article 18.

35 On this topic see Forlati, 'Nationality as a human right', pp. 19ff.

36 UDHR, 10 December 1948. Online. Available at: www.un.org (accessed 3 September 2012), Article 15; ACHR, adopted on 22 November 1969, OAS Treaty Series, No. 36, Article 20; ArCHR, adopted by the League of Arab States on 22 May 2004, reprinted in *Boston University International Law Journal*, 24, 2006, 147–64, Article 29; CRC, adopted on 20 November 1989, UNTS, vol. 1577, No. 27531, Article 7; ICCPR, adopted on 16 December 1966, UNTS, vol. 999, No. 14668, Article 24(3); ICRMW, adopted on 18 December 1990, UNTS, vol. 2220, No. 39481, Article 29; ECN, adopted on 6 November 1997, CETS 166, Article 4. In addition, some international instruments deal with the problem of the reduction of statelessness: the 1961 Convention, adopted on 30 August 1961, UNTS, vol. 989, No. 14458, and the 2006 Convention, adopted on 19 May 2006, CETS 200.

37 IACHR, *Proposed Amendments to the Naturalization Provisions of the Constitution of Costa Rica*, advisory opinion OC-4/84 of 19 January 1984, *Series A*, No. 4, para. 32.

38 General Comment No. 16, 'The right to respect of privacy, family, home and correspondence, and protection of honor and reputation (Art. 17)', 8 April 1988,

para. 4. See also UN secretary general, 'Human rights and arbitrary deprivation of nationality', 14 December 2009, UN Doc. A/HCR/13/34, paras 24–5.

39 General Comment No. 27, 'Freedom of movement (Art. 12)', 2 November 1999, CCPR/C/21/Rev.1/Add.9, para. 21.

40 See note 36 above.

41 Reference is made to the ECHR and to the ICCPR. In both cases the ECtHR and the HRC primarily refer to the right to respect of private and family life (Article 8 ECHR and Article 17 ICCPR respectively). However, the HRC has also referred to the right to return to one's own country, see case *Simalae and others v New Zealand*, views of 2 November 2000, CCPR/C/70/D/675/1995, para. 11.4.

42 IACHR, *Ivcher Bronstein v Peru*, judgment of 6 February 2001, *Series C*, No. 74, paras 85–97.

43 Inter-American Commission on Human Rights, *Nelson Ivan Serrano Saenz v. Ecuador*, report No. 84/09, 6 August 2009.

44 HRC, *Patricia Angela Gonzales v Guyana*, views of 25 March 2010, CCPR/C/98/D/1246/2004.

45 ECtHR, *Riener v Bulgaria*, No. 46343/99, judgment of 25 March 2006. See also the partly dissenting opinion of Judge Maruste.

46 IACHR, *Case of the Girls Yean and Bosico v The Dominican Republic*, judgment of 8 September 2005, *Series C*, No. 130, paras 156–8. However, it is to be noted that the national court had already rejected the interpretation given to the constitutional and legislative provisions by the state authorities, see in particular paras 153–4.

47 AComHPR, *John Modise v Botswana*, communication 97/93, decided at the 28th ordinary session, Oct/Nov 2000, *African Human Rights Law Reports*, 2000, para. 86.

48 ECtHR, *Genovese v Malta*, No. 53124/09, judgment of 11 October 2011. See also the case *Kurić v Slovenia*, No. 26828/06, judgment of 13 July 2012, where the Court criticized the internal law by adopting the same view of the Slovenian Constitutional Court, paras 364–73. However, we do not consider this case as directly linked to the right to nationality since the question of the withdrawal of nationality was declared inadmissible *ratione temporis* by the Court. See, in particular, para. 355 of the judgment. The same approach was reiterated also by the Grand Chamber in its recent judgment of 26 June 2012. See in particular paras 347–8.

49 IACHR, *Yean and Bosico*, para. 141. See also Forlati, 'Nationality as a human right', p. 24.

50 ILC, 'Report on the work of its forty-seventh session', 10 January 1996, UN Doc. A/CN.4/472/Add.1, para. 6.

51 Ibid., para. 8. See also J.L. Blackman, 'State succession and statelessness: the emerging right to an effective nationality under international law', *Michigan Journal of International Law* 19, 1997–8, 1141–94.

52 In view of this difference we prefer to use the term effective link, in this context, instead of genuine link or genuine connection utilized by the ICJ in *Nottebohm*. The ILC in the Commentary to Article 11, para. 9, of the Draft Articles on Nationality of Natural Persons in relation to the Succession of States (1999 Draft Articles, quoted below, note 52), refers to the term 'appropriate connection', considered broader than genuine link.

53 The text of the 1999 Draft Articles, together with the Commentaries, are contained in *Yearbook of the International Law Commission*, 1999, vol. II, Part II, pp. 23–47.
54 See note 36 above.
55 Article 1 reads as follows:

> Every individual who, on the date of the succession of States, had the nationality of the predecessor State, irrespective of the mode of acquisition of that nationality, has the right to the nationality of at least one of the States concerned, in accordance with the present draft articles.

56 See, for example, IACHR, *Proposed Amendments to the Naturalization Provisions of the Constitution of Costa Rica*, paras 61–2, and ECN, Article 5(2).
57 See Commentary to Article 5, para. 2.
58 2006 Convention, Article 5.
59 See para. 18 of the Explanatory Report to the 2006 Convention. Online. Available at: http://conventions.coe.int/Treaty/EN/Reports/Html/200.htm (accessed 15 February 2012).
60 1999 Draft Articles, Article 12.
61 Ibid., Article 15.
62 Ibid., Article 16.
63 Ibid., Article 17. See also Article 12 of the 2006 Convention, as well as Article 11 on the right to information and Article 8 on the rules of proof.
64 1999 Draft Articles, Article 11. See also Articles 20, 23 and 26 on the right of option in the context of specific categories of state succession.
65 2006 Convention, Article 7.
66 1999 Draft Articles, Article 11(2).
67 Commentary to Article 11 of the 1999 Draft Articles, paras 9–10.
68 2006 Convention, Article 7.
69 Commentary to Article 11 of the 1999 Draft Articles, para. 6. On the shift of the attention from the right to opt out to the right to opt in since 1990's see Y. Ronen, 'Option of Nationality,' *Max Planck Encyclopedia of Public International Law*. Online. Available at: www.mpepil.com (accessed 10 May 2012), p. 3, citing the example of USSR, Yugoslavia and Czechoslovakia, as well as the case of states relinquishing territory, such as during United Kingdom and France decolonization.
70 D.P. O'Connell, *The Law of State Succession*, Cambridge: Cambridge University Press, 1956, p. 250.
71 See, for example, C. Rousseau, *Droit international public*, Paris: Dalloz, 1987, pp. 174–5.
72 The ILC cites numerous treaties recognizing the right of option. See Commentary to Article 11, 1999 Draft Article, paras 2–4.
73 J.L. Kunz, 'L'option de nationalité', *Collected Courses of the Hague Academy of International Law* 31, 1930-I, 111–75, and 'Nationality and option clauses in the Italian Peace Treaty of 1947', *American Journal of International Law* 41, 1947, 622–31.
74 See Ronen, 'Option of Nationality,' p. 2 and A. Pellet, 'The Opinions of the Badinter Arbitration Committee: A Second Breath for the Self-Determination of Peoples', *European Journal of International Law* 3, 1992, 178–85 at 179.
75 See Articles 7 and 18(c) and Article 8(2), respectively.

76 UNTS, vol. 575, No. 8359.
77 Ibid., Article 25(a).
78 A. Broches, 'The Convention on the Settlement of Investment Disputes Between States and Nationals of other States', *Collected Courses of the Hague Academy of International Law* 136, 1972, 331–410 at 358.
79 Sloane, 'Breaking the Genuine Link', p. 18; S. Trevisanut, 'Nationality Cases before International Courts and Tribunals', *Max Planck Encyclopedia of Public International Law*. Online. Available at: http: www.mpepil.com (accessed 10 May 2012), para. 18.
80 ICSID, *Champion Trading Company Ameritrade International, Inc. v Arab Republic of Egypt*, No. ARB/02/9, decision on jurisdiction of 26 July 2001. Online. Available at: https://icsid.worldbank.org/ICSID/FrontServlet (accessed 2 September 2012).
81 Ibid., p. 288, *in fine*.
82 Ibid., p. 289.
83 ICSID, *Waguih Elie George Siag and Clorinda Vecchi v Arab Republic of Egypt*, No. ARB/05/15, decision on jurisdiction of 11 April 2007, *International Legal Materials* 46, 2007, 863–85.
84 See ICSID, *Hussein Nuaman Soufraki v United Arab Emirates*, No. ARB/02/7, 7 July 2004, as well as the following decision of the ad hoc Committee on the application for annulment of the award, 5 June 2007. Online. Available at: https://icsid.worldbank.org/ICSID/FrontServlet (accessed 2 September 2012), in particular paras 50–78.
85 ICSID, *Ioan Micula et al. v Romania*, No. ARB/05/20, decision on jurisdiction and admissibility of 24 September 2008, *International Legal Materials* 48, 2009, 51–78, in particular para. 95.
86 ICSID, 'Report of the Executive Directors on the Convention on the Settlement of Investment Disputes Between States and nationals of Other States', 18 March 1965, part III, para. 9, *ICSID Reports* 1, 1993, p. 23. See also Broches, 'The Convention on the Settlement of Investment Disputes', pp. 342–3 and Sloane, 'Breaking the genuine link', p. 24.
87 See R. Donner, *The Regulation of Nationality in International Law*, Irvington on Hudson, New York: Transnational Publishers, 1994, p. 350.
88 See Article 100 UN Charter, as well as the provision on the conferment of privileges and immunities, Article 105(2) of the Charter.
89 E.F. Ratshofen-Wertheimer, *The International Secretariat: A Great Experiment in International Administration*, Washington: Carnegie Endowment, 1945, p. 363. See also the position of the first UN Secretary General, T. Lie, *In the Cause of Peace: Seven Years with the United Nations*, New York: The Macmillan Company, 1954, p. 394.
90 On the case of officials seconded by a government see UNAT, *Qiu v United Nations Secretary General*, No. 482, judgment of 25 May 1990, UN Doc. AT/DEC/482.
91 UNAT, *Case No. 1383*, judgment No. 1300 of 29 September 2006, UN Doc. AT/DEC/1300.
92 UN Doc. ST/SGB/2009/7, 21 October 2009.
93 ILOAT, *Giuffrida*, judgment of 23 September 1960, *International Law Reports* 32, 1966, p. 513 and UNAT, *Julhiard*, No. 62, judgment of 3 December 1955, *International Law Reports* 22, 1955, p. 809.

94 See ECtHR, *Genovese v Malta*, paras 43–50.

95 See UNAT, *Case No. 1383*, para. VII.

96 Oppenheim in this respect stated that:

> notwithstanding the general principle that it is for each state to determine who are its nationals, a state's assertion that in accordance with its laws a person possesses its nationality is not conclusive evidence of that fact for international purposes
>
> R. Jennings and A. Watts, *Oppenheim's International Law*, 9th edn, Harlow: Longman, 1992, p. 854.

97 PCIJ, *Case Concerning Certain German Interests in the Polish Upper Silesia*, judgment of 25 August 1925, PCIJ *Series A*, No. 70, p. 19. See also P.-M. Dupuy, 'International Law and Domestic (Municipal) Law', *Max Planck Encyclopedia of Public International Law*. Online. Available at: www.mpepil.com (accessed 10 May 2012), paras 29–37.

98 See Brownlie, *Principles of Public International Law*, p. 39. The author also refers to the opinion of certain judges of the ICJ who have stated 'as a corollary of the proposition that "municipal laws are merely facts" that an international tribunal "does not interpret national law as such"'.

99 See the case decided by the Italian-United States Conciliation Commission, *Flegenheimer*, Decision No. 182, 20 September 1958, *UNRIAA*, vol. XIV, pp. 327–90 and the practice cited therein.

100 ICSID, *Hussein Nuaman Soufraki v United Arab Emirates*, decision of the ad hoc Committee, para. 59. See also PCIJ, *The Electricity Company of Sofia and Bulgaria (Preliminary Objection)*, judgment of 4 April 1939, PCIJ *Series A/B*, No. 77, p. 64; ICJ, *Aegean Sea Continental Shelf*, judgment of 19 December 1978, *ICJ Reports 1978*, p. 3.

101 ICSID, *Hussein Nuaman Soufraki v United Arab Emirates*, decision of the ad hoc Committee, para. 64.

102 In this sense see Brownlie, *Principles of Public International Law*, p. 39.

103 See, *ex multis*, ECtHR, *Busuioc v Moldova*, No. 61513/00, judgment of 21 December 2004, para. 54; see also *Amann v Switzerland*, No. 27798/95, judgment (GC) of 16 February 2000, paras 52–4, *Slivenko and Others v Latvia*, No. 48321/99, decision (GC) of 9 October 2003, para. 105, *Freitag v Germany*, No. 71440/01, judgment of 19 July 2007, para. 36.

104 Brownlie, *Principles of Public International Law*, p. 293.

5 Nationality and diplomatic protection

A reappraisal

Annemarieke Vermeer-Künzli

Introduction

In one particular area of international law, nationality comes with benefits: the law of diplomatic protection. This is the protection individuals may receive from their state of nationality when they suffer injury abroad. Diplomatic protection is an instrument for the invocation and implementation of state responsibility for injury to an individual by this individual's state of nationality.[1] The law on diplomatic protection prescribes three conditions for its lawful exercise: the individual must have suffered injury as a consequence of an internationally wrongful act attributable to the receiving state;[2] the individual must first exhaust the local remedies in this state; and the individual must possess the nationality of the protecting state.[3] This last requirement is often referred to as the nationality-of-claims rule.

This chapter will explore the nationality-of-claims rule and analyse how the changes to this rule reflect the changing role of nationality in the law of diplomatic protection. The second, and largest, section will discuss the nationality-of-claims rule as reflecting the bond of nationality between individuals and their states of nationality. It will demonstrate that the application of the rule has been increasingly flexible, in line with the changes to the bond between individuals and their states of nationality. This traditional bond has weakened due to migration and acquisition of second and third nationalities and the romantic[4] interpretation of nationality is no longer accurate (if it ever was). The third section will then continue by presenting a discussion on the additional exceptions to the nationality-of-claims rule that were included in the law on diplomatic protection by the International Law Commission (ILC). These are the protection of refugees and stateless persons, and the protection of ships' crews. Individuals in such cases technically do not possess the nationality of the protecting state. The fact that a non-national state may protect them decreases the exclusivity of nationality for the purpose of protection. The fourth section will present some general observations on the changes to the concept of nationality for the purpose of diplomatic protection.

The bond of nationality

The rationale for allowing states to protect their nationals abroad against the state to which those individuals had travelled or in which they were more or less permanently residing was the bond of nationality. This concept was famously expressed by the Permanent Court of International Justice (PCIJ) in the *Panevezys–Saldutiskis Railway* case. In this case, the Court stated that:

> This right [to exercise diplomatic protection] is necessarily limited to intervention on behalf of its own nationals because, in the absence of a special agreement, it is the bond of nationality between the state and the individual which alone confers upon the State the right of diplomatic protection, and it is as a part of the function of diplomatic protection that the right to take up a claim and to ensure respect for the rules of international law must be envisaged. Where the injury was done to the national of some other State, no claim to which such injury may give rise falls within the scope of diplomatic protection which a State is entitled to afford nor can it give rise to a claim which that State is entitled to espouse.[5]

This *dictum* was complemented some 20 years later by the successor to the PCIJ, the International Court of Justice (ICJ) in the *Nottebohm* case.[6] In this case the Court explained its view on nationality as follows: 'nationality must correspond with the factual situation.'[7] The Court further defined nationality as 'a legal bond having as its basis a social fact of attachment, a genuine connection of existence, interests and sentiments, together with the existence of reciprocal rights and duties.'[8] In addition, the Court stated that:

> Naturalization is not a matter to be taken lightly. To seek and to obtain it is not something that happens frequently in the life of a human being. It involves his breaking of a bond of allegiance and his establishment of a new bond of allegiance. It may have far-reaching consequences and involve profound changes in the destiny of the individual who obtains it.[9]

Although this last citation is about a particular way of acquiring nationality, naturalization, it demonstrates a few elements of nationality considered important by the Court. First, nationality is an expression of allegiance (as the PCIJ also explained). Second, this allegiance is based on attachment to the state of nationality and is not purely legal. Third, the rights and duties that derive from having a particular nationality will influence an individual's life greatly. The *Nottebohm* case has been criticized rather strongly, and rightly so, for its interpretation of these elements in view of the situation of Mr Nottebohm.[10] After all, the decision rendered Mr Nottebohm stateless: he had lost his German nationality, did not obtain Guatemalan nationality, and was denied his rights under the nationality of Liechtenstein. The *Nottebohm* case subsequently became known for the doctrine of 'genuine nationality'. The application of this in relation to dual nationality will be discussed below. At this stage, it is important to note the qualities attached by the Court to the bond of nationality, both in this case and in the previous *Panevezys–Saldutiskis* case.

The qualities attached to the bond of nationality are critical to the admissibility of a claim brought in the exercise of diplomatic protection. If the nationality of the individual is not of the requisite standard, the claim will fail. Changes to the requirements are thus important for the scope of diplomatic protection *ratione personae*. However, they also reflect views on the question of what nationality is and what purpose it would serve. Even if this chapter will not present a conclusive answer on those questions, the analysis presented here will be illustrative.

With the adoption of the Draft Articles on Diplomatic Protection (2006 Draft Articles) by the ILC, two important developments in the nationality-of-claims rule found their culmination. First, and contrary to earlier opinions such as the one found in *Nottebohm*, the requirement of genuineness or effectiveness of nationality was abandoned, allowing protection of individuals whose ties with the protecting states might not be absolutely genuine. Second, the exclusivity of nationality and the ensuing non-responsibility was abandoned, allowing the protection of dual nationals against a state of nationality.

Formal as opposed to genuine nationality

The exercise of diplomatic protection is premised on the nationality-of-claims rule. The issue then, of course, became whether nationality granted by one state would be recognized by another. Without entering into the issue of the rules on granting nationality, international law has always retained a balance between the sovereignty of a state to grant nationality in accordance with its own internal rules and the requirement of international law that this be done in good faith.[11] While international law has been rather reluctant to prescribe detailed rules on the granting of nationality, and it usually relies on saving clauses that the granting of nationality may not be contrary to international law,[12] over time ideas have vacillated on what a good nationality is. A certain paradox has arisen, since international law cannot predetermine the outcome of balancing two interests: the sovereignty of the state of nationality and the opposability of its decisions under international law. Principles of non-intervention and sovereignty have prohibited too restrictive rules on the granting of nationality, since this belongs to the 'reserved domain'.

On the other hand, international law clearly needs a means to withhold recognition of nationality that has been granted in an unacceptable manner.[13] Also, states could conclude treaties in which they limited their right to grant or withhold nationality. Examples of this principle are the UN Convention on the Elimination of All Forms of Discrimination Against Women (CEDAW), which provides rules on the acquisition of nationality by women upon marriage, and the Convention on the Reduction of Statelessness, which obliges states not to deprive individuals of their nationality if that would render them stateless.[14] In fact, a close reading of the ILC Commentary demonstrates an increasing consideration of human rights in issues related to the granting and recognition of nationality. While states retain their sovereignty, both to grant and to refuse to recognize nationality, international law now prescribes to what extent the granting or withholding of nationality may be to the detriment of the individual.[15] International obligations, then, will overrule states' liberty to accept or reject nationalities.

These developments are important, since international law increasingly determines which nationalities are valid under international law and which are not for the purpose of diplomatic protection. The international rules will mostly rely on formalities, rather than a substantive consideration. Thus, the CEDAW and other international conventions with rules on the granting or withholding of nationality usually consider the *effects* of particular rules on nationality, to avoid the imposition of an unwanted nationality, statelessness, or the granting of nationality contrary to the sovereignty of other states. They do not prescribe substantive criteria, such as nationality based on *jus soli* or *jus sanguinis*, habitual residence, family ties, language, or culture, which an individual must meet in order to qualify for nationality.

Such criteria underlie another doctrine that influenced views on the validity of nationality for the purpose of diplomatic protection in the past: the idea that a valid nationality should reflect real allegiance. Allegiance, it was thought, could only exist towards one state[16] and was to be real. States could only protect individuals who showed a genuine connection to their state of nationality. In a less globalized world, in which individuals travelled less, married mostly within their own state of nationality, and were generally less mobile, a requirement of real, almost physical, attachment might not have been problematic. The *Nottebohm* case of 1955 had already clearly demonstrated its limitations: the application of the requirement of genuine nationality, after all, rendered the cosmopolitan Mr Nottebohm stateless under international law. Today, however, insisting on a real bond between the state of nationality and the individual would deprive many of their nationality and the benefits this may bring under international law. As the ILC Special Rapporteur explained:

> [I]f the genuine link requirement proposed by *Nottebohm* was strictly applied it would exclude millions of persons from the benefit of diplomatic protection as in today's world of economic globalization and migration there are millions of persons who have moved away from their State of nationality and made their lives in States whose nationality they never acquired or have acquired nationality by birth or descent from states with which they have a tenuous connection.[17]

The idea that nationality must reflect a substantial and real link between the state granting nationality and the individual has thus been abandoned for individuals with only one nationality or in cases where the receiving state is not a state of nationality. The emphasis is now on the formal requirements, the rebuttable presumption being that the granting of nationality is within the reserved domain of states, provided their conduct in this regard does not conflict with applicable rules of international law. The matter is different in relation to individuals who possess more than one nationality, and in particular, if they also possess the nationality of the receiving state. This brings us to the rules on the protection of dual nationals, and it is in this regard that modern developments on nationality for the purpose of diplomatic protection have been the most complex.

Multiple nationality and non-responsibility

In its decision in *Nottebohm*, the ICJ relied on earlier case law of the various mixed-claims commissions.[18] This reliance is, however, not entirely convincing because the various mixed-claims commissions were often confronted with issues of dual nationality and weighing the various nationalities, rather than the appreciation of a single nationality. It is in relation to the protection of dual nationals that the nationality-of-claims rule was most controversial and culminated in the 2006 Draft Articles. In the analysis that follows, these Articles will provide the starting point to clarify how the requirements of nationality have modulated between absolute non-responsibility and application of the doctrine of pre-dominance.

The International Law Commission

Article 7 of the 2006 Draft Articles provides for diplomatic protection against a state of nationality by another state of nationality.[19] This provision was adopted on second reading in 2006. The same provision was included in the Draft Articles adopted on first reading.[20] The ILC Drafting Committee did not revisit this provision during its meetings preceding the adoption of the Draft Articles on second reading, and very few states commented on it. Some states called for a further qualification of the term 'predominant',[21] one state preferred the term 'effective' nationality instead of predominant nationality.[22] Italy suggested the introduction of a requirement of a genuine link with the claimant state, but this was not accepted by the ILC.[23] The only state explicitly raising concerns as to the status of the rule under international law was France. It stated that the doctrine of predominance had only been applied in massive settlement arrangements, such as the post-conflict Mixed-Claims Tribunals and the Iran–US Claims Tribunal, and it therefore questioned a general application to individual emigrants.[24] On the other hand, the Nordic States expressed strong support for the rule, which according to them was a codification of customary law.[25]

Article 7 is a departure from the earlier non-responsibility rule. This rule, which is derived from sovereignty and sovereign equality of states, essentially prescribes that states cannot be held responsible under international law for the treatment of their own nationals.[26] In addition, since nationality was traditionally considered to be an expression of permanent allegiance owed, it would be wrong to force a state to which allegiance is owed to defend its position before an international tribunal through the invocation of its responsibility by another state of nationality.[27] The rule, then, prohibits diplomatic protection against a state of nationality. It is an absolute rule that does not consider issues of effectiveness or predominance: the mere possession of nationality is sufficient. The rule is, for instance, contained in Article 4 of the 1930 Convention on Certain Questions relating to the Conflict of Nationality Laws.[28] Some case law supports non-responsibility, such as the *Reparation for Injuries* case.[29] The rule is espoused in legal scholarship[30] and earlier codification attempts of international law such as the Harvard Draft.[31] Yet, support for this rule has never been overwhelming and many cases, including very early case law of the Mixed-Claims Commissions established in the first half of the twentieth century, already proposed a weighing of nationality. The *Mergé* case, often cited in this regard, stated that:

> [t]he principle [of non-responsibility], based on the sovereign equality of States, which excludes diplomatic protection in the case of a dual national, must yield before the principle of effective nationality whenever such nationality is that of the claimant state.[32]

This concept was also applied by the Iran–US Claims Tribunal in a number of cases, which will be discussed below.

The ILC, therefore, did not introduce Article 7 as an exercise in progressive development, since it did not change existing law. The only novelty is the choice of the word 'predominant', rather than 'genuine', 'effective', or 'dominant'. This will be discussed below, but the choice of words does not affect the fundamental position that claims against a state of nationality are allowed. Even though some doubt may persist concerning the exact *application* of the rule pronounced in Article 7, in particular concerning the scope of the word 'predominant', states have accepted this principle.

The term 'predominant' was chosen by the ILC to express an element of relativity. Even if one nationality is the predominant nationality, the other nationality does not disappear or become invalid. The ILC has considered that the use of the terms 'effective' or 'dominant', as in older sources on the issue, are too absolute and suggest that the non-effective or non-dominant nationality disappears. The predominant nationality is the more important one for the purpose of diplomatic protection. Deciding which nationality, out of two or more, is the predominant nationality is based on a careful weighing. This is a relative weighing, and it assumes that both nationalities are 'effective' in the sense that they are both valid under international law, and can both be used by the individual holding them.[33]

Article 7 reflects this concept and provides for the protection of a dual national against a state of nationality by the state of the *predominant* nationality. The formulation of Article 7, which has a negative wording, is on purpose and shows that diplomatic protection against a state of nationality must be considered exceptional. The claimant state has the burden of proof regarding predominance. The ILC has decided against the use of 'effective' or 'dominant' and in favour of 'predominant' to 'convey the element of relativity and [to] indicate that the individual has stronger ties with one State rather than another'.[34] This means that it is not necessary to demonstrate that the nationality of the claimant state is particularly strong, that it is genuine, or that it is effective in an absolute sense, only that this nationality is stronger than the nationality of the respondent state. It is important to emphasise this point, since the determination of the admissibility of the claim, and its accordance with the nationality-of-claims rule, will in such cases depend on a comparison between the two nationalities, not on an evaluation of the independent strength of the claimant state's nationality.

This weighing must be based on a number of factors. The Commentary does not present an exhaustive list and refers to 'authorities' (without specifying which authorities in particular) to include the following elements:

> [H]abitual residence; the amount of time spent in each country of nationality; date of naturalization (i.e. the length of the period spent as a national of the protecting State before the claim arose); place, curricula and language of education; employment and financial interests; place of family life; family ties in each country; participation in social and public life; use of language; taxation, bank account, social security insurance; visits to the other State of nationality; possession and use of passport of the other State; and military service.[35]

The ILC added that these elements will not by themselves determine the issue and that the importance and relevance of each factor will depend on the particular case.[36] Thus, the mere fact that someone spent most of his life in one state does not make that state the predominant one, because this could be compensated for by an absence of visits to this state after the departure, an active political life in the new state, etc. As the ILC indicated, there may be other factors.

Case law on dual nationality

There is a rather rich body of case law in which tribunals decided which of the two nationalities of a given individual was to be considered the predominant one. Many, though by no means all, claims have been decided in favour of the respondent. However, the fact that all of these cases weigh the two nationalities and result in a decision on the predominant nationality (or dominant, or effective, depending on the language of the respective tribunal) clearly supports the principle of predominance, and defies a strict application of non-responsibility. It is not necessary in the present context to discuss each of these cases individually, but the most important ones will be singled out below.

In general, it is clear that all cases considered residence (sometimes called domicile) as the most important factor. In an early decision, Umpire Plumley already stated that:

> [W]here, as in this case, there appears to be a conflict of laws constituting Mrs Stevenson a British subject under British law and a Venezuelan under Venezuelan law the prevailing rule of public law, to which appeal must then be taken, is that she is deemed to be a citizen of the country in which she has her domicile.[37]

Similarly, in the *Mathison* case, it was decided that Mr Mathison was of Venezuelan nationality, since he was born in Venezuela and had always resided in Venezuela, despite the fact that he had British nationality by descent through his father.[38] These cases were relatively straightforward in the sense that the individuals concerned did not divide their time between two countries or acquired nationality by a voluntary decision for naturalization, but had dual nationality through birth, descent, or automatically through marriage.

More complicated was the *Canevaro* case between Italy and Peru.[39] The question was whether Mr Raphael Canevaro's dominant nationality was the Italian or the Peruvian nationality, because if it was the Italian nationality, Italy could exercise diplomatic protection. He had acquired Italian nationality by descent and Peruvian nationality by birth. The Tribunal did not state that either of the two would be inherently more important, but decided his nationality on his personal circumstances. As the tribunal stated:

> CANEVARO s'est, à plusieurs reprises, comporté comme citoyen péruvien, soit en posant sa candidature au Sénat où ne sont admis que les citoyens péruviens et où il est allé défendre son élection, soit surtout en acceptant les fonctions de Consul général des Pays-Bas, après avoir sollicité l'autorisation du Gouvernement, puis du Congrès péruvien [...].
>
> CONSIDÉRANT que, dans ces circonstances, quelle que puisse être en Italie, au point de vue de la nationalité, la condition de RAPHAEL CANEVARO, le Gouvernement du Pérou a le droit de le considérer comme citoyen péruvien et le lui dénier la qualité de réclamant italien.[40]

What this demonstrates is that, aside from residence, another important factor is how individuals use their nationalities. As we will see in the *Esphahanian* case, this is not an absolute rule, but in general, it will be the case that when an individual relies on a particular nationality to fulfil public functions, obtain favours, acquire goods, or pursue activities, and if this is only possible with that nationality (and not the other nationality), this will weigh in favour of the nationality used. Participation in the political life of a country will thus provide evidence of an interest in that country, which in itself supports the predominance of that particular nationality. Political participation may also be weighed if that participation is only possible when a national considers that nationality to be the predominant one.

Mrs Mergé was a US citizen by birth, and acquired Italian nationality through marriage. Her Italian husband was sent to Tokyo and Mrs Mergé accompanied him, travelling on her Italian passport. In Tokyo, however, she also registered at the American Consulate. In the aftermath of the Second World War, Mrs Mergé could have returned to the United States, but preferred to stay with her husband. Eventually, she did travel to the United States on a US passport issued for that purpose, but after nine months she returned to Italy on a visa granted by the Italian Consulate in the US to join her husband. Back in Rome, she registered with the American Embassy. In that context she stated that her only ties with the United States were her parents who lived in the United States and that she did not pay taxes to the United States. Later, she stated that her legal residence was in New York and that she intended to return to the United States permanently in the future. She was granted a US passport. When the claim arose, Mrs Mergé still lived in Italy.[41]

At first sight, these facts do not clearly present a predominant nationality. Unlike the earlier cases, there was no dispute about the possession of both nationalities. Rather, the Tribunal was to decide whether the claim was admissible, depending on the predominance of the US nationality. It stated on this point that:

> In order to establish the prevalence of the United States nationality in individual cases, habitual residence can be one of the criteria of evaluation, but not the only one. The conduct of the individual in his economic, social, political, civic and family life, as well as the closer and more effective bond with one of the two States must also be considered.[42]

The Tribunal ultimately concluded that:

> [T]he family did not have its habitual residence in the United States and the interests and the permanent professional life of the head of the family were not established there. In fact, Mrs Mergé has not lived in the United States since her marriage, she used an Italian passport in travelling to Japan from Italy in 1937, she stayed in Japan from 1937 until 1946 with her husband, an official of the Italian Embassy in Tokyo, and it does not appear that she was ever interned as a national of a country enemy to Japan.[43]

It is questionable whether the same line of reasoning would apply today. Surely, modern international law does not place so much emphasis anymore on the 'professional life of the head of the family' (i.e. the husband). Also, it seems a bit crude to argue that her predominant nationality was Italian since she was not interned in one of the camps in Japan. The diplomatic status of her husband must have played an important role in this respect. Nevertheless, the point of habitual residence remains and the picture that arises in the case of Mrs Mergé is that she did not use her US nationality as much as her Italian one, and did not participate in any meaningful way in the American society. In order for one nationality to be predominant in relation to the other, such predominance must be clear, which it was not in the case of Mrs Mergé. Absent such clarity, no protection can be exercised against the state of nationality.

The *Nottebohm* case, which was decided around the same time, is also relevant. It is important to note that this case did not concern dual nationality. However, the case is often referred to for support of a non-absolute approach to nationalities and the principle of predominance. In this case, the ICJ considered that:

> International arbitrators [. . .] have given their preference to the real and effective nationality, that which accorded with the facts, that based on stronger factual ties between the person concerned and one of the States whose nationality is involved. Different factors are taken into consideration, and their importance will vary from one case to the next: the habitual residence of the individual concerned is an important factor, but there are other factors such as the centre of his interests, his family ties, his participation in public life, attachment shown by him for a given country and inculcated in his children, etc.[44]

The list in this case is by now rather familiar; habitual residence, and certain social and business factors are taken into account as the more subjective element of the ties as perceived by the individual concerned.

In the context of the Iran–US Claims Tribunal, the most important case is the *Esphahanian* case. This case was followed by the *A/18* case, in which the question of nationality was specifically addressed. The Tribunal, in *A/18* confirmed its decision of the *Esphahanian* case. Other relevant cases are the *Golpira* case, the *Malek* case and the *Danielpour* case. These will all be discussed in turn.

The *Esphahanian* case is often considered to be the leading case. Mr Esphahanian was a naturalized US citizen with Iranian nationality by descent. He spent his childhood in Iran, but moved to the United State in his early 20s. He completed his education in the United States and served in the US Army. He had voted in the US and participated actively in cultural, civic, and business activities in the United States. During his professional life, he worked in Iran for a number of years, having been sent there by the American corporation for which he worked. While a resident in the United States, he continued to visit his family in Iran.[45] In this case, the Tribunal decided to apply the principle of predominance, or, in its own words, the rule of dominant and effective nationality.[46] The Tribunal considered that the question was as follows: '[w]ere Esphahanian's factual connections with the United States "in the period preceding, contemporaneous with and following" his naturalization as a United States citizen more effective than his factual connections with Iran during the same period?'.[47] The Tribunal acknowledged that Mr Esphahanian continued to entertain 'significant' contacts with Iran after his departure for the United States. These include family visits, the retention of his Iranian passport, and a stay for nine months per year from 1970 to 1979, accompanied by his wife and children.[48] In the final considerations, these did not outweigh the ties with the United States. His residence in Iran in the 1970s was due to the fact that his employer had sent him to Iran and he, in fact, spent a substantial amount of this time not in Iran, but in other Middle Eastern countries. More important was his use of his Iranian nationality when travelling to Iran and for the acquisition of property in Iran. As to the first point, the Tribunal decided that there were mitigating factors due to Iranian law. Individuals renouncing their Iranian nationality could thereafter travel to Iran only once. As the Tribunal stated:

> With respect to Esphahanian's use of an Iranian passport to enter and leave Iran, the Tribunal notes that the laws of Iran in effect forced such use. Once Esphahanian had emigrated to the United States and had become an American citizen, the only way he could return lawfully to Iran was as an Iranian national, using an Iranian passport. If he insisted on using his US passport to enter Iran, he would be turned away or, at least, his US passport would be confiscated and he would be admitted only as an Iranian. In effect, Iran told its citizens that, if they took foreign nationality, they must also retain their Iranian nationality – which in Iran would be considered their sole nationality – or they would be forever barred from returning to Iran.[49]

This is important to note. The Tribunal, rightly, was of the view that individuals will not be required to renounce their other state of nationality entirely and will be allowed to entertain some ties with it, as long as these are of less weight than the ties with the predominant state of nationality. Thus, the mere retention of a passport, and indeed its occasional use, will not be decisive. Although the Tribunal did not state this expressly, the conclusion must also be that family visits to a state of nationality, even when travelling on the passport of that state, do not undermine the predominance of the other state of nationality.

The decision in the *Esphahanian* case was not welcomed, to say the least, by the Iranian government. Iran, therefore, requested a principle decision by the full Tribunal, which was to become case *A/18*. This case involved a request to interpret the term 'national' in the Algiers Accords, in particular whether this term would include dual nationals with a nationality that includes the respondent state. The case, thus, essentially turned on the question of whether the Iran–US Claims Tribunal was allowed to apply the principle of predominance and not the principle of non-responsibility. The United States adhered to the principle of predominance, and Iran to the principle of non-responsibility. In its decision, the Tribunal found that 'the applicable rule of international law is that of dominant and effective nationality'.[50]

In the present context, it is important to note that the decision stated, first, that 'it is necessary to distinguish between different types of protection, whether consular or claims related'.[51] Second, that the Tribunal is an attempt 'to resolve a crisis in relations between Iran and the United States, not to extend diplomatic protection in the normal sense'.[52] These arguments were used to allow the Tribunal to move beyond Article 4 of the 1930 Convention, and to reject the rule of non-responsibility. However, a close reading of the judgment forces one to see through this second statement: in its analysis, the Tribunal relies exclusively on sources related to exercises of diplomatic protection. Since the Tribunal derived its conclusion that the principle of predominance must be applied from these sources, its conclusion is applicable beyond the judgment and to exercises of diplomatic protection.

In its decision, the Tribunal did not add new factors for determining predominance to those already mentioned in other case law. It supported the trend to give most weight to domicile, and having discussed the case law, it stated that it 'will consider all relevant factors, including habitual residence, center of interests, family ties, participation in public life and other evidence of attachment'.[53]

The *Golpira* case concerned an individual who was born and raised in Iran, but had lived in the United States more or less permanently from the age of 26. His Iranian nationality was based both on *jus soli* and *jus sanguinis*. Mr Golpira did use his Iranian nationality, which he retained, after becoming an American citizen in 1964. He travelled to Iran a few times and he used it to register his children at the Iranian Consulate in the United States. On this issue, the Tribunal applied the same reasoning as in the previous *Esphahanian* case. It stated:

> It should be noted that Iranian law permits renunciation of Iranian nationality only with the approval of the Council of Ministers. Any person who receives such approval is thereafter allowed to travel to Iran only once, in order to sell or transfer his properties. With respect to Golpira's use of an Iranian passport to enter and leave Iran, the Tribunal notes that the laws of Iran in effect forced such use.[54]

Thus the Tribunal applied exactly the same wording as in the *Esphahanian* case, cited above. Mr Golpira had also used his Iranian identification number for the purchase of certain shares, but this, according to the tribunal, 'does not mean that he concealed his American nationality in order to obtain benefits available only to Iranians'.[55] This supports the impression that the Tribunal was considering what nationality the individual himself considered the predominant one and whether this could be corroborated by facts.

In the *Malek* case, the Tribunal stated that, for the purpose of establishing predominant nationality 'the entire life of the Claimant, from birth, and all the factors which, during this span of time, evidence the reality and the sincerity of the choice of national allegiance he claims to have made, are relevant.'[56] The Tribunal added to this that:

> [T]he date of acquisition of the alleged dominant and effective nationality certainly deserves special attention, particularly if it demonstrates that this nationality was obtained at a time when the Claimant could foresee that its acquisition could better position him to assert a claim for his property.[57]

It is of further interest to note that Mr Malek did visit Iran while residing in the United States, but these visits were of a professional nature on the invitation of Iranian medical centres.[58] An important finding was also that while Mr Malek,

> [N]ever wholly severed his cultural and sentimental ties with country of his birth, as evidenced by his marriage and his visits to Iran, his conduct since the time he settled in the United States, in 1966, demonstrates that he fully and deliberately integrated into United States society.[59]

It was considered that he consciously and firmly decided to become an American citizen and, therefore, his predominant nationally was the US nationality.[60] This demonstrates that, in addition to more objective criteria such as habitual residence and education, self-identification with respect to nationality for the purpose of diplomatic protection will be considered.

The case of Mr Danielpour further supports this. In this case, the Tribunal decided that Mr Danielpour's predominant nationality was the US nationality, based on the following facts: he continuously resided in the United States, paid his taxes in the United States, and was employed by a US corporation, despite being offered a chance to take over his father's business in Iran.[61] Again, the Tribunal emphasised that Mr Danielpour had made a conscious decision: 'the Claimant had decided to live in the United States and to assert his United States nationality'.[62]

Concluding observations on dual nationality

The above analysis has demonstrated the complexities resulting from an increasingly globalizing world. Dual nationality is not an exception anymore, and neither is frequent commuting among the various states of nationality. In the early years of the twentieth century, the issues of dual nationality and diplomatic protection already gave rise to discussions, and the solution was often found in a weighing of the relevant nationalities. Not all authorities and states, however, accepted this, and some have insisted on the application of the non-responsibility rule prohibiting diplomatic protection against a state of nationality. In the light of recent developments, in particular in the context of the ILC, the absolute non-responsibility rule must be discarded in favour of the rule of predominant nationality. When faced with the application of a state on behalf of a national who also holds the nationality of the respondent state, a tribunal will engage in a balancing of the two nationalities, taking into account various factors, such as habitual residence, participation in public life, family ties, and financial ties. When this balancing results in a clear predominance of one nationality in favour of the other, this will determine the admissibility of the claim.

This approach has widened the scope of diplomatic protection *ratione personae* by including dual nationals. Not only will this increase the number of individuals who can be protected when injured abroad, but the changed rules on dual nationality also reflect on nationality as such. When the *lex lata* explicitly acknowledges the fact that individuals may possess more than one effective and valid nationality, and the case is for protection against a state of nationality, the nationalities will be weighed. Such a weighing may result in the conclusion that the nationalities are equally important, and nationality is no longer a testament of a bond defined by uniqueness. Protection against a state of nationality by another state of nationality is allowed when the bond with the latter state is *stronger*, which does not require that it is unique, nor that it is particularly strong. In theory it is possible that an individual is protected by a state of nationality against a state of nationality where neither of the nationalities are particularly relevant in the individual's life (for instance, because she lives in yet another state), but where the former nationality is still predominant. Even if one must criticize the dictum in the *Nottebohm* case for its insistence on the genuine attachment of individuals to their state of nationality in the 1950s, today such insistence is not supported by international law.

Inclusion of those traditionally excluded

The scope of diplomatic protection *ratione personae* was further widened by the ILC in its approach to stateless persons, refugees, and ships crews.[63] In an exercise of progressive development, the Special Rapporteur on Diplomatic Protection suggested the inclusion of Article 8 in the 2006 Draft Articles. This Article provides for the protection of refugees and stateless persons by the state in which they live.[64] Since it is an exercise in progressive development, the right to exercise such protection is restricted by a number of conditions. Nevertheless, it is quite revolutionary in the sense that Article 8 allows states to protect individuals who are not their nationals, and may not even have the intention to become their nationals, but who may require protection because no other state will be able or willing to do so. Their allegiance to the protecting state is based both on the conduct of the individual and on the conduct of the protecting state. Refugees and stateless persons must be 'lawfully and habitually' resident in the protecting state and refugees must in addition be recognized as such. The individual must therefore be habitually and physically present in the protecting state, but the protecting state must have taken steps to allow that person to be on its territory. For instance, the state must have granted a residence permit of some sort and granted refugees status in the case of refugees.

Without entering into too much detail on this provision regarding refugees, the rationale for including it is twofold. First, stateless persons have no nationality and refugees have a useless nationality.[65] Adhering to the requirement that states can only protect their nationals would render such individuals without protection. Second, by granting lawful residence to stateless persons and refugees, states consciously allow them to be part of their society. Although lawful residence is not equal to the granting of nationality, it will give rise to a bond between the individual and his/her state of residence. Such a bond, then, can also be established through other means than formal nationality. Even so, the nationality of a refugee does not entirely disappear. Comparatively, stateless persons by definition have no nationality. A state protecting a stateless person will therefore not offend another state which might consider this person its national. In this sense, the protection of stateless persons by their state of habitual and lawful residence will not be controversial. The matter is more complicated for refugees. Refugees by definition have the nationality of the state they have left for fear of persecution. While this nationality cannot be relied on by refugees for the purpose of protection, since that would risk their status as a refugee, it is a valid nationality under international law. Since it is a state's right to offer protection to a refugee, the ILC considered it as *de lege ferenda*,[66] and felt obliged to offer a limited provision: protection of a refugee may not be exercised against the state of nationality of the refugee.[67] The ILC offered two justifications for this limitation. First, it stated that 'nationality is the predominant basis for the exercise of diplomatic protection'.[68] To allow protection by the state in which the refugee is lawfully and habitually resident against the state of nationality would 'contradict' this approach.[69] On close reading, this explanation actually is not fully satisfactory. Obviously, a refugee will have only one nationality and the ILC considered allowing the exercise of protection against that state of nationality to be wrong. This is, however, based purely on a formality, which is somewhat contrary to the approach in other cases. For instance, as described above, the determination of the predominant nationality for dual nationals does not rely on formalities, as the Court in the *Nottebohm* case did not rely on formalities.[70] A different approach would, hypothetically, be possible: one could consider predominance of attachment, rather than nationality, and weigh the ties refugees have with their state of residence against the ties with the state of nationality, and decide that the state of residence can only exercise diplomatic protection when such ties are predominant. This approach will remain hypothetical, as can be concluded from the second justification offered in the Commentary to Article 8: the prohibition of protection against the state of nationality of a refugee is justified on 'policy grounds'. As the ILC explained:

> [M]ost refugees have serious complaints about their treatment at the hand of their State of nationality, from which they have fled to avoid persecution. To allow diplomatic protection in such cases would be to open the floodgates for international litigation. Moreover, the fear of demands for such action by refugees might deter States from accepting refugees.[71]

This argument is not unusual. It has been brought forward in the *Al-Adsani* case before the European Court of Human Rights, and has been explained in the concurring opinion of Judges Pellonpää and Bratza.[72] Even if the possession of nationality is no longer an absolute requirement for the purpose of diplomatic protection and even if the law on diplomatic protection has moved away from the position held in the 1931 *Dickson Car Wheel Company* case, in which protection against a state of nationality was strongly rejected,[73] diplomatic protection in case of absence of nationality, concurrent nationality or nationality which is not matched by strong factual ties will still be an exception. This is an accepted exception, but an exception no less.

Concluding observations

The discussion of the nationality-of-claims rule has demonstrated that international law's approach to the requirements of nationality for the purpose of the nationality-of-claims rule have developed over the course of the twentieth and twenty-first centuries. These changes are particularly relevant in cases where the evaluation of compliance with the nationality-of-claims rule is critical for the admissibility of the claim. For instance this evaluation is critical in the case of dual nationals and a claim against one state of nationality, and the case of diplomatic protection of stateless persons and refugees. Adherence to the non-responsibility rule, which recognized formal nationality of the respondent state as an obstacle to the exercise of diplomatic protection, has all but disappeared. In addition, the absence of (useful) nationality is also no longer an obstacle to such an exercise, as is the case with stateless persons and refugees.

What this demonstrates is a different perception of nationality for the purpose of diplomatic protection. Nationality is no longer considered to reflect a unique attachment that will belong exclusively to one state. The weighing of nationalities for the purpose of establishing the admissibility of a claim in the case of dual nationals will consider evidence of attachment, such as self-identification, residence, and participation in political, cultural, and social life. However, this is a relative weighing not intended to establish absolute attachment, but to determine to which of the two states an individual is more attached. This approach recognizes that individuals are able to hold more than one effective or genuine nationality. The law of diplomatic protection also recognizes this non-exclusivity in another sense: refugees generally possess a useless nationality, which they may nevertheless wish to retain in order to be able to return to their state of nationality at some point in the future. In the meanwhile, refugees may avail themselves of the protection of their state of lawful and habitual residence. Nationality, then, is non-exclusive in another sense: it is not the only bond of attachment between an individual and a state that may justify the exercise of diplomatic protection. In adopting these developments the ILC, in its 2006 Draft Articles, has acknowledged the changes to the constitution and nature of nationality, and has ensured the continuing protection of individuals travelling or residing abroad.

Notes

1 See Article 1 of the Draft Articles on Diplomatic Protection, adopted by the ILC on second reading in 2006. The text of the 2006 Draft Articles, together with the Commentaries, is contained in ILC, 'Report on the work of the fifty-eighth session', *UNGAOR, Sixty-first Session, Supplement No. 10*, UN Doc. A/61/10.

2 The term 'receiving state' or 'respondent state' will be used to designate the state which is allegedly responsible for the injury inflicted upon the individual.

3 See Articles 1, 3 and 14 of the 2006 Draft Articles.

4 See R.D. Sloane, 'Breaking the Genuine Link: The Contemporary International Legal Regulation of Nationality', *Harvard International Law Journal* 50, 2009, 1–60 at 17ff.

5 PCIJ, *Panevezys–Saldutiskis Railway (Estonia v Lithuania)*, judgment of 28 February 1939, PCIJ *Series A/B*, No. 76, p. 16.

6 ICJ, *Nottebohm Case (Second Phase) (Liechtenstein v Guatemala)*, judgment of 6 April 1955, *ICJ Reports 1955*, p. 4.

7 Ibid., p. 22.

8 Ibid., p. 23.

9 Ibid.

10 See in particular the excellent analysis by Sloane, 'Breaking the Genuine Link', and other criticism referred to therein.

11 2006 Draft Articles, Article 4 and accompanying Commentary.

12 See, e.g. the 1930 Convention, adopted on 12 April 1930, LNTS, vol. 179, No. 4137, Article 1; PCIJ, *Nationality Decrees Issued in Tunis and Morocco (French Zone)*, advisory opinion of 7 February 1923, PCIJ *Series B*, No. 4, p. 24; ECN, CETS 166, Article 3.

13 For examples and analysis of the limits imposed by international law on the granting of nationality see Sloane, 'Breaking the Genuine Link', pp. 3–8.

14 CEDAW, UNTS, vol. 1249, No. 20378, Article 9; 1961 Convention, UNTS, vol. 989, No. 14458, Article 8.

15 Commentary to Article 4, para. 8, referring to the *Namibia* advisory opinion, ICJ, *Legal Consequences for States of the Continued Presence of South Africa in Namibia (South West Africa) notwithstanding Security Council Resolution 276 (1970)*, advisory opinion of 21 June 1971, *ICJ Reports 1971*, p. 16 at 56.

16 In this context it is interesting to note current debates about allegiance and dual nationality. In the Netherlands (but also elsewhere), nationalist parties have moved to reduce the possibility of possessing more than one nationality arguing that allegiance was by definition exclusive. See for instance a motion served by a Dutch MP on changing the rules on nationality to the exclusion of dual nationality, *Kamerstukken* 31 813 (R1873), 19 January 2010, No. 23, Motie Fritsma: Wijziging van de Rijkswet op het Nederlanderschap met betrekking tot meervoudige nationaliteit en andere nationaliteitsrechtelijke kwesties (Amendment of the State Law on Dutch Nationality in relation to multiple nationality and other issues related to nationality, in Dutch).

17 Commentary to Article 4, para. 5.

18 ICJ, *Nottebohm*, pp. 21–3.

19 Article 7 provides:

> A State of nationality may not exercise diplomatic protection in respect of a person against a State of which that person is also a national unless the nationality of the former State is predominant, both at the date of injury and at the date of the official presentation of the claim.

20 ILC Draft Articles on Diplomatic Protection with Commentaries adopted on first reading, ILC, 'Report on the work of the fifty-sixth session', *UNGAOR, Fifty-ninth Session, Supplement No. 10*, UN Doc. A/59/10, 2004, p. 19.

21 El Salvador, Uzbekistan and Qatar, in: 'Diplomatic Protection: Comments and Observations Received from Governments', 27 January 2006, UN Doc. A/CN.4/561, pp. 22–3 (hereinafter: Government Comments and Observations), United Kingdom, in: 'Diplomatic Protection: Comments and Observations Received from Governments', 3 April 2006, UN Doc. A/CN.4/561/Add.1, p. 7, France, in: 'Report of the Secretary-General, Addendum, Comments and observations received from Governments', 2 August 2007, UN Doc. A/62/118/Add. 1, p. 4.

22 Morocco, 'Government Comments and Observations', p. 23.

23 'Diplomatic Protection: Comments and Observations Received from Governments', 12 April 2006, UN Doc. A/CN.4/561/Add.2, p. 4.

24 'Report of the Secretary-General, Addendum', p. 4.

25 'Government Comments and Observations', p. 4.

26 An obvious exception would be derived from human rights law, which makes no distinction on the basis of nationality, but *locus standi* in such cases would normally be derived from the *erga omnes* or *erga omnes partes* nature of the human rights obligation concerned. States wishing to exercise diplomatic protection in response to a human rights violation injuring their national must comply with the nationality-of-claims rule, see A. Vermeer-Künzli, 'A Matter of Interest: Diplomatic Protection and State Responsibility *Erga Omnes*', *International and Comparative Law Quarterly* 56, 2007, 553–81.

27 E.M. Borchard, *The Diplomatic Protection of Citizens Abroad*, New York: The Banks Law Publishing, 1919, (reprint William S. Hein 2003), p. 588.

28 It is interesting to note that this provision apparently reflects a compromise and that at the time various delegations preferred alternatives allowing the protection

of dual nationals. See on this R.W. Flournoy, 'Nationality Convention, Protocols and Recommendation adopted by the First Conference on the Codification of International Law', *American Journal of International Law* 24, 1930, 467–85 at 471.

29 ICJ, *Reparation for Injuries Suffered in the Service of the United Nations*, advisory opinion of 11 April 1949, *ICJ Reports 1949*, p. 174 at 186. There are other earlier cases, referred to in the Commentary to Article 7, but the interpretation of these cases varies among scholars and practitioners. An analysis actually supports the view that when faced with dual nationality, the nationalities would be weighed and if the nationality of the claimant state was not clearly dominant, the claim would be dismissed with reference to the non-responsibility rule. This structure actually supports the application of the doctrine of pre-dominance, rather than denying it.

30 See, e.g. Z.R. Rode, 'Dual Nationals and the Doctrine of Dominant Nationality', *American Journal of International Law* 53, 1959, 139–44 and E.L. Kelsey, 'Nationality of Claims, A Vista', *ASIL Proceedings* 63, 1969, 35–42.

31 Commentary to Article 7, paras 2–3.

32 US–Italy Conciliation Commission, *Mergé* claim, decision of 10 June 1955, *UNRIAA*, vol. XIV, pp. 236–48 at 247.

33 See on this also M. Aghahosseini, 'The Claims of Dual Nationals Before the Iran–United States Claims Tribunal: Some Reflections', *Leiden Journal of International Law* 10, 1997, 21–47 at 27–33.

34 Commentary to Article 7, para. 4.

35 Ibid.

36 Commentary to Article 7, para. 5.

37 Mixed Claims Commission Great Britain–Venezuela, *Stevenson* claim, 1903, *UNRIAA*, vol. IX, pp. 494–510 at 500.

38 Mixed Claims Commission Great Britain–Venezuela, *Mathison* claim, 1903, ibid., vol. IX, pp. 485–95 at 493.

39 Permanent Court of Arbitration, *Canevaro* claim, decision of 3 May 1912, ibid., vol. XI, pp. 397–410.

40 Ibid., p. 406:

> On several occasions, Mr Canevaro has behaved as a Peruvian citizen, by presenting his candidacy for the Senate to which only Peruvian citizens are admitted and more importantly by accepting the function of Consul general to the Netherlands, after having solicited the authorization first of the Peruvian government and subsequently its Congress [...]. Considering that, under these circumstances, whatever Mr Canevaro's status in Italy with respect to his nationality, the government of Peru has the right to consider him a Peruvian citizen and to deny him the status of Italian claimant.
>
> (translation by the author)

41 *Mergé* claim, pp. 237–8.

42 Ibid., p. 247.

43 Ibid., p. 248.

44 ICJ, *Nottebohm*, p. 22.

45 Iran–US Claims Tribunal, *Esphahanian v Bank Tejarat*, award No. 157, 29 March 1983, *Iran–U.S. Claims Tribunal Reports*, vol. 2, pp. 157–70.

46 Ibid., p. 161.

47 Ibid., p. 166.
48 Ibid., p. 167.
49 Ibid., p. 168.
50 Iran–US Claims Tribunal, *Iran v United States, Case No. A/18*, decision of 6 April 1984, *Iran-U.S. Claims Tribunal Reports*, vol. 5, pp. 251–67 at 260.
51 Ibid.
52 Ibid., p. 19.
53 Ibid., p. 25.
54 Iran–US Claims Tribunal, *Golpira v Iran*, award No. 211 of 29 March 1983, *Iran–U.S. Claims Tribunal Reports*, vol. 2, pp. 171–7 at 174.
55 Ibid.
56 Iran-US Claims Tribunal, *Malek v Iran*, award No. 193 of 23 June 1988, *Iran–U.S. Claims Tribunal Reports*, vol. 19, pp. 48–61 at 51.
57 Ibid., para. 15.
58 Ibid., para. 24.
59 Ibid., para. 25.
60 Ibid., paras 25–6.
61 Iran–US Claims Tribunal, *Danielpour v Iran*, award No. 169 of 16 June 1989, *Iran–U.S. Claims Tribunal Reports*, vol. 22, pp. 118–28, para. 12.
62 Ibid., para. 13.
63 The rules on the protection of ships' crews will not be explored in detail. Article 18 of the 2006 Draft Articles provides that concurrent protection by the state of nationality of the members of the crew of a ship and by the flag state of that ship is possible. This does not affect issues of nationality, but seeks to acknowledge the equal validity of the nationality of the individuals and the nationality of the ship for the purpose of diplomatic protection. See 2006 Draft Articles, Article 18 and Commentary.
64 Ibid., Article 8 and Commentary.
65 A refugee is commonly defined as a person who is unable or unwilling to obtain protection from his or her state of nationality. See Article 1(a)(2) of the 1951 Convention, adopted on 28 July 1951, UNTS, vol. 189, No. 2545.
66 Not only the ILC held this view: it was also pronounced in EWCA, *R (on the Application of Al Rawi & Others) v Secretary of State for Foreign Affairs and Another*, judgment of 12 October 2006, [2006] EWCA 972 (Admin), where the Court held in para. 63 that Article 8 was 'not yet part of international law'.
67 2006 Draft Articles, Article 8(3).
68 Commentary to Article 8, para. 10.
69 Ibid.
70 Applying the *Nottebohm* reasoning to refugees would actually mean that the state of nationality of the refugee could not exercise protection against the state of lawful and habitual residence.
71 Commentary to Article 8, para. 10.
72 ECtHR, *Case of Al-Adsani v the United Kingdom*, No. 35763/97, judgment (GC) of 21 November 2001, concurring opinion of Judges Pellonpää and Bratza, pp. 25–8.
73 Mexico–USA General Claims Commission, *Dickson Car Wheel Company (U.S.A.) v United Mexican States*, July 1931, *UNRIAA*, vol. IV, pp. 669–91 at 678.

6 Nationality and freedom of movement

Francesca De Vittor

Introduction

Article 13(2) of the Universal Declaration of Human Rights proclaims the right of everyone 'to leave any country, including his own, and to return to his country'.[1] This right is enshrined in a number of international human rights treaties, both at universal and regional levels,[2] and such a widespread recognition argues in favour of it being part of general international law.[3] Indeed, as asserted by the Human Rights Committee (HRC) 'Liberty of movement is an indispensable condition for the free development of a person'.[4] Nevertheless, freedom of movement is not an absolute right, and it is subject to restrictions provided by law and necessary to protect national security or other public values. Beside these classical restrictions, the right of every human being to decide freely where to live and eventually to emigrate from her or his own country is at variance with the sovereign authority of states over their territory and population, namely with the state's right to secure borders and to decide on conditions of entry and stay of foreigners.[5] In fact, neither customary international law, nor human rights treaties recognize a general right of aliens to enter or reside in the territory of a state.[6]

The aim of this chapter is to outline, in the absence of a comprehensive international legal regime which governs international migration,[7] how the intertwining of conventional and customary rules applying to the movement of people permits a normative balance between individuals' right to freedom of movement and sovereign authority in this matter.

The distinction among nationals and aliens is the necessary starting point when considering international migration. In fact, as sovereignty includes the 'right to exclude', the nationality link is the prime criterion to determine who cannot be excluded from the community, i.e., from the territory of the state. Thus, the analysis will move from the prohibition of expulsion (and the duty of admission) of nationals; the question of possible extension of this obligation towards foreigners to whom a particular status is granted will also be considered. After analysing the right of everyone to stay in her or his own country, the issue of the right to leave will be addressed; in this framework, the legitimacy of policies preventing emigration from the country of origin and transit of migrants, aiming to contrast illegal immigration in the destination country, will be challenged. Finally, attention will be paid to particular limitations imposed by international law to the right of the state to control its borders and to refuse admittance of aliens.

Despite the fact that the right to leave has been included in a number of international human rights treaties, the HRC is the international body that offers the most important practice concerning this right, both in the framework of general comments and individual cases. For this particular reason, combined with the widespread acceptance and ratification of the International Covenant on Civil and Political Rights (ICCPR), this paper mostly deals with the interpretation and application of Article 12 ICCPR. Second, whereas border control policies of European states will be challenged, particular attention will be paid to obligations deriving from the European Convention on Human Rights (ECHR).

Nationality as criterion for the determination of the only place where an individual always has the right to go and stay

In 1892, the *Institut du Droit International* in his 'Rules on Admission and Expulsion of Aliens' stated that '[i]n principle, a State may not prohibit either its nationals or persons who are no longer nationals of that State but have not acquired the nationality of any other State from entering or remaining in its territory'.[8]

The connection between nationality and territory is inherent to the very definition of the state as the entity exercising sovereign authority on people and space.[9] If it is accepted that states have a general right to refuse entry to individuals who are not their nationals and to expel them, conversely there is an obligation to admit nationals, thus avoiding the 'Flying Dutchman' phenomenon. In this framework, the right of nationals to enter and live in their own country[10] is sometimes understood as the mere functional consequence of the right of states to exclude foreigners from their territories.[11] There is no doubt that respect for other states' sovereignty is the traditional rationale for the customary obligation of states to grant residence to their own citizens. Nevertheless the right of individuals to live in their own country is, in contemporary international law, a human right enshrined both in treaties and customary rules. Indeed, the right to leave *any* country is always coupled by the right of everyone to return to *her or his own* country.

To acknowledge that the right of abode in one's own country is a human right of the individual, and not the mere consequence of an interstate obligation, has the important effect of limiting to exceptional cases – i.e. cases of public emergency threatening national security – the possibility for the state to expel its own nationals, even when another state is willing to receive them.[12] In other words the existence of a state willing to receive or admit the person is a *conditio sine qua non* for the expulsion, but does not, per se, allow the national state to expel or refuse entry to his citizens.

Expulsion of nationals is expressly forbidden by Article 3(1) of Protocol No. 4 to the ECHR, by Article 22(5) of the American Convention on Human Rights (ACHR), by Article 27(2) of the Arab Charter on Human Rights (ArCHR). Under Article 12(4) ICCPR, '[n]o one shall be arbitrarily deprived of the right to enter his own country'; this right also implies the right to remain in one's own country.[13] Even though the reference to arbitrariness seems to grant some margins of appreciation to states, the HRC 'considers that there are few, *if any*, circumstances in which deprivation of the right to enter one's own country could be reasonable'.[14] Moreover the right to enter and remain in the country is considered as a constitutional right inherent to citizenship by numerous national legislations.[15]

The hypothesis that the right to settle and reside in the territory of the state of nationality is an individual right inherent to nationality and not the mere consequence of an interstate obligation finds support in the International Law Commission's (ILC) work on expulsion of aliens. Specifically, this support is in the discussion concerning the expulsion of dual nationals, i.e., cases characterized by the existence of another state obliged to admit the person. In his third report, Special Rapporteur Kamto proposed Draft Article 4, codifying the prohibition of expulsion of nationals:

> 1. A State *may not* expel its own nationals. 2. However, if, for *exceptional reasons* it must take such action, it may do so only with the consent of a receiving State. 3. A national expelled from his or her own country shall have the right to return to it at any time at the request of the receiving State.[16]

On request by other ILC members, Special Rapporteur Kamto focused his fourth report on the question of the applicability of Draft Article 4 to dual or multiple nationals. Considering that in the case of multiple nationalities there is at least one other state obliged to admit the person, Special Rapporteur Kamto came to the conclusion that '[t]he principle of the non-expulsion of nationals does not apply to persons with dual or multiple nationality unless the expulsion can lead to statelessness'.[17] This conclusion has been sharply criticized by important members of the ILC, who considered that the number of nationalities possessed by an individual was irrelevant and dual or multiple nationals have exactly the same rights as other nationals.[18] The Working Committee established for that purpose came to the conclusion that 'the principle of non-expulsion of nationals also applied to persons who had legally acquired another or several nationalities'.[19] The question of expulsion of nationals was finally considered to fall outside the scope of the topic and consequently not included in the Draft Articles provisionally adopted by the Drafting Committee in May 2012 (2012 Draft Articles).[20]

Nevertheless, the protection of all nationals from expulsion is still implicit in Article 9, prohibiting deprivation of nationality for the sole purpose of expulsion.[21]

Assuming that the state cannot expel its own citizens, and that it is always obliged to admit them when they are expelled from other countries or choose to return,[22] leads to the conclusion that the territory of the state of nationality is the territory where an individual always has the right to enter and stay. Nevertheless, it remains questionable if, under particular circumstances, residents who are not nationals can claim a legitimate expectation to the same right. The ILC considered the situation of stateless persons and refugees. Under Articles 6 and 7 of the 2012 Draft Articles, a state shall not expel a stateless person or a refugee lawfully in its territory 'save on grounds of national security or public order'.[23] It seems relevant to note that the provision does not set forth any obligation of the state to find another state willing to admit the expelled refugee or stateless person;[24] such an obligation can nonetheless be deduced from the 'non-prejudice clause' provided for in Article 8.[25]

Finally, it has to be questioned if the right to enter and live in their own country can be extended to individuals who, while not nationals in a formal sense, can be compared to nationals for the special link they entertain with the country. In General Comment No. 27, the HRC considered that the language of Article 12(4) ICCPR 'permits a broader interpretation that might embrace other categories of long-term residents'.[26] This hypothesis was discussed in *Stewart v Canada*, where the HRC clarified the relationship between nationality and the notion of 'own country' under Article 12 of the Covenant. In the words of the Committee:

> The question in the present case is whether a person who enters a given state under that state's immigration laws, and subject to the conditions of those laws, can regard that state as his own country when he has not acquired its nationality and continues to retain the nationality of his country of origin. The answer could possibly be positive were the country of immigration to place unreasonable impediments on the acquiring of nationality by new immigrants. But when, as in the present case, the country of immigration facilitates acquiring its nationality, and the immigrant refrains from doing so, either by choice or by committing acts that will disqualify him from acquiring that nationality, the country of immigration does not become 'his own country' within the meaning of article 12, paragraph 4, of the Covenant.[27]

Despite moving towards a broader concept of 'own country' for the purposes of the ICCPR, these words show the strict relationship between the right to enter the territory and nationality. In fact, only '*unreasonable impediments on the acquiring of nationality* by new immigrants' could justify the extension of the obligation under Article 12(4) to long-term resident immigrants.

In the framework of the ECHR, Article 3 of Protocol No. 4 explicitly limits the prohibition of expulsion and the right to enter to 'the territory of the state of which [the person] is a *national*'.[28] The European Court of Human Rights (ECtHR) considers that for the purposes of this Article '"nationality" must be determined by reference to the national law concerning citizenship', excluding any broader interpretation of the provision.[29]

Refusal of renewal of residence permit and expulsion of long-term residents migrants may affect the right to respect for private and family life under Article 8 ECHR[30] (or Articles 17 and 23 in the framework of the ICCPR[31]). The length of the migrants' stay in the country from which they are to be expelled is one of the main criteria elaborated by the ECtHR in order to assess whether an expulsion measure is necessary in a democratic society and proportionate to the legitimate aim pursued.[32] Nevertheless, a wide margin of appreciation is left to the state in balancing the relevant interests, namely migrants' right to respect for their private and family life, on the one hand, and national security, public safety, economic well-being of the country, prevention of disorder or crime, protection of health or morals, and protection of the rights and freedoms of others, on the other.[33] The Court clearly stated that:

> [E]ven if a non-national holds a very strong residence status and has attained a high degree of integration, *his or her position cannot be equated with that of a national* when it comes to the [...] power of the Contracting States to expel aliens.[34]

This statement has only partially been muffled in the *Maslov* case, where the Court considered 'that for a settled migrant who has lawfully spent all or the major part of his or her childhood and youth in the host country *very serious reasons* are required to justify expulsion'.[35]

In conclusion, several exceptions notwithstanding, it seems accurate to say that the state of nationality is the only one where the individual *always* has a positive right to go or return, thus limiting, de facto, the possibilities of exercise of the right to leave.

State of nationality and the right to leave any country including one's own

The right to leave a country is granted to every individual, without distinguishing among citizens and non-citizens, or among lawful or unlawful resident aliens. Indeed, 'the freedom to leave a territory does not constitute a fundamental or distinguishing feature of nationality'.[36] Nevertheless, in practice, the state of nationality is the one usually burdened with the respect of this right, both concerning the negative obligation not to prevent departure, and the positive obligation to issue necessary travel documents. As a matter of fact, most people begin their migration by leaving their country of nationality: the exercise of the right to free movement is consequently conditional upon the permission by the state of nationality to leave freely the territory. Second, being the one competent to deliver passports, the state of nationality can interfere even with secondary movements; indeed, most cases involving freedom of movement relate to passport delivery procedures.[37]

The negative obligation not to raise obstacles to exit from the territory has traditionally been addressed in relation to policies, often adopted by non-democratic governments, aiming to prevent citizens from expatriating, or to limit their political activities abroad.[38] Important limitations on citizens' right to leave were imposed by former socialist countries, and this was an issue of particular concern for the Conference on Security and Cooperation in Europe, and one of the main points dealt with by the Helsinki Final Act of 1975.[39] Until recently, the necessity of exit visa (to be requested both by nationals and foreigners in order to leave the country) has been an obstacle to the exercise of the right to free movement in some countries, such as Saudi Arabia and Qatar (requiring exit visas for foreign workers), Nepal, Uzbekistan, Cuba, Belarus, and Ukraine (requiring exit visas for citizens who want to emigrate or travel abroad). This practice has been considered inconsistent with the right to leave any country by the HRC.[40] The Committee also noted that exit visa procedures are often used to stop human rights activists or political opponents from leaving their respective countries of nationality. In this case the violation of the right to leave is coupled by the violation of other human rights, such as freedom of expression and association.[41]

Concerning the positive obligation to issue necessary travel documents, state practice is characterized by manifold legal, bureaucratic, or financial barriers. These barriers include: difficult access to competent authorities, issuance of passports only on payment of high fees, unreasonable delays, restrictions on family members travelling together, requirement of a repatriation deposit or a return ticket, etc. Interpreting Article 12 ICCPR, the HRC made clear the scope of the positive obligation to deliver passports both in General Comment No. 27 and in views on individual communications.[42] In the Committee's words:

> Since international travel usually requires appropriate documents, in particular a passport, the right to leave a country must include the right to obtain the necessary travel documents. The issuing of passports is normally incumbent on the State of nationality of the individual. The refusal by a State to issue a passport or prolong its validity for a national residing abroad may deprive this person of the right to leave the country of residence and to travel elsewhere. It is no justification for the State to claim that its national would be able to return to its territory without a passport.[43]

In its views on the *Liechtensztejn* case, the Committee also observed that delivery of travel documents by the state of residence does not relieve the state of nationality of the obligation to deliver passports.[44] The Committee also specified that a *laissez-passer* allowing citizens that are resident abroad to return to their country of nationality, or other travel documents, cannot be considered a satisfactory substitute for a valid passport.[45] In conclusion, any obstacle to the issuance of passport by the national state is to be considered inconsistent with Article 12 ICCPR if it does not respect the conditions established by paragraph 3 of the same Article.[46]

As the issuing of passports is normally incumbent on the state of nationality of the individual, people belonging to national minorities to whom the state of permanent residence does not recognize citizen status are often subject to unlawful limitations of their right to free movement. This is because travel documents granted to non-citizens are not always accepted as valid passports by third countries.[47] Furthermore, it is difficult for non-citizens to obtain identity papers or travel documents by their state of residence, unless they are granted the status of stateless persons falling under the scope of Articles 27 and 28 of the International Convention relating to the Status of Stateless Persons.[48]

While passport restrictions and exit visas – established by states as part of policies aiming at restricting citizens' freedoms – have often been the object of decisions issued by the HRC and other human rights bodies, less attention has been paid, by judicial and quasi-judicial bodies, to restrictions on the right to leave that aim at preventing illegal immigration in other countries. Such restrictions are generally the result of agreements between countries of origin or transit of migrants and industrialized countries, especially the European Union (EU) and its member states, which intend to manage immigration and to prevent the entrance of 'illegal aliens'. A current priority of the EU is to establish a buffer zone of countries which not only readmit immigrants expelled from European countries, but also block or intercept them before they leave.[49] The introduction of stringent measures to control emigration is both the indirect result of the conclusion of a readmission agreement, and the direct effect of the integrated border management policy of the EU. Indeed, one of the pillars of the EU's Global Approach to Migration is to share border controls with neighbouring Mediterranean and Eastern European countries, providing them technical assistance and training for border guards and immigration officials to 'fight against illegal immigration and trafficking in human beings'.[50] Such cooperation is extended to African countries.[51] As a matter of fact, the control of emigration flows by the countries of origin or transit is a limitation to the right to leave those countries, that is often realized through measures of administrative retention of illegal migrants,[52] or even by criminalizing the so-called 'illegal emigration'.[53] The conformity of such practice with Article 12 ICCPR is questionable. However, in the absence of any decision or comment that specifically deals with these kinds of limitations, only some general considerations can be discussed here.

Article 12 ICCPR does not guarantee an unrestricted right to travel from one country to another. In particular, it confers no right for a person to enter a country other than her or his own, nor is such a right set forth by analogous dispositions in other human rights treaties. Responsibilities of receiving states and limits to the sovereign right to refuse foreigners access to territory will be addressed in the following section. Here a different issue will be addressed, namely the legitimacy of administrative or criminal rules preventing people from leaving a country in the absence of a visa enabling legal access to the destination territory. To the extent that such practice directly affects the right to leave granted by Article 12, it is consistent with that right only if it complies with the conditions set forth by paragraph 3 of the same Article. Assuming that such restrictive measures are provided by law, it must be verified if they 'are necessary to protect national security, public order, public health or morals or the rights and freedoms of others, and are consistent with the other rights recognized in the [...] Covenant'. Moreover, under General Comment No. 27, 'restrictions must not impair the essence of the right' to move freely;[54] they

> must conform to the principle of proportionality; they must be appropriate to achieve their protective function; they must be the least intrusive instrument amongst those which might achieve the desired result; and they must be proportionate to the interest to be protected.[55]

Finally, the Committee also made clear that 'the application of restrictions in *any individual case* must be based on clear legal grounds and meet the test of necessity and the requirements of proportionality'.[56] Controls on irregular migration pursue a legitimate aim under Article 12(3) if they are designed to prevent and punish criminal activities, such as smuggling or trafficking. Conversely, indiscriminate closure of borders and a generalized prevention of departure affecting citizens or migrants in transit, without an individual screening of necessity and proportionality, does not comply with these requirements. As stated by Goodwin-Gill: 'In the present state of the law, it is not unlawful to move or to migrate, any more than it is to seek asylum'.[57]

This interpretation is consistent with other relevant international conventions. Article 11 of the Protocol to Prevent, Suppress and Punish Trafficking in Persons, supplementing the United Nations Convention against Transnational Organized Crime, while binding states parties to 'strengthen, to the extent possible, such border controls as may be necessary to prevent and detect trafficking in persons', specifies that this must be '*without prejudice to international commitments in relation to the free movement of people*'.[58] An almost identical provision is included in Article 7 of the Council of Europe Convention on Action against Trafficking in Human Beings;[59] it is to be noted that Article 5(4) of the Convention recognizes that to 'take appropriate measures [...] to enable migration to take place legally' is a way to prevent trafficking in human beings.

Also Article 11 of the Protocol against the Smuggling of Migrants by Land, Sea and Air[60] specifies that border controls necessary to prevent and detect smuggling are to be strengthened 'without prejudice to international commitments in relation to the free movement of people'. Furthermore, while imposing strict control and cooperation measures among states in order to enforce criminal responsibility of smugglers and to detect false travel documents, the Protocol expressly excludes from criminal liability migrants 'for the fact of having been the object of conduct set forth in Article 6 of this Protocol' (Article 5). The case of smuggling is particularly interesting because, unlike trafficking, smuggled migrants take an active part by asking to be illegally brought to a state they have no right to enter, or by asking for fraudulent documents. Nevertheless the Protocol Against the Smuggling of Migrants stresses the centrality of upholding the rights of smuggled migrants,[61] which are always considered as *victims* of smugglers' criminal conduct. Thus the Protocol implicitly recognizes as legitimate the aspiration of migrants to leave in search for a better life, even though the Protocol itself does not accord to smuggled people any right to remain in the territory of the state they eventually succeed in reaching.[62] The right to enter and to stay in the receiving state may be granted according to other applicable domestic and international rules, including those stemming from international humanitarian law and international human rights law and, in particular, from the Convention relating to the Status of Refugees (1951 Convention), and from the principle of non-*refoulement*.[63]

In conclusion, international law instruments on smuggling and trafficking allow states to prevent their nationals from leaving using unauthorized or irregular means.[64] But such preventive measures have to be justified within the terms of Article 12(3) ICCPR. The state must demonstrate first, that these restrictions are provided by law; second, that they are for the purpose of fighting against smuggling and trafficking; third, that, in any individual case, they meet the test of necessity and the requirements of proportionality to the pursued scope; and fourth that the restrictions do not impair the very essence of the right.

In the light of these conditions, generalized prohibitions on leaving the territory and criminalization of irregular migrants would not be allowed. Moreover, even where restrictions on the right to leave are legitimate, they must be implemented in conformity with all other human rights. For instance, these restrictions must conform with: the right of judicial review in case of retention, the right not to be subject to torture or inhuman or degrading treatment, and the right to respect for human dignity. Unfortunately, some of the most heinous violations of fundamental human rights are documented in retention facilities for migrants set up outside the EU as a consequence of the cooperation policy described above.

The sovereign right of the state to control its borders and limit immigration of foreigners and the right of everyone to leave any country

As repeatedly acknowledged in previous sections, the universal recognition of the right to leave does not imply the right for people to enter a country other than their own. In other words, there is no universal right to immigrate corresponding to the universal right to emigrate, so that virtually there can be nowhere to go.[65] Nevertheless the sovereign right to deny access to territory to foreigners is subject to limitations imposed by human rights law and humanitarian law. As stated by the HRC (but the statement could apply to all human rights protection systems): 'aliens may enjoy the protection of the Covenant even in relation to entry or residence, for example, when considerations of non-discrimination, prohibition of inhuman treatment and respect for family life arise'.[66]

The prime limit is the principle of non-*refoulement*. Codified for refugees by Article 33 of the 1951 Convention, the principle has been extended by human rights treaties to protect every human being against the risk of being returned to a country where there are substantial grounds for believing that they would be in danger of being subject to violations of fundamental human rights.[67] The non-*refoulement* principle does not per se grant access to territory, but the impossibility of asylum seekers returning (and the difficulty of relocating them into a safe third country willing to accept them[68]) entails the right to stay in the territory and the recognition of the refugee status or another form of international protection. Furthermore, the applicability of the principle of non-*refoulement* outside territorial borders, and especially in search and rescue operations at sea, is no longer questionable.[69] Indeed refugee law and international protection law are unanimously considered as the most important limitations on the right of states to exclude foreigners from their territory.[70] Symmetrically, the right to leave can be considered as a necessary corollary of the right to seek asylum.

Second, the right to immigrate is, in particular circumstances, the consequence of the right to respect for private and family life. Even though some human rights treaties exhort states to foster family unity by favouring family reunification,[71] none entails a general obligation to authorize access to their territory for family members.[72] Nevertheless, restrictive immigration policies significantly affecting family union are to be considered an interference with family life. Although most of the practice in this matter deals with the expulsion of settled migrants,[73] the HRC has clearly asserted, with specific reference to admittance, that: 'to separate a spouse and children arriving in a State from a spouse validly resident in a State may give rise to issues under Articles 17 and 23 of the Covenant',[74] and that 'Article 23 of the Covenant guarantees the protection of family life including the interest in family reunification'.[75] Also the ECtHR considers that, in exceptional circumstances characterized by a particularly strong family link, such as the parental relationship, the interest of individuals prevails on the sovereign right of the state to control the entry of aliens into its territory.[76] Furthermore any regulation on admittance must respect the principle of non-discrimination.[77]

The literature on the scope of the principle of non-*refoulement* and international protection – both in refugees and human rights law – is unlimited, and so is the literature on private and family rights of migrants. Thus, it does not seem useful to provide here further analysis on this point. Rather, it seems timely to question if the right to leave any country may, *in itself*, be understood as a limit to the 'extraterritorial' management of border control by states of destination.

As mentioned in the previous section, one of the pillars of the contemporary EU's Global Approach to Migration is to share border controls with countries of origin or transit of migrants, in order to prevent people from starting their journey to Europe. This 'externalization' of border controls is accomplished by shifting the responsibility of controls on the countries of origin, and by setting up maritime border control operations in the high seas adjacent those countries, or even in their territorial waters.

The consistency of maritime interdiction operations with the right to leave any country has been raised before the ECtHR in the *Xhavara* case. In 1997, the Italian and Albanian authorities, faced with the wave of Albanian citizens immigrating illegally into Italy, took, jointly, a number of measures to discourage further Albanians from leaving. A naval interdiction programme was set up and an agreement authorizing the Italian navy to board and search Albanian boats was signed by the two governments. On 28 March 1997, an Albanian boat transporting migrants, the *Kater I Rades*, sank in international waters following a collision with an Italian warship whose crew was attempting to board and search it. Some survivors applied to the ECtHR alleging the violation of several Convention rights, including the right to leave under Article 2(2) of Protocol No. 4. The Court considered that the latter provision was not applicable in that case because 'the purpose' of the naval interdiction was not to deprive applicants of their right to leave Albania, but rather to prevent them from entering Italy.[78] Based exclusively on the *declared purpose* of measures, the decision offers no indication of objective elements to establish when, if ever, pre-border operations fall under the scope of the rule.

This interpretative loophole seems more serious taking into account the trend to move migration control far away from European borders. The evolution of Frontex Hera operations offers an example of the downsides of the 'purpose criterion'. The first module of the operation, Hera I, started on July 2006 with the deployment of experts from France, Germany, Italy, Portugal, the Netherlands, Norway, and the United Kingdom into the Canary Islands to assist Spanish authorities in identifying migrants landed in the Islands and determining their status. Thus, it was an almost traditional border control operation, preventing irregular access to Spanish territory, rather than affecting the exercise of the right of migrants to leave their countries of origin. Hera II and the subsequent operations were completely different.[79] In fact, the latter consisted of joint patrols by several European states, carried out within Senegalese and Mauritanian territorial seas, on the base of bilateral agreements between these two states and Spain. The migrants' vessels were intercepted, hundreds of kilometres away from the Canary Islands, before they left the territorial waters of those Western African countries, and diverted back to their point of departure, in the absence of any individual screening of personal situations and status.[80] The purpose of these operations was to prevent landing on Canary Island, rather than leaving Senegal or Mauritania. Nevertheless they ended up making these individuals' right to leave entirely illusory. Thus, it is doubtful whether the right of the state to prevent irregular immigration can be exercised in such a way as to impair 'the very essence' of the individual right to leave any country.

It seems more accurate to apply to pre-borders operations, carried out into the territorial sea of the country of origin or transit and preventing migrants from leaving that country, the same criteria proposed in relation to emigration control. To the extent that such operations constitute a restriction to the right of everyone to leave any country, they have to comply with the conditions codified under Article 12(3) ICCPR. To control irregular migration by sea, thus preventing useless and dangerous journeys and tackling smuggling and trafficking, is a legitimate purpose. Nevertheless, the conduct of operations and the rules of engagement of patrols must be clearly regulated by law. Furthermore, the externalization of control cannot be used to avoid individual screening of intercepted migrants; indeed, in every case in which migrants can claim a legitimate expectation to obtain legal access when reaching the borders of their destination country, the limitation of their right to leave does not seem proportionate.

The obligation of individual screening in extraterritorial border controls finds support also in the *Hirsi* judgment of the ECtHR. The Court established that the prohibition of collective expulsion of aliens provided for by Article 4 of Protocol No. 4 does not only apply to the removal of aliens from the territory of the state, but also to push-back operations carried out outside national territory. The Court takes on the premise that:

> [T]he purpose of Article 4 of Protocol No. 4 is to prevent states being able to remove certain aliens without examining their personal circumstances and, consequently, without enabling them to put forward their arguments against the measure taken by the relevant authority.[81]

The ECtHR further considers that if the Article were to apply only to collective expulsions from the national territory, 'migrants having taken to the sea, often risking their lives, and not having managed to reach the borders of a State, would not be entitled to an examination of their personal circumstances before being expelled'.[82] On that premise, the Court considers that:

> [T]he removal of aliens carried out in the context of interceptions on the high seas by the authorities of a State in the exercise of their sovereign

> authority, the effect of which is to prevent migrants from reaching the borders of the State or even to push them back to another State [...] engages the responsibility of the State in question under Article 4 of Protocol No. 4.[83]

Thus, under the ECHR, the restrictive interpretation of the right to leave adopted in *Xhavara* is balanced by an extensive interpretation of the prohibition of collective expulsion leading to the analogous result of requiring the screening of each migrant's individual situation.[84]

Concluding remarks

This article starts from the traditional premise that the prime responsibility to respect the right to leave any country, including one's own, is on the state of nationality of the individual. That state is in fact the only place where the individual always has the right to stay, go, and return. Often this state represents the starting point of migration, and it is the one usually burdened with issuing passports. Conversely, other states have the sovereign right to exclude, meaning the right to establish their own immigration policies, and to deny foreigners access to their territory.

Despite this premise, the burden of respecting the right to leave is far from being limited to the state of nationality. Indeed, the review of relevant international instruments has demonstrated that the normative content of the right to leave cannot be reduced to the obligation on the state of nationality to avoid restrictive emigration policies and to issue all necessary documents. Upon every state, international law imposes a balance of relevant interests, namely between the sovereign right to exclude and the legitimate expectation of the individual to flee toward a better life, enshrined in the recognition of the right to leave.

Particularly, in the management of their border controls, *wherever and whenever realized*, states cannot 'impair the very essence' of the right at issue. Thus, contemporary policies of extraterritorial border controls, adopted by destination countries or negotiated with countries of origin and transit of migrants, aiming to decreasing illegal immigration by preventing emigration, are consistent with the right to leave only if an individual screening assessing the legitimate expectation of the migrant to be admitted in the country of destination on the basis of refugee law or other substantive and procedural human rights obligations *of the latter country* is provided. In the absence of such an individual assessment, any measure preventing people from leaving must be considered disproportionate and thus inconsistent with the right to leave.

Notes

1 'Freedom of movement' also includes the right to liberty of movement and freedom to choose residence *within the territory* of the state where anyone lawfully

lives. Nevertheless, for the purpose of this contribution only *international* movements are to be considered.

2 Among universal instruments, see ICCPR, UNTS, vol. 999, No. 14668, Article 12(2); CERD, UNTS, vol. 660, No. 9464, Article 5(d)(ii); CRC, UNTS, vol. 1577, No. 27531, Article 10(2); ICRMW, 18 December 1990, UNTS, vol. 2220, No. 39481, Article 10(1); International Convention on the Suppression and Punishment of the Crime of Apartheid, UNTS, vol. 1015, No. 14861, Article II(c). Among regional instruments, see Protocol No. 4 to the ECHR, ETS 46, Article 2(2); ESC, ETS 163, Article 18(4); ACHR, OAS Treaty Series, No. 36, Article 22(2); ACHPR, UNTS, vol. 1520, No. 26363, Article 12; ArCHR, reprinted in *Boston University International Law Journal* 24, 2006, 147–64, Article 27(1) (cf. also Article 21 of the 1994 Charter).

3 See, among others, for a comprehensive historical and philosophical reconstruction of the principle, H. Hannum, *The Right to Leave and Return in International Law and Practice*, Dordrecht–Boston: M. Nijhoff, 1987; J. Juss, 'Free Movement and the World Order', *International Journal of Refugee Law* 16, 2004, 289–335; R. Higgins, 'The Right in International Law of an Individual to Enter, Stay in and Leave a Country', *International Affairs* 49, 1973, 341–57. For an historical doctrine perspective, see F. Rigaux, 'La liberté de mouvement dans la doctrine du droit de gens', in V. Chetail (ed.) *Globalization, Migration and Human Rights: International Law under Review*, Brussels: Bruylant, 2007, pp. 137–60. It is relevant that freedom of movement had been proclaimed since 1975 in the Helsinki Final Act; even though the Act did not provide for binding obligations, the fact that it has been signed even by traditional opponents to the right to leave such as the Soviet Union and other communist states would seem to show a general recognition of the right (see D. Turack, 'Freedom of Transnational Movement: The Helsinki Accord and Beyond', *Vanderbilt Journal of Transnational Law* 11, 1978, 585–608; V. Chetail, 'Freedom of Movement and Transnational Migrations', in A. Aleinikoff and V. Chetail (eds) *Migration and International Legal Norms*, The Hague: T.M.C. Asser Press, 2003, p. 53).

4 HRC, General Comment No. 27, 'Freedom of movement (Art.12)', 2 November 1999.

5 This paradox allows Juss to affirm that 'although the right to free movement has normative force, it is not unequivocally recognized as a fundamental human right by positive law' ('Free Movement and the World Order', p. 291). Even though we do not share this postulate in its terms as we consider that the question is one of balance between different rights and principles rather than one of recognition by positive law, the assertion of Juss gives a good image of reality. See also, S. McGrath Dale, 'The Flying Dutchman Dichotomy: *The International Right to Leave v. The Sovereign Right to Exclude*', *Dickinson Journal of International Law* 9, 1991, 359–85.

6 This contribution is centered on the international human right dimension of freedom of movement, whereas regional integration mechanisms fall outside the scope of the analysis.

7 UN Secretariat, 'Expulsion of aliens. Memorandum by the Secretariat', 10 July 2006, UN Doc. A/CN.4/565, p. 21. An attempt to provide such a comprehensive legal framework, at least for economic migration, is the ICRMW. Unfortunately, among the 46 states parties no one is an industrialised country, major destination of international migrant workers.

8 Institut du droit international, 'Règles internationales sur l'admission et

l'expulsion des étrangers', 9 September 1982, *Annuaire de l'Institut de droit international*, vol. XII, 1892–4, p. 219.

9 See S. Wiessner, 'Blessed by the Ties That Bind: The Nexus between Nationality and Territory', *Mississippi Law Journal* 56, 1986, 447–534; D. Kochenov, 'The Right to Leave Any Country', forthcoming in R. Plender (ed.) *International Migration Law*, The Hague: M. Nijhoff, 2012. Online. Available at: http://ssrn.com/abstract=1847769 (accessed 20 August 2012).

10 For the purposes of this contribution, and unless otherwise indicated, we will consider the concept of 'own country' as synonymous of 'country of nationality'. Nevertheless it has to be acknowledged that 'own country' is a broader concept covering sometimes non-nationals who have a strong connection with the country, as long-time residents.

11 See, among others, P. Weis, *Nationality and Statelessness in International Law*, 2nd edn, Alphen aan den Rijn: Sijthoff & Noordhoff, 1979, p. 45; K. Doehring, 'Aliens, Expulsion and Deportation', in R. Bernhardt (ed.) *Encyclopedia of Public International Law*, Amsterdam: Elsevier Science Publishers, vol. 1, 1992, p. 110; W.T. Worster, 'International Law and the Expulsion of Individuals with More than One Nationality', *UCLA Journal of International Law and Foreign Affairs* 14, 2009, 425. For further references see UN Secretariat, 'Expulsion of aliens', p. 35, notes 57 and 58.

12 Deportation of nationals is also possible in the framework of extradition procedures, but the latter fall outside the present study.

13 HRC, General comment No. 27, para. 19.

14 Ibid., para. 21 (emphasis added).

15 See ILC, 'Expulsion of Aliens. Comments and information received from Governments', 26 August 2008, UN Doc. A/CN.4/604 (Russian Federation and Switzerland), and 26 April 2010, UN Doc. A/CN.4/628 (Malaysia). See also, for references to other national legislations, UN Secretariat, 'Expulsion of aliens', p. 36, note 60.

16 M. Kamto, 'Third report on the expulsion of aliens', 19 April 2007, UN Doc. A/CN.4/581, p. 21 (emphasis added). In his Memorandum, the UN Secretariat considered that 'international law does not appear to prohibit the expulsion of nationals in general' ('Expulsion of aliens', p. 34, and note 53 for references). Nevertheless, subsequent works of the ILC evidenced the existence of such a general rule. Previously see also G. Gaja, 'Expulsion of Aliens: Some Old and New Issues in International Law', in J. Cardona Lloréns (ed.) *Cursos Euromediterráneos Bancaja de Derecho Internacional*, Aranzadi: Elcano, Vol. III, 1999, p. 292.

17 M. Kamto, 'Fourth report on the expulsion of aliens', 24 March 2008, UN Doc. A/CN.4/594, 2008, p. 5.

18 See ILC, 'Summary Record of the 2972nd meeting, held on 5 June 2008', 14 July 2008, UN Doc. A/CN.4/SR.2972, notably for the opinions of Niehaus, Escarameia and Gaja, and 'Summary Record of the 2973rd, held on 6 June 2008', 6 February 2009, UN Doc. A/CN.4/SR.2973, notably for the opinions of Nolte, Jacobsson, Vasquez-Bermudes, who put particularly emphasis on the human right nature of the right not to be expelled from the country of nationality.

19 ILC, 'Summary Record of the 2984th meeting, held on 24 July 2008', 8 August 2008, UN Doc. A/CN.4/SR.2984, p. 29.

20 ILC, 'Expulsion of Aliens. Statement of the Chairman of the Drafting Committee, Mr. Mahmoud D. Hmoud', 29 May 2012. Online. Available at: http://untreaty.un.org/ilc/sessions/64/ExpulsionOfAliensDCstatement%282012%29.pdf (accessed 20 August 2012), p. 10.

21 ILC, 'Expulsion of aliens. Texts of draft articles 1–32 provisionally adopted on first reading by the Drafting Committee at the sixty-fourth session of the International Law Commission', 24 May 2012, UN Doc. A/CN.4/L.797 (2012 Draft Articles). The question of denationalization and expulsion had been previously addressed by the Eritrea–Ethiopia Claims Commission. The latter established that the denationalization of Ethiopian nationals of Eritrean origin who participated to the referendum deciding Eritrea independence (and acquired Eritrean nationality), and their subsequent expulsion for security reasons as citizens of belligerent country did not violate international law (*Partial Award, Civilians Claims, Eritrea's Claims 15, 16, 23 & 27–32*, of 17 December 2004. Online. Available at: www.pca-cpa.org/ (accessed 20 August 2012). Nevertheless such conclusion can hardly be generalized as the same Commission underlined the 'exceptional wartime circumstances' of the case (para. 75). Moreover it has to be noted that denationalization and expulsion has been considered legitimate only in relation to people against whom there was at least minimum evidence they threatened Ethiopian security. On this issue see further S. Forlati, 'Nationality as a human right', *supra*, p. 27.

22 Basing on an accurate analysis of state practice and legal theory, G. Noll, 'Return of Persons to States of Origin and Third States', in Aleinikoff and Chetail (eds) *Migration and International Legal Norms*, pp. 60–74, maintains that under international customary law states are bound to readmit only citizens who voluntarily return, whereas the obligation to readmit citizens forcibly expelled is negotiated in the framework of readmission agreements. This statement confirms that the right to return is a right of the individual (who '*voluntarily*' returns) rather than an interstate obligation connected to states' right to expel foreigners. It should be noticed, however, that this is a minority approach (see K. Hailbronner, 'Readmission agreements and the obligation on states under public international law to readmit their own and foreign nationals', *Zeitschrift für ausländisches öffentliches Recht und Völkerrecht* 57, 1997, 1–49, especially at 11–14; N. Coleman, *European Readmission Policy: Third Country Interests and Refugee Rights*, The Hague: M. Nijhoff, 2009, pp. 28–33; M. Marchegiani, 'L'accordo di riammissione quale strumento integrato di cooperazione tra Stati per il contrasto all'immigrazione irregolare', in G. Palmisano (ed.) *Il contrasto al traffico di migranti. Nel diritto internazionale, comunitario ed interno*, Milano: Giuffré, 2008, pp. 19–26).

23 Article 6(2) of the 2012 Draft Articles extends the prohibition of expulsion to refugees who, albeit unlawfully present in the territory of the receiving state, have applied for recognition of refugee status, while such application is pending.

24 The initial proposal by Special Rapporteur Kamto provided for a paragraph 2 of the Article concerning expulsion of a stateless person establishing that the state

> shall allow such person a reasonable period within which to seek legal admission into another country. [However, if after this period it appears that the stateless person has not been able to obtain admission into a host country, the State may [, in agreement with the person,] expel the person to any State which agrees to host him or her].
>
> Kamto, 'Third report on the expulsion of aliens', p. 32

25 According to Article 8 of the 2012 Draft Articles: 'The rules applicable to the expulsion of aliens provided for in the present draft articles are without prejudice to other rules on the expulsion of refugees and stateless persons provided for by law.' Under Article 31(3) of the 1954 Convention: 'The Contracting States shall

allow such a stateless person a reasonable period within which to seek legal admission into another country'.

26 HRC, General comment No. 27, para. 20.

27 HRC, *Charles E. Stewart v Canada*, views of 1 November 1996, CCPR/C/58/D/538/1993, para. 12.5. For some criticism on this decision see Gaja, 'Expulsion of aliens', p. 293.

28 Emphasis added.

29 See ECtHR, *Slivenko and Others v Latvia*, No. 48321/99, decision (GC) of 23 January 2002, para. 77.

30 To cite only the leading cases, see ECtHR, *Moustaquim v Belgium*, No. 12313/86, judgment of 18 February 1991; *Beldjoudi v France*, No. 12083/86, judgment of 26 March 1992. In *Boultif v Switzerland*, No. 54273/00, judgment of 2 August 2001, the Court elaborated the relevant criteria which it would use in order to assess whether an expulsion measure is necessary in a democratic society and proportionate to the legitimate aim pursued, with reference to 'family life'. In *Üner v the Netherlands*, No. 46410/99, judgment (GC) of 18 October 2006, para. 59, the Court specified that:

> the totality of social ties between settled migrants and the community in which they are living constitute part of the concept of 'private life' within the meaning of Article 8. Regardless of the existence or otherwise of a 'family life', therefore, the Court considers that the expulsion of a settled migrant constitutes interference with his or her right to respect for private life.

31 See HRC, *Winata v Australia*, views of 26 July 2001, CCPR/C/72/D/930/2000, para. 7.3; *Jonny Rubin Byahuranga v Denmark*, views of 1 November 2004, CCPR/C/82/D/1222/2003, para. 11.5.

32 ECtHR, *Boultif v Switzerland*, para. 48.

33 In ECtHR, *Boughanemi v France*, No. 22070/93, judgment of 24 April 1996, para. 39, the deportation of a 34-year old man lawfully living in France since the age of eight was considered proportionate to the pursued aim (protection of public order and prevention of crime). It is to be noted that the Court took note of the circumstance that the applicant 'had not sought French nationality'.

34 ECtHR, *Üner v the Netherlands*, para. 56, (emphasis added).

35 ECtHR, *Maslov v Austria*, No. 1638/03, judgment of 23 June 2008, para. 75.

36 Wiessner, 'Blessed by the Ties That Bind', p. 512.

37 See literature and practice cited by Kochenov, 'The Right to Leave Any Country', pp. 22ff. It has to be noted that quite often the violation of the right to leave is combined with discriminatory procedures, for example when passport regulations establish that a married woman will not be issued a passport without her husband's consent (see HRC, General Comment No. 28, 'Equality of rights between men and women (article 3)', 29 March 2000, para. 16; CEDW, 'Concluding Comments: Uganda', 23 August 2002, UN Doc. A/57/38, para. 141).

38 For example, despite the proclamation of the right to leave and return by Article 68 of Vietnamese Constitution, Article 91 of Vietnamese Criminal Code sanctions with three to twelve years of imprisonment 'those who flee abroad or defect overseas with a view to opposing the people's administration' (See CtERD, 'Concluding Observations: Viet Nam', 9 March 2012, CERD/C/VNM/CO/10–14, para. 18).

39 See Turack, 'Freedom of Transnational Movement', p. 585.

40 See HRC, 'Consideration of reports by states parties: Belarus', UN Doc. A/47/40 (1992), pp. 124ff. at para. 560. For extensive citations of HRC observations, and

an analysis of exit visa practice from an human rights perspective see C. Harvey and R.P.J. Barnidge, 'Human Rights, Free Movement, and the Right to Leave in International Law', *International Journal of Refugee Law* 19, 2007, 1–21 at 16–18.

41 See HRC, 'Concluding Observations: Uzbekistan', 26 April 2005, UN Doc. CCPR/CO/83/UZB, para. 19.

42 HRC, *Montero v Uruguay*, views of 31 March 1981, CCPR/C/OP/2, pp. 136ff., para. 9.4; *Vidal Martins v Uruguay*, views of 23 March 1982, UN Doc. A/37/40, pp. 157ff. at para. 7; *Lichtensztejn v Uruguay*, views of 31 March 1983, CCPR/C/OP/2, pp. 102ff., para. 8; *Loubna El Ghar v Libyan Arab Jamahiriya*, views of 29 March 2004, CCPR/C/82/D/1107/2002, para. 7.3.

43 HRC, General comment No. 27, para. 9.

44 HRC, *Lichtensztejn v Uruguay*, para. 8.3.

45 HRC, *Loubna El Ghar v Libyan Arab Jamahiriya*, para. 7.2. For a commentary see Harvey and Barnidge, 'Human Rights, Free Movement, and the Right to Leave in International Law', p. 7.

46 HRC, General comment No. 27, para. 17.

47 An example is the case of Latvian 'non-citizens' under the Law on the Status of Former Soviet Citizens who are not Citizens of Latvia or any Other State of 1995. See K. Krūma, *EUDO Citizenship Observatory. Country Report: Latvia*, 2010. Online. Available at: http://eudo-citizenship.eu/docs/CountryReports/Latvia.pdf (accessed 20 August 2012).

48 It is to be noted that also Articles 27 and 28 of the 1951 Convention, adopted on 28 July 1951, UNTS, vol. 189, No. 2545, requires states to issue identity papers and travel documents to refugees.

49 Coleman, *European Readmission Policy. Third Country Interests and Refugee Rights*, p. 61; E. Brouwer, 'Extraterritorial Migration Control and Human Rights: Preserving the Responsibility of the EU and its Member States', in B. Ryan and V. Mitsilegas (eds) *Extraterritorial Immigration Control. Legal Challenges*, Leiden: M. Nijhoff, 2010, p. 209. At the Seville summit, the European Council stressed 'the importance of ensuring the cooperation of countries of origin and transit in joint management and in border control as well as on readmission' and considered that 'insufficient cooperation by a country could hamper the establishment of closer relations between that country and the Union' (Seville European Council of 21 and 22 June 2002, 'Presidency Conclusions', 24 October 2002, Doc. 13463/02, paras 34–5). In the following Thessaloniki summit, the European Council recognised 'the importance of developing an evaluation mechanism to monitor relations with third countries which do not cooperate with the EU in combating illegal immigration' (Thessaloniki European Council of 19 and 20 June 2003, 'Presidency Conclusions', 1 October 2003, Doc. 11638/03, para. 19).

50 European Commission, 'Communication from the Commission to the European Parliament, the Council, the European Economic and Social Committee and the Committee of the Regions – Applying the Global Approach to Migration to the Eastern and South-Eastern Regions Neighbouring the European Union', 8 June 2007, COM (2007)247 final/2. See, among numerous documents, European Council, 'The Stockholm Programme – An open and secure Europe serving and protecting citizens', 16 October 2009, *Official Journal of the European Union* C 115, 4 May 2010, 1–38, para. 6.1.6; European Commission, 'Communication from the Commission to the European Parliament and the Council, An area of freedom, security and justice serving the citizen', 10 June 2009, COM (2009) 262 final,

para. 5.1.1; 'Conclusions of the European Council of 23–24 June 2011', 29 September 2011, Doc. EUCO 23/1/11 REV 1, para. 25.

51 Agreements among the EU (or EU member states) and third-countries generally focus on readmission. Nevertheless prevention of illegal migration is also at issue, see for example Article 13(5)(a) of the ACP–EC Partnership Agreement signed in Cotonou on 23 June 2000 (further revised in Luxembourg on 25 June 2005, and in Ouagadougou on 22 June 2010).

52 Retention facilities for illegal migrants are reported in Eastern European countries (Belarus, Ukraine, Moldova, Turkey), in Mediterranean countries (Libya, Morocco, Tunisia, Algeria), and even in the Atlantic coast of Africa (Mauritania) (Online. Available at: www.migreurop.org/rubrique266.html?lang=fr (accessed 20 August 2012)). Concerning retention centres in Maghreb see K. Debbeche, 'La protection des migrants en Mediterranée', in A. Millet-Devalle (ed.) *L'Union européenne et la protection des migrants et des réfugiés*, Paris: Pedone, 2010, p. 148.

53 Moroccan Law No. 02–03 of 11 November 2003, Articles 50–2, severely punishing whoever *leaves* or helps people to 'illegally leave' Moroccan territory; see C. Rodier, 'Emigration illégale: une notion à bannir', 13 June 2006. Online. Available at: www.migreurop.org/article922.html?lang=fr (accessed 20 August 2012).

54 HRC, General Comment No. 27, para. 13.

55 Ibid., para. 14.

56 Ibid., para. 16 (emphasis added).

57 G.S. Goodwin-Gill, 'Migrants Rights and "Managed Migration"', in Chetail (ed.) *Globalization, Migration and Human Rights*, p. 167.

58 Protocol to Prevent, Suppress and Punish Trafficking in Persons, Especially Women and Children, supplementing the United Nations Convention against Transnational Organized Crime, 15 November 2000, UNTS, vol. 2237, No. 39574 (emphasis added).

59 Council of Europe Convention on Action against Trafficking in Human Beings, 16 May 2005, CETS 197.

60 Protocol against the Smuggling of Migrants by Land, Sea and Air, supplementing the United Nations Convention against Transnational Organized Crime, 15 November 2000, UNTS, vol. 2241, No. 39574.

61 See Articles 2, 4, 9, 14, 15, 16, and 19 of the Protocol.

62 Under Article 18(1) of the Protocol:

> Each State Party agrees to facilitate and accept, without undue or unreasonable delay, the return of a person who has been the object of conduct set forth in article 6 of this Protocol and who is its national or who has the right of permanent residence in its territory at the time of return.

Still, paragraph 5 of the same Article binds each state involved to 'take all appropriate measures to carry out the return in an orderly manner and with due regard for the safety and dignity of the person.

63 See the saving clause provided for by Article 19 of the Protocol.

64 See Harvey and Barnidge, 'Human Rights, Free Movement, and the Right to Leave in International Law', p. 14.

65 J. Purcell, 'A Right to Leave, but Nowhere to Go: Reconciling an Emigrant's Right to Leave with the Sovereign's Right to Exclude', *University of Miami Inter-American Law Review* 39, 2007, 177–205.

66 HRC, General Comment No. 15, 'The position of aliens under the Covenant', 11 April 1986, para. 5.

67 First, the rule has been developed and codified to prevent the risk of being tortured or being subject to inhuman and degrading treatments. Further, both the HRC and the ECtHR have extended the application of the principle to other human rights as the right to life, the right to fair process, the right not to be arbitrarily detained. For an outline of the relevant jurisprudence see V. Chetail, 'Migration, droits de l'homme et souveraineté: le droit international dans tous ses états', in Chetail (ed.) *Globalization, Migration and Human Rights*, pp. 79ff.

68 See, for example, the well-known Australian 'Pacific Solution'. This policy program, introduced in 2001 by the Australian government in the wake of the *Tampa* episode, denied access to the Australian territory to asylum seekers, diverting them to New Zealand, Nauru, and Papua New Guinea (see M.N. Fornari, 'Soccorso di profughi in mare e diritto di asilo: questioni di diritto internazionale sollevate dalla vicenda della nave Tampa', *La Comunità internazionale* 57, 2002, 61–78). Criticized by NGOs and institutions, this policy was abandoned in 2008 (see UNHCR, 'UNHCR welcomes close of Australia's Pacific Solution', briefing notes of 8 February 2008. Online. Available at: www.unhcr.org/47ac3f9c14.html (accessed 20 August 2012).

69 UNHCR, 'Extraterritorial Application of Non-Refoulement Obligations under the 1951 Convention relating to the Status of Refugees and its 1967 Protocol', advisory opinion of 26 January 2007. Online. Available at: www.unhcr.org/refworld/docid/45f17a1a4.html (accessed 21 August 2012). ECtHR, *Hirsi Jamaa and Others v Italy*, No. 27765/09, judgment (GC) of 23 February 2012. On the *Hirsi* case, see A. Liguori, 'La Corte europea dei diritti dell'uomo condanna l'Italia per i respingimenti verso la Libia del 2009: Il caso *Hirsi*', *Rivista di diritto internazionale* 95, 2012, 415–43; N. Napoletano, 'La condanna dei "respingimenti" operati dall'Italia verso la Libia da parte della Corte europea dei diritti umani: molte luci e qualche ombra', *Diritti umani e diritto internazionale* 6, 2012, 436–47 (Online. Available at: www.sidi-isil.org/?page_id=468 (accessed 20 August 2012)); M. Tondini, 'The Legality of Intercepting Boat People Under Search and Rescue and Border Control Operations: With Reference to Recent Italian Interventions in the Mediterranean Sea and the ECtHR Decision in the *Hirsi* Case', *Journal of International Maritime Law* 18, 2012, 59–74.

70 See G.S. Goodwin-Gill and J. McAdam, *The Refugee in International Law*, 3rd edn, Oxford: Oxford University Press, 2007, p. 383; A. Hurwitz, *The Collective Responsibility of States to Protect Refugees*, Oxford: Oxford University Press, 2009, p. 212; Chetail, 'Migration, droits de l'homme et souveraineté', p. 83; Purcell, 'A Right to Leave, but Nowhere to Go: Reconciling an Emigrant's Right to Leave with the Sovereign's Right to Exclude', p. 198.

71 See Article 10 CRC. In General Comment No. 19, 'Protection of the family, the right to marriage and equality of the spouses (Art. 23)', 27 July 1990, para. 5, the HRC declared that

> the possibility to live together implies the adoption of appropriate measures, both at the internal level and as the case may be, in cooperation with other States, to ensure the unity or reunification of families, particularly when their members are separated for political, economic or similar reasons.

72 Article 44 ICRMW is more specific in content, establishing that states parties 'shall take appropriate measures to ensure the protection of the unity of the families of migrant workers', and 'shall take measures that they deem appropriate and that fall

within their competence to facilitate the reunification of migrant workers with their spouses [...], as well as with their minor dependent unmarried children'. However, the reluctance of industrialized states to ratify the Convention precludes a significant impact of this rule.

73 See above.

74 HRC, *Bakhtiyari v Australia*, views of 29 October 2003, CCPR/C/79/D/1069/2002, para. 9.6.

75 HRC, *Ngambi and Nébol v France*, decision on admissibility of 16 July 2004, CCPR/C/81/D/1179/2003, para. 6.4; but the case was considered inadmissible.

76 ECtHR, *Şen v the Netherlands*, No. 31465/96, judgment of 21 December 2001. See also *Rodrigues da Silva and Hoogkamer v the Netherlands*, No. 50435/99, judgment of 31 January 2006 and *Nunez v Norway*, No. 55597/09, judgment of 28 June 2011, as examples of regularization of irregular migrants in the interest of the child. EU Council Directive 2003/86/EC of 22 September 2003 on the right to family reunification, *Official Journal of the European Union* L 251, 3 October 2003, 12, guarantees that right in broader terms than the ECtHR case law does.

77 In *Abdulaziz, Cabales and Balkandali v the United Kingdom*, Nos. 9214/80, 9473/81 and 9474/81, judgment of 28 May 1985, the ECtHR considered that the refusal of residence permit to husbands of the applicants was not per se in breach of Article 8 (para. 69), but that the applicants were victims of discrimination on the ground of sex (para. 83).

78 ECtHR, *Xhavara and Others v Italy and Albania*, No. 39473/98, decision of 11 January 2001, para. 3.

79 Hera operations were maintained since 2011; at present, the area continues to be patrolled by Spanish means with the active participation of Senegalese and Mauritanian authorities. Concerning Hera II and III, see S. Trevisanut, 'L'Europa e l'immigrazione clandestina via mare: Frontex e il diritto internazionale', *Il diritto dell'Unione europea* 13, 2008, 379ff.

80 EU Council Decision 2010/252/EU of 26 April 2010 supplementing the Schengen Borders Code as regards the surveillance of the sea external borders in the context of operational cooperation coordinated by the European Agency for the Management of Operational Cooperation at the External Borders of the Member States of the European Union, *Official Journal of the European Union* L 111, 4 May 2010, 20, provides some guarantees and guidelines to ensure that Frontex operations are conducted in accordance with fundamental rights (Parts I and II of Annex). Nevertheless, individual screening is difficult to conceive when the vessel transporting migrants is escorted back without disembarking people. The Decision was annulled by ECJ, C-355/10, *European Parliament v Council of the European Union*, judgment (GC) of 5 September 2012; nevertheless the ECJ maintained the effects of the Decision until the entry into force of new rules.

81 ECtHR, *Hirsi v Italy*, para. 177.

82 Ibid., para. 177.

83 Ibid., para. 180.

84 In *Hirsi* migrants where rescued at sea and embarked on an Italian warship. Nevertheless, it seems possible to apply the same conclusion also when the border guard ship diverts the migrant's vessel escorting it back, as it is established – until new rules enter into force – in Part I of the Annex to EU Council Decision 2010/252/EU (see, *mutatis mutandis*, ECtHR, *Medvedyev and others v France*, No. 3394/03, judgment of 29 March 2010, para. 67).

7 Nationality and political rights

Delia Rudan

Introduction

The right of every individual to a nationality[1] is recognized in various international instruments for the protection of human rights, like the Universal Declaration of Human Rights (UDHR) (Article 15) and the American Convention on Human Rights (ACHR) (Article 20), whereas the European Convention on Human Rights (ECHR) does not provide for this specific right.[2] However, the Council of Europe (CoE) has dealt with the issue in many other instruments, the most important of which is the 1997 European Convention on Nationality (ECN) that embodies the principle of individual right to a nationality (Article 4).[3]

The term 'nationality' is sometimes distinguished from 'citizenship'; the latter term specifically indicates the faculty to exercise political rights (i.e. the right to vote and the right to stand as a candidate), whereas 'nationality' generally refers to the legal relationship existing between an individual and a given state, through which the individual has access to the political and economic rights and privileges conferred by that state.[4] There still exist states, like Honduras, Bolivia, Mexico, and Latvia, which expressly distinguish between 'nationals' and 'citizens'.[5]

As acknowledged by the Inter-American Court of Human Rights (IACHR):

> [T]he importance of nationality is that, as the political and legal bond that connects a person to a specific State, it allows the individual to acquire and exercise rights and obligations inherent in membership in a political community. As such, nationality is a requirement for the exercise of specific rights.[6]

As a matter of fact, political rights constitute a fundamental feature of the modern idea of citizenship.[7] Both the right to vote and the right to hold public office can be restricted on the basis of nationality.[8]

An exception to the traditional idea of citizenship is represented by the European Union (EU) system where an effective link between political rights holders and the exercise of political power is not required: the rights to vote and to stand as a candidate both in municipal and European elections granted to every EU citizen resident in a member state (even if different from their own state of nationality) is not considered a real political right, but rather a 'legal status' accorded to EU citizens in order to facilitate freedom of movement and establishment and to implement the principle of non-discrimination.[9]

Discrimination on grounds of nationality

The European Court of Human Rights' (ECtHR) case law shows clearly that the main problem stemming from nationality, or its absence, is the different treatment of citizens and foreigners in the enjoyment of rights and freedoms protected by the ECHR.[10] Many international instruments for the protection of human rights do not expressly prohibit discriminations on the grounds of citizenship, but only those based on national origin.[11] Also Article 14 ECHR and Protocol No. 12 include 'national origin' among the expressly prohibited reasons for discrimination. As the ECtHR has observed in the *Lucksaz v Poland* case, a difference in treatment on the basis of nationality falls within the non-exhaustive list of prohibited grounds for discrimination contained in Article 14.[12] For the purposes of Article 14, a difference in treatment between persons in analogous or similar positions is discriminatory if it has no objective and reasonable justification.[13] However, the ECtHR has held that strong reasons would have to be put forward before it could regard a difference in treatment based exclusively on grounds of nationality as compatible with the Convention.[14] This means that the ECtHR does not exclude categorically any difference in treatment between nationals and foreigners: the possession of a given nationality may, on certain conditions, be considered an appropriate reason to justify a difference of treatment.[15]

The ECHR system does not totally overtake the distinction between citizens and foreign nationals. This is confirmed by the presence in the Convention of various provisions that differentiate between the positions of these two groups.[16] The most important indication in this sense is represented by Article 16 ECHR, according to which 'nothing in Articles 10, 11 and 14 shall be regarded as preventing the High Contracting Parties from imposing restrictions on the political activity of aliens'.[17] Such a provision is nowadays considered outdated as it no longer corresponds to the needs of current society.[18] It is particularly revealing that the Parliamentary Assembly of the CoE has expressly called for the elimination of Article 16.[19]

Besides, within the CoE, there have been significant improvements in the direction of the attribution of political rights to non-citizens;[20] the Convention on Participation of Foreigners to Public Life at Local Level (1992 Convention) is an important instrument for partially overcoming the distinction among citizens and foreigners in the political rights field, but this convention has limited effects because of its application only at a local level.

Moreover, only eight state parties to the ECHR have ratified the 1992 Convention, and two of those states, namely Italy and Albania, have not accepted chapter C, related to the right of every foreign resident to vote and stand for election in local authority elections.[21]

Interestingly, in the framework of the International Covenant on Civil and Political Rights (ICCPR) there have been improvements in this direction. Even if Article 25 ICCPR expressly guarantees rights of political participation to citizens of states parties, in its General Comment No. 25 the Human Rights Committee (HRC) acknowledged that non-citizens can be granted rights of political participation at local level.[22] Moreover, the UN Working Group on Minorities established by the UN Sub-Commission on the Promotion and Protection of Human Rights (WGM), after acknowledging that citizenship is still 'an important condition for full and effective participation',[23] urged states to reduce the obstacles to acquisition of citizenship for minorities. In particular, the WGM stated that 'forms of participation by resident non-citizens should also be developed, including local voting rights after a certain period of residence and inclusion of elected non-citizen observers in municipal, regional and national legislative and decision-making assemblies'.[24]

Nationality and the right to vote

The ECHR expressly distinguishes between the position of citizens and foreigners for the purposes of participation in political life and the right to elective representation. In this regard a prominent position is assigned to the right to free elections protected by Article 3 of Protocol No. 1.[25] Such a provision establishes the obligation for the High Contracting Parties 'to hold free elections at reasonable intervals by secret ballot, under conditions which will ensure the free expression of the opinion of the people in the choice of the legislature'. Therefore the express aim of this article is to guarantee the free expression of people's opinion in the choice of the legislature.

In this connection, it must be noted that the notion of 'people' is not clarified by the ECHR, nor has it ever been analysed by the ECtHR. Political rights can be limited to citizens only, although every state is free to extend political rights to non-citizens.[26] According to the principle of the most-favourable-treatment, incorporated into many human rights treaties, a state cannot appeal to the norms of a certain convention in order to curtail or to preclude the application of rights acknowledged in its national legislation or of other rights established by international law. This means that, in principle, nothing in the ECHR prevents states parties from establishing a most favourable condition for non-citizens by granting them the rights to vote and to stand for election within their state of residence.

A significant step towards the acknowledgement of political rights to aliens is the judgment delivered by the European Court of Justice (ECJ) in the case *Spain v United Kingdom*. The ECJ held that the definition of the persons entitled to vote and stand as a candidate for elections to the European Parliament fell within the competence of each member state in compliance with European Community Law. The relevant articles of the EC Treaty did not preclude a member state from granting that right to vote and to stand as a candidate to persons who have close links to it, even if they are not that member state's own nationals or EU citizens resident in their territory.[27]

According to the Preamble of the ECHR, human rights and fundamental freedoms are best guaranteed by effective political democracy.[28] Article 3 of Protocol No. 1, therefore, enshrines a principle of primary importance in the ECHR system.[29] Free elections are the keystone of representative democracy, which is the only political model contemplated by the Convention and compatible with it.[30] Even if this provision does not expressly recognize individual rights, the ECtHR, with regard to the preparatory work and the interpretation of the Convention as a whole, has established that it confers individual rights, such as the right to vote and the right to stand for election.[31]

The right to take part in the government of one's country, directly or through freely chosen representatives, is recognized in Article 21(1) UDHR, in Article 25 ICCPR, in Article 29 of the Commonwealth of Independent States Convention on Human Rights (CIS Convention),[32] and in Article 24 of the Arab Charter on Human Rights (ArCHR)[33] as well. According to Article 21(1) UDHR, the right to take part in the government of one's country, directly or through freely chosen representatives, and the right of equal access to public service in one's own country is reserved to citizens.[34]

The right in question, provided for and guaranteed in Article 13 of the African Charter on Human and Peoples' Rights (ACHPR), is subject to the same limitation, in so far as this provision grants such a right only to citizens.[35] In *Mouvement Ivoirien des Droits Humains (MIDH) v Côte d'Ivoire*, the African Commission on Human and People's Rights (AComHPR) recognized that it is:

> [F]or the states to determine criteria for eligibility for those who can vote and those who can stand for elections to whatever positions. [...] However, these criteria must be reasonable, objective and justifiable. They must not seek to take away the already accrued rights of the individual.[36]

Even if Article 25 ICCPR does not contain a specific limitation clause, the right to vote is not considered to be an absolute right and the HRC stated that any condition that applies to the exercise of political rights 'should be based on reasonable and objective criteria'.[37] As acknowledged by the HRC, 'the right to vote at elections and referenda must be established by law and may be subject only to reasonable restrictions, such as setting a minimum age limit for the right to vote'.[38]

Likewise, the individuals' rights stemming from Article 3 of Protocol No. 1 are not absolute, but may be subject to restrictions:[39] Article 3 does not determine these rights in express terms, but there is room for implied limitations.[40] Given that the contracting parties legislation on electoral matters varies from place to place and from time to time, they enjoy a wide margin of appreciation in this area.[41] The rules on granting the right to vote, reflecting the need to ensure both citizen participation and knowledge of the particular situation of the region in question, vary according to the historical and political factors and are peculiar to each state.[42] So it is for the Court to determine, as a last resort, whether the member state has complied with the requirements of Article 3 of Protocol No. 1.[43] The requirements are: first, national measures limiting the rights to vote and to stand for elections may not impair the essence of these rights; second, the conditions imposed by states must pursue a legitimate aim; and, finally, the means employed must be proportionate.[44]

Within the ACHR system, the enjoyment of political rights is guaranteed by Article 23, a provision similar to Article 25 ICCPR. The exercise of the rights to be elected and to vote is the expression of the individual and social dimensions of political participation.[45] Also according to the IACHR, political rights 'are not absolute and may be subject to limitations. Their regulation should respect the principles of legality, necessity and proportionality in a democratic society'.[46] For what specifically concerns the right to vote, the principle of equality of treatment of all citizens in the exercise of their right to vote is encompassed in Article 3 of Protocol No. 1, Article 25 ICCPR, as well as in Article 23 ACHR.[47]

As the ECtHR declared in *Russian Conservative Party of Entrepreneurs v Russia*, 'freedom of suffrage is the cornerstone of the protection afforded by Article 3 of Protocol No. 1'.[48] However, the ECtHR has allowed restrictions on the right to vote of certain categories of voters if reasonably justified.[49] For example, the European Commission of Human Rights (EComHR) has upheld the deprivation of the right to vote as a consequence of conviction for uncitizenlike conduct, pronounced by a Special Dutch Court after the Second World War.[50] On the contrary, in *Hirst v the United Kingdom*, the ECtHR held that the exclusion from voting imposed on convicted prisoners in detention established by the British legislation amounted to a violation of Article 3 of Protocol No. 1 because 'such a general, automatic and indiscriminate restriction on a vitally important Convention right must be seen as falling outside any acceptable margin of appreciation'.[51]

Similarly, the HRC has affirmed that Hong Kong's laws that disenfranchise detainees for periods up to 10 years 'may be a disproportionate restriction of the rights protected by article 25'.[52] In *Landinelli Silva v Uruguay*, the HRC went beyond and considered that the deprivation of the right to engage in any activity of a political nature for a term of 15 years imposed on members of opposition parties constituted a violation of Article 25 ICCPR, as Uruguay had unreasonably restricted the rights stemming from such provision.[53] Besides, concerning restrictions on the right to vote grounded on national origin, the HRC, in its concluding observations on Kuwait, has expressed concern for the particular situation of Bedoons (included in the category of stateless persons) in Kuwait.[54] In particular, the HRC asked Kuwait to 'confer its nationality on a non-discriminatory basis and ensure that those who are granted Kuwaiti nationality are treated equally with other Kuwaiti citizens with regard to voting rights'.[55]

In particular regarding limitations on the right to vote on grounds of national origin, in the *Aziz v Cyprus* case, the ECtHR noted that even if:

> States enjoy a considerable latitude to establish rules within their constitutional order governing parliamentary elections and the composition of the parliament [. . .] these rules should not be such as to exclude some persons or groups of persons from participating in the political life of the country and, in particular, in the choice of the legislature.[56]

In consequence, the ECtHR held that the situation of the applicant, a member of the Turkish-Cypriot community, a resident in the non-occupied territory of Cyprus, and completely deprived of the opportunity to express his opinion in the choice of the Cypriot Parliament, was in breach of Article 3 of Protocol No. 1 because the very essence of his right to vote was impaired.[57]

However, nowadays there are states that impose restrictions on the right to vote for dual nationals on the basis of residence; in fact many dual nationals are excluded from voting as non-residents of states in which they hold citizenship.[58] This exclusion from voting is not determined by their dual nationality status, but rather by their non-residence status in the second state.[59] In this regard, the EComHR considered that the residence requirement provided for in the electoral law of the United Kingdom cannot be regarded as unreasonable or arbitrary. Thus the electoral law of the United Kingdom is not contrary to Article 3 of Protocol No. 1, as it is not discriminatory to citizens residing abroad.[60] Also in the ICCPR system, residence requirements are permitted, provided that they are reasonable.[61]

Nationality and the right to stand for election

Passive electoral rights protect both the right to stand as a candidate and, once elected, the right to sit as a MP.[62] The ECtHR has often emphasized the considerable latitude that states enjoy in establishing criteria on the eligibility to stand for election and limited its review to a 'check on the absence of arbitrariness in the domestic procedures leading to disqualification of an individual from standing as a candidate'.[63]

With regards to the limitations on the right to stand for election, the EComHR upheld the exclusion of a political party from municipal elections because of the parties' political propaganda on racial discrimination. Article 17 does not permit the use of Article 10 to spread racially discriminatory ideas, nor does Article 3 of Protocol No. 1 support a candidature based on a platform of racial discrimination.[64] Also, the restrictions on certain political activities of local public servants imposed by the British legislation were upheld by the ECtHR as such measures constituted a justified requirement for the maintenance of officers' impartiality.[65]

Regarding restrictions on the right to stand as a candidate motivated by national origin, in *Mouvement Ivoirien des Droits Humains (MIDH) v Côte d'Ivoire* the AComHPR found:

> [T]he requirement that an individual can only exercise the right to stand for the post of a President not only if he/she is born in Côte d'Ivoire, but also that his parents must be born in Côte d'Ivoire unreasonable and unjustifiable.[66]

The AComHPR considered it 'an unnecessary restriction on the right to participate in government guaranteed under 13 of the African Charter'.[67] Moreover, in *Modise v Botswana*, the author of the communication alleged that, although he was a national of Botswana by descent, the Government of Botswana declared him an 'undesirable immigrant' and subsequently deported him because of his political activity. After many years, the government granted him citizenship by registration; however, this latter form of citizenship precluded him from running as candidate for the presidency of the Republic of Botswana. Therefore, the AComHPR decided that denying nationality by birth to the complainant, due to his political opinions, amounted to a violation of Article 13 ACHPR.[68] However, this pronouncement builds upon the particular situation of the complainant. After recalling that the deportation of Mr Modise occured soon after he founded an opposition political party and with the intent to hinder his political activity, the AComHPR affirmed that 'granting the Complainant citizenship by registration has therefore gravely deprived him of one of his most cherished fundamental rights, the right to freely participate in the government of his country, either directly or through elected representatives'.[69] The AComHPR, however, refrained from affirming that the distinction between citizens by registration and citizens by birth amounted in this case to a violation of the rights embodied in the ACHPR. Thus, the AComHPR confirmed that states enjoy a wider margin of appreciation in relation to limitations on the right to stand for elections as compared to the right to vote.

In the ICCPR framework, and according to the HRC, 'any restrictions on the right to stand for election, such as minimum age, must be justifiable on objective and reasonable criteria'.[70] For example, the Committee holds that it is unreasonable to require candidates to be members of parties or specific parties.[71]

The ECtHR dealt with the right to stand for election of individuals with dual or multiple citizenship in the *Tanase v Moldova* case. This case concerned the electoral legislation in Moldova, according to which Moldavian citizens with dual or multiple nationality were allowed to stand as candidates in legislative elections, but if elected, they were required to renounce to the foreign nationalities in order to obtain the validation of their mandates by the Constitutional Court. Here the ECtHR took into account the provisions of the ECN, the reports of the Commission against Racism and Intolerance, the European Commission for Democracy through Law (Venice Commission), and the resolutions of the Parliamentary Assembly of the CoE to decide if the Moldavian law was proportionate. After observing that all the above-mentioned human rights bodies criticized this provision for its discriminatory nature, the ECtHR recalled that any restriction on electoral rights should not exclude some persons or groups of persons from participating in the political life of the country. According to the ECtHR, the contested measure had a detrimental impact on the ability of opposition parties to participate effectively in the political process of the country.[72]

Pluralism and democracy must be based on dialogue and a spirit of compromise, which necessarily entails various concessions by individuals or groups of individuals that are justified in order to maintain and promote the ideals and values of a democratic society. For this reason, it is important to ensure access to the political arena for opposition parties and to allow them to represent their electorate and defend their interests.[73] Any measure that appears to operate solely, or principally, to the disadvantage of the political opposition shall be scrutinized by the Court with particular care because similar restrictions limit the rights protected by Article 3 of Protocol No. 1 and impair their essence.[74] In the light of these observations, the ECtHR considered the Moldavian law preventing the election of individuals with multiple nationalities to Parliament to be disproportionate and to violate Article 3 of Protocol No. 1.

Refugees and political rights

The Convention relating to the Status of Refugees (1951 Convention) does not encompass specific provisions on political rights of refugees.[75] However, according to Article 7(1), 'except where this Convention contains more favourable provisions, a Contracting State shall afford to refugees the same treatment as is accorded to aliens generally', regarding the right to association with trade unions and non-political bodies.[76] An identical provision is embodied in Article 7(1) of the Convention relating to the Status of Stateless Persons (1954 Convention), requiring stateless persons to be treated not less favourably than aliens generally. This indicates that both refugees and stateless persons are granted the same political rights as other aliens in the country of asylum or residence. Besides, it follows that the country of asylum or residence is entitled to restrict the exercise of political rights of refugees and stateless persons present in its territory.[77]

No specific recommendation on this matter comes from the 1984 Cartagena Declaration on Refugees. This instrument is limited to affirming that Central American States 'establish a minimum standard of treatment for refugees, on the basis of the provisions of the 1951 Convention and 1967 Protocol and of the American Convention on Human Rights, taking into consideration the conclusions of the UNHCR Executive Committee'.[78] Therefore, the legal framework for refugees and political rights issues mainly from international human rights law.[79]

As said before, Article 25 ICCPR recognizes the rights to vote and to stand for election only to citizens, while no such right is granted to foreign residents.[80] This approach is confirmed also in other provisions of human rights treaties, like Article 23 ACHR and Article 13 ACHPR. Even if the ECtHR has not explicitly limited the application of Article 3 of Protocol No. 1 to citizens, according to Article 16 of the Convention, states can impose restrictions on the political activity of aliens, including refugees and stateless persons. In fact Article 16 ECHR seems to be an attempt 'to protect the discretion of States to restrict electoral rights'.[81]

State practice shows that the majority of states do not enfranchise aliens, including refugees.[82] Nevertheless, there are some exceptions, like the United Kingdom[83] and New Zealand, that grant certain aliens the right to vote in national elections, and a few states allow foreign residents to vote in local elections.[84] In many of these states, refugees are granted the same voting rights recognized to resident aliens, if they have complied with the residence requirement for a certain period of time.[85] As such, the right to vote and to be elected is bestowed only on citizens, and both refugees and stateless persons are left outside the electoral process of their country of asylum or residence.

For what concerns 'quasi-political rights' instead, refugees are entitled to the same freedom of expression, association, and assembly as citizens.[86]

Democracy and political rights

Finally, some obsevations must be made on the links between political rights and the idea of democracy. The promotion and preservation of democracy is one of the ECHR's objectives and the reference to the 'democratic society' contained in the limitations clauses of Articles 8 through 11 demonstrates the prominent role given to democracy in the balance between individual claims and community needs. The concept of democratic society is a unifing thread in the entire Convention.[87] The ECtHR state at various times that 'free elections and freedom of expression, particularly freedom of political debate, together form the bedrock of any democratic system'.[88]

Also in the ICCPR system there is an essential link between freedom of expression and the exercise of electoral rights and democratic participation.[89] Citizens also take part in the conduct of public affairs by exerting influence through public debate and dialogue with their representatives or through their capacity to organize themselves. This participation is supported by ensuring freedom of expression, assembly, and association.[90] In order to ensure the full enjoyment of rights protected by Article 25, the free communication of information and ideas about public and political issues among citizens, candidates, and elected representatives is essential.[91] This implies a free press and other media able to comment on public issues without censorship or restraint and to inform public opinion. Therefore states have to guarantee the:

> [F]reedom to engage in political activity individually or through political parties and other organizations, freedom to debate public affairs, to hold peaceful demonstrations and meetings, to criticize and oppose, to publish political material, to campaign for election and to advertise political ideas.[92]

In this regard, it is significant to stress that the protection of freedom of expression, assembly, and association is not limited to citizens, but is recognized to aliens and refugees as well, extending the guarantee of the rights of participation.[93]

The importance of the interrelationship between democracy and human rights protection is emphasized by international monitoring bodies. The IACHR maintains that 'representative democracy is the form of State organization explicitly espoused by the member states of the Organization of American States'.[94] According to the ECtHR, 'there can be no democracy without pluralism'.[95] It is for that reason that freedom of expression is applicable, not only to information or ideas that are favourably received, regarded as inoffensive, or treated with indifference, but also to those that offend, shock, or disturb.[96] As the ECtHR has acknowledged, the state is the ultimate guarantor of the principle of pluralism.[97] Therefore, political parties play an essential role in ensuring pluralism and the proper functioning of democracy.[98] Political parties make an irreplaceable contribution to political debate: 'it is of the essence of democracy to allow diverse political programmes to be proposed and debated, even those that call into question the way a State is currently organised, provided that they do not harm democracy itself'.[99] Finally, for the ACHR system, the IACHR has developed an innovative guarantee to the right to political participation by admitting that political parties are not the only entities that could participate in elections and by recognizing the right of indigenous communities to participate in the democratic process.[100]

Concluding remarks

Nationality is still considered to be an important criterion for the grant of political rights. In fact, both at a universal level and at a regional level, it is legitimate to exclude non-citizens (including refugees) from the rights to vote and to stand for election.[101] More specifically, the absence of political rights, as well as 'quasi-political rights', from the 1954 Convention clearly shows that states are fully entitled to exclude non-citizens from these rights; the exclusion of such rights from the final text of the Convention was justified by the will to allow states to restrict the political activity of stateless persons on their territory.[102] Besides, from the above analysis it is evident that refugees do not have the rights to vote or to stand for election in the country of asylum.

This notwithstanding, there is a tendency, in particular in the European context, to recognize voting rights to foreigners at a local level, provided that they have complied with a residence requirement for a certain period of time.[103] Significant improvements in this direction are represented by Article 6 of the 1992 Convention, as well as by Recommendation 1500 (2001) on participation of immigrants and foreign residents in political life in the Council of Europe member states, adopted by the Parliamentary Assembly of the CoE. Further improvements in this sense come from the Venice Commission and the Advisory Committee on the Framework Convention for the Protection of National Minorities, that urge states parties to grant foreigners belonging to national minorities the opportunity to vote and stand as candidates in local elections.[104]Although no customary rule has developed to acknowledge political rights for non-citizens, not even at a local level, all the above-mentioned instruments clearly show that state actions in this direction are increasing[105] and indicate the possibility of future changes.

Notes

1 On the right of every individual to a nationality see S. Forlati, 'Nationality as a human right', *supra*, pp. 18–36.

2 J.Y. Carlier, 'Droits de l'homme et nationalité', *Annales de droit de Louvain* 63, 2003, 243–57 at 246; M. De Salvia, 'Nazionalità in senso formale e nazionalità in senso sostanziale nella Convenzione europea dei diritti dell'uomo', *Rivista internazionale dei diritti dell'uomo* 8, 1995, 9–22 at 9; S. Forlati, 'Discriminazione sulla base della cittadinanza e Convenzione europea dei diritti umani', in L. Desanti, P. Ferretti and A.D. Manfredini (eds) *Per il 70. compleanno di Pierpaolo Zamorani. Scritti offerti dagli amici e colleghi di facoltà*, Milano: Giuffré, 2009, pp. 231–45 at 238; L. Panella, 'La cittadinanza nel diritto internazionale: potere dello Stato o diritto del singolo?', in G. Venturini and S. Bariatti (eds) *Diritti individuali e giustizia internazionale. Liber Fausto Pocar*, Milano: Giuffré, 2009, pp. 649–62 at 659; C. Thiele, 'Citizenship as a Requirement for Minorities', *European Human Rights Law Review* 10, 2005, 276–89 at 286; EComHR, *X. v Austria*, No. 5212/71, decision of 5 October 1972; ECtHR, *Slivenko and others v Latvia*, No. 48321/99, decision (GC) of 23 January 2002, para. 77.

3 The right of every individual to a nationality is stated in Article 2 of the 2006 Convention and in Article 1 of the 1961 Convention. This right is affirmed moreover in Conference for Security and Cooperation in Europe, *The Challenges on Change*, Helsinki, 9–10 July 1992, part VI, para. 55. Online. Available at: www.osce.org/mc/39530?download=true (accessed 20 June 2012) and in

Venice Commission, 'Consequences of State Succession for Nationality', report of 14 September 1996. Online. Available at: www.venice.coe.int (accessed 20 June 2012), para. 28.

4 See R. Cordova, 'Third report on the elimination or reduction of statelessness', 11 March 1954, *Yearbook of the International Law Commission*, 1954, vol. II, para. 32; according to Special Rapporteur Cordova:

> nationality does not, by itself, include the status of citizenship. A citizen is a national who enjoys political rights; but there are many nationals who are not citizens in the sense that they do not enjoy political rights. That is the case with minors in all countries and, in some of them, with women, the mentally incapacitated and convicted criminals.

5 See, for example, Article 36 of the Constitution of Honduras ('Son ciudadanos todos los hondureños mayores de dieciocho años'). Online. Available at: www.honduras.net/honduras_constitution2.html (accessed 25 July 2012). See Immigration and Refugee Board of Canada, *Bolivia: Difference between nationality and citizenship in Bolivia; rights and obligation attached to each*, 22 August 2000, BOL35164.E. Online. Available at: www.unhcr.org/refworld (accessed 25 July 2002); CtRC, 'Summary record of the 106th meeting: Mexico', 14 January 1994, CRC/C/SR.106, paras 35–8. Online. Available at: www.unhchr.ch/tbs/doc.nsf (accessed 25 July 2012); HRC, 'Concluding Observations: Latvia', 6 November 2003, CCPR/CO/79/LVA, paras 17–18. Online. Available at: www.unhchr.ch/tbs/doc.nsf (accessed 25 July 2012).

6 IACHR, *Case of the Girls Yean and Bosico v Dominican Republic*, judgment of 8 September 2005, *Series C*, No. 130, para. 137.

7 P. Spiro, 'Political Rights and Dual Nationality', in D.A. Martin and K. Hailbronner (eds) *Rights and Duties of Dual Nationals. Evolution and Prospects*, The Hague–London–New York: Kluwer Law International, 2003, pp. 135–52 at 135; C. Tiburcio, *The Human Rights of Aliens under International and Comparative Law*, The Hague: M. Nijhoff, 2001, p. 177.

8 Ibid. See J. Fitzpatrick, J. Brotman and S. Brotman, *The Human Rights of Migrants*, paper presented at the Conference on International Legal Norms and Migration, Geneva, 23–25 May 2002. Online. Available at: www.baliprocess.net/files/ConferenceDocumentation/The%20Human%20Rights%20of%20Migrants_%202002.pdf (accessed 2 July 2002), p. 5.

9 F. Del Conte, 'CEDU e UE a confronto: la Corte di Lussemburgo si pronuncia sulla titolarità del diritto di voto per le elezioni del Parlamento europeo', *Diritto pubblico comparato ed europeo*, 2006, pp. 1525–9 at 1526. This is confirmed by the EU Council Directive 93/109/EC of 6 December 1993 laying down detailed arrangements for the exercise of the right to vote and stand as a candidate in elections to the European Parliament for citizens of the Union residing in a Member State of which they are not nationals, *Official Journal of the European Communities* L 329, 30 December 1993, 34, and by the ECJ, C-145/04, *Kingdom of Spain v United Kingdom of Great Britain and Northern Ireland*, judgment (GC) of 12 September 2006, *ECR*, 2006, p. I-7917, para. 66.

10 De Salvia, 'Nazionalità', p. 12. On the topic of discrimination on grounds of nationality in the ECHR see Forlati, 'Discriminazione', pp. 231–45.

11 Ibid., p. 232. See notably: Article 2 UDHR (adopted on 10 December 1948. Online. Available at: http://www.un.org (accessed 20 April 2012)); Article 2(1)

and Article 26 ICCPR (adopted on 16 December 1966, UNTS, vol. 999, No. 14668); Article 2(2) ICESCR (adopted on 16 December 1966, UNTS, vol. 993, No. 14531); Article 1(1) ACHR (adopted on 22 November 1969, OAS Treaty series, No. 36) and Article 2 ACHPR (adopted on 27 June 1981, OAV DOC. CAB/LEG/67/3 rev.5 (1981)).

12 ECtHR, *Luczak v Poland*, No. 77782/01, judgment of 27 November 2007, para. 46.

13 ECtHR, *Abdulaziz, Cabales and Balkandali v the United Kingdom*, No. 9214/80, judgment of 28 May 1985, para. 72; ECtHR, *Andrejeva v Latvia*, No. 55707/00, judgment (GC) of 18 February 2009, para. 81. See Forlati, 'Discriminazione', p. 234; C. Ovey and R.C.A. White, *Jacobs, White and Ovey. The European Convention on Human Rights*, 5th edn, Oxford: Oxford University Press, 2010, p. 547.

14 ECtHR, *Gaygusuz v Austria*, No. 17371/90, judgment of 16 September 1996, para. 42; ECtHR, *Andrejeva v Latvia*, para. 87.

15 Forlati, 'Discriminazione', p. 234; De Salvia, 'Nazionalità', p. 13. In the same direction see also Protocol No. 12 to the ECHR, Explanatory Report, para. 19. Online. Available at: http://conventions.coe.int (accessed 20 June 2012).

16 Forlati, 'Discriminazione', p. 234; De Salvia, 'Nazionalità', p. 11.

17 On Article 16 ECHR see A. De Guttry, 'Art. 16. Restrizione all'attività politica degli stranieri', in S. Bartole, B. Conforti and G. Raimondi (eds) *Commentario alla Convenzione europea per la tutela dei diritti dell'uomo e delle libertà fondamentali*, Padova: Cedam, 2001, pp. 443–53; S. Granata Menghini, 'Art. 16. Restrizioni all'attività politica degli stranieri', in S. Bartole, P. De Sena and V. Zagrebelsky (eds) *Commentario breve alla Convenzione europea dei diritti dell'uomo*, Padova: Cedam, 2012, pp. 564–70; P. Mascagni, 'Le restrizioni alle attività politiche degli stranieri consentite dalla Convenzione europea dei diritti dell'uomo', *Rivista di diritto internazionale* 60, 1977, 526–39.

18 De Guttry, 'Art. 16', p. 452; Granata Menghini, 'Art. 16', p. 570.

19 Parliamentary Assembly of the CoE, Recommendation No. 799 (1977) on the political rights and position of aliens, 25 January 1977. Online. Available at: www.assembly.coe.int (accessed 20 June 2012).

20 Parliamentary Assembly of the CoE, Recommendation No. 903 (1980) on the right of aliens to vote and stand in local authority elections, 30 September 1980. Online. Available at: www.assembly.coe.int (accessed 20 June 2012); Recommendation No. 1500 (2001), Participation of immigrants and foreign residents in political life in the Council of Europe member states, 26 January 2001. Online. Available at: www.assembly.coe.int (accessed 20 June 2012). See also: CoE, Congress of Local and Regional Authorities of Europe, Recommendation No. 76 (2000) on the participation of foreign residents in local public life, 24 May 2000. Online. Available at: www.coe.int/t/congress/default_en.asp (accessed 26 June 2012).

21 Forlati, 'Discriminazione', p. 236.

22 HRC, General Comment No. 25, 'The right to participate in public affairs, voting rights and the right of equal access to public service', 12 July 1996, CCPR/C/21/Rev.1/Add.7, para. 3; see S. Joseph, J. Schultz and M. Castan, *The International Covenant on Civil and Political Rights. Cases, Materials and Commentary*, Oxford: Oxford University Press, 2000, p. 496.

23 WGM, 'Commentary of the Working Group on Minorities to the United

Nations Declaration on the Rights of Persons Belonging to National or Ethnic, Religious and Linguistic Minorities', 4 April 2005, UN Doc. E/CN.4/Sub.2/AC.5/2005/2, para. 50.

24 Ibid. See A. Verstichel, 'Understanding Minority Participation and Representation and the Issue of Citizenship', in M. Weller and K. Nobbs (eds) *Political Participation of Minorities. A Commentary on International Standards and Practice*, Oxford: Oxford University Press, 2010, pp. 72–94 at 92.

25 Protocol to the Convention for the Protection of Human Rights and Fundamental Freedoms, Paris, 20 March1952, CETS No. 9.

26 A. Eide, 'Citizenship and the Minority Rights of Non-Citizens', 15 April 1999, UN Doc. E/CN.4/Sub.2/AC.5/1999/WP.3, para. 50.

27 ECJ, *Spain v United Kingdom*, para. 78.

28 ECtHR, *United Communist Party of Turkey and others v Turkey*, No. 19392/92, judgment of 30 January 1998, para. 45; A. Mowbray, 'The Role of the European Court on Human Rights in the Promotion of Democracy', *Public Law*, 1999, 703–25 at 703; R. O'Connell, 'Towards a Stronger Conception of Democracy in the Strasbourg Convention', *European Human Rights Law Review* 11, 2006, 281–93 at 283.

29 ECtHR, *Mathieu-Mohin and Clerfayt v Belgium*, No. 9267/81, judgment of 2 March 1987, para. 47; ECtHR, *Krasnov and Skuratov v Russia*, No. 17864/04, judgment of 19 July 2007, para. 39; M. Kaiser, 'Le droit à des élection libres. L'application timide d'une disposition ambitieuse', in *Les droits de l'homme au seuil du troisième millénaire. Mélanges en hommage à Pierre Lambert*, Bruxelles: Bruylant, 2000, pp. 435–65 at 437–38; O'Connell, 'Towards a Stronger Conception', p. 283.

30 ECtHR, *Refah Partisi (the Welfare Party) and others v Turkey*, No. 41340/98, judgment (GC) of 13 February 2003, para. 86; ECtHR, *Zdanoka v Latvia*, No. 58278/00, judgment (GC) of 16 March 2006, para. 98. See C. Pinelli, 'Le sens de la démocratie politique dans le système conventionnel', *Diritto pubblico comparato ed europeo*, 2004, 1325–32 at 1325; F. Salerno, '"Sovranità liquida" ovvero il diritto alla democrazia rappresentativa tra sovranità costituzionale ed obblighi internazionali', in Desanti, Ferretti and Manfredini, *Per il 70. compleanno*, pp. 363–90 at 371.

31 ECtHR, *Mathieu-Mohin and Clerfayt v Belgium*, paras 46–51; ECtHR, *Hirst v the United Kingdom (No. 2)*, No 74025/01, judgment (GC) of 6 October 2005, para. 57; Forlati, 'Discriminazione', p. 235; D.J. Harris, M. O'Boyle and C. Warbrick, *Law of the European Convention on Human Rights*, Oxford: Oxford University Press, 2009, p. 712; Salerno, 'Sovranità liquida', p. 378; M. Starita, 'Art. 3 Diritto a libere elezioni', in Bartole, De Sena and Zagrebelsky (eds) *Commentario*, pp. 832–57 at 833; M. Starita, 'Il "diritto di voto" secondo la Corte comunitaria e secondo la Corte europea dei diritti dell'uomo', *Diritti umani e diritto internazionale* 1, 2007, 507–43 at 525; V. Huet, 'Vers l'emergence d'un principe de légitimité démocratique en droit international?', *Revue trimestrielle des droits de l'homme* 67, 2006, 547–73 at 568.

32 Article 29 of the CIS Convention reads:

> In accordance with national legislation, everyone shall have the right and opportunity and in the State of which he is a citizen: (a) to take part in the management and conduct of public affairs, either directly or through freely chosen representatives; (b) to vote and to be elected at elections held on the basis of universal and equal suffrage by secret ballot, that guarantees the free expression of the will of voters; c) to have access, on general conditions of equality, to the public service of his country.

33 According to Article 24 ArCHR:

> Every citizen has the right: 1. To freely pursue a political activity. 2. To take part in the conduct of public affairs, directly or through freely chosen representatives. 3. To stand for election or choose his representatives in free and impartial elections, in conditions of equality among all citizens that guarantee the free expression of his will. 4. To the opportunity to gain access, on an equal footing with others, to public office in his country in accordance with the principle of equality of opportunity. 5. To freely form and join associations with others. 6. To freedom of association and peaceful assembly. 7. No restrictions may be placed on the exercise of these rights other than those which are prescribed by law and which are necessary in a democratic society in the interests of national security or public safety, public health or morals or the protection of the rights and freedoms of others.

34 Granata Menghini, 'Art. 16', p. 565; A. Rosas, 'Article 21', in G. Alfredsson and A. Eide (eds) *The Universal Declaration on Human Rights: A Common Standard of Achievement*, The Hague–Boston–London: M. Nijhoff, 1999, pp. 431–51 at 438.

35 AComHPR, *Mouvement Ivorien des Droits Humaines (MIDH) v Côte d'Ivoire*, Communication 246/02, decided at the 5th extraordinary session, 21–29 July 2008. Online. Available at: www.achpr.org/files/sessions/5th-eo/comunications/246.02/achpreo5_246_02_eng.pdf (accessed 22 August 2012), paras 76–7. See M.K. Mbondenyi, 'The Right to Participate in the Government of One's Country: An Analysis of Article 13 of the African Charter on Human and Peoples' Rights in the Light of Kenya's 2007 Political Crisis', *African Human Rights Law Journal* 9, 2009, 183–202 at 185.

36 AComHPR, *Mouvement Ivorien des Droits Humaines (MIDH) v Côte d'Ivoire*, para. 83.

37 HRC, General Comment No. 25, para. 4. On Article 25 ICCPR see A. Conte and R. Burchill, *Defining Civil and Political Rights. The Jurisprudence of the United Nations Human Rights Committee*, Farnham: Ashgate, 2009, pp. 97–110.

38 HRC, General Comment No. 25, para. 10.

39 ECtHR, *Gitonas v Greece*, No. 18747/91, judgment of 1 July 1997, para. 39; C. Pinelli, 'Art. 3 Diritto a libere elezioni', in Bartole, Conforti, Raimondi (eds) *Commentario*, pp. 845–61 at 852.

40 ECtHR, *Zdanoka v Latvia*, para. 103; ECtHR, *Yumak v Turkey*, No. 10226/03, judgment (GC) of 8 July 2008, para. 109. See Harris, O'Boyle and Warbrick, *Law of the European Convention*, p. 713; Starita, 'Art. 3', p. 842.

41 Harris, O'Boyle and Warbrick, *Law of the European Convention*, p. 714; ECtHR, *Py v France*, No. 66289/01, judgment of 11 January 2005, para. 46.

42 ECtHR, *Py v France*, para. 46.

43 ECtHR, *Labita v Italy*, No. 26772/95, judgment (GC) of 6 April 2000, para. 201.

44 ECtHR, *Podkolzina v Latvia*, No. 46726/99, judgment of 9 April 2002, para. 33; ECtHR, *Hirst v the United Kingdom (No. 2)*, para. 62. See Pinelli, 'Art. 3', pp. 849–50; Starita, 'Il diritto di voto', pp. 526–7.

45 IACHR, *Yatama v Nicaragua*, judgment of 23 June 2005, *Series C*, No. 127, para. 197.

46 Ibid., para. 206.

47 ECtHR, *Mathieu-Mohin and Clerfayt v Belgium*, para. 54; HRC, 'Concluding Observations (Hong Kong): United Kingdom of Great Britain and Northern

Ireland', 9 November 1995, CCPR/C/79/Add.57, para. 19; IACHR, *Yatama v Nicaragua*, para. 198. See Salerno, 'Sovranità liquida', p. 379; Joseph, Schultz, Castan, *The International Covenant*, p. 504.

48 ECtHR, *Russian Conservative Party of Entrepreneurs v Russia*, No. 55066/00, judgment of 11 January 2007, para. 71.

49 ECtHR, *Aziz v Cyprus*, No. 69949/01, judgment of 22 June 2004, para. 28; ECtHR, *Zdanoka v Latvia*, para. 105. See Starita, 'Il diritto di voto', p. 538. In this regard see also AComHPR, *Purohit and Moore v Gambia*, Communication 241/01, adopted at the 33rd ordinary session, 15–29 May 2003. Online. Available at: www.achpr.org/files/sessions/33rd/communications/241.01/achpr33_241_01_eng.pdf (accessed 22 August 2012), para. 75.

50 EComHR, *X. v the Netherlands*, No. 6573/74, decision of 19 December 1974, pp. 89–90; Pinelli, 'Art. 3', p. 853.

51 ECtHR, *Hirst v the United Kingdom (No. 2)*, para. 82; Harris, O'Boyle and Warbrick, *Law of the European Convention*, p. 717.

52 HRC, 'Concluding observations (Hong Kong): United Kingdom of Great Britain and Northern Ireland', para. 19.

53 HRC, *Jorge Landinelli Silva v Uruguay*, views of 8 April 1981, UN Doc. A/36/40, para.10. See also HRC, *Lucia Sala de Touron v Uruguay*, views of 31 March 1981, CCPR/C/12/D/32/1978, para. 11.

54 HRC, 'Concluding Observations: Kuwait', 27 July 2000, CCPR/CO/69/KWT, para. 26.

55 Ibid., para. 29.

56 ECtHR, *Aziz v Cyprus*, para. 28.

57 Ibid. pp. 136–7.

58 Spiro, 'Political Rights', p. 135.

59 Ibid., pp. 136–7.

60 EComHR, *X. v the United Kingdom*, No. 7566/76, decision of 11 December 1976, pp. 122–3; Pinelli, 'Art. 3', p. 852.

61 HRC, General Comment No. 25, para. 11.

62 ECtHR, *Sadak and others v Turkey (No. 2)*, No. 25144/94, judgment of 11 June 2002, para. 33.

63 ECtHR, *Zdanoka v Latvia*, para. 115.

64 EComHR, *Glimmerveen and Hagenbeek v the Netherlands*, No. 8348/78, decision of 11 October 1979. See Pinelli, 'Art. 3', p. 853.

65 ECtHR, *Ahmed and others v the United Kingdom*, No. 22952/93, judgment of 2 September 1998, para. 63; Mowbray, 'The Role of the European Court', pp. 708–11.

66 AComHPR, *Mouvement Ivorien des Droits Humaines (MIDH) v Côte d'Ivoire*, para. 86.

67 Ibid. See also AComHPR, *Legal Resources Foundation v Zambia*, Communication 211/98, decided at the 29th ordinary session, 23 April–7 May 2001. Online. Available at: http://www.achpr.org/files/sessions/29th/communications/211.98/achpr29_211_98_eng.pdf (accessed 22 August 2012), paras 71–2.

68 AComHPR, *Modise v Botswana*, Communication 97/93, decided at the 28th ordinary session, 26 October–6 November 2000. Online. Available at: http://www.achpr.org/files/sessions/28th/communications/97.93_14ar/achpr28_97_14ar_eng.pdf (accessed 22 August 2012). See Mbondenyi, 'The Right to Participate', pp. 188–9.

69 AComHPR, *Modise v Botswana*, para. 97.
70 HRC, General Comment No. 25, para. 15.
71 Conte and Burchill, *Defining Civil and Political Rights*, p. 104.
72 ECtHR, *Tanase v Moldova*, No. 7/08, judgment (GC) of 27 April 2010, paras 168–9. On this judgment see J.F. Flauss, 'Le droit du Conseil de l'Europe au service d'élections libres et de la double nationnalité', *Revue trimestrielle des droits de l'homme* 79, 2009, 851–66.
73 ECtHR, *Tanase v Moldova*, paras 177–8.
74 Ibid., para. 179.
75 UNHCR, 'Political Rights of Refugees', November 2003, PPLA/2003/04, p. 1. Online. Available at: www.unhcr.org/refworld (accessed 16 July 2012).
76 De Guttry, 'Art. 16', pp. 445–6; Granata Menghini, 'Art. 16', p. 567.
77 Ibid.
78 'Cartagena Declaration on Refugees, Colloquium on the International Protection of Refugees in Central America, Mexico and Panama', 22 November 1984. Online. Available at: www.unhcr.org/refworld/docid/3ae6b36ec.html (accessed 22 August 2012), para. III(8).
79 UNHCR, 'Political Rights of Refugees', p. 1.
80 Ibid., p. 3.
81 Ibid., p. 7.
82 Ibid., p. 17.
83 In the United Kingdom, all resident Commonwealth and Irish citizens are able to vote in national elections.
84 Among the countries that grant foreign residents the right to vote in local elections, we can mention Denmark, Ireland, Finland, Norway, Sweden and Iceland.
85 UNHCR, 'Political Rights of Refugees', p. 18. See European Council on Refugees and Exiles, 'Position on the Integration of Refugees in Europe', 1 December 2002, paras 26–9. Online. Available at: www.unhcr.org/refworld (accessed 16 July 2012).
86 UNHCR, 'Political Rights of Refugees', pp. 6–8.
87 O'Connell, 'Towards a Stronger Conception', p. 283.
88 ECtHR, *Bowman v the United Kingdom*, No. 24839/94, judgment of 19 February 1998, para. 42. See Mowbray, 'The Role of the European Court', p. 704.
89 Conte and Burchill, *Defining Civil and Political Rights*, p. 85.
90 HRC, General Comment No. 25, para. 8.
91 See Starita, 'Art. 3', p. 839.
92 HRC, General Comment No. 25, para. 25.
93 UNHCR, 'Political Rights of Refugees', pp. 6–8.
94 Inter-American Commission on Human Rights, *Annual Report 1990–91*. Online. Available at: www.oas.org/en/iachr/ (accessed 2 July 2012), Chapter V, para. III.
95 ECtHR, *United Communist Party of Turkey and others v Turkey*, para. 43.
96 ECtHR, *Refah Partisi (the Welfare Party) and Others v Turkey*, para. 89.
97 ECtHR, *Yumak v Turkey*, para. 106.
98 ECtHR, *United Communist Party of Turkey and others v Turkey*, para. 43; HRC, General Comment No. 25, para. 26.
99 ECtHR, *Socialist Party and others v Turkey*, No. 21237/93, judgment of 25 May 1998, para. 47.

100 IACHR, *Yatama v Nicaragua*, paras 217–20. See L. Burgorgue-Larsen and A. Ubeda De Torres, *The Inter-American Court of Human Rights. Case Law and Commentary*, Oxford: Oxford University Press, 2011, p. 595.

101 Verstichel, 'Understanding Minority', p. 92; Venice Commission, 'Report on Non-Citizens and Minority Rights', 18 January 2007, CDL-AD (2007)001, para. 139. Online. Available at: www.venice.coe.int (accessed 2 July 2012); D. Weissbrodt, 'Final report on the rights of non-citizens', 26 May 2003, UN Doc. E/CN.4/Sub.2/2003/23/Add.3, para. 22; Advisory Committee on the Framework Convention for the Protection of National Minorities, 'Commentary on the Effective Participation of Persons Belonging to National Minorities in Cultural, Social, and Economic Life and in Public Affairs', 27 February 2008, ACFC/31/DOC(2008)001. Online. Available at: www.coe.int (accessed 2 July 2012), para. 101.

102 L. van Waas, *Nationality Matters. Statelessness under International Law*, Antwerp-Oxford-Portland: Intersentia, 2008, p. 289.

103 Verstichel, 'Understanding Minority', p. 92; Venice Commission, 'Report on Non-Citizens and Minority Rights', para. 39.

104 Advisory Committee on the Framework Convention for the Protection of National Minorities, 'Commentary on the Effective Participation', para. 101.

105 In fact, an increasing number of States grant non-national residents the rights to vote or to be elected in local elections. See van Waas, *Nationality Matters*, p. 293.

8 Nationality and social rights

Alessandra Annoni[1]

Introduction

According to the traditional classification developed by Karel Vasak in 1977, human rights fall into three categories: the first generation of human rights concerns 'negative rights' (i.e. civil and political rights), calling on the state not to interfere with individual liberties; the second generation of rights – including social, economic, and cultural rights – requires the implementation by states of positive actions, in order to improve the living conditions of individuals and ensure substantive equality among them; finally, the third generation of human rights aims at improving solidarity among mankind, calling on states, international organizations, and private individuals to ensure sustainable development, a healthy environment, peace, and the protection of the common heritage of mankind.[2]

Vasak's classification, however, is in some ways artificial, as the boundaries between the different categories of human rights are often blurred. The right to form or join trade unions, for instance, is usually treated as a social right, but has much in common with the right to peaceful association, which is indisputably a civil right. The right to social security, moreover, may either be considered as an economic right or as a social one, and the right to education could be classified both as a cultural and as a social right. For the purpose of this chapter, social rights will be considered to include: the right to work, the right to enjoy just and favourable working conditions, the right to form or join trade unions, the right to health, and the right to social security.

The personal scope of social rights and the relevance of non-discrimination clauses

Social rights were the first to attract the attention of the international community.[3] The very creation of the International Labour Organization (ILO), in 1919, reflected the idea that durable peace could be accomplished only if it was based upon social justice.[4] Pursuant to its Constitution, the ILO developed a comprehensive system of labour standards, laid down both in international conventions open for ratification by member states and in non-binding recommendations.

According to Principle 9(a) of the ILO Non-Binding Principles and Guidelines for a Rights-Based Approach to Labour Migration, 'all international labour standards apply to migrant workers, unless otherwise stated'.[5] Several instruments, especially those dealing with the social security of migrant workers, however, operate on the basis of reciprocity, so that non-nationals may enjoy the rights enshrined therein only if both their country of origin and their country of residence have ratified the relevant convention.[6] ILO Convention No. 111 on Discrimination in Respect of Employment and Occupation, moreover, does not include nationality amongst the prohibited grounds of discrimination.

On the other hand, the special condition of migrant workers prompted the development of international rules specifically addressing their needs. Several conventions have been adopted to this effect, under the auspices of the ILO,[7] of the United Nations (UN),[8] and of the Council of Europe (CoE).[9] Most of these instruments, however, have been sparsely ratified, and some western countries remain unbound by the most advanced, universal treaties.[10] Furthermore, the enjoyment of the social rights enshrined in the migrant workers conventions is often reserved for foreigners regularly admitted in the receiving country.[11]

With the adoption of the Universal Declaration of Human Rights (UDHR) in 1948, the International Covenant on Economic, Social and Cultural Rights (ICESCR) in 1966,[12] the African Charter of Human and Peoples' Rights (ACHPR) in 1982,[13] the Protocol of San Salvador to the American Convention of Human Rights in the Area of Economic, Social and Cultural Rights in 1988,[14] and the Arab Charter on Human Rights (ArCHR) in 1994 (revised in 2004[15]), social rights were given the status of human rights. As such, they must be granted to *every individual*, without distinction of any kind, such as race, colour, sex, language, religion, political or other opinion, national or social origin, property, birth, or other status.[16] Although neither nationality nor immigration status are specifically mentioned amongst the prohibited grounds of discrimination, the reference to 'other status' is flexible enough to capture situations in which people are granted a differential treatment on these basis.[17]

Guaranteeing that social rights will be exercised without discrimination implies, first of all, eliminating *formal discriminations*, abrogating laws and policies that expressly deny social security benefits to foreign workers, and taking effective measures to ensure that private individuals, such as landlords and housing agencies, refrain from engaging in discriminatory practices.[18] States, however, must also address *substantive discriminations*, adopting all necessary positive measures to eradicate any situation or condition which may have a disproportionate impact on the enjoyment of social rights by certain categories of people.[19] This involves taking into consideration the different cultural attitude of foreigners, their specific linguistic and financial problems, and adopting targeted strategies to address their peculiar needs.[20]

Not all types of differentiation, however, should be deemed discriminatory. According to the Committee on Economic, Social and Cultural Rights (CESCR), differential treatment based on prohibited grounds will not be viewed as discriminatory if the justification for differentiation is *reasonable* and *objective*.[21] Any differential treatment, in particular, must pursue a legitimate aim and its effects must be strictly proportioned to that aim.[22] States, moreover, may limit the social rights of a certain category of beneficiaries, but only for the purpose of promoting the general welfare in a democratic society,[23] and provided that the measures adopted do not lead to the exclusion of any person from the core content of social rights,[24] and do not detract from the protection accorded to fundamental human rights by other human rights treaties.[25]

It is against this legal framework that this chapter will assess if – and to what extent – states may legitimately differentiate among nationals and non-nationals, or among different categories of non-nationals concerning the enjoyment of social rights.

Permissible scope of distinction among nationals and non-nationals

According to Article 1 of the Convention on the Elimination of All Forms of Racial Discrimination (CERD), distinctions, restrictions, or preferences made by states among nationals and non-nationals do not amount to racial discrimination.[26] In its General Recommendation No. 30, however, the Committee on the Elimination of Racial Discrimination (CtERD) made clear that this provision 'must be construed so as to avoid undermining the basic prohibition of discrimination; hence, it should not be interpreted to detract in any way from the rights and freedoms recognized [in other human rights instruments]'.[27]

In order not to be considered discriminatory, differential treatment as to the enjoyment of social rights based on alienage must pursue a legitimate aim and be strictly necessary to achieve it. States, for example, may prevent non-nationals from accessing certain categories of employment, where this is necessary in the interest of the state.[28] The need to ensure the security of the nation may, for instance, justify limitations on the right of aliens and stateless people to seek employment in the public service. In order to be proportionate, however, the exclusion of non-nationals should be limited to posts that involve the exercise of public authority, or that are strictly connected to the preservation of a national interest, presuming 'on the part of those occupying them the existence of a special relationship of allegiance to the State and reciprocity of rights and duties which form the foundation of the bond of nationality'.[29] If foreign nationals are hired for a public service, moreover, they must be granted the same treatment their fellow workers enjoy.[30] Consistently applied by the European Court of Justice (ECJ) in the interpretation of Article 39 of the Treaty establishing the European Community (TEC), now Article 45 of the Treaty on the Functioning of the European

Union (TFEU), concerning discrimination against workers coming from other member states,[31] these principles are generally considered valid in respect to all non-national workers.[32]

In times of economic distress, states may be tempted to further limit the right of foreigners to work, reserving certain jobs for nationals. Paragraph 18 of part I of the revised European Social Charter (ESC)[33] seems to uphold this attitude, making the right of non-nationals to engage in any gainful occupation on a footing of equality with nationals subject to restrictions based on cogent economic or social reasons. The European Committee of Social Rights (ECSR), however, maintained that, although state parties may make foreign nationals' access to employment on their territory subject to the possession of a valid work permit,[34] 'the only jobs from which foreigners may be banned [...] are those that are inherently connected with the protection of the public interest or national security and involve the exercise of public authority'.[35]

This reading of paragraph 18 is in line with the interpretation of the non-discrimination clause included in Article 2 ICESCR upheld by the CESCR. According to the latter:

> A failure to remove differential treatment on the basis of a lack of available resources is not an objective and reasonable justification unless every effort has been made to use all resources that are at the State party's disposition in an effort to address and eliminate the discrimination, as a matter of priority.[36]

This principle applies to all the rights enshrined in the ICESCR, preventing states from invoking scarcity of available recourses as a justification for concentrating their efforts on the fulfilment of the social, cultural, and economic needs of nationals at the expense of non-nationals.

Article 2(3) ICESCR provides for an exception, allowing 'developing countries, with due regard to human rights and their national economy, [to] determine to what extent they would guarantee the economic rights recognised in the [...] Covenant to non-nationals'. A lack of sufficient resources may hence only justify developing countries limiting the enjoyment of *economic rights* by non-nationals. As we have seen, however, the distinction among economic rights and social rights is not always easy to draw; doubts may arise, in particular, in respect to the qualification of the right to accede to social security benefits.[37] If economic rights are defined as those that 'enable a person to earn a living or that relate to that process',[38] moreover, Article 2(3) may also affect the right to work enshrined in Article 6 ICESCR, notwithstanding the fact that the latter is generally considered a social right.[39]

Countries which are unable to rely on the exception provided by Article 2(3) must provide another objective and reasonable justification, if they wish to limit non-nationals' access to work or to social benefits. Aliens' access to the labour market, for instance, could be validly constrained in order to maintain control over immigration fluxes. Hence, in an attempt to discourage abuses of their immigration laws, states could lawfully restrict the ability of foreigners holding a temporary work permit to change their job, or limit their access to a certain remunerated activity in pursuance of a policy of granting priority to nationals.[40] In order to be proportional, however, similar measures should be limited in time.[41]

Limitations on aliens' access to social security benefits may seem even easier to justify. As pointed out by the European Court of Human Rights (ECtHR), states enjoy a wide margin of appreciation when it comes to allocating 'resource-hungry' public benefits, even when this leads to the exclusion of certain categories of people.[42] The Court, however, has also held that 'very weighty reasons would have to be put forward before it could regard a difference of treatment based exclusively on the grounds of nationality as compatible with the Convention'.[43] States, therefore, may lawfully restrict access to public health care, housing, and other social benefits to aliens which show a strong connection with the state's social fabric[44] and who concurred, either directly or indirectly, to fund such services.[45] A differential treatment among nationals and fully integrated long-term migrants, however, would be very hard to justify.[46] States, moreover, should always allow short-term migrants' access to 'core benefits'[47] (i.e. those necessary to ensure an adequate standard of living,[48] fulfilling primary needs such as food, clothing, water, and adequate housing[49]), as failing to do so may result in a violation of underogable human rights, such as the right to life or the prohibition of torture.[50]

Preferential treatment accorded to certain categories of aliens

Some bilateral and multilateral treaties require states parties to ensure 'national treatment' to nationals of the other states parties.[51] This has led some states to afford a preferential treatment to the latter, for example granting them access to social benefits otherwise precluded to aliens, or exempting them from the required qualification periods or other similar conditions. Article 81 of the International Convention on the Protection of the Rights of All Migrant Workers and Members of Their Families (ICRMW) expressly upholds similar practices. Nevertheless, in the *Koua Poirrez* case, the ECtHR considered that 'the difference in treatment regarding entitlement to social benefits between [...] nationals of a country having signed a reciprocity agreement and other foreign nationals was not based on any "objective and reasonable justification"'.[52] The HRC, though, followed a more cautious approach, affirming that:

> [Although] an international agreement that confers preferential treatment to nationals of a State party to that agreement might constitute an objective and reasonable ground for differentiation, no general rule can be drawn [to that effect]. Rather, it is necessary to judge every case on its own facts.[53]

Conversely, the legitimacy of differentiations between citizens of the European Union (EU) and third-country migrants within the EU is peacefully recognized even by the ECtHR. In the *Ponomaryovi* case, the latter upheld the exemption from school fees granted by Bulgaria to EU citizens, emphasizing that 'the Union forms a special legal order, which has, moreover, established its own citizenship'.[54]

Similarly, the preferential treatment accorded to refugees and to stateless persons on the basis of relevant international treaties[55] could be deemed to be based on 'reasonable and objective criteria', since these two categories of aliens are not in a position to avail themselves of the protection and assistance of their country of nationality.[56]

The status of irregular migrants

Several treaties protecting social rights expressly exclude irregular migrants from their personal scope of application.[57] The ESC, for example, applies to foreigners 'only in so far as they are nationals of other Parties lawfully resident or working regularly within the territory of the Party concerned'.[58] Under Article 32 of ILO Convention No. 130 on Medical Care and Sickness Benefits, adopted in 1969, moreover, states parties must ensure equality of treatment with their own nationals as regards the rights enshrined in the Convention only to non-nationals 'who normally reside or work' within their territory. Similarly, the non-discrimination clause included in Article 6 of ILO Convention No. 97 applies exclusively to 'immigrants lawfully within [a foreign state's] territory'. The same approach was maintained by the UN General Assembly's Declaration on the Human Rights of Individuals Who Are Not Nationals of the Country in Which They Live, adopted in 1985, which reserved to '[a]liens lawfully residing in the territory of a State' the enjoyment of labour rights, of the right to join trade unions and of the right to health protection and social security.[59]

Other international treaties, while including irregular migrants in their personal scope of application, endow regular migrants with more extensive guarantees. Article 1 of ILO Convention No. 143, for instance, provides that 'Each Member for which this Convention is in force undertakes to respect the *basic* human rights of all migrant workers',[60] while part II of the Convention – concerning 'equality of opportunity and treatment' – applies solely to individuals 'regularly admitted' as migrant workers.[61] The ICRMW enshrines, in its third part, the human rights of all migrant workers and members of their families, whereas the additional guarantees provided in part IV only apply to migrants and their families who are 'documented or in a regular situation'.

By granting a differential treatment to irregular migrants, states pursue the legitimate aim of discouraging violations of their immigration laws. In order to be acceptable under human rights law, however, the measures that states adopt to this effect must be proportionate and must not detract from the protection afforded to fundamental human rights by other treaties.[62] The application of these standards ends up legitimizing extensive limitations on certain social rights, leaving others almost untouched.

The right to freely choose an employment

Although Article 6 ICESCR ensures to '*everyone* [. . .] the opportunity to gain his living by work which he freely chooses or accepts',[63] no one disputes the right of states to prevent irregular migrants from acceding employment, including the possibility of criminalizing the act of providing work for undocumented foreigners.[64] This right may be inferred, *a contrario*, from Article 9(4) of ILO Convention No. 143, according to which: 'Nothing in this Convention shall prevent Members from giving persons who are illegally residing or working within the country the right to stay and to take up legal employment'. Articles 52–3 ICRMW, moreover, expressly confine the right to free choice of employment to legal migrants.

Besides, as seen above, the legitimate aim of securing states' control over their immigration fluxes may even justify limitations on the right to freely choose an employment in respect of regular migrants.

Labour rights

Whether, and to what extent, states may reserve to irregular migrants a differential treatment in the enjoyment of labour rights is highly controversial. Article 25 ICRMW enshrines the right of all migrant workers to enjoy treatment 'not less favourable than that which applies to nationals of the State of employment', in respect of conditions of work and the termination of the employment relationship, and of other terms of employment. Nevertheless, under Articles 54–5, full equality of treatment with nationals, including as for what concerns protection against dismissal, is only granted to migrant workers in a regular situation. Analogously, Article 26 ICRMW provides all migrant workers with the right to join trade unions, to participate in their activities, and to seek their assistance, whereas Article 40 grants only migrants in a regular situation the right to form trade unions.

This approach follows the pattern of ILO Convention No. 143, which ensures irregular migrants and members of their families 'equality of treatment [. . .] in respect of rights arising out of past employment as regards remuneration, social security and other benefits',[65] but requires state parties to guarantee full 'equality of opportunity and treatment in respect of employment and occupation [. . .] and of trade unions' only for migrants who are lawfully within their territories.[66]

In assessing the proportionality of these limitations compared to the legitimate aim of thwarting illegal immigration, one should bear in mind that, while granting certain rights only to regular migrant workers may encourage non-nationals to comply with immigration regulations, forcing employers to guarantee equal treatment to all workers – irrespective of their immigration status – is likely to reduce the demand for irregular migrants' labour.[67] This consideration led the IACHR to affirm, in an advisory opinion rendered in 2003 at the request of Mexico, that, although

> the State and the individuals in a State are not obliged to offer employment to undocumented migrants [...], if undocumented migrants are engaged, they immediately become possessors of the labor rights corresponding to workers and may not be discriminated against because of their irregular situation.[68]

The same conclusion was reached the following year by the CtERD, in its General Recommendation No. 30,[69] and reiterated in 2011 by the Human Rights Council, in its Resolution No. 18/21.[70]

Several states with high immigration rates, however, are still reluctant to recognize full equality of treatment in employment to irregular migrants.[71] Article 15(3) of the Charter of Fundamental Rights of the European Union (EU Charter) – according to which only '[n]ationals of third countries who are authorised to work in the territories of the Member States are entitled to working conditions equivalent to those of citizens of the Union' – is a clear indication of this attitude, which was maintained also in the recent Directive 2011/98/EU setting a common framework of rights for third-country workers legally residing in a Member State.[72] Most European states, moreover, refused to ratify Protocol No. 12 to the ECHR, which endorses a definition of prohibited discrimination broad enough to encompass distinctions as to the enjoyment of employment rights based on nationality or immigration status.[73]

This negative attitude led some scholars to conclude that the principle according to which workers may not be discriminated against because of their irregular situation is not yet recognized under general international law.[74] Nevertheless, even assuming that irregular migrant workers could be granted a differential treatment, the restrictions imposed on their employment rights would still need to be proportional and to comply with core labour standards and other underogable human rights obligations, especially those concerning the prohibition of slavery, servitude, and forced and compulsory labour.[75]

Right to health care

Curbing undocumented migrants' access to health care may be a powerful deterrent for illegal immigration. The right to health, however, is strictly related with the preservation of human dignity and of other human rights,[76] including the right to life and the prohibition of torture,[77] which do not admit any kind of derogation nor limitation. In order to meet their international obligations, states must therefore ensure that at least the 'minimum essential level' relating to the right of health is fulfilled also in relation to undocumented migrants.[78]

According to some states, this standard is met as long as irregular migrants have access to emergency health care.[79] Endorsed in the ICRMW,[80] this restrictive approach has been contested not only by the CESCR,[81] according to which Article 12 ICESCR[82] prohibits states from 'denying or limiting equal access for all persons, including [. . .] illegal immigrants, to preventive, curative and palliative health services',[83] but also by the ECSR. Notwithstanding the clear limitation as to the personal scope of application of the ESC provided in the Appendix, the Committee accepted the request to consider a claim concerning access to health care by irregular migrants in France, in order to assess the compliance of the relevant domestic legislation with other international obligations, including those arising from the ECHR and the Convention on the Rights of the Child.[84] In this context, the Committee maintained that any differential treatment among regular and irregular migrants for the purpose of access to health care should take the special needs of children into due account.[85] Hence, French legislation which admitted illegal immigrants to the medical assistance scheme only after a certain time, meanwhile ensuring them only treatment for emergencies and life threatening conditions, was considered illegitimate, to the extent that it was applied to adults and children alike.[86] Following the same line of reasoning, the CoE Commissioner for Human Rights held that

> where access to antenatal care is normally free, but made dependant on payment in the case of irregular migrants, issues of discrimination in the enjoyment of the right to life, to protection from inhuman treatment, and to family life arise.[87]

Social security and assistance

According to Article 27 ICRMW, with respect to social security, all migrant workers (including irregular ones) shall enjoy the same treatment granted to nationals 'in so far as they fulfil the requirements provided for by the applicable legislation of [the state of employment] and the applicable bilateral and multilateral treaties'. This *caveat* allows states parties to introduce significant limitations to the rights of irregular migrants.[88] Being unable to engage lawfully in a paid occupation, the latter are usually banned from all contributory schemes of social security. Domestic legislations, moreover, tend to reserve for regulars most publicly funded benefits. In order to meet the terms of the principle of non-discrimination enshrined in human rights law, however, similar limitations must comply with the 'reasonableness and proportionality' test.

Limitations upon the right of undocumented migrants to social security are certainly reasonable.[89] Allowing all migrants, irrespective of their immigration status, to access social benefits would act as a magnet for low-income foreigners, inducing them to breach immigration laws precisely to abuse the system of social security.[90] On the other hand, irregular migrants are amongst the most vulnerable sectors of the society, and social assistance could represent the only way for them to gain access to essential goods, such as food, water, clothing, and adequate housing. Depriving unlawful migrants that lack sufficient resources of access to any form of public assistance is then disproportionate.[91] Moreover, it would entail a violation of their right to an adequate standard of living and – in extreme situations, such as when children or disabled people are involved – it could expose them to an inhuman or degrading treatment or even place their lives in danger.[92]

International rules restricting access to social security benefits to legal migrants should be read in light of these considerations. Thus, in its recent case law, the ECSR maintained that – notwithstanding the Appendix to the Charter – the right of homeless people to a shelter, enshrined in Article 31(2), should be guaranteed to every child, regardless of residence status.[93] Similar considerations should favour the disjoint reading of Articles 34(2) and 34(3) of the EU Charter – enshrining, respectively, the right of '*[e]veryone residing and moving legally within the European Union* [...] to social security benefits and social advantages' and 'the right to social and housing assistance so as to ensure a decent existence *for all those who lack sufficient resources*'.[94]

Conclusions

Social rights are, to all effects, 'human rights' and as such they should be equally enjoyed by every human being. International law, however, does not prevent states from differentiating between nationals and non-nationals, nor among different categories of non-nationals, provided that differential treatments are based on reasonable and objective criteria.

The need to maintain control over immigration fluxes, the opportunity to reserve 'resource-hungry' social benefits to those who have significantly contributed to funding them or who have a stronger link with the social fabric, and the will to thwart illegal immigration may all constitute reasonable basis for differentiation. The principle of proportionality, however, calls on the state to restrict the rights of non-nationals only to the extent strictly necessary to achieve these legitimate goals. Limitations upon social rights, moreover, should never jeopardize the enjoyment of other underogable human rights, such as the right to life or the prohibition of torture.

Ensuring that non-nationals be 'legally entitled' to certain social rights, however, is not the end of the problem. First of all, states should take positive actions to inform aliens of their rights, and to put them in a position to effectively enforce them. Hence, for instance, language assistance and cultural mediation should be provided in hospitals and in other premises supplying public services; stateless people should be issued identification documents;[95] and irregular migrants should be reassured they will not face the risk of detention or deportation while they make use of public services to which they are entitled.[96] A serious effort should be made, moreover, to tackle 'indirect discriminations', such as those that could result from an excessively restrictive legislation on recognition of diplomas and qualifications.[97] Finally, states should take positive actions in order to thwart discrimination by private individuals, such as employers or landlords.

Notes

1 I wish to thank Dr Kathleen Cavanaugh and all the staff of the Irish Centre for Human Rights for their hospitality while I was writing this chapter.

2 K. Vasak, 'A Thirty-Year Struggle: The Sustained Efforts to Give Force of Law to the Universal Declaration of Human Rights', *UNESCO Courier* 30, 1977, No. 11, 29–32.

3 Quite the opposite, the primal concern of national constitutionalism was to ensure the protection of civil and political rights, and domestic constitutions started to enshrine social, economic, and cultural rights only at the beginning of the twentieth century. Hence the traditional qualification of the latter rights as 'second generation human rights'. See C. Tiburcio, *The Human Rights of Aliens under International and Comparative Law*, The Hague–Boston–London: M. Nijhoff, 2001, p. 145.

4 See the preamble of the ILO Constitution, adopted by the Peace Conference in April 1919. Online. Available at: www.ilo.org/public/english/bureau/leg/download/constitution.pdf (accessed 14 August 2012).

5 ILO, 'Multilateral Framework on Labour Migration. Non-binding Principles and Guidelines for a Rights-Based Approach to Labour Migration', 2006. Online. Available at: www.ilo.org/public/english/protection/migrant/download/multilat_fwk_en.pdf (accessed 14 August 2012). See also R. Cholewinski, 'Human Rights of Migrants: The Dawn of a New Era?', *Georgetown Immigration Law Journal* 24, 2009–10, 585–615 at 589.

6 See, for example, Social Security (Minimum Standards) Convention, 1952 (No. 102), Article 68; Equality of Treatment (Social Security) Convention, 1962 (No. 118), Articles 5–7; Maintenance of Social Security Rights Convention, 1982 (No. 157). The texts of all ILO Conventions can be retrieved on the website of the Organization. Online. Available at: www.ilo.org (accessed 23 July 2012).

7 Migration for Employment Convention (Revised), 1949 (No. 97); Migrant Workers (Supplementary Provisions) Convention, 1975 (No. 143).

8 ICRMW, 18 December 1990, UNTS, vol. 2220, No. 39481.

9 ECLSMW, 24 November 1977, CETS 93.

10 ILO Conventions No. 97 and No. 143 have so far been ratified, respectively, by 49 and 23 states (data retrieved from the Information System on International Labour Standards. Online. Available at: www.ilo.org/dyn/normlex/en (accessed 19 November 2012)). ICRMW is currently in force between 46 parties, none of which is a high-income country (Online. Available at: http://treaties.un.org (accessed 23 July 2012)), and ECLSMW between 5 (Online. Available at: www.conventions.coe.int (accessed 23 July 2012)).

11 See below.

12 Adopted on 16 December 1966, UNTS, vol. 993, No. 14531.

13 Adopted on 27 June 1981, OAU Doc. CAB/LEG/67/3 rev. 5 (1981).

14 Adopted on 16 November 1988, OAS Treaty Series, No. 69.
15 22 May 2004, reprinted in *Boston University International Law Journal* 24, 2006, 147–64.
16 See Article 2 UDHR, Article 2(2) ICESCR, Article 2 ACHPR. The scope of the non-discrimination clause included in the ArCHR has been reduced as a consequence of the 2004 revision. Article 3 ArCHR now only forbids distinctions on grounds of race, colour, sex, language, religious belief, opinion, thought, national or social origin, wealth, birth, or physical or mental disability. Article 3 of the Protocol of San Salvador is also rather restrictive, as it forbids discrimination only for reasons related to race, colour, sex, language, religion, political or other opinions, national or social origin, economic status, birth, or any other social condition. Non-discrimination clauses are also included in most human rights treaties dealing with specific categories of individuals (see, for example, Article 2 CRC).
17 CESCR, General Comment No. 20, 'Non-Discrimination in Economic, Social and Cultural Rights (art. 2, para. 2)', 2 July 2009, para. 30. See also, *mutatis mutandis*, HRC, *Ibrahima Gueye et al. v France*, views of 6 April 1989, CCPR/C/35/D/196/1985, para. 9.4.
18 See CtERD, *F.A. v Norway*, decision of 21 March 2001, CERD/C/58/D/18/2000, urging Norway to take action to put an end to the practice of housing advertisement containing discriminatory requirements. Cf. also D. Weissbrodt, *The Human Rights of Non-Citizens*, Oxford: Oxford University Press, 2008, p. 65.
19 CESCR, General Comment No. 20, para. 8.
20 R. Cholewinski, *Migrant Workers in International Human Rights Law: Their Protection in Countries of Employment*, Oxford: Oxford University Press, 1997, p. 121.
21 CESCR, General Comment No. 20, para. 13. Along the same lines cf. HRC, *F.H. Zwaan-de Vries v Netherlands*, views of 9 April 1987, CCPR/C/29/D/182/1984, para. 13. See also Protocol No. 12 to the ECHR, Explanatory Report, para. 19.
22 Office of the high commissioner for human rights, *The Rights of Non-Citizens*, New York and Geneva: UN, 2006. Online. Available at: www.ohchr.org/Documents/Publications/noncitizensen.pdf (accessed 23 July 2012).
23 Article 4 ICESCR.
24 UN high commissioner for human rights, 'Report on the economic, social and cultural rights of migrants', 1 June 2010, UN Doc. E/2010/89, para. 14.
25 Article 5 ICESCR. See also World Conference on Human Rights, 'Vienna Declaration and Programme of Action', 12 July 1993, UN Doc. A/CONF.157/23, para. 5, according to which: '[a]ll human rights are universal, indivisible and interdependent and interrelated'.
26 See also EU Council Directive 2000/43/EC implementing the principle of equal treatment between persons irrespective of racial or ethnic origin, 29 June 2000, *Official Journal of the European Communities* L 180, 19 July 2000, 22, para. 3(2): 'This Directive does not cover difference of treatment based on nationality and is without prejudice [. . .] to any treatment which arises from the legal status of the third-country nationals and stateless persons concerned'.
27 CtERD, General Recommendation No. 30, 'Discrimination against Non-Citizens', 1 October 2004, para. 2.
28 See Article 14(c) of ILO Convention No. 143 and Article 52(2)(a) ICRMW.
29 ECJ, C-149/79, *Commission v Belgium*, judgment of 17 December 1980, *ECR*, 1980, p. 3881, para. 10.

30 ECJ, C-152/73, *Sotgiu v Bunderspost*, judgment of 12 February 1974, *ECR*, 1974, p. 153.

31 ECJ, C-149/79, *Commission v Belgium*; C-4/91, *Bleis v Ministère de l'Education Nationale*, judgment of 17 November 1991, *ECR*, 1991, p. I-5627; C-473/93, *Commission v Luxemburg*, judgment of 2 July 1996, *ECR*, 1996, p. I-3207; C-173/94, *Commission v Belgium*, judgment of 2 July 1996, *ECR*, 1996, p. I-3265; C-290/94, *Commission v Greece*, judgment of 2 July 1996, *ECR*, 1996, p. I-3285. See also Commission of the European Communities, 'Free movement of workers – achieving the full benefits and potential', communication of 11 December 2002, COM (2002) 694 final, p. 21.

32 See, among others, Supreme Court (USA), *Sugarman v Dougall*, 25 June 1973, 413 U.S. 634 (1973), and *Foley v Connelie*, 22 March 1978, 435 U.S. 291 (1978); Tribunale Imperia (Italy), judgment of 12 September 2004. Online. Available at: www.meltingpot.org (accessed 13 August 2012); Tribunale Perugia (Italy), order of 29 September 2006, ibid.; Tribunale Bologna (Italy), order of 25 October 2007, *Rivista critica di diritto del lavoro* 17, 2008, 175ff.; Tribunale Genova (Italy), order of 3 June 2008. Online. Available at: www.meltingpot.org (accessed 13 August 2012); Corte d'appello Firenze (Italy), decree of 28 November 2008, *Rivista critica di diritto del lavoro* 18, 2009, 311ff.; Tribunale Milano (Italy), order of 11 January 2010. Online. Available at: www.meltingpot.org (accessed 13 August 2012). See however Cassazione, Labour Section (Italy), judgment of 13 November 2006, No. 24170, *Corriere Giuridico* 3, 2007, 357, basing its conclusions on the alleged non self-executing character of the relevant ILO Conventions, but failing to assess the compliance of the Italian legislation banning non-nationals from public employment with the ICESCR. See also G.S. Goodwin-Gill, 'Immigration, nationality and the standards of international law', in A. Dummet (ed.) *Towards a Just Immigration Policy*, London: Cobden Trust, 1986, pp. 3–32 at 14.

33 Strasbourg, 3 May 1996, CETS 163. The original version of the ESC was adopted on 18 October 1961, CETS 35. The ESC is often referred to as the natural complement to the ECHR, which only protects civil and political rights. The fact that the Charter operates on the basis of reciprocity, and that irregular migrants are excluded from the personal scope of application of most of its provisions (see Appendix to the Charter), however, makes it difficult to classify this instrument as a human rights treaty.

34 The right of foreigners to engage in a gainful occupation on a footing of equality with nationals cannot imply an obligation for states to grant aliens admission on their territory to this effect. Under international law, states are free to refuse access to their territory to aliens, unless the latter are asylum seekers or migrants coming from a state with which an establishment treaty is in force (see G.S. Goodwin-Gill, *International Law and the Movement of Persons between States*, Oxford: Oxford University Press, 1978, pp. 136–97).

35 ECSR, 'Conclusions: Romania', in *Conclusions 2006*, vol. 2, Strasbourg: Council of Europe, 2006, p. 737.

36 CESCR, General Comment No. 20, para. 13. See also CESCR, General Comment No. 3, 'The nature of States parties obligations (Art. 2, par. 1)', 14 December 1990, para. 1, according to which the obligation to ensure that rights will be exercised without discrimination is of immediate effect, hence its fulfilment should not depend on the availability of resources.

37 See above.

38 E.V.O. Dankwa, 'Working Paper on Article 2(3) of the International Covenant on Economic, Social and Cultural Rights', *Human Rights Quarterly* 9, 1987, 230–49 at 240.

39 Cholewinski, *Migrant Workers in International Human Rights Law*, p. 59. Cf. High Court of Kenya, *Kenya v Minister For Home Affairs and ors, ex p Leonard Sitamze*, decision of 18 April 2007, *Oxford Reports on International Law*, ILDC 1094 (KE 2007). Online. Available at: www.oxfordlawreports.com (accessed 27 July 2012), para. 77.

40 See Article 14(a) of ILO Convention No. 143 and Article 52(3) ICRMW. For a clear example of such limitations see Beschäftigungsverfahrensverordnung (Employment Procedure Ordinance, Germany), 22 November 2004, *Bundesgesetzblatt*, I S. 2934, as amended on 1 June 2012.

41 Cf. Cholewinski, *Migrant Workers in International Human Rights Law*, pp. 108–11 and 161–3. See also High Court of Justice (Israel), *Kav LaOved Worker's Hotline and others v Israel and others*, No. 4542/02, judgment of 30 March 2006. Online. Available at: http://elyon1.court.gov.il/files_eng/02/420/045/o28/02045420.o28.pdf (accessed 31 July 2012). According to the Court, the Israeli policy of making the granting of residency licenses conditional upon the foreign worker being employed by the particular employer who invited him imposed a disproportioned limitation on the right to work of foreigners, who were indefinitely prevented from seeking another job.

42 See, among others, ECtHR, *Stec and others v the United Kingdom*, Nos. 65731/01 and 65900/01, judgment of 12 April 2006, para. 52. The right to social security is not enshrined, as such, in the ECHR. According to the Court, however, a state's legislation providing for the payment of a welfare benefit – whether on the basis of a contributory scheme or relying on public funding – generates 'a pecuniary interest falling within the ambit of Article 1 of Protocol No. 1 [enshrining the right to peaceful enjoyment of possessions] for persons satisfying its requirements' (ECtHR, *Andrejeva v Latvia*, No. 55707/00, judgment (GC) of 18 February 2009, para. 77. See also ECtHR, *Stec and others v the United Kingdom*, paras 54–5).

43 ECtHR, *Gaygusuz v Austria*, No. 17371/90, judgment of 16 September 1996, para. 42.

44 In order to prove their attachment to the country, aliens are often required to prove their knowledge of the local language, history and culture. These conditions are based on the assumption – refuted by some scholars – that individuals must share a common heritage of customs and values in order to stick together as 'a people'. The issue is thoroughly discussed by H.P. Hestermeyer, '*Staatsvolk* and homogeneity: from Weimar to the *Maastricht* decision of the German Federal Constitutional Court and beyond', *supra*, pp. 1–17.

45 Access to certain benefits may for example be granted only once a reasonable 'qualifying period' has lapsed (CESCR, General Comment No. 19, 'The right to social security (art. 9)', 4 February 2008, para. 37).

46 S. Forlati, 'Discriminazione sulla base della cittadinanza e Convenzione europea dei diritti umani', in L. Desanti, P. Ferretti, A.D. Manfredini (eds) *Per il 70. compleanno di Pierpaolo Zamorani. Scritti offerti dagli amici e dai colleghi di facoltà*, Milano: Giuffrè, 2009, pp. 231–45 at 243. See, however, Article 11(4) of EU Council Directive 2003/109/EC concerning the status of third-country nationals who are long-term residents, which allows member states to limit equal

treatment in respect of social assistance and social protection to 'core benefits' (25 November 2003, *Official Journal of the European Union* L 16, 23 January 2004, 44). It is worth mentioning, in this respect, that the ECJ favoured a restrictive interpretation of this provision, holding that

> a public authority [...] can rely on the derogation provided for in Article 11(4) of Directive 2003/109 only if the bodies in the Member State concerned responsible for the implementation of that directive have stated clearly that they intended to rely on that derogation.
>
> (ECJ, C-571/10, *Kamberaj*, judgment (GC) of 24 April 2012, para. 87)

47 CESCR, General Comment No. 19, para. 59(a).

48 CESCR, 'Concluding Observations: Ukraine', 7 December 1995, UN Doc. E/1996/22, para. 266. The right to an adequate standard of living is enshrined in Article 25 UDHR, Article 11 ICESCR, Article 14(2)(h) CEDAW and in Article 27 CRC.

49 CESCR, General Comment No. 12, 'The right to adequate food (art. 11)', 12 May 1999; General Comment No. 15, 'The right to water (arts. 11 and 12)', 20 January 2003; General Comment No. 4, 'The right to adequate housing (Art. 11(1))', 13 December 1991.

50 See, in this respect, the case law of the IACHR, which recognizes the right to a 'vida digna' as part of the right to life (cf. F. Costamagna, 'Corte interamericana e tutela dei diritti economici, sociali e culturali: il diritto ad una "vida digna"', in F. Bestagno (ed.) *I diritti economici, sociali e culturali. Promozione e tutela nella comunità internazionale*, Milano: Vita e Pensiero 2009, pp. 137–69). See also, High Court (Ghana), *Asare and others v Ga West District Assembly and Attorney General*, decision of 2 May 2008, *Oxford Reports on International Law*, ILDC 1488 (GH 2008). Online. Available at: www.oxfordlawreports.com (accessed 14 August 2012), para. 29, considering the right to life under Article 4 of the ACHPR to encompass 'all other rights that make the enjoyment of the right complete and meaningful'.

51 This is the case, for example, of some ILO conventions operating on the basis of reciprocity, see above, note 6.

52 ECtHR, *Koua Poirrez v France*, No. 40892/98, judgment of 30 September 2003, para. 49. Cf. D.G. Simmala, 'Nationalité et discrimination: la problématique de l'accès aux droits de l'homme', in SFDI, *Droit international et nationalité – Colloque de Poitiers*, Paris: Pedone, 2012, pp. 337–58 at 350.

53 HRC, *Karakurt v Austria*, views of 4 April 2002, CCPR/C/74/D/965/2000, para. 8.4.

54 ECtHR, *Panomaryovi v Bulgaria*, No. 5335/05, judgment of 21 June 2011, para. 54.

55 See, in particular, the 1951 Convention, adopted on 28 July 1951, UNTS, vol. 189, No. 2545 and the 1954 Convention, adopted on 28 September 1954, UNTS, vol. 360, No. 5158. See also L. van Waas, *Nationality Matters. Statelessness under International Law*, Antwerp–Oxford–Portland: Intersentia, 2008, pp. 301–57.

56 CESCR, General Comment No. 19, para. 38; ECtHR, *Andrejeva v Latvia*, para. 88.

57 For the purpose of this paper, the terms 'irregular migrants' and 'undocumented migrants' will be used interchangeably, to describe non-nationals lacking legal status, whether because they were never authorised to enter their host country, or because they lost title to remain therein.

58 ESC, Appendix. See also Article 1(1) ECLSMW.
59 UN Doc. A/RES/40/144 of 13 December 1985, Article 8.
60 Emphasis added.
61 See Article 1(1) of ILO Convention No. 143.
62 G. Palmisano, 'Trattamento dei migranti clandestini e rispetto degli obblighi internazionali sui diritti umani', *Diritti umani e diritto internazionale* 3, 2009, 509–39.
63 Emphasis added.
64 See EU Parliament and Council Directive 2009/52/EU of 18 June 2009 providing for minimum standards on sanctions and measures against employers of illegally staying third-country nationals, *Official Journal of the European Union* L 168, 30 June 2009, 24.
65 ILO Convention No. 143, Article 9.
66 Ibid., Article 10.
67 ICRMW, preamble.
68 IACHR, *Juridical Condition and Rights of Undocumented Migrants*, advisory opinion OC-18/03 of 17 September 2003, *Series A*, No. 18, paras 135–6. See Cholewinski, 'Human Rights of Migrants', p. 593; C. Favilli, 'I diritti dell'immigrato non regolarmente soggiornante', in P. Benvenuti (ed.) *Flussi migratori e fruizione dei diritti fondamentali*, Ripa di Fagnano Alto: Il Sirente, 2008, pp. 291–304 at 299ff.
69 CtERD, General Recommendation No. 30, para. 35.
70 Human Rights Council, Resolution No. 18/21, 'The Human Rights of Migrants', 17 October 2011, A/HRC/RES/18/21, para. 10. See also the Statement by Ivan Simonovic, UN Assistant Secretary General for Human Rights, 22 July 2010, New York. Online. Available at: www.ohchr.org/EN/NewsEvents/Pages/DisplayNews.aspx?NewsID=10231&LangID=E (accessed 28 July 2012).
71 Palmisano, 'Trattamento dei migranti clandestini', pp. 527–8.
72 EU Parliament and Council Directive 2011/98/EU of 13 December 2011 on a single application procedure for a single permit for third-country nationals to reside and work in the territory of a Member State and on a common set of rights for third-country workers legally residing in a Member State, *Official Journal of the European Union* L 343, 23 December 2011, 1, Article 12.
73 Protocol No. 12 to the ECHR, 4 November 2000, CETS 177, Article 1(1).
74 R. Baratta, 'Spunti di riflessione sulla condizione del migrante irregolare nella giurisprudenza internazionale', in Benvenuti (ed.) *Flussi migratori e fruizione dei diritti fondamentali*, p. 19.
75 Cf. ECtHR, *Siliadin v France*, No. 73316/01, judgment of 26 July 2005, where the Court held that the treatment reserved to an irregular migrant employed as a domestic worker violated her right not to be subjected to slavery, servitude nor forced or compulsory labour. See also EU Charter, Article 31(1), according to which: '*Every worker* has the right to working conditions which respect his or her health, safety and dignity' (emphasis added).
76 CESCR, General Comment No. 14, 'The right to the highest attainable standard of health (article 12)', 11 August 2000, para. 3.
77 In ECtHR, *D v the United Kingdom*, No. 30240/96, judgment of 2 May 1997, the Court held that the 'abrupt withdrawal of medical treatment caused by the deportation' could expose migrants 'to a real risk of dying under most distressing circumstances and would thus amount to inhuman treatment' (paras 53–4). The HRC and the CAT reached similar conclusions (see, respectively: HRC, *C. v Australia*,

views of 28 October 2002, CCPR/C/76/D/990/1999, para. 6, and CAT, *G.R.B. v Sweden*, views of 15 May 1998, CAT/C/20/D/83/1997, para. 6.7).

78 CERD, 'Concluding Observations: Netherlands', 19 November 2010, E/C.12/NDL/CO/4–5, para. 25.

79 Cf. D. Vitiello, 'The European Doorway to Social Rights for Undocumented Migrants. A Comparative Perspective', *AWR Bulletin* 48, 2010, 110–20, highlighting how several European states, while not de jure barring access to health care by foreigners, enact de facto policies which discourage the latter from availing themselves of such services, for example requiring the exhibition of an ID or compelling the medical staff to report illegal migrants to the police. For up-to-date information on national legislations regulating access to health care by undocumented migrants cf. Online. Available at: www.nowhereland.info (accessed 30 July 2012).

80 According to Aricle 28 ICRMW, undocumented migrants should not be refused medical care 'urgently required for the preservation of their life or the avoidance of irreparable harm to their health'. Under Articles 43(1)(e) and 45(1)(c), however, only legal migrants and members of their families must be guaranteed full equality of treatment with nationals of the state of employment in relation to access to health services.

81 CESCR, 'Concluding Observations: Belgium', 4 January 2008, E/C.12/BEL/CO/3, paras 21 and 35, and 'Concluding Observations: France', 16 May 2008, E/C.12/FRA/CO/3, paras 26 and 46.

82 Article 12 ICESCR recognizes the 'right of everyone to the enjoyment of the highest attainable standard of physical and mental health'.

83 CESCR, General Comment No. 14, para. 34. This broad understanding of the principle of equality in respect to the right to health has been also endorsed by the CtRD, in its General Recommendation No. 30, para. 36, but is rarely upheld by domestic laws (see however Article 8 of the Argentinian Migration Law, No. 25.871 (2004)).

84 ECSR, *International Federation of Human Rights Leagues (FIDH) v France*, No. 14/2003, decision of 8 September 2004. The ECSR made express reference to the '*vacuum* theory', as developed by the ECtHR on the basis of Article 31(3(c) VCLT. As pointed out by Mr Rolf Birk in his dissenting opinion, however, reference to Article 31(3(c) VCLT 'cannot [...] set aside the clear wording of the Appendix to the revised European Social Charter'.

85 The special condition of undocumented migrant children was recognised also by the CESCR, in its General Comment No. 20, para. 30: 'all children within a State, including those with an undocumented status, have a right to receive education and access to adequate food and affordable health care' and by the CtRC, General Comment No. 6, 'Treatment of unaccompanied and separated children outside their country of origin', 1 September 2005, CRC/GC/2005/6, para. 22.

86 ECSR, *FIDH v France*, paras 35–7.

87 CoE commissioner for human rights, 'The human rights of irregular migrants in Europe', Comm DH/Issue Paper (2007)1, 17 December 2007, p. 16.

88 M. Hasenau, 'Setting Norms in the United Nations System: The Draft Convention on the Protection of the Rights of All Migrant Workers and their Families in Relation to ILO in Standards on Migrant Workers', *International Migration Review* 28, 1990, 133–58 at 143.

89 Belgian Constitutional Court (Cour d'arbitrage), No. 51/94, judgment of 29 June 1994, *Moniteur Belge*, 14 July 1994, upholding the federal legislation excluding illegal immigrants from social assistance and welfare.

90 ECtHR, *Bah v the United Kingdom*, No. 56328/07, judgment of 27 September 2011, paras 47–9.

91 CMW, 'Concluding Observations: Argentina', 28 September 2011, CMW/C/ARG/CO/1 para. 30(c), inviting member states to '[c]onsider extending non-contributory social benefits to migrant workers and members of their families in an irregular situation in cases of extreme social vulnerability'.

92 See also above, text corresponding to note 50.

93 ECSR, *Defence for Children International (DCI) v the Netherlands*, No. 47/2008, decision of 20 October 2009, paras 46–8. See also Parliamentary Assembly of the CoE, Resolution No. 1509/2006, 'Human rights of irregular migrants', 27 June 2006. Online. Available at: http://assembly.coe.int (accessed 22 August 2012), para. 13.1.

94 Emphasis added.

95 See D. Weissbrodt and C. Collins, 'The Human Rights of Stateless Persons', *Human Rights Quarterly* 28, 2006, 245–276 at 264ff. A valid ID is not only essential to apply for a job, but is also usually required to access social benefits and health care services. Article 27 of the 1954 Convention binds contracting states to 'issue identity papers to any stateless person in their territory who does not possess a valid travel document'. Only 74 states, however, have so far ratified this instrument (Online. Available at: http://treaties.un.org (accessed 10 August 2012)).

96 Cholewinski, *Migrant Workers in International Human Rights Law*, p. 190; R. Pisillo Mazzeschi, 'The relationship between human rights and the rights of aliens and immigrants', in U. Fastenrath, R. Gelger, D.E. Khan, A. Paulus, S. von Schorlemer and C. Vedder (eds) *From Bilateralism to Community Interest: Essays in Honour of Judge Bruno Simma*, Oxford: Oxford University Press, 2011, pp. 552–73 at 566–7. See also the Statement by Ivan Simonovic quoted above.

97 By subjecting the recognition of foreign diplomas and qualification to the fulfilment of certain standards – such as the successful completion of a given period of training – states pursue the legitimate aim of preventing unqualified migrants from engaging in occupations or professions which are considered as particularly 'sensitive'. Harsh conditions for the recognition of foreign qualifications, however, may also serve as a deterrent to immigration, or as a surreptitious means for reserving certain jobs for nationals. When the state's approach to the recognition of foreign qualifications is unduly narrow, however, aliens may suffer a disproportionate limitation to their right to work (see, in this respect, CtERD, *B.M.S. v Australia*, opinion of 10 May 1999, CERD/C/54/D/8/1996, para. 11.1).

9 Determining the nationality of companies in ICSID arbitration

Giulia D'Agnone

Introduction

Nationality represents a gateway to gaining access to the protection offered both by diplomatic protection and by the dispute settlement mechanism established by the Convention on the Settlement of Investment Disputes (ICSID Convention). As is well known, these two fields of international law are strictly interconnected: Article 27 of the ICSID Convention prohibits resort to diplomatic protection when the dispute has been, or should have been, submitted to arbitration under the Convention. In addition, general international law treats investment law as a distinct set of rules having the status of *lex specialis*.[1]

The present chapter will focus on the tension – common to both systems – between formal and substantive criteria for determining corporate nationality. Formal criteria are based on an act of incorporation or on the presence of a company's legal seat in a given state; to the contrary, substantive criteria give relevance to the origin of capital or to the concrete management of the corporation. The analysis will concentrate on Article 25 of the ICSID Convention, which defines the meaning of the notion 'national of another Contracting state' for the purposes of the Convention, but it will also take into account the law applicable for the purposes of diplomatic protection.

After a brief overlook of the criteria used to determine corporate nationality respectively in the framework of diplomatic protection and in the system of the International Centre for Settlement of Investment Disputes (ICSID), particular attention will be devoted to the role of the control test through an examination of some problematic cases faced by ICSID tribunals that show the tension between formal and substantive nationality's *criteria individuationis*. This will help to identify different interpretations of Article 25 of the ICSID Convention and question whether control could play a major role in the determination of corporate nationality in order to preserve the international character of the ICSID dispute settlement system.

The criteria for determining corporate nationality: a comparison between diplomatic protection and the ICSID system

International law has no rule of its own for defining the nationality of a corporation and must consequently turn to municipal law for guidance on this subject. However, it is for international law to determine the circumstances in which a state may exercise diplomatic protection on behalf of a corporation or in which a certain dispute can be settled under the auspices of settlement mechanisms such as ICSID.

As is well known, for the purposes of diplomatic protection international law privileges formal criteria for determining the nationality of companies. In the famous *Barcelona Traction* case, the International Court of Justice (ICJ) firmly acknowledged that the state under the laws of which the company is incorporated and in whose territory it has its registered office is the state having the right to exercise diplomatic protection.[2] In the Court's view, veil piercing for determining the nationality of corporations is possible in only three cases: first, when the rights of the shareholders are directly infringed;[3] second, in the event of a legal demise of the company, because otherwise shareholders would be deprived of 'the possibility of a remedy available through the company';[4] and third, when the corporation's state of nationality is the wrongdoing state.[5]

The incorporation criterion was also retained in the Articles on Diplomatic Protection (2006 Draft Articles) drafted by the International Law Commission (ILC). Article 9, which concerns the identification of the 'State of nationality of a corporation', provides: 'For the purposes of the diplomatic protection of a corporation, the State of nationality means the State under whose law the corporation was incorporated'.[6] The second part of the same Article introduces, however, an exception to the general rule of incorporation. Under this exception, the state enabled to exercise diplomatic protection can be a state different from the state of incorporation under three circumstances to be satisfied cumulatively: the legal entity is controlled by nationals of another state, it has no substantial business activities in the state of incorporation, and the seat of management and financial control of the corporation are both located in another state.[7] As stated in the Commentary to the 2006 Draft Articles:

> Policy and fairness dictate such a solution. It is wrong to place the sole and exclusive right to exercise diplomatic protection in a State with which the corporation has the most tenuous connection as in practice such a State will seldom be prepared to protect such a corporation.[8]

Notwithstanding the introduction of a substantive test of nationality, control still remains an exception to the formal criterion of incorporation. Moreover, Article 9 surrounds the element of control with a series of other conditions to be satisfied in order to resort to it.

The rules on diplomatic protection are not the only ones that make use of formal criteria for the purposes of determining corporate nationality. Article 25(2)(b) of the ICSID Convention, which refers to the notion of a 'national of another Contracting State' for the purposes of determining the scope of the Centre's jurisdiction, provides that this notion includes in the first place 'any juridical person which had the nationality of a Contracting State other than the State party to the dispute'.

Article 25, therefore, does not indicate criteria for determining corporate nationality but leaves states free to determine them. However, treaties and national laws commonly have recourse to formal criteria of incorporation and to the main seat of the business (*siège social*) for defining corporate nationality.[9] Moreover, it has been observed that 'ICSID tribunals have uniformly adopted the test of incorporation or seat rather than control when determining the nationality of a juridical person'.[10] Therefore, the ICSID system appears to be anchored to traditional formal criteria to define the nationality of legal entities. In this respect, it does not differ from general international law.

The role of the control test in the ICSID Convention

As seen in the previous paragraph, the general rule of the first part of Article 25(2)(b) of the ICSID Convention leaves states free to define nationality's *criteria individuationis*. However, the second part of the Article provides an exception to the general rule. Drafters of the Convention introduced a second part to Article 25 in order to address a common phenomenon in business activity. Host states often require investments to be made through locally incorporated companies. In those cases, many corporations would not qualify as foreign investors and then would not benefit from the protection granted by the ICSID system. Therefore, Article 25 provides that '*national of a Contracting State*' can be considered:

> [A]ny juridical person [. . .] which had the nationality of the Contracting State party to the dispute on that date and which, because of foreign control, the parties have agreed should be treated as a national of another Contracting State for the purposes of this Convention.[11]

The meaning of this provision is that locally incorporated companies, which formally have the nationality of the host state, can be considered to be nationals of another state party to the Convention if an agreement exists between the parties to the dispute which gives relevance to foreign control. This agreement can be given in three ways. It can be contained in the agreement between the investor and the host state.[12] Second, it may be contained in a provision in the national legislation of the host state (often in its investment code); in this case the mere existence of the provision in national legislation will not suffice and the investor may accept the offer made by the state through national legislation usually by simply instituting the arbitral proceeding before the Centre. The third method to agree with the use of the control test is through a treaty between the host state and the investor's state of nationality. As in the previous case, the agreement will be perfected when the investor accepts the offer made by the state.[13] Tribunals have been quite flexible as to the form of the agreement. They acknowledged that the insertion of the ICSID arbitration clause in the contract between the private investor and the host state may imply an agreement to treat the local company as a foreign national, arguing that otherwise the ICSID forum selection clause would have been nonsensical.[14]

The ICSID Convention does not define the term 'control'. As pointed out by Schreuer:

> [T]he existence of foreign control is a complex question requiring the examination of several factors such as equity participation, voting rights and management. In order to obtain a reliable picture, all these aspects must be looked at in connection. There is no simple mathematical formula based upon shareholding or votes alone.[15]

Basically, one can imagine that 'foreign control' under the terms of Article 25(2)(b) of the ICSID Convention is to be identified with the management or the ownership of the majority stake.[16] Indeed, elements for the identification of 'foreign control' cannot be drawn from the general rules on diplomatic protection. First, it must be noted that, notwithstanding the fact that the ILC refers to the control test for determining corporate nationality for diplomatic protection purposes, in the 2006 Draft Articles the issue of exact qualification of the term 'control' has not been resolved.[17] More importantly, given the different function of nationality for diplomatic protection purposes from nationality within the ICSID system, it would be questionable whether criteria elaborated in the first field can be applied to the latter.

Uncertainty also surrounds the degree of control needed in order to fulfil the requirement of Article 25(2)(b). As it has been noted:

> ICSID practice [...] has shown certain disagreement on how far a tribunal may go in the shareholding structure of the juridical person, for the purposes of the second clause of Article 25(2)(b), in order to determine whether the foreign control requirement is fulfilled.[18]

While some ICSID tribunals have considered the control test to be satisfied where there is direct control,[19] others seek to reconstruct the entire chain of control in order to identify who has effective control.[20]

The ICSID case law: the controversial *Tokios Tokelés* and *Rompetrol* cases

Notwithstanding the fact that the ICSID Convention leaves states great latitude to determine the criteria for defining nationality, one could question whether the Convention places some limitations, or if, on the contrary, it imposes no restrictions at all on the freedom of states. The answer to this question is fundamental in order to analyse the role of the control test within the ICSID system.

ICSID tribunals have been called upon to address this issue in two cases: the *Tokios Tokelés*[21] and the *Rompetrol* cases.[22] In the *Tokios Tokelés* case, where the issue was addressed for the first time, Ukrainian investors incorporated a company in Lithuania and then used that entity to invest in Ukraine. Although the company was 99 per cent Ukrainian-owned, it was protected by the Lithuania–Ukraine Bilateral Investment Treaty (BIT), which defined nationality by reference to the place of incorporation. Ukraine objected to the Tribunal's jurisdiction, asserting that because of foreign control the company was actually claiming against its home state. The Tribunal ruled that the company was entitled to bring a claim against Ukraine because under the Lithuania–Ukraine BIT incorporation was the criterion to be applied for the determination of the status of 'investor'.[23] The President of the Tribunal, Prosper Weil, strongly dissented to the outcome of the proceeding.

A very similar case occurred four years later. In the *Rompetrol* case, the claimant was a company incorporated in the Netherlands but ultimately controlled by a Romanian national. Romania argued that the Tribunal had to dismiss the case since *Rompetrol* was not a 'foreign investor'. Once again the Tribunal refused to look behind formal criteria stating that the Netherlands–Romania BIT did not allow veil piercing.[24] These two emblematic cases show the reluctance of ICSID tribunals to apply substantive criteria in order to define corporate nationality in the absence of an explicit allowance by the parties to the dispute.[25]

However, in so doing the two Tribunals allowed domestic controversies to benefit from the protection offered by the ICSID Convention. The crucial point is that the ICSID Convention was clearly meant to offer a dispute settlement system for *international* controversies (Article 25 refers to controversies 'between a Contracting State and a national of another Contracting State'). In some cases, if the element of control is not taken into account, the international character of the ICSID system risks being put in jeopardy.

Therefore, a tension clearly emerges between the freedom enjoyed by states under the ICSID Convention to determine nationality and the need to preserve the international character of the system. In this context, the element of control may play a crucial role. In particular, in cases such as the above-mentioned ones, the control test is the key element to discover the real nature of the dispute – whether it is genuinely international or not. Once it has been ascertained that a dispute is substantially domestic, one could question whether the ICSID system should apply to disputes that only apparently satisfy the international character of the system.

The interpretation of Article 25(2)(b) of the ICSID Convention: teleological vs. literal approach

The question concerning the role of control within the ICSID system reflects an interpretative problem that is raised in connection to Article 25 of the Convention. In this regard, the outcome of this interpretative problem appears to be different, depending on the methods of interpretation which one applies. Reference is made here to the literal and the teleological methods of interpretation, both provided by the first paragraph of Article 31 of the Vienna Convention on the Law of Treaties.[26]

A teleological interpretation endeavours to analyse Article 25 in light of the object and purpose of the Convention. In this respect, reference may be made to the Report of the Executive Directors on the Convention, which clearly states that:

> [T]he creation of an institution designed to facilitate the settlement of disputes between States and foreign investors can be a major step toward promoting an atmosphere of mutual confidence and thus stimulating a larger flow of private international capital into those countries which wish to attract it.[27]

According to the Report, the Convention is not intended to settle purely domestic controversies related to investments, but disputes between a state and a national of another state – in other words, international controversies.[28] Article 25 is clear in this respect when it provides that 'national of a Contracting State' means 'any juridical person which had the nationality of a Contracting State *other* than the State party to the dispute'.

However, allowing a company formally incorporated in a State A but controlled by nationals of State B (such in the *Tokios Tokelés* and the *Rompetrol* cases) to act against the latter state actually means that domestic disputes come under ICSID's scope, where only formally dressed up as international controversies. This is clearly not what the drafters of the Convention had in mind and leaves room for inconsistency. Thus, the solution adopted by the Tribunals in these two cases appears to run counter to Article 25 if one interprets this provision teleologically. This teleological interpretation was strongly supported by Prosper Weil in his dissenting opinion in the *Tokios Tokelés* case. He clearly stated that:

> The ICSID arbitration mechanism is meant for international investment disputes, that is to say, for disputes between States and foreign investors. It is because of their international character, and with a view to stimulating private international investment, that these disputes may be settled, if the parties so desire, by an international judicial body. The ICSID mechanism is not meant for investment disputes between States and their own nationals.[29]

The President of the Tribunal turned also to the relationship between the ICSID Convention and BITs, declaring that:

> It is within the limits determined by the basic ICSID Convention that the BITs may determine the jurisdiction and powers of the ICSID tribunal, and it is not for the Contracting Parties in their BIT to extend the jurisdiction of the ICSID tribunal beyond the limits determined by the Convention.[30]

In his opinion, the notion of nationality used in a BIT cannot depart from the 'outer limits'[31] set by the Convention. Therefore, the provisions of the ICSID Convention, and not the provisions of the investment treaty, should prevail. According to his view, in order to establish whether a dispute can be settled by an ICSID tribunal, one will first prove that the requirements of Article 25 of the Convention are satisfied and, in a second stage, that a company is a 'national' under the BIT provisions, not the contrary. Under this interpretation, in order to fulfil the object and scope of the Convention, the above-mentioned tribunals should have dismissed the case, because the reference to foreign control clearly demonstrated that it was a purely domestic controversy.

Literal interpretation of Article 25 leads to completely different results. Under a literal interpretation, which is favoured by the great majority of authors,[32] it is hard to deny that Article 25 leaves states free to determine the criteria of corporate nationality and that therefore, when applying this provision, ICSID tribunals must look primarily at the criteria set forth in the BIT. As observed by the Tribunal in *Rompetrol*:

> [G]iven the latitude granted to States under the ICSID Convention to settle the applicable nationality criteria, there is nothing illogical in looking first of all to whether the nationality criteria set forth in the BIT are satisfied before going on to examine whether there is anything in Article 25 of the Convention which stands in the way of giving effect to that.[33]

In *Tokios Tokelés* and *Rompetrol*, arbitrators considered that the nationality requirements provided by the relative BITs (which both referred to formal criteria for determining nationality) were satisfied. They underlined that under Article 25(2)(b) of the ICSID Convention, states are free to determine nationality's *criteria individuationis*, and therefore if the company satisfies the BIT's requirements of nationality, there is nothing inconsistent with the Convention. Therefore the two Tribunals granted the companies in question access to the ICSID system, relying on formal criteria of nationality without giving relevance to the substantive dimension of the investment. The Tribunals decided to adhere to the explicit wording of the second phrase of Article 25(2)(b), which requires that an express agreement must exist in order to treat the locally incorporated company as a national of another state party to the Convention. Because of the absence of agreement, the control test could not be applied by the two Tribunals. For example, in *Tokios Tokelés* the Tribunal asserted that:

> [T]he second clause of Article 25(2)(b) provides that parties can, by agreement, depart from the general rule that a corporate entity has the nationality of its state of incorporation. [...] This exception to the general rule applies only in the context of an agreement between the parties. [...] In the present case, the Claimant is not a national of the host State nor have the parties agreed to treat the Claimant as a national of a State other than its state of incorporation.[34]

While the solution retained by the two Tribunals found support in the literal interpretation of Article 25, it remains that, if one looks carefully at the circumstances of the disputes at issue, it is hard to say that these disputes had a genuinely international character. Article 25(2)(b) was introduced in the Convention in order to address a very specific situation: the case in which investors are required to conduct their business through locally incorporated companies. By virtue of incorporation, the legal entity acquires the nationality of the host state and thus the investor loses standing before the Centre. Thus the drafters' intention is to avoid situations in which foreign investors are unduly excluded from the jurisdiction of the Centre.[35] The use of the control test is then limited to that specific circumstance. However, in *Tokios Tokelés* and *Rompetrol* the problem was not that locally incorporated companies were injured by a wrongful act of their formal state of nationality, which is the phenomenon addressed by the second part of Article 25(2)(b). Rather, the cases involved companies formally having the nationality of a certain state, but that because of control were claiming against their state of substantive nationality. Therefore, in this case, one could question whether the control test could play a role in order to avoid the risk of jeopardizing the international character of the ICSID Convention.

As already mentioned, the rationale of Article 25(2)(b) is to grant protection to investors when the state of nationality is the wrongdoing state and incorporation in that state is a precondition for making investments. This provision and the rules on corporate nationality for the purposes of diplomatic protection have much in common. The rules on diplomatic protection give relevance to the element of control only in the circumstance in which local incorporation is imposed and the state of formal nationality is the wrongdoing state.

This rule was first developed in the *Barcelona Traction* case, where the ICJ recognized that 'a theory has been developed to the effect that the State of the shareholders has a right of diplomatic protection when the State whose responsibility is invoked is the national State of the company'.[36] Although the Court declared that the rule was not applicable in the case at issue, Judges Jessup,

Fitzmaurice and Tanaka expressed strong support for this rule in their separate opinions.[37] In particular, Judges Fitzmaurice and Jessup considered that such a rule was particularly needed when incorporation was required as a precondition for doing business in the state of incorporation.[38] The exception at issue is limited to what has been called 'Calvo corporation', which is defined as 'a corporation whose incorporation, like the Calvo Clause, is designed to protect it from the rules of international law relating to diplomatic protection'.[39]

Nowadays, the rule has been explicitly included in Article 11(b) of the 2006 Draft Articles. In this case, veil piercing is allowed – and therefore the state of nationality of shareholders is entitled to exercise diplomatic protection in respect of such shareholders – if '[t]he corporation had, at the date of injury, the nationality of the State alleged to be responsible for causing the injury, and incorporation in that State was required by it as a precondition for doing business there.' A clear parallel can be drawn between Article 11 of the 2006 Draft Articles and the second part of Article 25(2)(b) of the ICSID Convention. Both rules justify veil piercing in order to grant protection to companies locally incorporated in a state that is responsible to them for committing a wrong. However, it should be noted that rules on diplomatic protection use the control test not, as the ICSID Convention does, for determining corporate nationality, but to extend diplomatic protection to shareholders in cases in which the exceptional circumstance described in Article 11 recurs.[40] Indeed, Special Rapporteur Dugard envisaged the possibility of introducing the control test in order to determine the state entitled to exercise diplomatic protection.[41] However, he ultimately considered that:

> [T]he wisest course seems to be to formulate articles that give effect to the principles expounded in Barcelona Traction. The following articles endorse both the primary rule in the Barcelona Traction — namely that the State of incorporation of a company enjoys the right to exercise diplomatic protection on behalf of the company — and the exceptions to this rule, recognized, to a greater or lesser extent, by the Court.[42]

The need for a genuine connection between the state of nationality and the company

It has been shown that Article 25(2)(b) shares the same rationale as Article 11 of the 2006 Draft Articles. However, it can be questioned whether the control test could play a role, not only in the case described in the second part of Article 25(2)(b), but also in the case where a company is formally incorporated in a certain state but that, because of control, is de facto a national of the state against which it is actually bringing a claim. ICSID tribunals answered the question negatively.[43] As we have seen, a literal interpretation of Article 25(2)(b) supports the view that the control test can be applied only in the specific circumstance described in the provision. The rules on diplomatic protection confirm this approach.

This limited relevance of the control test for the purposes of determining corporate nationality has evident shortcomings. The real dimension of the investment made through the corporation is neglected. Moreover, 'the worry is that the ICSID Convention's laudable framework for international arbitration might be jeopardized by the manipulation of nationality'.[44] If control is not taken into account, foreign investors are in fact authorized to establish corporations in certain states (the so-called 'mailbox companies') for the sole purpose of taking advantage of nationalities of convenience and, therefore, of the system of protection of investments established by the ICSID Convention.[45]

The question is whether genuine nationality can play a role in a situation of this kind. In its judgment in the *Nottebohm* case, the ICJ recognized that a state's rules on nationality may be ignored when nationality is conferred without regard to any effective link between the state and the individual.[46] The genuine link theory developed by the Court applies exclusively to individuals,[47] and in *Barcelona Traction* the Court pointed out that 'in the particular field of the diplomatic protection of corporate entities, no absolute test of the "genuine connection" has found general acceptance'.[48] However, the Court recognized the need for some 'permanent and close connection' between the state exercising diplomatic protection and the corporation.[49]

Leaving aside the rules on diplomatic protection, the question is whether it is possible to look for some genuine connection between a company and the state of nationality within the ICSID system. ICSID arbitrators explicitly acknowledged the relevance of some genuine link between a company and the state concerned for the purpose of determining the company's nationality. An indication that supports the need for a genuine connection can be inferred from the fact that both the Tribunals in *Tokios Tokelés* and *Rompetrol* explicitly considered whether the companies had abused their legal personality.[50] In both instances, arbitrators found that the two corporations did not abuse their formal nationalities. However, the fact that the Tribunals themselves addressed the matter is a clear sign that the arbitrators acknowledged the need for some genuine connection between companies and states of nationality.

The importance attached by arbitrators to the notion of 'abuse of nationality' shows that there may be at least two different techniques in order to assess the genuineness of a company's connection to the state of nationality and, as a consequence, the international character of the dispute submitted to ICSID tribunals. The first technique is to emphasize the element of control under Article 25(2)(b) of the ICSID Convention; the second technique is to apply the abuse-of-rights doctrine.

When addressing the problem of the genuineness of the nationality, ICSID tribunals limit themselves to assessing whether an abuse of process took place.[51] As asserted by El Salvador in the recent ICSID case *Pac Rim Cayman*:

> The doctrine of Abuse of Process, also called Abuse of Right, exists to protect parties from misuse of international arbitration system. The doctrine is rooted in the universal requirement of good faith and in the inherent powers of arbitral tribunals to determine their own jurisdiction and to protect the integrity of the international arbitration system.[52]

While resort to the abuse-of-rights doctrine may provide judges with a useful tool to assess the genuineness of the link of nationality, reliance on this doctrine cannot be regarded as sufficient to address all the situations in which the problem of a genuine link arises. In this respect, the abuse-of-rights doctrine presents certain shortcomings. The first shortcoming is represented by the fact that abuse of process is an elusive concept, and it is not well established in international law.[53] Above all, cases which raise the problem of abuse of process do not necessarily coincide with cases characterized by a lack of a genuine link between a state and a corporation. The first set of cases appear to be more restricted than the latter. In particular, an allegation of abuse of rights requires proof of a deceitful intention on the part of the company, while the lack of genuine link appears to be an objective situation. Thus, for instance, when the change of nationality took place as a consequence of the restructuring of a corporation, arbitrators denied the possibility of abuse of rights in cases in which the change of nationality took place before the date on which the dispute arose.[54] This implies that if corporate restructuring occurs before any dispute arises or if there is not a deceitful intention when incorporating or placing a company's legal seat in a certain state, the abuse of rights doctrine provides little assistance with the problem of genuine nationality.

Therefore, in light of ICSID case law, the abuse-of-rights doctrine is a technique that has a limited area of application and does not seem to provide an effective alternative to a teleological interpretation of Article 25 as a means of coping with the problem of genuine corporate nationality. Consequently, the abuse-of-rights doctrine has limited application to the problem of preserving the international character of the dispute.

Concluding remarks

Even if, in principle, the ICSID system should reflect better than diplomatic protection the economic reality of business activity and take into account business strategies, control remains a residual and exceptional criterion for determining corporate nationality. However, recent cases have underlined that the international character of the system is endangered when formal nationality legitimizes domestic controversies to be settled under the aegis of the ICSID Convention. Control should therefore play an active role in determining corporate nationality. So far, ICSID tribunals have demonstrated their reluctance to apply it. However, the time is ripe to improve the criteria of a more genuine connection between companies and states of nationality.

Notes

1 As it was observed by the ICJ, the

> developments in question [bilateral investment treaties and lump sum settlements] have to be viewed as distinctive processes, arising out of circumstances peculiar to the respective situations. To seek to draw from them analogies or conclusions held to be valid in other fields is to ignore their specific character as lex specialis and hence to court error.
>
> (*Barcelona Traction, Light and Power Company, Limited, Judgment (Belgium v Spain)(New application:1962)*, judgment of 5 February 1970, *ICJ Reports 1970*, p. 40, para. 62)

On the relationship between diplomatic protection and the ICSID system, see J. Kokott, 'Interim Report on "The Role of Diplomatic Protection in the Field of the Protection of Foreign Investment"', in International Law Association, *Report of the Seventieth Conference, New Delhi*, London: International Law Association, 2002, pp. 259–77. See also B. Juratowitch, 'The Relationship between Diplomatic Protection and Investment Treaties', *ICSID Review – Foreign Investment Law Journal* 23, 2008, 10–35.

2 ICJ, *Barcelona Traction, Light and Power Company, Limited*, para. 70.

3 Ibid., para. 47.

4 Ibid., paras 64–8.

5 Ibid., para. 92.

6 ILC, Draft Articles on Diplomatic Protection, Article 9. The text of the 2006 Draft Articles, together with the Commentaries, is contained in ILC, 'Report on the work of the fifty-eighth session', *UNGAOR, Sixty-first Session, Supplement No. 10*, UN Doc. A/61/10.

7 The second part of Article 9 provides that

> when the corporation is controlled by nationals of another State or States and has no substantial business activities in the State of incorporation, and the seat of management and the financial control of the corporation are both located in another State, that State shall be regarded as the State of nationality.

8 2006 Draft Articles, Commentary to Article 9.

9 See C.H. Schreuer, *The ICSID Convention: A Commentary*, Cambridge: Cambridge University Press, 2001, p. 279, stating that:

> Under traditional international law, there are several possible criteria for the determination of a juridical person's nationality. The most widely used test looks at the place of incorporation or registered office. Alternatively, the place of the central administration or effective seat (siège social) is considered decisive.

See also the statement by the ICSID Tribunal in *Société Ouest Africaine des Bétons Industriels {SOABI} v State of Senegal*, No. ARB/82/1, decision on jurisdiction of 1 August 1984, *ICSID Reports* 2, 1994, p. 181:

> As a general rule, States apply either the head office or the place of incorporation criteria in order to determine nationality. By contrast, neither the nationality of the company's shareholders nor foreign control, other than over capital, normally govern the nationality of a company, although a legislature may invoke these criteria in exceptional circumstances.

10 Schreuer, *The ICSID Convention: A Commentary*, p. 281.

11 Ibid., p. 290:

> Incorporation in the host state makes the investor technically a national of that state according to the most common test for nationality of juridical persons. This would exclude all investors that operate through local companies from the ambit of the ICSID Convention. A large and important part of foreign investment would then be outside the Convention's scope. The second clause of Article 25(2)(b) is designed to accommodate this problem by creating an exception to the diversity of nationality requirement.

12 See ICSID Model Clauses, Online. Available at: http://icsid.worldbank.org/ICSID/FrontServlet?actionVal=ModelClauses&requestType=ICSIDDocRH (accessed 22 August 2012), Clause 7:

> It is hereby agreed that, although the Investor is a national of the Host State, it is controlled by nationals of name(s) of other Contracting State(s) and shall be treated as a national of [that]/[those] State[s] for the purposes of the Convention.

13 See Schreuer, *The ICSID Convention: A Commentary*, p. 294, stating that:

> The Convention does not require any specific form for an agreement to treat a juridical person that has the host State's nationality as a national of another Contracting State because of foreign control. Since such an agreement is closely linked to consent, it will normally be recorded in the consent agreement.

14 See, for example, ICSID, *Klöckner Industrie-Anlagen GmbH and others v United Republic of Cameroon and Société Camerounaise des Engrais*, No. ARB/81/2, award of 21 October 1983, *ICSID Reports* 2, p. 16; ICSID, *Liberian Eastern Timber Corporation (LETCO) v Republic of Liberia*, No. ARB/83/2, interim award of 24 October 1984, *ICSID Reports* 2, 349–53.

15 See Schreuer, *The ICSID Convention: A Commentary*, p. 391.

16 The most common way of controlling a locally incorporated entity is represented by the ownership of shares: see ICSID, *LETCO v Liberia*, p. 351; *Klöckner Industrie v United Republic of Cameroon and Société Camerounaise des Engrais*, p. 145. However, see P. Acconci, 'Determining the Internationally Relevant Link between a State and a Corporate Investor, Recent Trends concerning the Application of the "Genuine Link" Test', *The Journal of World Investment & Trade* 5, 2004, 139–75 at 141, considering that

> testing to discover a 'genuine link' gives rise to a further question, since it must be decided whether the subject of this test is the link between the company and the general economic environment of the country where the company operates or the link between the company and the country to whose legal system the company's most important basic elements can be ascribed. In the first case, any circumstance linking a company to a certain country is relevant, for instance the contribution given by the company activities to the economics of that country, the residence of the company for tax purposes and also the place where the shares and bonds of the company are issued. In the second case, when the corporate veil is lifted in order to identify the most effective link, relevance is alternatively given to the nationality of the company's shareholders, the owners of its bonds, or of its directors or creditors.

17 See J. Dugard, 'Fourth report on diplomatic protection', 13 March 2003, UN Doc. A/CN.4/530, paras 34–5:

> Defining control is not an easy task [...] State practice is not uniform. Some treaties define control in terms of majority shareholding. Others simply refer to control and leave it to the relevant tribunal to determine this requirement in all the circumstances, including shareholding. Economic control as the test for the nationality of a corporation for the purposes of diplomatic protection is open to several criticisms in addition to that of imprecision in relation to the concept of control.

See however C.F. Amerasinghe, *Jurisdiction of Specific International Tribunals*, Leiden: M. Nijhoff, 2009, p. 480: 'In the case of diplomatic protection, as understood by some authorities before the Barcelona Traction case, the concept of "control" appears to have been associated entirely with the nature of shareholding', referring to L. Caflisch, *La Protection de Sociétés Commerciales et des Intérets Indirects en Droit International Public*, The Hague: M. Nijhoff, 1969, p. 89 and J.M. Jones, 'Claims on behalf of Nationals who are Shareholders in Foreign Companies', *British Year Book of International Law* 26, 1949, p. 225.

18 R. Castro de Figueiredo, 'ICSID and Non-Foreign Investment Disputes', *Transnational Dispute Management* 5, 2007, p. 13. Online. Available at: www.transnational-dispute-management.com (accessed 22 August 2012).

19 ICSID, *Amco Asia Corporation and others v Indonesia*, No. ARB/81/1, decision on jurisdiction of 25 September 1983, *International Legal Materials* 23, 1984, p. 351.

20 See, for example, ICSID, *Société Ouest Africaine des Bétons Industriels v Senegal*, pp. 182–3; *LETCO v Liberia*, p. 351 and, recently, *TSA Spectrum de Argentina S.A. v Argentine Republic*, No. ARB/05/5, award of 19 December 2008. Online. Available at: www.arbitration.fr/resources/ICSID-ARB-05–5-Award-English.pdf (accessed 22 August 2012), stating that

> [i]t would not be consistent with the text, if the tribunal, when establishing whether there is foreign control, would be directed to pierce the veil of the corporate entity national of the host State and to stop short at the second corporate layer it meets, rather than pursuing its objective identification of foreign control up to its real source, using the same criterion with which it started.
>
> (para. 147)

21 ICSID, *Tokios Tokelés v Ukraine*, No. ARB/02/18, decision on jurisdiction of 29 April 2004, *ICSID Review—Foreign Investment Law Journal* 20, 2005, p. 205.

22 ICSID, *The Rompetrol Group N.V. v Romania*, No. ARB/06/3, decision on jurisdiction and admissibility of 18 April 18 2008. Online. Available at: http://icsid.worldbank.org (accessed 22 August 2012).

23 ICSID, *Tokios Tokelés v Ukraine*, para. 40. It has been correctly noted that '[t]he Tokios arbitration places in stark relief the relative weight of substantive control versus corporate form of the investment vehicle' (C. McLachlan, L. Shore and M. Weiniger, *International Investment Arbitration Substantive Principles*, New York: Oxford University Press, 2010, p. 145).

24 ICSID, *The Rompetrol Group N.V. v Romania*, paras. 79–84.

25 See the assertion in *Tokios Tokelés*, para. 36: 'it is not for tribunals to impose limits on the scope of BITs not found in the text.'

26 VCLT, 23 May 1969, UNTS, vol. 1155, No. 18232, Article 31, entitled 'General rule of interpretation' states as follows: 'A treaty shall be interpreted in good faith in accordance with the ordinary meaning to be given to the terms of the treaty in their context and in the light of its object and purpose'.

27 'Report of the Executive Directors on the Convention on the Settlement of

Investment Disputes between States and Nationals of Other States', par. 9. Online. Available at: http://icsid.worldbank.org/ICSID/StaticFiles/basicdoc/CRR_English-final.pdf (accessed 22 August 2012).

28 See Schreuer, *The ICSID Convention: A Commentary*, p. 290, affirming that: 'The Convention is designed to facilitate the settlement of investment disputes between States and nationals of other States. It is not meant for disputes between States and their own nationals'.

29 ICSID, *Tokios Tokelés v Ukraine*, dissenting opinion, *ICSID Review – Foreign Investment Law Journal* 20, 2005, 245, para. 5.

30 Ibid., para. 13.

31 This successful expression was coined by A. Broches, 'The Convention on the Settlement of Investment Disputes Between States and Nationals of other States', *Collected Courses of the Hague Academy of International Law* 136, 1972, 331–410 at 361.

32 R.L. Astorga, 'The Nationality of Juridical Persons in the ICSID Convention in Light of Its Jurisprudence', *Max Planck Yearbook of United Nations Law* 11, 2007, p. 472; Schreuer, *The ICSID Convention: A Commentary*, p. 278.

33 ICSID, *The Rompetrol Group N.V. v Romania*, para. 82.

34 ICSID, *Tokios Tokelés v Ukraine*, paras 44–5.

35 Schreuer, *The ICSID Convention: A Commentary*, p. 276.

36 ICJ, *Barcelona Traction, Light and Power Company, Limited*, para. 92.

37 *ICJ Reports 1970*, respectively pp. 191–3, 72–5, 134. See the statement of Judge Fitzmaurice:

> It seems that, actually, in only one category of situation is it more or less definitely admitted that intervention by the Government of foreign shareholders is allowable, namely where the company concerned has the nationality of the very State responsible for the acts or damage complained of, and these, or the resulting circumstances, are such as to render the company incapable de facto of protecting its interests and hence those of the shareholders.
>
> (p. 72, para. 14)

38 See, for example, Judge Jessup asserting that the rationale for the exception 'seems to be based largely on equitable considerations and the result is so reasonable it has been accepted in State practice.' He explained that '[t]he equities are particularly striking when the respondent State admits foreign investment only on condition that the investors form a corporation under its law', but he did not limit the exception to such circumstances see *ICJ Reports 1970*, pp. 191–2.

39 2006 Draft Articles, Commentary to Article 11.

40 F. Orrego Vicuña, 'Changing Approaches to the Nationality of Claims in the Context of Diplomatic Protection and International Dispute Settlement', *ICSID Review – Foreign Investment Law Journal* 15, 2000, 340–61 at 357: 'These additional criteria have been rightly described not as conferring nationality, but as creating an equivalent connection which on occasion is considered to provide enough ground for the exercise of diplomatic protection'.

41 Dugard, 'Fourth report on diplomatic protection', paras 30, 32–43.

42 Ibid., para. 47.

43 The Tribunal in *Tokios Tokelés v Ukraine*, para. 50, reached exactly this conclusion, stating that 'ICSID jurisprudence also confirms that the second clause of Article 25(2)(b) should not be used to determine the nationality of juridical entities in the absence of an agreement between the parties'.

44 R.D. Sloane, 'Breaking the Genuine Link: The Contemporary International Legal Regulation of Nationality', *Harvard International Law Review* 50, 2009, 41.

45 It could be argued that formal interpretation favours the predictability of the outcome regarding the jurisdiction *ratione personae*. However, the author does not agree with the conclusion that in such case predictability could stimulate the international capital flow (see the conclusion on this point by A. Sironi, 'Nationality of individuals in public international law: a functional approach', *supra*, pp. 54–75). The ICSID system was thought for providing a neutral forum where international investment disputes could be settled. The economic development which derives to states through the adherence to the system is only a consequence thereof. Prevalence of forms over the economic dimension of corporate structure jeopardizes the international character of the dispute settlement mechanism of the ICSID Convention and its reputation.

46 *Nottebohm Case (Second Phase) (Liechtenstein v Guatemala)*, judgment of 6 April 1955, *ICJ Reports* 1955, p. 4 at 23. The ICJ stated:

> According to the practice of States, to arbitral and judicial decisions and to the opinion of writers, nationality is the legal bond having as its basis a social fact of attachment, a genuine connection of existence, interests and sentiments, together with the existence of reciprocal rights and duties. It may be said to constitute the juridical expression of the fact that the individual upon whom it is conferred, either directly by the law or as the result of an act of the authorities, is in fact more closely connected with the population of the State conferring nationality than with that of any other State. Conferred by a State, it only entitles that State to exercise protection vis-à-vis another State, if it constitutes a translation into juridical terms of the individual's connection which has made him its national.

47 However, even for individuals it is questionable whether the genuine link principle is still relevant: see the conclusions on this point of Sironi, 'Nationality of individuals in public international law: a functional approach' and A. Vermeer-Künzli, 'Nationality and diplomatic protection: a reappraisal', *supra*, respectively, pp. 54–75 and pp. 76–95.

48 ICJ, *Barcelona Traction, Light and Power Company, Limited*, para. 70.

49 Ibid., para. 71.

50 ICSID, *Tokios Tokelés v Ukraine*, para. 56 and *The Rompetrol Group N.V. v Romania*, para. 115.

51 On the abuse of process and illegitimate corporate planning, see ICSID, *Phoenix Action Ltd. v Czech Republic*, No. ARB/06/5, award of 15 April 2009. Online. Available at: http://icsid.worldbank.org (accessed 22 August 2012); ICSID, *Mobil Corporation and others v Bolivarian Republic of Venezuela*, No. ARB/07/27, decision on jurisdiction of 10 June 2010, Online. Available at: http://icsid.worldbank.org (accessed 22 August 2012); ICSID, *Pac Rim Cayman LLC v Republic of El Salvador*, No. ARB/09/12, decision on jurisdiction of 1 June 2012. Online. Available at: http://icsid.worldbank.org (accessed 22 August 2012), para. 11.

52 ICSID, *Pac Rim Cayman LLC v Republic of El Salvador*, para. 11.

53 M. Gestri, 'Considerazioni sulla teoria dell'abuso di diritto alla luce della prassi internazionale', *Rivista di diritto internazionale* 78, 1994, p. 57.

54 See ICSID, *Mobil Corporation and others v Bolivarian Republic of Venezuela,* para. 204; see also ICSID, *Tokios Tokelés v Ukraine*, para. 56.

10 Nationality and regional integration

The case of the European Union

Pierluigi Simone

Introduction

The term 'nationality', when used in reference to individuals, commonly indicates the legal relations that bind a person to a given state, and determine the sphere of enforcement of a basic set of social and political rights and obligations.[1] Nationality is regarded as an inalienable right of every human being. Thus, the Universal Declaration of Human Rights (UDHR) of 10 December 1948 declares in Article 15 that 'everyone has the right to a nationality' and that 'no one shall be arbitrarily deprived of his nationality'.[2] Nationality is of essential importance because through it the individual enters the scope of international law and accedes to the political and economic rights and privileges conferred onto nationals in modern states. Nationality must also be distinguished from 'citizenship', which is a narrower term that denotes various relations between an individual and a state that do not necessarily confer political rights, but do imply other privileges, particularly protection abroad. Citizenship is commonly used in international law to denote the status of those nationals who have full political privileges and all persons whom a state is entitled to protect.[3]

Several international legal instruments, both at the universal and regional levels, refer to nationality and citizenship. Among the first type of instruments is the International Convention on the Protection of the Rights of All Migrant Workers and Members of their Families (ICRMW) of 18 December 1990, which provides in Article 25 that migrant workers shall enjoy treatment not less favourable than that which applies to nationals of the state of employment in respect of remuneration and other conditions of work.[4] Among the regional instruments, Protocol No. 4 to the European Convention for the Protection of Human Rights and Fundamental Freedoms (ECHR) of 16 September 1963, guarantees that 'no one shall be expelled, by means either of an individual or of a collective measure, from the territory of the state of which he is a national' and that 'no one shall be deprived of the right to enter the territory of the State of which he is a national'.[5] The American Convention on Human Rights of 22 November 1969 lists the rights that belong to each person as distinguished from the rights belonging to citizens.[6] The Convention on the Participation of Foreigners in Public Life at Local Level, adopted by the Council of Europe (Strasbourg, 5 February 1992), explains in its Preamble the reasons why some rights traditionally reserved to citizens should also be granted today to non-nationals.[7] The Arab Charter on Human Rights of 22 May 2004, finally, lists in Article 24 the rights of every citizen, and adds in Article 37 the right for citizens to participate in the development, and contribute to and enjoy the benefits, of their goods and the fruits of their labour.[8]

Nationality and citizenship are also relevant under the various regional integration processes currently in place. In such contexts, the concept of citizenship transcends state borders, working as a mechanism to enhance and consolidate these processes. In this regard, it is worth mentioning specifically the examples of the Southern Common Market (Mercosur) and the Southern African Development Community (SADC).[9] Despite the limitations of the founding Treaty of Asunción, which did not include the free movement of individuals in its provisions, the subsequent evolution of Mercosur has brought significant modifications in terms of freedom of movement and migrant workers' rights, and has opened a debate that led to the signing of the Regularization and Residence Agreements of 5 and 6 December 2002.[10] These Agreements represent a step forward in the direction of guaranteeing legal status to Mercosur citizenship, and contain a series of fundamental rights to be respected (such as non-discrimination, the right to family reunification, the right to receive an equal treatment, the right to transfer remittances, and the right to access social security). The same Agreements, however, entered into force only in 2009 and still denote a lack of enforcement that undoubtedly hampers the efforts to ensure free movement and residence to Mercosur citizens in the region.[11] The Constitutive Protocol of the Parliament of the Mercosur (Montevideo, 9 December 2005) also attributed a right to direct election, stating in Article 6(1) that '[t]he Parliamentarians will be chosen by the citizens of the respective States Parties, through direct suffrage, universal and secret'.[12] As for the SADC, the Protocol on the Facilitation of Movement of Persons of 18 August 2005 was established to drive the agenda of that regional cooperation away from an economic and state-centred coordination towards a deep and people-centred integration.[13] The Protocol aims to transform progressively the regional labour market and migration patterns in a way that would create a common and integrated labour market; the Protocol also promotes and protects the rights of all nationals of a SADC member state to enter other member states freely and without a visa, and to reside, establish, and work in the territory of another member state.[14]

The most prominent example of regional integration is however provided by the European Union (EU), which has adopted since 1992 a particular citizenship status of its own. Nationality, as a determining factor in international relations, is closely related to the concept of sovereignty. With a changing perception of sovereignty as a result of a globalized interdependent world and national regimes, nationality has lost many of its functions as the expression of membership of a nation as a political community, and can no longer be considered the only and exclusive legal bond between an individual and a country.[15] In this respect, the citizenship of the EU has widely contributed to a changed perception, as nationality of member states is increasingly undermined and partially exceeded by processes of transnational interdependence and internationalization of institutional and economic structures. EU citizenship involves people in the European integration process, launches a political message, and gives the EU a source of legitimacy that only individuals can provide, as they vote in elections and in *referenda* organized in the member states to ratify changes to the founding Treaties; EU citizenship is in fact intended for the development of a supranational identity.[16] It presupposes the existence of a political relationship between European citizens based on the European political area from which rights and duties emerge.[17]

The concept of citizenship is usually described as a gradual substitution of important elements of the nationality of the member states. The citizenship of the EU is no longer limited to economic freedoms, but already implies, although to a limited extent, political rights and a right of residence, which is becoming independent from traditional requirements of alien law.[18] This chapter seeks to point out the main characteristics that EU citizenship has acquired over time. The relationship among EU citizenship and the nationalities of individual member states will be discussed. Finally, the chapter will examine recent judgments of the European Court of Justice (ECJ) which, even with the limitations that will be highlighted, are particularly important in strengthening the transnational character of the EU.

The citizenship of the EU: an overview

The citizenship of the EU was introduced by the Treaty of Maastricht in order to increase the protection of the rights of nationals of member states in a time when the development of the European Community (EC) into a political and economic union was taking a very significant step forward. The debate within the Intergovernmental Conference, which led to the adoption of the Treaty of Maastricht, was fuelled by the awareness of a marked democratic *deficit* in the EC decision-making processes and involved the submission of proposals to improve democratic legitimacy.[19] In the same period and in the past years, the ECJ case law on the free movement of persons and services surpassed the economic aspects of the common market in order to make nationals of member states more integrated within the social context of the host country even in their human dimension.[20]

As already stated in Article 17 of the Treaty establishing the European Community (TEC), in the text following the entry into force of the Treaty of Amsterdam, EU citizenship derives from nationality of a member state and is then automatically acquired.[21] It is complementary and does not replace national citizenship. Nationality of a member state is thus a necessary condition for the enjoyment of the status of Union citizen and of the rights conferred in this regard. The Treaty of Lisbon, in Article 9 of the Treaty on European Union (TEU), states that 'citizenship of the Union shall be additional to and not replace national citizenship'.[22]

The citizens of the EU hold the rights currently set out in Article 20 of the Treaty on the Functioning of the European Union (TFEU),[23] and clarified in Articles 21–4: the rights to move and reside freely within the territory of the member states, subject to the limitations and conditions laid down in the Treaties and by the measures adopted to give them effect;[24] the rights to vote and to stand as candidates in elections to the European Parliament and in municipal elections in their member state of residence, of which they may not be nationals, under the same conditions as nationals of that state;[25] the right to enjoy the protection of the diplomatic or consular authorities of any member state, on the same conditions as the nationals of that state, in the territory of a country outside of the EU, if the member state of which they are nationals is not represented;[26] the rights to petition the European Parliament and to apply to the European Ombudsman, in accordance with Articles 227 and 228 of the TFEU itself;[27] and the right to write to any of the institutions and bodies of the EU in one of the official languages and to have an answer in the same language.[28] Not less than one million citizens who are nationals of a significant number of member states may also take the initiative of inviting the European Commission, within the framework of its powers, to submit any appropriate proposal on matters on where citizens consider that a legal act of the Union is required for the purposes of implementing the Treaties.[29]

The catalogue of Article 20 TFEU, however, is not exhaustive; on one hand, it can be expanded under Article 25 TFEU (stipulating that the Council, acting unanimously in accordance with a special legislative procedure and after obtaining the consent of the European Parliament, may adopt provisions to strengthen or to add to those rights); on the other hand, the same Article 20 states that citizens of the EU shall enjoy the rights and be subject to the duties provided for in the Treaties.[30] Therefore, EU citizens also have additional rights: the right to non-discrimination on grounds of nationality or based on sex, racial or ethnic origin, religion or belief, disability, age, or sexual orientation;[31] the right to exercise fundamental economic freedoms, such as freedom of movement for workers, the right of establishment, and the freedom to provide services;[32] the right to equal pay for male and female workers for equal work or work of equal value;[33] and the protection offered by legislation adopted under the provisions of the Treaty on social policy. Moreover, while some of the rights listed in Article 20 TFEU may be exercised directly against the institutions of the EU, member states themselves must guarantee to the citizens of the EU within their territories a great many of the rights that derive from their status as EU citizens. This aspect emphasizes even more the unique and complex nature of EU citizenship.[34]

European citizenship is also envisaged by Articles 39–46 of the Charter of Fundamental Rights of the European Union (EU Charter) proclaimed in Strasbourg on 12 December 2007.[35] Title V of the EU Charter ('Citizens' Rights') incorporates and arranges the same rights enumerated in Article 20 TFEU. The right to good administration and the right of access to documents of the institutions, bodies, offices, and agencies of the Union, are added to the rights of the TFEU.[36]

Nationality of a member state and citizenship of the EU

The ECJ has dealt many times with the issue of the citizenship of the EU, with particular reference to its definition, legal scope, and the many aspects related to the rights of movement and residence, the right to vote, the principle of equal treatment, and the prohibition of discrimination on grounds of nationality. Very often, the judgments of the ECJ argue that:

> Union citizenship is destined to be the fundamental status of nationals of the Member States, enabling those who find themselves in the same situation to enjoy the same treatment in law irrespective of their nationality, subject to such exceptions as are expressly provided for.[37]

This statement should be seen as a further token of the constitutionalization of EU citizenship, of the evolving nature of that status, and of the effects it can have on European law.

The ECJ has also dealt with the relationships among the citizenship of the EU and the nationalities of member states. In this regard, when the citizenship of the EU was introduced, some member states feared that it might interfere with state competence concerning the conditions for the acquisition and loss of national citizenship, even if exercised in conformity with international law.[38] Consequently, in the Declaration on nationality of a member state annexed to the Final Act of the Treaty of Maastricht, it was clearly indicated:

> The Conference declares that, wherever in the Treaty establishing the European Community reference is made to nationals of the Member States, the question whether an individual possesses the nationality of a Member State shall be settled solely by reference to the national law of the Member State concerned. Member States may declare, for information, who are to be considered their nationals for Community purposes.[39]

A decision of the heads of state and government, meeting within the European Council of Edinburgh of 11 and 12 December 1992, concerning problems raised by Denmark on the TEU, also declared that:

> The provisions of Part Two of the Treaty establishing the European Community relating to citizenship of the Union give nationals of the

> Member States additional rights and protection as specified in that Part. They do not in any way take the place of national citizenship. The question whether an individual possesses the nationality of a Member State will be settled solely by reference to the national law of the Member State concerned.[40]

The *Micheletti* case is very interesting in this respect.[41] A Spanish judge, the *Tribunal Superior de Justicia* of Cantabria, asked the Court to determine if the then Articles 3(c), 7, 52, 53, and 56 of the Treaty establishing the European Economic Community (TEEC), the Council Directive 73/148/EEC on the abolition of restrictions on movement and residence within the Community for nationals of member states with regard to establishment and the provision of services,[42] and the relevant provisions of secondary law on the free movement of persons and freedom of establishment could be interpreted

> as being compatible and thus as allowing the application of domestic legislation which does not recognize the 'Community rights' inherent to a person's status as a national of another Member State of the EEC merely because that person simultaneously possesses the nationality of a non-member country and that country was the place of his habitual residence, his last residence or his actual residence.[43]

The ECJ stated that, in accordance with international law, it is for each member state, having due regard to EC (now EU) law, to lay down the conditions for the acquisition and loss of nationality. The need to exercise state competences in respect of EU law is expressed in *Micheletti*, which prohibits the legislation of a member state from restricting the effects that flow from the grant of the nationality of another member state by imposing an additional condition for recognition of that nationality, with a view to the exercise of the fundamental freedoms provided for in the Treaties.[44]

The clarification contained in the *Micheletti* case was later emphasized in many other judgments concerning the free movement of persons, such as *Mesbah*, *Kaur*, and *Zhu and Chen*.[45] In particular, in *Zhu and Chen* the Court took care of the difficulties that can arise in relations among the rights of free movement and residence, as a result of the acquisition of the nationality of a member state, and the competence of that state. By accepting the opinion of Advocate-General Antonio Tizzano,[46] the ECJ, on the basis of the TEC provisions on EU citizenship, recognized the rights of movement and residence in the member states to a Chinese woman, the mother of a four-year-old Irish child. Mrs Chen, together with her husband, also a Chinese national, decided to have a second child, in contrast with the policy of containment of births (the one-child policy) implemented by the People's Republic of China. To escape such a policy, Mrs Chen entered the United Kingdom when she was about six months pregnant. The birth being near, she went to Belfast, where her daughter was born on 16 September 2000.

The choice of Belfast was made with a very specific purpose. Under section 6(1) of the Irish Nationality and Citizenship Act of 1956, which was amended in 2001 and applies retroactively from 2 December 1999, Ireland allows any person born on the island of Ireland to acquire Irish nationality. Under section 6(3), a person born on the island of Ireland is an Irish citizen from birth if he or she is not entitled to citizenship of any other country. The intent of Mrs Chen was to give birth to an Irish daughter and then to settle with her in the United Kingdom (which, unlike Ireland, does not award citizenship *jure soli*). The secretary of state for Home Department of the United Kingdom, however, refused to grant Mrs Chen and her daughter a long-term residence permit, considering that Mrs Chen was not entitled to reside in the United Kingdom under regulations of the TEC, and her daughter was not exercising any rights arising from the TEC such as those laid down by Regulation 5(1) of the Immigration (European Economic Area) Regulations 2000.[47]

For the ECJ, the acquisition of the Irish nationality in these circumstances is not unlawful, in accordance with the principle already established in *Micheletti*, according to which a member state is not permitted to limit the effects resulting from the attribution of the nationality by another member state by imposing an additional condition for recognition of that nationality, with a view of the exercise of fundamental freedoms provided for in the Treaty. Therefore, Article 18 TEC and Council Directive 90/364/EEC[48] confer the right of residence for an indefinite period on a young minor who is a national of a member state, is covered by appropriate sickness insurance, and is in the care of a parent who is a third-country national having sufficient resources for that minor not to become a burden on the public finances of the host member state. Those same provisions allow a parent who is that minor's primary caretaker to reside with the child in the host member state.[49]

The complexity of the connections that exist among the nationality of a member state and the citizenship of the EU has been further emphasized by the *Rottmann* case.[50] *Rottmann* was the first opportunity of the ECJ to examine the extent of the autonomy that member states have in establishing the conditions for acquisition and loss of their national citizenship. The case also assessed whether member states can, or cannot, exercise their discretionary power outside of the control of the EU. The ECJ was asked to clarify if the decision of a member state (Germany) to withdraw the naturalization of Mr Rottmann, an Austrian national, would be contrary to EU law in general, and to Article 17 TEC (Article 20 TFEU) in particular. The decision to withdraw Mr Rottmann's German citizenship made him stateless, and caused him to lose EU citizenship and the rights derived from that citizenship. Mr Rottmann lost his original citizenship as a result of an application for naturalization, pursuant to the laws on nationality in force at that time in the state of his former nationality and in the state of naturalization. Withdrawal of Mr Rottmann's citizenship by Germany was due to a deception committed by the applicant during the naturalization procedure, as he failed to mention the proceedings opened against him in Austria for suspected, serious fraud on an occupational basis in the exercise of his profession.[51] Reaffirming the principle that member states are competent to establish rules concerning the acquisition and loss of their nationality, even though they must still act in accordance with European law, the ECJ held that the member state of naturalization is entitled to withdraw it if acquired fraudulently. The ECJ stated, however, that any decision to withdraw nationality must observe the principle of proportionality, without specifying if, under Article 17 TEC, national authorities wishing to withdraw naturalization could be forced to suspend the withdrawal procedure to allow citizens of the EU to seek to recover their original citizenship.[52] The *Rottmann* case can be considered as a confirmation of the complementary nature of EU citizenship in respect of nationalities of member states; building upon the obligations incumbent on the member states with regard to the principle of proportionality, the case pointed out how European citizenship affects the sovereigns' right to define their nationals.[53]

A new stage in defining the significance of the citizenship of the EU: the *Ruiz Zambrano* case

Other more recent judgments on citizenship are particularly important in strengthening the supranational character of the EU. The ECJ took a very significant stance in the *Ruiz Zambrano* case, also in the path of development that seeks to give meaning to the above-mentioned statement, according to which 'Union citizenship is destined to be the fundamental status of nationals of the Member States'.[54] The *Ruiz Zambrano* case seems to emphasize a new approach to EU citizenship and the rights that stem from that citizenship, since the case aims at overcoming the privileged connection with the exercise of freedom of movement and opens up some new perspectives. The applicant, a third-country national, was father of two children that were born in Belgium. Both children had acquired Belgian nationality, and were therefore citizens of the EU even though they had never exercised their freedom of movement. The Belgian authorities refused to grant the applicant and his wife a residence permit in their capacity as ascendants of Belgian nationals, thus Mr Ruiz Zambrano claimed instead to be holder of a right of residence directly by virtue of the TEC or at least, of a derived right of residence, recognized in the above mentioned *Zhu and Chen* case for the ascendants of a minor child who is a national of a member state.[55]

On the one hand, *Ruiz Zambrano* stands in continuity with *Zhu and Chen*, because of the recognition of the rights stemming from citizenship of the EU in favour of a minor, in connection with the request made by a third-country national, who is the caretaker of the child, to be granted a right of residence in a member state. On the other hand, however, unlike *Zhu and Chen*, whose situation appeared, at least formally, to fulfil a requirement of transnationality, the Ruiz Zambrano family had never moved from Belgium. For this reason, the questions referred for a preliminary ruling from the *Tribunal du travail* of Brussels show the difficulty of breaking away from the logic that binds the rights associated with EU citizenship to the exercise of freedom of movement and residence. The referring Court from Brussels asked essentially whether the provisions of the TFEU on EU citizenship are to be interpreted to confer on a third-country national, and ascendant relative of minors with EU citizenship, a right of residence in the member state of which they are nationals and in which they reside; also, the Court was asked whether the third-country nationals were exempt from having to obtain a work permit in that member state.[56] Any reference to the exercise of freedom of movement and residence is therefore avoided, while the reasoning is solely set on the basis of Article 20 TFEU, which recognizes EU citizenship to all those who have the nationality of a member state. By virtue of the national law, Mr Ruiz Zambrano's children legitimately acquired Belgian nationality, and consequently the status of Union citizens. On this aspect, therefore, the ECJ focused its arguments in order to give substance to the statement that Union citizenship is destined to be the fundamental status of nationals of the member states.[57]

Recalling *Rottmann*, the Court stated that Article 20 TFEU precludes national measures which have the effect of depriving EU citizens of the genuine enjoyment of the substance of the rights conferred by virtue of their status of citizens of the Union. A refusal to grant a right of residence to a third-country national with dependent minor children in the member state where those children are nationals and reside, and also a refusal to grant such a person a work permit, lead to a situation where those children, citizens of the Union, would have to leave the territory of the Union in order to accompany their parents. Similarly, if a work permit is not granted to such persons, they would risk not having sufficient resources to provide for themselves and their families, which would also result in the children, citizens of the Union, having to leave the territory of the Union. In these circumstances, those citizens of the Union 'would, in fact, be unable to exercise the substance of the rights conferred on them by virtue of their status as citizens of the Union'.[58]

Through the interpretation of Article 20 TFEU, therefore, the Court directly recognizes rights, stemming from the citizenship of the EU, which can be applied even against one's own member states. In this respect, the opinion of Advocate-General Eleanor Sharpston is relevant; she tried to define exactly what is involved in the Union citizenship and what these rights mean.[59] Advocate-General Sharpston considered the role of the freedom of movement and the possibility to invoke the rights connected to citizenship even in relation to 'purely internal situations'. She also considered the issues of equal treatment in terms of reverse discriminations against nationals of the member state and the implications of the protection of fundamental rights on the provisions of the Treaty concerning European citizenship. Through an extensive analysis of the relevant case law,

Advocate-General Sharpston suggested that, despite the undeniable importance due to the freedom of movement, the exercise of rights deriving from citizenship of the EU is not 'always inextricably and necessarily bound up with physical movement'.[60] The interpretation of 'the right to move and reside freely within the territory of the Member States', enshrined in Articles 20(2)(a) and 21(1) TFEU, is thus not confined to situations in which the citizen of the EU has first moved to another member state. On the contrary, the terms 'move' and 'reside' can be read disjunctively so that a European citizen is not disbarred from invoking such rights when he resides (without prior movement) in his member state of nationality.[61]

The *McCarthy* case

Does the logic of *Ruiz Zambrano*, which made reference to the rights of citizens under the age of majority and, consequently, to the position of parents who take care of them, also apply in other situations, such as those concerning the spouse of a third-country national or another family member? The opportunity to answer this question arrived with the *McCarthy* case.[62] The case involved a national of the United Kingdom, Mrs McCarthy, also an Irish national, who was born and always lived in the United Kingdom, and had never argued she has been a worker, self-employed person, or self-sufficient person, so that she enjoyed social benefits. In 2002, Mrs McCarthy married a Jamaican national who had no right to remain in the United Kingdom under the immigration rules of that member state. Following her marriage, Mrs McCarthy applied for the first time for an Irish passport, and obtained it. Later, in 2004, she applied with her husband to the British authorities for a residence permit and a residence document under EU law as, respectively, a citizen of the EU and the spouse of a citizen of the EU. The application was refused by the secretary of state for the Home Department on the ground that Mrs McCarthy was not a 'qualified person' (i.e. not a worker, self-employed or self-sufficient person) and, accordingly, her husband was not the spouse of a 'qualified person'. Mrs McCarthy appealed against this decision before the Asylum and Immigration Tribunal, then before the Court of Appeal (Civil Division) (England and Wales), and finally before the Supreme Court of the United Kingdom.[63] First, the matter was referred to the ECJ in order to know if a person of dual Irish and British nationality, who has resided for her entire life in the United Kingdom, could be regarded as 'beneficiary' within the meaning of Article 3 of the European Parliament and Council Directive 2004/38/EC on the right of citizens of the Union and their family members to move and reside freely within the territory of the member states.[64] Second, the case was referred to the Court in order to determine if such a person 'resided legally' within the host member state for the purpose of Article 16 of that Directive in circumstances where she was unable to satisfy the requirements of Article 7 of the same Directive.[65]

These events are the obvious attempt of Mrs McCarthy to obtain recognition of the right of residence under European law in her national country where she always resided, in order to allow her husband, a third-country national, to obtain the right of residence under Directive 2004/38/EC as a family member of a European citizen, right that he would not be entitled to have under national legislation. The peculiarity is that Mrs McCarthy enjoyed dual nationality, and under this circumstance asked for the implementation of Directive 2004/38/EC, despite never having exercised freedom of movement, and with reference to the member state of which she was a national and where she had always resided. In her opinion, Advocate-General Juliane Kokott maintained that Mrs McCarthy's hypothesis can be seen as a sort of 'cherry picking' because, thanks to dual nationality, EU citizens enjoy the advantages of Directive 2004/38/EC as regards family reunification in respect of their spouses, without meeting the objectives of the Directive (namely to give effect to and facilitate free movement), and without being subject to any of the Directive's conditions, i.e. the requirement of economic self-sufficiency under Article 7(1) of the same Directive.[66]

The brief description of the events show that the rejection of Mrs McCarthy's request was indeed caused by the failure to meet the criteria imposed by the Directive for the residence in the host country (especially in terms of economic resources), an aspect to which the second question proposed by the national court refers. The ECJ, however, focused on the broader issue underlying this case, that is, reformulating the first question to ask

> whether Article 3(1) of Directive 2004/38 or Article 21 TFEU is applicable to the situation of a Union citizen who has never exercised his right of free movement, who has always resided in a Member State of which he is a national and who is also a national of another Member State.[67]

As in *Ruiz Zambrano*, then, the prospect re-emerges of an extensive enforcement of Article 21 and Directive 2004/38/EC in order to ensure the enjoyment of the rights conferred by these legal instruments, even against the state of residence and nationality, regardless of the exercise of freedom of movement. In this case, the Court addressed the issue in a direct and articulate way, and concluded, with regard to the applicability of Article 3(1) of Directive 2004/38/EC to a person like Mrs McCarthy, that 'a literal, teleological and contextual interpretation of that provision leads to a negative reply to the question'.[68]

As a preliminary point, the ECJ emphasizes two details that help to define the relationship among the rights conferred by national citizenship and those arising from European citizenship. On the one hand, citizenship of the Union confers to each Union citizen a primary and individual right to move and reside freely within the territory of the member states, subject to the limitations and restrictions laid down by the Treaties and the secondary legislation. Freedom of movement for persons is, moreover, one of the fundamental freedoms of the internal market, which is also reaffirmed in Article 45 of the EU Charter. Directive 2004/38/EC aims to facilitate the exercise of such a primary and individual right.[69] On the other hand, the Court held that a principle of international law, reaffirmed in Article 3 of Protocol No. 4 to the ECHR mentioned above, 'that European Union law cannot be assumed to disregard in the context of relations between Member States, precludes a Member State from refusing its own nationals the right to enter its territory and remain there for any reason', and 'also precludes that Member State from expelling its own nationals from its territory or refusing their right to reside in that territory or making such right conditional'.[70] In this framework, according to the Court, Directive 2004/38/EC cannot be interpreted in the terms envisaged by Mrs McCarthy. It covers the conditions for the exercise of freedom to move and reside freely within the territory of the member states and, therefore, 'cannot apply to a Union citizen who enjoys an unconditional right of residence due to the fact that he resides in the Member State of which he is a national'.[71] According to the Court, 'the residence to which it refers is linked to the exercise of the freedom of movement for persons',[72] and this conclusion does not change if citizens of the EU possess a dual nationality, because the fact that Union citizens are nationals of more than one member state does not mean that they have made use of their right of freedom of movement.[73]

Then, reversing the logical order that one might have expected, the Court addresses the question of applicability of Article 21 TFEU, by extending its reasoning to Article 20 TFEU and to the interpretation carried out in *Ruiz Zambrano*. Explicitly confirming a settled case law and a unitary reading of Article 21 focused on the freedom of movement, it stated that the Treaty rules governing freedom of movement for persons and the measures adopted to implement them 'cannot be applied to situations which have no factor linking them with any of the situations governed by European Union law and which are confined in all relevant respects within a single Member State'.[74] However, and this is a confirmation of *Ruiz Zambrano*, 'the situation of a Union citizen who, like Mrs McCarthy, has not made use of the right to freedom of movement cannot, for that reason alone, be assimilated to a purely internal situation'.[75] Once again, the fundamental role of the status of European citizen is reaffirmed, with the result that Article 20 TFEU must be interpreted to mean that the Article precludes national measures which have the effect of depriving Union citizens of the real and effective enjoyment of the substance of the rights conferred by virtue of that status.[76]

Citizenship of the EU and the Charter of Fundamental Rights: the *Dereci and Others* case

With the judgment in the *Dereci and Others* case, the Grand Chamber of the ECJ faced again the claim of the status of EU citizen by persons that have not yet exercised their right to free movement.[77] The reference for a preliminary ruling, proposed by the Austrian *Verwaltungsgerichtshof*, originated from five proceedings with similar problems in terms of the possible relevance of EU law. All the applicants were third-country nationals (coming from Nigeria, Serbia, Sri Lanka, and Turkey) who wished to live with their respective family members that were Austrian nationals (i.e. EU citizens) residing in Austria. As in *Ruiz Zambrano*, none of the citizens of the Union concerned had yet exercised the right to free movement. However, unlike *Ruiz Zambrano*, there was no risk that the EU citizens would be deprived of their means of subsistence; rather, in two of those cases, the applicants were in a situation of economic dependence from the citizen of the Union. All the applicants in the main proceedings had their applications for residence in Austria rejected. In addition, the applicants already residing in Austria had been subject to expulsion and to individual removal orders from the Austrian territory.[78] In this context, the national court asked to ascertain whether the refusal to grant the third-country nationals a right of residence could be interpreted as leading to a denial of the genuine enjoyment of the substance of the rights conferred to their family members by virtue of their status as citizens of the EU.[79]

It is clear that the reference was intended by the Austrian judge to clarify whether the fundamental right to respect for private and family life under Article 7 of the EU Charter and Article 8(1) ECHR, constitutes an integrant part of the status of EU citizen. As in *McCarthy*, the ECJ reiterated the need for a strict reading of the *Ruiz Zambrano* case. First, the Court excluded the possibility of applying the Council Directive 2003/86/EC on the right to family reunification,[80] as well as Directive 2004/38/EC.[81] The Court also considered whether, notwithstanding this inapplicability, the Union citizens concerned by the disputes could rely on the provisions of the Treaty regarding citizenship of the EU.[82] It should be noted that, although the appellants in the main proceedings were third-country nationals, the Court's attention turned to their family members, citizens of the Union. It is well known that the Treaty rules governing freedom of movement of persons and the measures adopted to implement them cannot be applied to situations that have no factor linking them with any of the situations governed by EU law and that are confined in all relevant respects within a single member state.[83] However, whereas the citizenship of the EU is meant to become the fundamental status of nationals of the member states, the situation of a Union citizen who has not made use of the right to freedom of movement cannot, for that reason alone, be assimilated to a purely internal situation. Still, the Court reiterated that Article 20 TFEU precludes national measures that have the effect of depriving Union citizens of the genuine enjoyment of the substance of the rights conferred by that status.[84] The Court further clarified that the criterion relating to the denial of the genuine enjoyment of the substance of the rights ascribed to EU citizens is specific in character and refers exceptionally to situations in which, although secondary legislation on the right of residence of third-country nationals is not applicable, a right of residence may not be refused. Otherwise, citizens of the EU may be forced to leave not only the territory of the member state of which they are nationals, but also the territory of the Union as a whole.[85]

Therefore, EU law and its provisions on citizenship of the EU do not preclude a member state from refusing to allow third-country nationals to reside on its territory, even when third-country nationals wish to reside with a member of their family, who is a citizen of the Union and a resident and national of that member state, but who has never exercised the right to freedom of movement. This scenario is permitted, provided that such a refusal does not lead, for the Union citizens concerned, to the denial of the genuine enjoyment of the substance of the rights conferred by virtue of their status as a citizen of the Union, which is a matter for a national court to verify.[86]

As regards the right to respect for private and family life, the ECJ confirms that, if EU law applies, Article 7 of the EU Charter should be respected, recalling that the meaning and scope of Article 7 are to be the same as those laid down by Article 8(1) ECHR, as interpreted by the case law of the European Court of Human Rights. The provisions of the EU Charter are, according to Article 51(1) thereof, addressed to the member states only when they are implementing EU law. The EU Charter does not extend the field of application of EU law, nor does it establish new powers or tasks for the Union itself, or modify such powers and tasks as defined in the Treaties. Accordingly, the Court has been called upon 'to interpret, in the light of the Charter, the law of the European Union within the limits of the powers conferred on it'.[87] Moreover, according to the ECJ, if the referring court had considered, in the light of the circumstances of the disputes in the main proceedings, that the situation of the applicants was covered by EU law, it should have examined whether the refusal of their right of residence undermines the right to respect for private and family life provided for in Article 7 of the EU Charter. On the other hand, if the referring court took the view that that situation was not covered by EU law, it should undertake that analysis in the light of Article 8(1) ECHR.[88] The significance of the statement by the ECJ is rather unclear, especially taking into account, as the ECJ expressly asked to do, the circumstances of the disputes in the main proceedings. In the first part of its argument, in fact, the Court already excluded that the applicants' situation could fall under Directive 2003/86/EC or Directive 2004/38/EC. The statement could then have a general character and be aimed at reaffirming the obvious: if the situation falls within the EU law, fundamental rights guaranteed by it are relied upon/referred to. However, the double reference to the circumstances of the disputes seems to exclude this interpretation. Given that the preliminary ruling originated from five separate national proceedings, it can be assumed that the Court has asked the national judge to verify the factual circumstances of the different applicants' position, possibly distinguishing among them, in order to assess whether in some of these cases the denial of the residence permit would actually have the effect of forcing the family member, who is also a Union citizen, to leave the territory of the Union itself.

Concluding remarks

The concept of EU citizenship is obviously becoming more elaborate thanks to the ECJ case law, which uses this concept as a means to expand the substantive scope *ratione materiae* and *ratione personae* of EU law.[89] In this sense, the citizenship of the EU puts into action the rights and freedoms recognized by the Treaties. In the past, this transformation did not occur due to citizenship itself, but due to an additional condition, the movement of the citizen or any other link between member states, without which situations were classified as 'purely internal' and were thus excluded from the scope of application of EC (now EU) law.[90] Currently, it is possible to see a gradual erosion of the link between citizenship of the EU and Article 18 TFEU (Article 12 TEC). Whereas at first, EU citizens enjoyed only the rights to move and reside without discrimination, the Court seems now to admit that an actual or even a potential obstacle to citizens' rights to move and reside are probably contrary to EU law, despite the non-discriminatory character they could have.[91] In this regard, *Rottmann* is a very relevant example. Advocate-General Miguel Poiares Maduro stressed that the *Rottmann* case had a link with EU law, inasmuch as it had been caused by the movement of an Austrian national to Germany.[92] The Court, however, did not consider this factor. Rather, the Court emphasized that an act which constitutes a deprivation of citizenship was, because of its nature and its consequences, part of EU law and would have affected the rights conferred by EU law. In *Ruiz Zambrano*, the situation of the children, equally, is far from being 'purely internal', because the denial of residence and work permits to their father is a clear obstacle to their potential and future movements. The reasoning of *Rottmann* is thus transposable to *Ruiz Zambrano*. The minors, in fact, were not in danger of losing their status as EU citizens. Their citizenship would remain intact, as well as, in theory, the rights relating to it, although it is undoubted that, after the refusal of Belgian authorities, the minors would not have been able to enjoy these rights. The intention of the ECJ to introduce a new category of rights attached to EU citizenship is also confirmed by *McCarthy*.

Rottmann, *Ruiz Zambrano*, and *McCarthy*, however, lend themselves to various criticisms, because even the significant openings to promote the European integration process are moderated by immediately subsequent passages characterized by a greater prudence. *Rottmann* shows a very cautious attitude in the Court. On the one hand, a decision withdrawing naturalization because of deception corresponds to a reason relating to a public interest recognized both by EU and international law (Convention on the Reduction of Statelessness of 30 August 1961; European Convention on Nationality of

6 November 1997).[93] The legitimacy of the withdrawal is thus admitted even when it results in statelessness for the citizen of the EU involved. In this regard, the test of proportionality is used to limit and to control the discretionary power of member states in giving or withdrawing their nationality.[94] On the other hand, the Court asked the national court (the German *Bundesverwaltungsgericht*) to verify the compliance with the principle of proportionality as regards the consequences for the person involved and to assess whether the observance of the principle of proportionality should delay the effectiveness of the withdrawal in order to allow the EU citizen to try to recover his nationality of origin.[95] In this regard, it is possible to wonder about how national authorities can evaluate the degree of proportionality of the decisions on the permanent withdrawal of citizenship that will be issued. The Court also did not clarify whether Article 17 TEC (Article 20 TFEU) obliges or not member states to interpret their national law so as to avoid the loss of EU citizenship and to allow the revival of the national citizenship previously possessed.[96]

The above-mentioned judgment is thus a missed opportunity, as it could have been better to emphasize the autonomy of the legal and political notion of 'citizenship of the EU' than that of 'national citizenship'. The clear autonomy of the citizenship of the EU is also a landmark achievement of the Treaty of Lisbon, since, under Article 9 TEU and Article 20 TFEU, EU citizenship 'shall be additional' to national citizenship (and no longer a 'complement' to national citizenship, as Article 17 TEC previously stipulated), and would so acquire its own self-expressive value of specific rights and duties.[97] A situation in which the withdrawal of national citizenship determines the statelessness of the person (a former European citizen) is not compatible either with this evolution, or with the new emphasis with which the Treaty of Lisbon addresses the citizenship of the EU and all its related aspects. Through the loss of national citizenship, member states deprive individuals of their rights of direct and indirect democratic participation. Statelessness has also a negative effect on the system of protection of fundamental rights and freedoms (such as equality and free movement rights) and on the protection of social rights guaranteed to EU citizens.[98]

A degree of caution was also taken by the Court in the *McCarthy* case. The national decisions against Mrs McCarthy were in fact not deemed to infringe the rights stemming from EU citizenship, in particular the right to move and reside freely within the territory of the member states under Article 21 TFEU. The comparison with *Ruiz Zambrano*, which confirms the fundamental role played by freedom of movement and residence in defining the content of EU citizenship, is particularly interesting. While, as seen above, the measures taken by the Belgian authorities could either force the minors to leave the Union, or deprive them of the support of their parents who were their caretakers, *McCarthy* did not demonstrate a situation of this type, since Mrs McCarthy, by virtue of national citizenship, had an unconditional right of residence in the United Kingdom.[99]

The Court confirms the approach followed in *Ruiz Zambrano*, but does not provide in *McCarthy* further food for thought. It is not clear what rights, beyond the rights of movement and residence, can be asserted directly against the member state on the basis of the citizenship of the EU. Only with reference to minor children it is probably possible to imagine situations that force the European citizen to leave the Union, and which Article 20 TFEU precludes. However, it might also be asked what conditions of life the EU should guarantee to EU citizens residing in its territory, or whether the right of residence in the Union could imply the recognition of a similar right for the spouse who is a third-country national, in order to ensure family reunification and the right to family life. In *Ruiz Zambrano* and *McCarthy* the Court chose to ground its reasoning on the interpretation of Article 20 TFEU and therefore on EU citizenship, but did not seem to be ready to define EU citizenship beyond the freedom of movement and residence and the prohibition of being forced to leave the Union.[100]

The *Dereci and Others* case confirms that there are exceptional situations in which citizens of the EU would effectively be deprived of the enjoyment of their rights because of the refusal to grant a residence permit to their family members who are third-country nationals, and where this refusal would therefore be contrary to EU law. The Court also notes that Article 7 of the EU Charter can be activated only under Article 51(1) of the EU Charter. It is therefore necessary that there is an implementation of EU law by member states (excepting a purely internal situation or a non-application of EU law), and that a national court considers the positions of national applicants subject to European law.[101] Because of this clarification, the applicability of fundamental rights is even more specific, and this could make it more difficult for applicants to assert fundamental rights in favour of their claim to residence.[102]

A link with the EU Charter in this regard has also been suggested very recently by Advocate-General Verica Trstenjak in her opinion on the case *Iida*; while recalling that the EU Charter applies only in connection with the implementation of EU law,[103] she upheld the right of residence of a third-country national in order to guarantee fundamental rights in an effective manner.[104] In the light of the fundamental rights under Article 6(1) and (3) TEU, and of those enshrined in Articles 7 and 24(3) of the EU Charter, Advocate-General Trstenjak asserted that a parent who has a right of custody and is a third-country national could have, in order to maintain a personal relationship and a direct parental contact on a regular basis, a right of residence in the member state of origin of his child, who is a Union citizen, under Articles 20 and 21 TFEU, if the child has moved from there to another member state, by exercising his right of free movement.[105]

Dereci and Others seems to refer to the rights of European citizenship as a whole. This clearly implies the Court's decision to supply a literal, teleological, and contextual interpretation of the scope of EU citizenship,[106] and further indicates the willingness of judges to interpret freely the text of the

Treaties for the pursuit of European citizenship as the 'fundamental status' for nationals of member states.[107] *Dereci and Others*, therefore, does not make a distinction between family relationships in applying the criterion of 'genuine enjoyment'. While *Ruiz Zambrano* may have suggested the dependence of the child on a parent, and *McCarthy* the importance of the marital relationship, this distinction has no place in *Dereci and Others*, since the family members of the applicants had all reached the age of majority or were economically independent.[108] The judgment also does not resolve the ambiguity (pointed out in *Ruiz Zambrano*) surrounding the application of the 'sufficient resources' criterion imposed on the third-country national, who is a family member of the citizen of the EU, as an essential requirement for a family reunification.[109] It is to be hoped that the Court will provide for a further clarification on this point with the expected decisions regarding the currently pending cases *O and S* and *L*, in which the Finnish Supreme Administrative Court (*Korkein hallinto-oikeus*) has asked to determine if Article 20 TFEU precludes a third-country national from being refused a residence permit because of lack of means of subsistence, in a family situation in which a child, who is a citizen of the Union, is cared for by the third-country national's spouse, but the third-country national is not that child's parent or caretaker.[110]

Notes

1 See 'Nationality', in *Encyclopaedia Britannica.* Online. Available at: www.britannica.com (accessed 20 April 2012).

2 UDHR, 10 December 1948. Online. Available at: www.un.org (accessed 20 April 2012).

3 See 'Citizenship', in *Encyclopaedia Britannica.* Online.

4 ICRMW, 18 December 1990, UNTS, vol. 2220, No. 39481.

5 See Article 3 of the Protocol No. 4 to the ECHR, 16 September 1963, CETS 46.

6 See ACHR, 22 November 1969, OAS Treaty Series, No. 36, Article 23.

7 1992 Convention, CETS 144.

8 League of Arab States, ArCHR, 22 May 2004, reprinted in *Boston University International Law Journal* 24, 2006, 147–64.

9 Mercosur is an economic and political agreement among Argentina, Brazil, Paraguay, Uruguay and Venezuela (Bolivia, Chile, Colombia, Ecuador and Peru currently have an associate member status). Founded by the Treaty of Asunción of 26 March 1991, which was later amended and updated by the Treaty of Ouro Preto of 16 December 1994, it has the purpose to promote free trade and the fluid movement of goods, persons and currency. SADC, a successor of the former Southern African Development Coordination Conference, is an intergovernmental organization that intends to pursue a further socio-economic cooperation and integration as well as a political and security cooperation among 15 southern African states (Angola, Botswana, Democratic Republic of the Congo, Lesotho, Madagascar, Malawi, Mauritius, Mozambique, Namibia, Seychelles, South Africa, Swaziland, Tanzania, Zambia and Zimbabwe). It complements the role of the African Union.

10 Regularization and Residence Agreements (International Migratory Regularization of Mercosur Citizens; International Migratory Regularization of Citizens of Mercosur, Bolivia and Chile; Residence for Nationals of the Member States of Mercosur; Residence for Nationals of the Member States of Mercosur, Bolivia and Chile), 5 and 6 December 2002. Online. Available at: www.mercosur.int (accessed 28 April 2012).

11 See M.B. Olmos Giupponi, 'Citizenship, Migration and Regional Integration: Re-shaping Citizenship Conceptions in the Southern Cone', *European Journal of Legal Studies* 4, 2011, 104–36.

12 Constitutive Protocol of the Parliament of the Mercosur, 9 December 2005. Online. Available at: www.mercosur.int (accessed 28 April 2012).

13 Protocol on the Facilitation of Movement of Persons, 18 August 2005. Online. Available at: www.sadc.int (accessed 2 May 2012).

14 Articles 12–20 of the Protocol on the Facilitation of Movement of Persons of 2005. See K. Matlosa, 'Human Movements, Common Regional Citizenship and Identity in Southern Africa', *Policy, Issues & Actors* 19, 2006, 1–20.

15 K. Hailbronner, 'Nationality in Public International Law and European Law', in R. Bauböck, E. Ersbøll, K. Groenendijk and H. Waldrauch (eds) *Acquisition and Loss of Nationality, Policies and Trends in 15 European Countries*, Amsterdam: Amsterdam University Press, 2006, p. 36.

16 C. Closa, 'The Concept of Citizenship in the Treaty on European Union', *Common Market Law Review* 29, 1992, 1143–50 and 1168–9.

17 See F.G. Jacobs, 'Citizenship of the European Union: A Legal Analysis', *European Law Journal* 13, 2007, 591–610; D. Kostakopoulou, 'The Evolution of European Union Citizenship', *European Political Science* 7, 2008, 285–95; A. Dashwood, M. Dougan, B. Rodger, E. Spaventa and D. Wyatt, *Wyatt and Dashwood's European Union Law*, 6th edn, London: Sweet & Maxwell, 2011, pp. 461–96; F. Wollenschläger, 'A New Fundamental Freedom beyond Market Integration: Union Citizenship and Its Dynamics for Shifting the Economic Paradigm of European Integration', *European Law Journal* 17, 2011, 1–34.

18 Hailbronner, 'Nationality', p. 37.

19 Closa, 'The Concept of Citizenship', pp. 1153–7; F. Laursen and S. Vanhoonacker (eds) *The Intergovernmental Conference on Political Union: Institutional Reforms, New Policies and International Identity of the European Community*, Maastricht: Institute of Public Administration, 1992.

20 ECJ, C-9/74, *Casagrande v Landeshauptstadt München*, judgment of 3 July 1974, *ECR*, 1974, p. 773; C-293/83, *Gravier v Ville de Liège*, judgment of 13 February 1985, *ECR*, 1985, p. 593; C-186/87, *Cowan v Trésor public*, judgment of 2 February 1989, *ECR*, 1989, p. 195.

21 TEC (consolidated version 1997), *Official Journal of the European Communities* C 340, 10 November 1997.

22 TEU (consolidated version 2010), *Official Journal of the European Union* C 83, 30 March 2010.

23 TFEU (consolidated version 2010), *Official Journal of the European Union* C 83, 30 March 2010.

24 Article 21 TFEU.

25 Article 22 TFEU.

26 Article 23 TFEU.

27 Article 24 TFEU.

28 Article 24 TFEU. Moreover, the rights listed there are not all exclusively reserved for citizens of the EU. The right to petition the European Parliament and to apply to the European Ombudsman are guaranteed to all persons residing in the Union. The ECJ has expressly recognized that the rights listed in Article 20 do not depend all on EU citizenship or the nationality of a member state. The Union citizenship, as the fundamental status of nationals of member states, would not necessarily mean that the rights recognized by the TFEU are limited only to EU citizens. Although the right to vote and to stand as candidates in elections to the European Parliament and in municipal elections is included in Article 20 as a right of EU citizens, the definition of persons enjoying such rights falls under the competence of member states, with the result that they may possibly extend this right also to third-country nationals who have no more contacts with their country of origin.

29 Article 11(4) TEU.

30 However, the fact that EU citizens hold rights and duties (the latter ones, unspecified), is also recalled in the Preamble of the EU Charter (see below, note 35).

31 Articles 18 and 19 TFEU.

32 Articles 45, 49, and 56 TFEU.

33 Article 157 TFEU.

34 J. Shaw, 'Citizenship: Contrasting Dynamics at the Interface of Integration and Constitutionalism', in P. Craig and G. de Búrca (eds) *The Evolution of EU Law*, 2nd edn, Oxford: Oxford University Press, 2011, p. 575.

35 EU Charter, *Official Journal of the European Union* C 83, 30 March 2010.

36 Articles 41 and 42 of the EU Charter.

37 This principle was stated first in ECJ, C-184/99, *Grzelczyk v Centre public d'aide sociale d'Ottignies-Louvain-la-Neuve*, judgment of 20 September 2001, *ECR*, 2001, p. I-6193, para. 31.

38 Closa, 'The Concept of Citizenship', pp. 1153–7; S. O'Leary, *The Evolving Concept of Community Citizenship: From the Free Movement of Persons to Union Citizenship*, 2nd edn, The Hague–Boston: Kluwer Law International, 1996, p. 30.

39 Declaration on nationality of a member state, annexed to the Final Act of the Treaty of Maastricht, *Official Journal of the European Communities* C 191, 29 July 1992. See O'Leary, 'The Evolving Concept', pp. 39–40.

40 'Decision of the heads of state and government, meeting within the European Council of Edinburgh of 11 and 12 December 1992, concerning problems raised by Denmark on the Treaty on European Union', *Official Journal of the European Communities* C 21, 25 January 1993.

41 ECJ, C-369/90, *Mario Vicente Micheletti and Others v Delegación del Gobierno en Cantabria*, judgment of 7 July 1992, *ECR*, 1992, p. I-4258.

42 Council Directive 73/148/EEC of 21 May 1973, *Official Journal of the European Communities* L 172, 28 June 1973, 14.

43 ECJ, *Micheletti*, para. 6.

44 Ibid., paras 10 and 15. See also H.U. Jessurum d'Oliveira, 'Case C-369/90, *M. V. Micheletti and others v Delegación del Gobierno en Cantabria*, Judgment of 7 July 1992', *Common Market Law Review* 30, 1993, 623–37.

45 ECJ, C-179/98, *Belgian State v Fatna Mesbah*, judgment of 11 November 1999, *ECR*, 1999, p. I-7983; C-192/99, *The Queen v Secretary of State for the Home Department, ex parte Manjit Kaur*, judgment of 20 February 2001, *ECR*, 2001, p. I-1237; C-200/02, *Kunqian Catherine Zhu and Man Lavette Chen v Secretary of*

State for the Home Department, judgment (FC) of 19 October 2004, *ECR*, 2004, p. I-9925.

46 Opinion of Advocate-General Tizzano, delivered on 18 May 2004, *ECR*, 2004, p. I-9927.

47 ECJ, *Zhu and Chen*, paras 7–10.

48 Council Directive 90/364/EEC of 28 June 1990, on the right of residence, *Official Journal of the European Communities* L 180, 13 July 1990, 26.

49 ECJ, *Zhu and Chen*, paras 39 and 41. See also J.Y. Carlier, 'Case C-200/02, *Kunqian Catherine Zhu, Man Lavette Chen v Secretary of State for the Home Department*', *Common Market Law Review* 42, 2005, 1121–31; B. Hofstötter, 'A Cascade of Rights, or Who Shall Care for Little Catherine? Some Reflections on the Chen Case', *European Law Review* 30, 2005, 548–58; B. Kunoy, 'A Union of National Citizens: the Origins of the Court's Lack of Avant-Gardisme in the Chen Case', *Common Market Law Review* 43, 2006, 179–90.

50 ECJ, C-135/08, *Janko Rottmann v Freistaat Bayern*, judgment (GC) of 2 March 2010, *ECR*, 2010, p. I-1449.

51 Ibid., paras 22–35.

52 Ibid., paras 39, 59 and 64.

53 See D. Kochenov, 'Case C-135/08, *Janko Rottmann v Freistaat Bayern*, Judgment of the Court (Grand Chamber) of 2 March 2010', *Common Market Law Review* 47, 2010, 1831–46; A. Seling, 'Case C-135/08 *Janko Rottmann v Freistaat Bayern*, Judgment of the Court of Justice (Grand Chamber) of 2 March 2010, nyr-Towards a direct "droit de regard"?', *Maastricht Journal of European and Comparative Law* 17, 2010, 470–8; G.R. de Groot and A. Seling, 'Decision of 2 March 2010, Case C-135/08, *Janko Rottmann v Freistaat Bayern* – Case Note II – The Consequences of the Rottmann Judgment on Member State Autonomy – The European Court of Justice's Avant-Gardism in Nationality Matters', *European Constitutional Law Review* 7, 2011, 150–60; H.U. Jessurum d'Oliveira, 'Decision of 2 March 2010, Case C-135/08, *Janko Rottmann v Freistaat Bayern* – Case Note I – Decoupling Nationality and Union Citizenship?', *European Constitutional Law Review* 7, 2011, 138–49.

54 ECJ, C-34/09, *Gerardo Ruiz Zambrano v Office national de l'emploi (ONEm)*, judgment of 8 March 2011.

55 Ibid., paras 14–34.

56 Ibid., paras 35 and 36.

57 See K. Hailbronner and D. Thym, 'Case C-34/09, *Gerardo Ruiz Zambrano v Office national de l'emploi (ONEm)*, Judgment of the Court of Justice (Grand Chamber) of 8 March 2011', *Common Market Law Review* 48, 2011, 1253–70; R. Morris, 'European Citizenship and the Right to Move Freely: Internal Situations, Reverse Discrimination and Fundamental Rights', *Maastricht Journal of European and Comparative Law* 18, 2011, 179–89; H. van Eijken and S.A. de Vries, 'A New Route into the Promised Land? Being a European Citizen after Ruiz Zambrano', *European Law Review* 36, 2011, 704–21.

58 ECJ, *Ruiz Zambrano*, paras 42–4.

59 Opinion of Advocate-General Sharpston, delivered on 30 September 2010.

60 Ibid., para. 77.

61 Ibid., para. 81.

62 ECJ, C-434/09, *Shirley McCarthy v Secretary of State for the Home Department*, judgment of 5 May 2011.

63 Ibid., paras 14–20.
64 Council Directive 2004/38/EC of 29 April 2004, *Official Journal of the European Union* L 158, 30 April 2004, 77.
65 ECJ, *McCarthy*, para. 21.
66 Opinion of Advocate-General Kokott, delivered on 25 November 2010, para. 56.
67 ECJ, *McCarthy*, para. 26.
68 Ibid., para. 31.
69 Ibid., paras 27 and 28.
70 Ibid., para. 29.
71 Ibid., para. 34.
72 Ibid., para. 35.
73 Ibid., para. 41.
74 Ibid., para. 45.
75 Ibid., para. 46.
76 Ibid., para. 47. See P. van Elsuwege, 'European Union Citizenship and the Purely Internal Rule Revisited. Decision of 5 May 2011, Case C-434/09 *Shirley McCarthy v Secretary of State for the Home Department*', *European Constitutional Law Review* 7, 2011, 308–24; N.N. Shuibhne, 'Case C-434/09, *Shirley McCarthy v Secretary of State for the Home Department*, Judgment of the Court of Justice (Third Chamber) of 5 May 2011; Case C-256/11, *Dereci and Others v Bundesministerium für Inneres*, Judgment of the Court of Justice (Grand Chamber) of 15 November 2011', *Common Market Law Review* 49, 2012, 349–80.
77 ECJ, C-256/11, *Murat Dereci, Vishaka Heiml, Alban Kokollari, Izunna Emmanuel Maduike and Dragica Stevic v Bundesministerium für Inneres*, judgment (GC) of 15 November 2011.
78 Ibid., paras 22–32.
79 Ibid., para. 37.
80 Council Directive 2003/86/EC of 22 September 2003, *Official Journal of the European Union* L 251, 3 October 2003, 12.
81 ECJ, *Dereci and Others*, paras 46–8 and 50.
82 Ibid., para. 59.
83 Ibid., para. 60.
84 Ibid., paras 61, 62 and 64.
85 Ibid., paras 66, 67 and 68.
86 Ibid., para. 74. For some general commentaries on the *Dereci and Others* case, see S. Adam and P. van Elsuwege, 'Citizenship Rights and the Federal Balance between the European Union and its Member States: Comment on *Dereci*', *European Law Review* 37, 2012, 176–90; Shuibhne, 'Case C-434/09', pp. 349–80.
87 ECJ, *Dereci and Others*, paras 70 and 71.
88 Ibid., para. 72.
89 For an analysis of this phenomenon see S. Besson and A. Utzinger, 'Introduction: Future Challenges of European Citizenship Facing a Wide-open Pandora's Box', *European Law Journal* 13, 2007, 573–90; Jacobs, 'Citizenship of the European Union', p. 591; E. Spaventa, 'Seeing the Wood Despite the Trees? On the Scope of Union Citizenship and its Constitutional Effects', *Common Market Law Review* 45, 2008, 13–45; Wollenschläger, 'A New Fundamental Freedom', p. 1.

90 ECJ, C-148/02, *García Avello v Belgian State*, judgment of 2 October 2003, *ECR*, 2003, p. I-11613; C-403/03, *Schempp v Finanzamt München V*, judgment (GC) of 12 July 2005, *ECR*, p. I-6421; C-127/08, *Metock and Others v Minister for Justice, Equality and Law Reform*, judgment (GC) of 25 July 2008, *ECR*, 2008, p. I-6241.

91 For an example of this trend see ECJ, C-224/98, *D'Hoop v Office national de l'emploi*, judgment of 11 July 2002, *ECR*, 2002, p. I-6191; C-152/05, *Commission v Germany*, judgment of 17 January 2008, *ECR*, 2008, p. I-39; C-353/06, *Grunkin and Paul*, judgment (GC) of 14 October 2008, *ECR*, 2008, p. I-7639; C-208/09, *Sayn-Wittgenstein v Landeshauptmann von Wien*, judgment of 22 December 2010.

92 Opinion of Advocate-General Poiares Maduro, delivered on 30 September 2009, para. 13.

93 ECJ, *Rottmann*, para. 52.

94 Ibid., para 55.

95 Ibid., paras 55 and 58.

96 T. Konstadinides, 'La Fraternité européenne? The Extent of National Competence to Condition the Acquisition and Loss of Nationality from the Perspective of EU Citizenship', *European Law Review* 35, 2010, 409–14.

97 See above, text corresponding to note 22.

98 J. Shaw, 'The Treaty of Lisbon and Citizenship', *Federal Trust* 1, 2008, 3–4. Online. Available at: www.fedtrust.co.uk (accessed 20 May 2012); M. La Torre, 'Citizenship and European Democracy: Between the European Constitution and the Treaty of Lisbon', in P. Birkinshaw and M. Verney (eds) *The European Union Legal Order after Lisbon*, Alphen aan den Rijn: Kluwer Law International, 2010, pp. 206–7.

99 Shuibhne, 'Case C-434/09', p. 380.

100 H. Wray, 'Family Life and EU Citizenship: A Commentary on McCarthy C-434/09 5 May 2011', pp. 1–6. Online. Available at: http://eudo-citizenship.eu (accessed 10 June 2012).

101 ECJ, *Dereci and Others*, paras 71–2.

102 'This position of the Court is in keeping with its established case law on the scope of fundamental rights as recognised by Advocate-General Sharpston in her opinion on *Ruiz Zambrano*': see A. Lansbergen, 'Case Summary and Comment: Case C-256/11, *Dereci and Others v Bundesministerium für Inneres*'. Online. Available at: http://eudo-citizenship.eu (accessed 24 July 2012), pp. 4–5.

103 ECJ, C-40/11, *Yoshikazu Iida v Stadt Ulm*, opinion of Advocate-General Trstenjak delivered on 15 May 2012, para. 72. The judgment of the Court was issued on 8 November 2012, when this book was already in print.

104 Ibid., paras 70–87.

105

> For such a right of residence to exist, the denial thereof must have a restrictive effect on the child's right to freedom of movement and must be regarded as amounting to a disproportionate interference with fundamental rights in the light of the abovementioned fundamental rights. This is a matter for assessment by the referring court.
>
> (See ibid., para. 88)

106 ECJ, *Dereci and Others*, para. 54.

107 Lansbergen, 'Case Summary and Comment: Case C-256/11', p. 5.
108 Ibid.
109 Ibid., pp. 5–6; A. Lansbergen and N. Miller, 'European Citizenship Rights in Internal Situations: An Ambiguous Revolution? Decision of 8 March 2011, Case C-34/09 *Gerardo Ruiz Zambrano v Office national de l'emploi (ONEM)*', *European Constitutional Law Review* 7, 2011, 287–307.
110 ECJ, C-356/11, *O and S v Maahanmuuttovirasto*; C-357/11, *Maahanmuuttovirasto v L*, references for a preliminary ruling, lodged on 7 July 2011, *Official Journal of the European Union* C 269, 10 September 2011. See also Lansbergen, 'Case Summary and Comment: Case C-256/11', p. 6. The Court's judgment was issued on 6 December 2012, when this book was already in print.

11 The evolving role of nationality in private international law

Pietro Franzina

Introduction

Since the beginning of the nineteenth century, nationality has played a prominent role within the domestic systems of private international law (PIL) of several countries, especially in Continental Europe, South America and East Asia, as well as in a number of international conventions. Nationality serves both as a connecting factor designating the law applicable to legal relationships with a foreign element,[1] and as a head of jurisdiction determining whether the courts of a given state may entertain civil claims with cross-border implications.[2] References to nationality may be found, most of the time, in rules dealing with the personal status of individuals, including issues such as legal capacity and personal identity.

Today, the point is frequently made among scholars that the golden days of nationality in PIL are over. Some speak squarely of a decline of nationality, noting that the latter is gradually losing ground to other personal connecting factors, such as domicile and habitual residence.[3] Nationality has actually competed with other personal connecting factors since it first entered the PIL stage, de facto requiring lawmakers to decide among clearly alternative options and charging practitioners with the task of solving delicate technical issues arising out of the coexistence, and the possible interplay, of opposing paradigms.[4]

In some of the legal systems where nationality has traditionally occupied a key position, recent codifications tend to follow a more balanced approach, with nationality being replaced by (or coupled with) other connecting factors in some fields.[5] Multilateral international conventions, especially those negotiated within The Hague Conference on Private International Law and those issued from the Specialized Conferences hosted by the Organization of American States, rely today almost systematically on habitual residence, leaving little or no room for nationality.[6] Similar remarks may be made as regards the uniform rules of PIL enacted by the European Union (EU) as part of the measures relating to 'judicial cooperation in civil matters'.[7]

The purpose of this chapter is to trace the evolution of the role of nationality in PIL and discuss the main factors behind this development.

The rise of nationality

Although the first provisions relying on nationality for the purpose of regulating jurisdiction and the conflict of laws appeared as early as 1803, in the French Civil Code,[8] it was not until the 1850s that a scientific reflection on the relevance of nationality to PIL was fully elaborated. The most impressive contributions in this regard have been provided by Pasquale Stanislao Mancini (1817–1888).[9] His work has represented a long-lasting source of inspiration both for domestic legislators and those engaged in the international unification of PIL.

In the following paragraphs, we will give a short account of the theoretical background against which the said development has occurred; we will then explore the political significance of the option in favour of nationality in PIL and outline the technical advantages associated with the use of nationality as a connecting factor and a head of jurisdiction.

The theoretical background

At the time of Mancini, the theory of PIL relied to a large extent on two assumptions. On one side, following the teachings of Friedrich Carl von Savigny (1779–1861), the idea was generally accepted that issues relating to the conflict of laws (and, subject to certain qualifications, issues in respect of adjudicatory jurisdiction) could most conveniently be addressed through a 'geographical' approach, i.e. by determining the localization of the situation at stake.[10] It was believed that legal relationships could be regarded as being situated in a given place: in Savignian parlance, the 'seat' of the relationship.[11] By identifying the seat of the relationship at stake, one could determine its governing law and, possibly, the authorities entitled to exercise their powers in connection with it.

On the other side, it was common ground that the only 'space' in which a legal relationship could be situated for PIL purposes was a space delimited by reference to state sovereignty. Positivism, the then prevailing legal doctrine, regarded power as being ultimately vested in states. Accordingly, legal relationships could be situated in no other space, or environment, than a *state's* legal order. PIL, thus understood, appeared to perform an 'allocating' function by providing the standards according to which sovereign powers should be distributed among states in cross-border situations. Unsurprisingly, many at that time, including Mancini himself, considered PIL to be closely linked to public international law, with common principles lying at the heart of the two disciplines.[12]

The boundaries of a state's sovereignty could be drawn in different ways for the purpose of localizing legal relationships. Needless to say, since sovereignty is territorial in essence, territory was naturally considered to be a relevant standard. However, the relevance of other standards was asserted, too.

This is where nationality comes into play. Nation states tend to see themselves as entities engaged in the government of a community, the members of which are bound together by a unique set of shared values and a common culture, on the basis of which a form of political loyalty is built and preserved. Within nation states, the exercise of power follows a pattern which is completely different from those underlying other forms of government. On one hand, nation states are different from empires, in that they provide an experience of membership based on a distinctive culture, a common language and, possibly, a particular religion, as opposed to a combination of historically diverse ethnic or political components. On the other hand, nation states are different from tribes and other locality-tied forms of government, since the idea of membership they are based upon does not rely on the fact that members live in the same geographical context and share the same resources. On the contrary, as suggested by Benedict Anderson, a nation may be understood as an 'imagined community', where individuals take part in a group of which they do not know most of the participants.[13]

The use of nationality in PIL may be seen as reflecting the peculiar idea of membership just described. A rule whereby issues that arise in connection with the personal status of individuals must be decided in accordance with their *lex patriae*, (i.e. the law of his or her nationality) rests on the assumption that their status may be meaningfully localized in that particular country, no matter whether according to other elements – e.g. the domicile or the habitual residence of the individual at stake – the situation might appear to be more significantly connected with a different place. This reasoning is premised on the idea that, when it comes to determining the identity of an individual, nationality is a key element. One may actually belong to a wide range of social groups (a family, a clan, a guild, etc.), but – according to this view – the most relevant form of membership is the membership in a nation. Nationality is seen, in fact, as a particularly meaningful status: it is politically meaningful, since it is associated with ideas such as allegiance, loyalty and participation in decision-making; and it is legally meaningful, because it embodies a set of entitlements vis-à-vis state authorities. Due to these features, nationality is a key factor for determining the identity of an individual. The latter, in this perspective, is first and foremost a member of a given national community. The idea of subjecting the individuals in question to the regulatory and adjudicatory jurisdiction of their national state, whenever an issue arises in connection with their personal status, is but the corollary of the preceding assumptions.

The politics of nationality seen through the prism of private international law

It is clear, in light of the foregoing, that the decision to make nationality the core element of one or more PIL rules reflects, in principle, strong political motivations.[14] As a matter of fact, what explains the fortune of nationality as a connecting factor and a head of jurisdiction is, to a large extent, the fact that nationality has been perceived as a notion capable of serving the political needs of a significant number of states, at least at a given stage of their historical development.

The use of nationality for PIL purposes may actually underlie two political strategies. The first strategy is concerned with the definition and the reinforcement of the geo-political identity of the state. Political entities rely on the cohesion among the individuals (and groups) that form their social basis. For the reasons stated above, this is particularly true for nation states. As Rogers Brubaker puts it, nation states are built upon a 'social closure', i.e. a clear separation dividing those entitled to enjoy the benefits of membership (in terms of political participation, protection by state authorities, etc.), and those who are not.[15] Recently born states, as well as states governing highly diversified societies (as is the case with colonial states or states issued from the unification of former sovereign entities, each possessing some distinctive social and cultural features) may want to consolidate their authority and enhance the efficiency of their action by raising the awareness of membership among those subject to their jurisdiction. For this, they may be interested, *inter alia*, in legal devices capable of sharpening, to the eyes of the members of the community, the distinction between those who belong to the community, and those who are alien to it ('us' and 'them'). The regulation of legal relationships in the realm of private law, especially where personal and family interests are at stake, represents a field in which this goal may be pursued in a particularly effective way. As a matter of fact, family and personal issues tend to arise more frequently than any other legal issue, and involve, by their nature, any member of the community.

In this connection, by deciding that all nationals, no matter whether they live, are subject to one and the same law (the *lex patriae*) and are entitled to enjoy the protection of one and the same body of authorities (those of the country of nationality), the state is stressing the said distinction, emphasising for the interested individuals the legal consequences of being part of a particular community. For those possessing a certain nationality, including newcomers born elsewhere and people who have left the country to settle down abroad (while retaining a cultural tie with their country of origin), the use of nationality for PIL purposes corroborates political loyalty to the state (what is at stake here is the 'vertical' dimension of nationality) and strengthens the bonds of solidarity among community members (the 'horizontal' dimension).[16]

The second political strategy underpinning the use of nationality in PIL has to do with the intercourse among states and the 'quality' thereof. States, by asserting the nationality of those belonging to the community they govern, acknowledge by implication that non-nationals possess, in principle, the nationality of another state. From a PIL perspective, this implies that the state of the forum accepts to refrain from systematically claiming jurisdiction in respect of foreigners and that, where jurisdiction is asserted, it is ready to instruct its courts to decide the relevant issues in accordance with foreign law, i.e. in accordance with the law of the country of which the individual in question is a national.[17] This way, the forum state displays an attitude of self-restraint and a sort of deference to the equal sovereignty of other states, an attitude which is all the more politically significant where no treaty obligation exists requiring the state in question to follow such a course of action in the circumstances. In a way, by conforming to the requirements of comity in the absence of strictly legal prescriptions, the forum state affirms its awareness that dialogue is needed among sovereign entities and that isolation should be avoided. For states seeking international recognition or desiring to develop cooperation with other countries, this attitude may prove strategically useful.

The technical advantages associated with using nationality as a connecting factor or a head of jurisdiction

Nationality, as used for PIL purposes, has been generally credited for ensuring the smooth functioning, in several respects, of the rules on jurisdiction and the conflict of laws. It is not surprising that at a time in which PIL scholars strived to build a discipline with sound scientific foundations[18] and legislators sought to provide efficient solutions to problems of increasing practical relevance, those features that promote a technically proper operation of rules have been regarded as an important asset.

The technical advantages stemming from the use of nationality as a connecting factor and a head of jurisdiction may be grouped under four headings: material consistency; temporal continuity; avoidance of conflicts; and international harmony.

Within the continental tradition of PIL, jurisdiction and applicable law are often required to be determined on an issue-by-issue basis. Different provisions, each dealing with a specific class of claims or questions, may come into play when complex relationships are at stake. For example, two separate conflict-of-laws rules may be needed in order to make an overall assessment of the consequences of a contract concluded by an adult who is not in a position to protect his or her interests: one rule may be needed to deal with the aspects regarding capacity and another rule may be needed to address issues relating to the protection of the adult in question. Where the different sides of the relationship at stake are closely inter-related, a technically convenient solution is to ensure that one and the same law is designated to govern all issues, thus promoting the 'internal' consistency of the applicable substantive regulation.[19] Consistency may in principle be achieved by employing the same connecting factor for determining the law applicable to a wide range of (diverse, but possibly) interconnected issues. Nationality is an asset in this connection, since – for the reasons stated above – it presents itself as the single (or main) relevant factor for the whole area of family law and the law of persons.

Legal relationships may last for a long period of time. Where the relevant connecting factor or head of jurisdiction is likely to change over time, a *conflit mobile* may arise and the laws of different countries (or the authorities of different states) may be successively called upon to govern the matter.[20] The difficulties that this may cause can be avoided at the outset by opting for a stable connecting factor. Stability is, in principle, one of the intrinsic features of nationality: the latter is conceived as a permanent status, since it is subject to few or no changes during the life span of most individuals.

The operation of a rule of PIL based on the geographical approach may be problematic whenever the factual circumstances identified as the relevant connecting factor or head of jurisdiction occur (or may otherwise be localized) in two or more sovereign spaces, thus leading to the designation of multiple laws or to positive conflicts of jurisdiction. Nationality has often been credited for being capable of significantly reducing this risk, on the assumption that most individuals possess just one nationality or at least one nationality at a time.

The use of nationality as a connecting factor has further been presented as a choice favouring the international harmony of solutions. Harmony is achieved when a given relationship is dealt with consistently (i.e. in accordance with one and the same law) in all countries where the relationship itself may be at issue. International harmony may be ensured at the outset when the PIL rules of the countries in question employ the same connecting factor.[21] Nationality, seen from the point of view of Mancini and his followers, may be regarded as 'naturally' contributing to this goal, since it represents, at least in the field of personal and family law, a connecting factor based on rational grounds.[22] As such, it should be capable, for its proponents, of gaining support almost universally.[23]

The decline of nationality

The idea of nationality and the patterns of nation states have undergone significant changes since they first made their appearance within the legal and political discourse. Some general trends of this evolution have affected the role of nationality in PIL as well. In the following pages we will try to identify some of the factors of change specifically relating to that discipline.

In parallel with the previous section, we will start by determining whether the changes that occurred in the theory of PIL, especially starting from the second half of the twentieth century, have had an impact on the role played by nationality. We will go on to establish to what extent the political significance of nationality is still relevant to today's PIL. Finally, we will verify, in light of what we have called the technical advantages of nationality, whether the use of nationality in PIL still represents a technically appealing option.

The changed theoretical landscape

The theoretical foundations of today's PIL differ considerably from those existing at the time of Savigny and Mancini. Of course, the idea of localization has not disappeared and, actually, present-day legislators still appear to be persuaded that legal relationships may, in principle, be conveniently situated within a geographical context for PIL purposes, at least in some circumstances. Yet, the geographical approach is no longer 'the' paradigm of the discipline, and different methods are currently followed by rule makers using an increasingly diversified toolbox.[24]

For our present purposes, three general (and closely interconnected) trends may be mentioned in this respect. The first trend is the 'materialization' of PIL rules.[25] This trend has different facets and may manifest itself through the use of a range of different techniques. The basic idea is that the rules on the conflict of laws (and possibly the rules on jurisdiction, although in a peculiar technical fashion) may be designed and applied in such a way as to ensure *immediately* the achievement of certain substantive interests, such as the personal and educational welfare of children or the protection of maintenance creditors. Where substantive policies so require, localization may either be adjusted (so as to rectify its outcomes, whenever these appear to be inconsistent with the selected substantive goals) or be superseded altogether. It is worth stressing that the interests pursued through such material or 'substantively flavoured' provisions are to a large extent, as in the previous examples, interests of a private nature ascribed directly to individuals.

This leads us to the second trend that is worth recalling here. PIL is experiencing something akin to an 'individualist turn'. Legal pluralism is no longer regarded as posing essentially a problem of sovereignty. The crux is, rather, how pluralism should be 'ordered', or 'managed', so that the rights of the individuals may effectively be protected within a fragmented and diversified legal landscape. PIL, seen from this angle, acquires a new *raison d'être*, since it may be essential in the forum – according to the circumstances – for safeguarding fundamental rights when these are threatened by foreign rules, and for ensuring the unfettered (and 'spatially continuous') enjoyment of such rights for persons moving across borders.[26]

The third trend is the 'flexibilization' of PIL.[27] This trend, too, manifests itself in various ways (e.g. through the use of safeguard clauses, or *clauses d'exception*, in the conflict of laws), but the point basically is that the actual operation of PIL rules is considered, in principle, to be open to those adjustments that may turn out to be necessary, or convenient, in the circumstances of the case. Abstract provisions regulating jurisdiction and the conflict of laws, without some flexibility, are felt to be less and less capable of properly addressing the issues posed by an increasingly complex reality.

In a way, each of these trends implies a challenge to the role of nationality in PIL. Materialization takes nationality, as well as other factors traditionally employed for localizing legal relationships, out of the limelight: substantive interests, not mere geographical factors, tend to occupy the centre of the stage. Individualism implies a reallocation of values within PIL, with state policies – such as those embodied in nationality – being recognized as having a lesser status. Flexibilization is at odds with the idea that the operation of rules based on nationality is 'naturally' rigid, since nationality is a status 'objectively' conferred by a state's rules: it is essentially outside the reach of the individual's autonomy and judicial authorities enjoy little or no discretion in its ascertainment and regulation.

The place of nationality in the contemporary politics of PIL

Nation states, as those upon which the principle of nationality has originally been moulded, do not exist anymore. Contemporary states, while retaining some of their features, have gradually evolved into something different.

As the nation state is often regarded as an expression of modernity, the evolution we are talking about may be described by referring to what represents the 'antagonist' of the nation state: the post-modern state.[28] Drawing on the analysis of Jacques Chevallier,[29] we will focus on some common characteristics of post-modern states in an attempt to establish how these characteristics influence the politics of PIL (just like the basic features of nation states influenced the development of PIL at the time of Mancini), and ultimately affect the role of nationality as a connecting factor and a head of jurisdiction. Two characteristics will be considered.

In the first place, an evolution may be detected regarding the functions that states are engaged to perform. Globalization has led states to allow other entities, such as international organizations, to perform functions traditionally associated with statehood (e.g. in the field of criminal justice or currency).[30] In the meanwhile, private entities, such as multinational corporations and non-governmental organizations, have gradually gained social and political weight and tend to 'compete' with states as regards, *inter alia*, market regulation and social welfare. Within this changing landscape, post-modern states tend to reduce the scope of their action and concentrate their efforts on certain objectives. One of these objectives is social cohesion.[31] In this connection, pressed by the growth of economic inequalities and the increased relevance of the phenomenon of migration, states appear particularly keen on ensuring integration. With this in mind, they provide core public utility services in the area of education, health, fighting discrimination, etc.[32]

This shift in priorities results in a renewed interest of states for those who live in their territory and are thus directly involved in the social dynamics that state agencies are asked to govern. The fact that they are nationals, foreigners or stateless persons tends to be unessential. Conversely, people whose ties to the national community are mainly of a cultural nature, such as nationals having migrated abroad and their descendants, tend to leave the centre of the stage.

As far as PIL is concerned, the transformation just illustrated helps in understanding the growing importance of a personal connecting factor, like habitual residence, to the detriment of nationality. In principle, the habitual residence of an individual is in the place where the latter entertains most of his social relationships.[33] This place may normally be identified by looking at the professional activity of the person in question or at his or her family ties (e.g. the place where his or her children go to school may be one of the relevant indicia). Actually, all 'localizable' interests of the person in question may call for consideration when it comes to determining his or her habitual residence.

PIL rules relying mainly on habitual residence and less (or in no way at all) on nationality, as far as personal and family matters are concerned, convey the idea of a state whose priority is to govern social integration, not to assert its geo-political identity or build a community with distinctive cultural features. The focus being on social governance, habitual residence enhances among those who reside in the state territory the awareness of being part of a community that may well be culturally diversified, but should be socially coherent.[34] By making habitual residence the key connecting factor or head of jurisdiction as regards issues of family law or the law of persons, PIL rules ensure that the degree of protection of the rights of the individuals in these fields is substantially the same for all individuals belonging to a given social environment. The latter individuals are thus encouraged to represent themselves as part of the community, each on an equal standing. In the end, this is meant to reinforce the ties of loyalty towards the state on whose territory the community is settled, and the solidarity among its members (regardless of the nationality of each of them).

The second characteristic of post-modern states we shall focus on has to do with the sources of law. The monopoly of the state regarding the production of norms, a key principle of modern states, is no longer a dogma in the post-modern era. Domestic provisions stand side-by-side with international and supranational rules and with prescriptions elaborated within non-national or sub-national contexts (such as religious law, regional law, local customs, etc.).[35] The competition among sources is particularly clear as far as family law and the law of persons are concerned. National rules are challenged both from above, e.g. by international conventions on the protection of human rights; in Europe, one may think of the relevance of Article 8 of the European Convention on Human Rights (ECHR) on the rules of the contracting states concerning the relationship between parents and children); and from below, e.g. by religious standards claiming recognition in respect of the substantive regulation of marriage.

Seen from a PIL perspective, these developments affect the ability of nationality (and other personal connecting factors) to perform effectively their functions.

On one side, whenever the *lex patriae* of the individual concerned is designated as the applicable law, the actual application of its rules may still be challenged through the public policy exception, as may happen on account of their non-conformity with the relevant international or supranational human rights standards. As a matter of fact, the forum state may be bound by the relevant international and supranational rules to secure the fundamental rights in question to 'everyone within its jurisdiction' (as stated in Article 1 ECHR), regardless of nationality and other personal qualifications. Regional integration may similarly play a role in this respect. In principle, private law rules enacted by the EU are meant to apply 'objectively' to all situations relevant to the area of integration (be it the internal market or the 'area of freedom of security and justice'), no matter whether EU citizens or other individuals are concerned.

On the other side, where the *lex patriae* consists of (or refers to) a plurality of sub-national regulations, based either on territorial or personal standards, i.e. local laws or rules addressing those belonging to a given ethnic group, nationality (as much as other connecting factors) may end up playing a marginal role. While nationality may still come into play in the process leading to the identification of the rules governing the matter, those rules will not necessarily be 'national' rules, as they may reflect a different membership of the individuals at stake (rules reflecting a shared religious belief, rules elaborated within a local community, etc.).

The residual relevance of the technical advantages associated with nationality

One may wonder whether nationality, while losing ground for political reasons to other connecting factors, may still be an appealing concept thanks to the technical advantages illustrated above. In answering this question, it should be considered that the technicalities of PIL have considerably developed over the last few decades. Along the lines of the methodological renewal that has previously been mentioned, the 'engineering' of PIL rules seems to be definitely more sophisticated today than it was at the time of Mancini. This implies that some of the advantages associated with nationality may now be achieved through technical means that only recently have been elaborated and practically experienced.

Material consistency and international harmony, for example, are no longer pursued only, or chiefly, by ensuring that domestic rules on the conflict of laws employ but one connecting factor for a wide range of interrelated issues. These goals may in fact be achieved through uniform rules of PIL aimed at addressing, in an integrated fashion, the whole set of issues that may arise in connection with a given relationship, i.e. issues relating to jurisdiction, applicable law, and the recognition of judgments.[36] 'Integrated' rules, provided they are binding upon a significant number of states, may efficiently serve the goals mentioned above without having to be rigid. As a matter of fact, the efficiency of PIL solutions is no longer seen as depending essentially on the intrinsic qualities of the connecting factors and heads of jurisdiction employed, but rather on the way in which the different components of the PIL regulation of a certain legal institution work together. In this manner, domestic legislators may be ready to abandon connecting factors they have traditionally cherished (as may be the case of nationality), in favour of integrated solutions leading to better overall results. These remarks may help to explain why, in the field of family law and other areas, states where nationality has long been a reference in PIL, have decided to become parties to international conventions based on the so-called jurisdictional approach. These are conventions which provide that conflict-of-laws issues are to be decided, as a rule, in accordance with the law of the forum (which may not correspond to the *lex patriae*, especially where, as it is frequently the case, the default ground for jurisdiction is habitual residence).[37]

Party autonomy is a tool that PIL has long been using with extreme caution and is now rapidly expanding its reach, including in the field of family law.[38] It is now considered as a device capable of ensuring, where properly employed, the achievement of some of the technical goals traditionally pursued through nationality. This is the case, for example, with temporal continuity. Long-lasting relationships may, in principle, be made subject to one law by an agreement, ensuring that the substantive regulation of the relationship in question remains the same, in spite of any change in the relevant 'objective' connecting factors (such as habitual residence, or nationality itself).[39]

At the same time, it appears that one of the technical advantages traditionally associated with nationality in PIL is gradually losing its practical relevance and may even turn into a drawback. As mentioned earlier, nationality used to provide univocal designations, since individuals normally possess but the nationality of one state. The positive attitude displayed by several national legislators regarding dual nationality has resulted in an increased number of individuals possessing two or more nationalities. Without uniform solutions to deal with conflicts of nationality for PIL purposes, situations like this may become a source of uncertainty and could possibly result in contrasting decisions and limping situations.[40] Furthermore, dual nationality cases may prove to be politically sensitive where, as in the EU, discrimination on grounds of nationality is prohibited (at least for those possessing certain nationalities), by rules of primary law reflecting the needs of regional integration.[41]

The combined operation of the technical developments illustrated so far generally results in the use of nationality for PIL purposes being often 'relativized'. References to nationality, where not suppressed altogether, become the elements of structurally complex rules featuring a variety of connecting factors or heads of jurisdiction and more than one methodological option.[42]

Concluding remarks

The role of nationality in the area of PIL has undergone deep transformations over the last two centuries. The evolution that this chapter has been outlining, however, is not over. While traditional rules enjoy a certain degree of inertia, allowing nationality to keep a prominent role in several domestic systems of PIL and in a number of international conventions, some of the factors of change we have mentioned have not yet expressed their full potential. This may be said, in particular, for the increasing influence exerted upon PIL by rules on the protection of human rights, to the extent that they disregard nationality, and for the interplay among PIL and the rules governing regional integration, insofar as the latter are intended to meet the needs of a supranational area where the nationals of different countries are allowed in principle to move freely.[43]

That said, claiming that nationality is experiencing a decline in PIL is not the same thing as saying that it has become totally unable to reflect present-day values and perform important regulatory functions.

Arguments have recently been put forward with a view to demonstrating, from a general perspective, that nationality, once deprived of its 'nationalistic' implications, is an important component of a model of government based on representative democracy and the rule of law, and may still represent, as such, an ideal for contemporary states and a factor on which the significance of borders may be reappraised.[44] More specifically, as far as PIL is concerned, it has been contended that the effective protection of fundamental human rights requires *inter alia* an effort by domestic legislators and other regulators to ensure that individuals may effectively claim their identity and enjoy the protection of the marks of such identity.[45] In cross-border situations, this implies that the need still exists to treat the personal status of individuals as a unitary and permanent condition, at least in principle, and that the largely mandatory nature of the domestic substantive rules relating to such status must be safeguarded through appropriate PIL devices. This view recognizes that the personal status of individuals performs a 'structuring function' (*fonction structurante*) in respect of the identity of individuals, in the framework of which nationality may still have a role to play.[46] While nationality is no longer vested with the 'publicistic' task of extending a certain idea of power and political membership into the private law arena, it represents a means by which the identity of individuals may be safeguarded at a time of globalization and increased cross-border mobility of persons.

Nationality remains, in fact, an expression of cultural identity. It is one of the factors capable of differentiating one individual from another, while embodying a bundle of socially and historically meaningful ties between the individual concerned and a larger reality where part of the individual's roots may be found.[47] As a matter of fact, the diversity of national cultures is an aspect of cultural diversity: the expressions of diversity enjoy international protection[48] and may be preserved, *inter alia*, through the operation of PIL.[49]

Notes

1 See, e.g.: Article 9(1) of the Austrian Federal Statute of 1978 on Private International Law: 'The law governing the personal status of a natural person shall be the law of the state to which that person belongs'; Munich Convention on the Law Applicable to Surnames and Forenames, 5 September 1980, UNTS, vol. 1553, No.

26995, Article 1(1): 'The surnames and forenames of a person shall be determined by the law of the State of which he or she is a national' (unofficial translations).

2 See, e.g.: Article 32 of the Belgian Code of Private International Law of 2004:

> Except where otherwise provided for in this code, Belgian courts shall have jurisdiction in matters of status or capacity of a natural person [. . .] if [. . .] (2) the person in question is a national of Belgium at the time when proceedings are instituted.
>
> Hague Convention relating to the Deprivation of Civil Rights and Similar Measures of Protection, 17 July 1905

Online. Available at: www.hcch.net/index_en.php?act=text.display&tid=18 (accessed 28 August 2012), Article 2: 'Guardianship may only be granted by the competent authorities of the country of which the ward is a national' (unofficial translations).

3 See generally L.I. Winter, 'Nationality or Domicile: The Present State of Affairs', *Collected Courses of the Hague Academy of International Law* 128, 1969, 347–503. See further R. De Nova, 'Recenti sviluppi in diritto internazionale privato', *Diritto internazionale* 22, 1968, I, 20–61 at 55, and, more recently, F. Mosconi, 'Sul criterio della cittadinanza: da Mancini ai giorni nostri', *Rivista di diritto internazionale privato e processuale* 47, 2011, 634–41, advocating a 'thorough reconsideration' of the role of nationality within the Italian system of PIL.

4 Attempts have been made to lay down uniform provisions to deal with cases where the conflict-of-laws rules of the country of domicile of the individual at stake rely on nationality, while the conflict-of-laws rules of the country of nationality employ domicile as a connecting factor, and similar situations. These attempts, which resulted, *inter alia*, in the Hague Convention relating to the Settlement of the Conflicts Between the Law of Nationality and the Law of Domicile (15 June 1955. Online. Available at: www.hcch.net/index_en.php?act=conventions.text&cid=35 (accessed 15 August 2012)), had in fact little or no success.

5 That is the case of Belgium, among other states. See M.J. Verwilghen, 'La place de la nationalité dans le Code de droit international privé belge', in *En hommage à Francis Delpérée: itinéraires d'un constitutionnaliste*, Bruxelles: Bruylant, 2007, pp. 1687–701.

6 See, e.g. Inter-American Convention on Support Obligations, 15 July 1989, OAS, Treaty Series, No. 71, Article 8:

> At the option of the creditor, support claims may be heard by the following judicial or administrative authorities: (a) those of the State of domicile or habitual residence of the creditor; (b) those of the State of domicile or habitual residence of the debtor; or (c) those of the State to which the debtor is connected by personal links such as possessing property, receiving income or obtaining financial benefits.

7 See, e.g. EU Council Regulation 1259/2010/EU implementing enhanced cooperation in the area of the law applicable to divorce and legal separation, 20 December 2010, *Official Journal of the European Union* L 343, 29 December 2010, 10, Article 8:

> In the absence of a choice [by the spouses], divorce and legal separation shall be subject to the law of the State: (a) where the spouses are habitually resident at the time the court is seized; or, failing that (b) where the spouses were last habitually

resident, provided that the period of residence did not end more than 1 year before the court was seized, in so far as one of the spouses still resides in that State at the time the court is seized; or, failing that (c) of which both spouses are nationals at the time the court is seized; or, failing that (d) where the court is seized.

8 See, e.g. Article 3(3) of the French *Code Civil*: 'French provisions on status and capacity of persons apply to French nationals, no matter whether the latter resides in a foreign country'; Article 14:

> A foreigner, no matter whether he is not a resident of France, may be sued before French courts as regards the performance of obligations undertaken in France towards a French national; he may also be sued before French courts as regards the performance of obligations undertaken in a foreign country towards French nationals
>
> (unofficial translations)

9 P.S. Mancini, *Della nazionalità come fondamento del dritto delle genti: prelezione al corso di dritto internazionale e marittimo pronunziata nella R. Università di Torino*, Torino: Tipografia Eredi Botta, 1851. On Mancini and the principle of nationality in PIL, see generally, among others, E. Jayme, 'Pasquale Stanislao Mancini (1817–1888) – Die Nation als Rechtsbegriff im Internationalen Privatrecht', in E. Jayme, *Gesammelte Schriften – Band 3. Internationales Privatrecht und Völkerrecht*, Heidelberg: Müller Verlag, 2003, pp. 64–75.

10 See generally P. Picone, 'Les méthodes de coordination entre ordres juridiques en droit international privé', *Collected Courses of the Hague Academy of International Law* 276, 2000, 9–296 at 35ff.

11 The contribution of Savigny to the theory of PIL has been the object of several detailed studies. A synthetic illustration of his thought may be found in F.K. Juenger, 'General Couse on Private International Law', *Collected Courses of the Hague Academy of International Law* 193, 1985, 119–387 at 159ff.

12 See generally A. Nussbaum, 'Rise and Decline of the Law-of-Nations Doctrine in the Conflict of Laws', *Columbia Law Review* 42, 1942, 189–206.

13 B. Anderson, *Imagined Communities. Reflections on the Origin and Spread of Nationalism*, New York: Verso, 1991, pp. 2ff.

14 There is a wide consensus among scholars, today, that PIL rules, despite their technical appearance, express political ideas and accordingly lend themselves to be examined, among various possible approaches, from the standpoint of the political goals they pursue. See generally on this matter A.V.M. Struycken, 'Co-ordination and Co-operation in Respectful Disagreement', *Collected Courses of the Hague Academy of International Law* 311, 2004, 9–551 at 195ff.

15 R. Brubaker, *Citizenship and Nationhood in France and Germany*, Cambridge, Massachusetts: Harvard University Press, 1992, pp. 21ff. In the words of P. Lagarde, 'Nationalité', in D. Alland and S. Rials (eds) *Dictionnaire de la culture juridique*, Paris: Presse Universitaires de France, 2003, pp. 1051–6 at 1052, 'le droit de la nationalité est intrinsèquement un droit d'exclusion'.

16 F. Terré, 'Réflexions sur la notion de nationalité', *Revue critique de droit international privé* 64, 1975, 197–214.

17 The first conflict-of-laws rules relying on nationality, such as Article 3(3) of the French *Code Civil*, were originally intended to apply in a mere unilateral way, so

as to ensure the application of the *lex fori* to those possessing the nationality of the forum state. See R. Cassin, 'La nouvelle conception du domicile', *Collected Courses of the Hague Academy of International Law* 34, 1930, 655–809 at 659 and 708f. As a matter of fact, Article 3(3) of the French *Code Civil* has soon been 'bilateralized' by courts. On the theoretical premises of bilateralization, implying a reappraisal of the role of the state in the regulation of private law relationships, see R. De Nova, 'Historical and Comparative Introduction to Conflict of Laws', *Collected Courses of the Hague Academy of International Law* 118, 1966, 435–612 at 572ff.

18 See generally B. Oppetit, 'Le droit international privé, droit savant', *Collected Courses of the Hague Academy of International Law* 234, 1992, 331–433.

19 Similar remarks apply to jurisdiction in cases where, due to the connection existing between two or more claims, it is advisable to have one court deciding all aspects of litigation.

20 Regarding the relevance of the passing of time on the functioning of conflict-of-laws rules, see generally M. Souleau-Bertrand, *Le conflit mobile*, Paris: Dalloz, 2005.

21 Where this is not the case, harmony may be pursued through devices intended to come into play after the relevant conflict-of-laws rule has made its designation. One of these devices is *renvoi*.

22 See, e.g. P. Esperson, *Il principio di nazionalità applicato alle relazioni civili internazionali*, Pavia: Tipografia dei Fratelli Fusi, 1868, pp. IIIff.

23 It is worth mentioning, however, that Mancini himself, far from relying on the intrinsic capacity of nationality to appeal to national legislators, pragmatically advocated the unification of some core PIL solutions by means of international conventions: P.S. Mancini, 'De l'utilité de rendre obligatoires pour tous les États sous la forme d'un ou de plusieurs traités internationaux, un certain nombre de règles générales du droit international privé, pour assurer la décision uniforme des conflits entre les différentes législations civiles et criminelles', *Journal du droit international privé* 1, 1874, 221–85.

24 On the methodological mutations of contemporary PIL see, among others, D. Bureau, H. Muir Watt, *Droit international privé*, 2nd edn, Paris: Presses Universitaires de France, 2010, pp. 356ff.

25 J.D. González Campos, 'Diversification, spécialisation, flexibilisation et matérialisation des règles de droit international privé', *Collected Courses of the Hague Academy of International Law* 287, 2000, 9–426 at 309ff.

26 On the relationship between PIL and human rights, see generally P. Kinsch, 'Droits de l'homme, droits fondamentaux et droit international privé', *Collected Courses of the Hague Academy of International Law* 318, 2005, 9–331, and E. Jayme, 'Menschenrechte und Theorie des Internationalen Privatrechts', in E. Jayme, *Gesammelte Schriften – Band 3*, pp. 95–109. See also L. d'Avout, 'Droits fondamentaux et coordination des ordres juridiques en droit privé', in E. Dubout and S. Touzé (eds) *Les droits fondamentaux: charnières entre orders et systèmes juridiques*, Paris: Pedone, 2010, pp. 165–98, and, regarding a particular aspect of the topic, P. Franzina, 'Some Remarks on the Relevance of Article 8 of the ECHR to the Recognition of Family Status Judicially Created Abroad', *Diritti umani e diritto internazionale* 5, 2011, 609–16.

27 González Campos, 'Diversification, spécialisation, flexibilisation et matérialisation', pp. 214ff.

28 Post-modernity has proved to be a particularly useful approach to studying the evolution of PIL following the seminal contribution of E. Jayme, 'Identité

culturelle et intégration: le droit international privé postmoderne', *Collected Courses of the Hague Academy of International Law* 251, 1995, 9–267.

29 J. Chevallier, *L'État post-moderne*, 3rd edn, Paris: LGDJ, 2008.

30 Ibid., pp. 32ff.

31 Ibid., pp. 52ff.

32 See A. Annoni, 'Nationality and social rights', *supra*, pp. 135–52.

33 See generally: P. Stone, 'The Concept of Habitual Residence in Private International Law', *Anglo-American Law Review* 29, 2000, 342–67; P. McEleavy, 'La résidence habituelle, un critère de rattachement en quête de son identité: perspectives de *common law*', *Travaux du Comité Français de droit international privé*, 2008–2010, 127–46. See also D. Baetge, *Der gewohnliche Aufenthalt im internationalen Privatrecht*, Tübingen: Mohr, 1994.

34 Seen from this standpoint, the option in favour of habitual residence reflects the evolving patterns (and, ultimately, the elusiveness) of the socio-political notion of 'homogeneity'. See, generally, H.P. Hestermeyer, '*Staatsvolk* and homogeneity: From Weimar to the *Maastricht* decision of the German Federal Constitutional Court and beyond', *supra*, pp. 1–17.

35 J. Guillaumé, *L'affaiblissement de l'État-Nation et le droit international privé*, Paris: LGDJ, 2011, pp. 51ff.

36 Among recent instruments relying on an integrated regulatory strategy, see, e.g. The Hague Convention on the International Protection of Adults, 13 January 2000. Online. Available at: www.hcch.net/index_en.php?act=conventions.text&cid=71 (accessed 15 August 2012), or EU Parliament and Council Regulation 650/2012/EU on jurisdiction, applicable law, recognition and enforcement of decisions and acceptance and enforcement of authentic instruments in matters of succession and on the creation of a European Certificate of Succession, 4 July 2012, *Official Journal of the European Union* L 201, 27 July 2012, 107.

37 This trend, already noticed by H. Batiffol,'Le pluralisme des méthodes en droit international privé', *Collected Courses of the Hague Academy of International Law* 139, 1973, 75–148 at 85ff., has been studied more recently by Y. Lequette, 'Le droit international privé de la famille à l'épreuve des conventions internationales', *Collected Courses of the Hague Academy of International Law* 246, 1994, 9–233 at 54ff.

38 E. Jayme, 'Party Autonomy in International Family and Succession Law: New Tendencies', *Yearbook of Private International Law* 11, 2009, pp. 1–10.

39 One may see here a peculiar expression of the 'prophylactic function' that party autonomy – as suggested by O. Kahn-Freund, 'General Problems of Private International Law', *Collected Courses of the Hague Academy of International Law* 143, 1974, 139–474 at 341ff. – is basically intended to perform in PIL. Actually, allowing the parties to choose the governing law prevents at the outset a technical inconvenience (or discontinuity) that would otherwise stem from the operation of the objective conflict-of-laws provisions applicable in the circumstances.

40 Under several domestic legislations, should an individual possess two or more nationalities, he or she will be considered to be a national of the country with which the most significant connection exists, unless one of those nationalities is the nationality of the forum, in which case the latter shall prevail. See, e.g. Article 4(b) and (c) of the Turkish Statute on Private International Law of 2007, and Article 3(1) of the Korean Statute on Private International Law of 1962, as amended in 2001. Claims regarding the same legal relationship instituted in two

countries following this rule shall thus be decided in accordance with two different laws whenever the individual in question is a national of such two countries. The individual concerned may, in practice, be recognized as having certain status in one country but not in the other.

41 See generally, in recent literature: J. Basedow, 'Le rattachement à la nationalité et les conflits de nationalités en droit de l'Union Européenne', *Revue critique de droit international privé* 99, 2010, 427–56; O. Vonk, *Dual Nationality in the European Union*, Leiden-Boston: M. Nijhoff, 2012. Recent EU legislation in the field of PIL tend to provide specific solutions to deal with cases of dual and multiple nationalities; where this happens, the domestic rules of the member states play a residual role, or none at all. See, e.g. Article 22(1) of Regulation 650/2012/EU on succession, mentioned above.

42 As far as conflict-of-laws rules are concerned, one technique is frequently resorted to with a view to ensuring the coexistence of different connecting factors, possibly including nationality: we refer to the so called Kegel's ladder. The expression is used to designate rules providing for two or more factors and establishing that the subsequent one(s) will come into play only where the first one(s) cannot be resorted to. An example is provided by Article 8 of Regulation 1259/2010/EU, mentioned above.

43 See for further developments M. Bogdan, 'The EC Treaty and the Use of Nationality and Habitual Residence as Connecting Factors in International Family Law', in J. Meeusen *et al.* (eds) *International Family Law for the European Union*, Antwerpen: Intersentia, 2007, pp. 303–17.

44 T. Baudet, *The Significance of Borders*, Leiden–Boston: M. Nijhoff, 2012.

45 See generally D. Gutmann, *Le sentiment d'idéntité – Étude de droit des personnes et de la famille*, Paris: LGDJ, 2000.

46 For further developments, see M. Hunter-Hénin, *Pour une redéfinition du statut personnel*, Aix-en-Provence: Presses Universitaires d'Aix-Marseille, 2004.

47 See generally A. Gogos-Gintrand, *Les statuts des personnes – Études de la différenciation des personnes en droit*, Paris: IRJS, 2011.

48 UNESCO Convention on the Protection and Promotion of the Diversity of Cultural Expressions, 20 October 2005, UNTS, vol. 2440, No. 43977.

49 A. Malatesta, 'Cultural Diversity and Private International Law', in G. Venturini and S. Bariatti (eds) *Liber Fausto Pocar*, Milano: Giuffrè, 2009, pp. 643–57.

12 Conclusions

Francesco Salerno

This book draws an overall picture of the new approach of contemporary international law to the relationship among States and the complex of people that relate to their territory with a certain degree of stability, i.e. at the three levels of nationality, residence, and irregular presence. These three situations reflect sovereign power as being full within the territory and may thus be all categorized under the general notion of 'subjection'. The latter, however, is inherently linked to the doctrine of the absolute sovereignty of the state, as originally shaped around the idea of a sovereign suffering no limitations in its domination over a given territory and over all the people residing therein, even if on different grounds and with various degrees of social attachment. A violent break with this scheme is brought about by the French Enlightenment, introducing the concept of *citoyen*, or 'citizen', as a uniform condition of equality for those who take active part in the social contract that is the basis of the state itself. German and Italian romantic culture merges this link under the collective notion of 'People' (*Volk* or *Nazione*), that becomes simultaneously the engine of the formation of the state and a part of the state itself. Along these lines, the private international law of Italy and other countries translates the link of nationality into a universal value.[1] Contemporary states revert to this approach in that they construe their own constitutions as an expression of the sovereign will of the people; thus, a particular emphasis lies in the full, constitutional autonomy with which states define the conditions for acquiring nationality and mould – through nationality – the bond of allegiance such individuals owe them.[2] Whatever its precise contours, that bond shapes the homogeneity of a state's social basis.[3]

The evolution of political theory between the second half of the eighteenth century and the first half of the twentieth century influenced the evolution of classical international law. Conversely, international law, as an autonomous legal order, developed institutes and rules concerning nationality that now limit states' constitutional discretion in regulating the acquisition and contents of the *status civitatis*.

The bond of nationality, as we currently understand it, developed at the beginning of the nineteenth century in the context of diplomatic protection, i.e. the situation in which a state puts forward an international claim to protect 'its own' individuals and legal persons as against a foreign state that allegedly affected their interests. Classical international law grants states unfettered discretion in this regard, but sets a requirement for submitting the claim, namely the bond of nationality between the claiming state and the interested individual or legal person (a further requirement being prior exhaustion of local remedies offered by the state allegedly responsible of infringing the individual's internationally protected interests). The growing mobility of individuals contributes to a possible overlap among legal orders of different states as regards nationality, so that a given individual may be granted more than one nationality. Nonetheless, situations of double or multiple nationality stemming from the exercise of states' domestic jurisdiction imply the need to identify an international legal criterion regulating the exercise of diplomatic protection. This actually does not interfere in states' domestic jurisdiction: international law simply draws from the exercise of such domestic jurisdiction some consequences as to the exercise of an entitlement (or *faculté*) on the international plane, and regulates those consequences.[4] As Article 6(2) of the ILC Draft Articles on Diplomatic Protection (2006 Draft Articles) shows, there is no hindrance to the joint exercise of diplomatic protection if the various claims coincide; in any case, there is a preference for the state whose nationality is 'predominant' at the moment both of the infringement of the private party's rights and of the exercise of diplomatic protection (Article 7 of the 2006 Draft Articles). Under such circumstances, international law allows a state of nationality to advance a claim as against another state of nationality, setting aside the bond of allegiance that should, at least in theory, link the individual to the latter state. The need to ensure coherence of the international legal order leads to the conclusion that the same criterion should apply if two or more states of nationality put forward competing claims against a third state: i.e. the claim of the state of predominant nationality should prevail, unless there is a waiver or the concerned states agree otherwise.

As Sironi aptly observes,[5] the parameter relied upon by the ILC does not correspond to the notion of 'genuine link', which the ICJ referred to in a number of cases: a given nationality may be 'predominant' even if it does not give rise to a fully genuine link. Nonetheless, the link of predominant nationality, as outlined in the 2006 Draft Articles better suits the current context of cross-border mobility of persons. This is even truer since, as Simone points out, in the context of the European Union (EU) there is no need for a nationality bond to be genuine in order for it to display its cross-border effects. This evolution of international law bears an influence on domestic legal rules, which were originally inspired by the genuine link parameter, in that it binds states to interpret them, *infra* or *praeter legem*, in such a way as to ensure their compatibility with the new international legal framework. Thus, for instance, any reference to the state of nationality with which the individual is 'most closely connected' (see Article 19(2) of the Italian Statute on Private International Law No. 218/1995) should not be read any longer as referring to the genuine link criterion, but rather to the predominant link.

Even more significant, in this regard, is the way in which international law, in order to fulfill its own regulatory aims, affects the constitutive aspect of nationality, thus eroding the sphere of domestic jurisdiction. This *emprise* depends mainly on the way in which international human rights law has developed. The growing role of the human being in international law inevitably affects the regulation of nationality, since civil, political, and social rights are enjoyed mainly on the basis of the *status civitatis*, which best ensures a situation of legal certainty for individuals. Therefore, international law binds states to limit, as far as possible, the grounds that justify the loss of nationality, especially when this depends on historical circumstances that are regulated by international legal rules. For instance, in the case of state succession the affected entities are bound to preserve the nationality of individuals that previously possessed one, e.g. by relying on the bond with the state of residence[6] or by respecting those individuals' option.[7] In order to avoid statelessness, international law develops its own form of protection by requiring states to grant nationality, and construing nationality as part of the fundamental human rights. The most significant example in this regard concerns the right of the child to a nationality,[8] but this protective function emerges in all the circumstances in which the principle of non-discrimination binds the state to grant nationality, unless differences in treatment may be reasonably justified under international law.[9]

Finally, due to the growing level of protection it affords to human rights, international law also interferes with the constitutional contract among individuals and states, affecting the content of the *status civitatis*, specifically with regard to political, social, and cultural rights.

These three different aspects of the international regulation of nationality show – as stressed by Sironi[10] – that the traditional approach, according to which nationality is a fact that international law should merely take note of, cannot be accepted any longer. International law, on one hand, rationalizes this 'fact' within its own, autonomous, legal order – as in the case of diplomatic protection. This aspect finds only a partial correspondence as regards the nationality of legal entities.[11] On the other hand, international law draws nationality within the realm of human rights, thus setting forth obligations that states must transpose into domestic legal rules. This opens new, extremely relevant perspectives, upon which political and legal discourse should dwell for their constitutional implications. Indeed, this new international element in the determination of the personal and material scope of the social contract between individuals and states has become crucial for the historical determination of this contract, thus altering the latter's previously purely domestic nature. This contamination is all the more significant whenever the constitution of a country sets forth a requirement to respect international law, thus introducing an element that may potentially undermine the constitutional identity of that state. On the other hand, international obligations in this field are still drafted in a rather cautious way, in order to respect, as far as possible, states' discretion in framing the specificities of their own social contract with nationals. This is shown, for instance, by the absence of specific international rules on attribution of nationality even if the state would, in principle, be bound to grant it, e.g. concerning children.[12] Similarly, states still enjoy a broad margin of appreciation in conferring political, social, and cultural rights.[13] The tension among the international and the domestic levels of the *status civitatis* can be best appreciated with reference to the regional frameworks of partial supranational integration, as is well exemplified by the, at times difficult, decisions taken by the German Constitutional Court – and, to a lesser extent, by the Italian Constitutional Court – on the interrelationship between domestic and EU law. The EU has actually set up a form of European citizenship that, while stemming from the nationality of a member state, has attained a partially autonomous content as part of the EU legal order.[14]

Precisely, EU law confirms that the bond of nationality is an inescapable, primary constituent element of the individuals' *status civitatis*. It is around this bond that every state builds its constitutional structure and develops a privileged core of individual rights. The distinction between nationals and foreigners in this regard is so clear that international law upholds it, especially with regards to the right of free movement of persons.[15] Nonetheless, as it broadens its interest in regulating the status of human beings regardless of nationality, international law relies on other kinds of bonds that may better apply to situations that it regulates directly. The traditional approach, according to which nationality is the exclusive gateway to protection of individual rights,[16] may thus be overcome, e.g. in the case of refugees, by relying on the bond of residence, which is at the basis of some forms of international protection. As regards EU law, the tendency to treat foreigners legally present in a state's territory on an equal footing with nationals is even more striking. But the principle of equal treatment applies, at times, also under international law, such as in the international regulation of the status of legal migrants, or as regards the minimum core rights that should be ensured for irregular migrants in order to respect their human dignity.[17] Also uniform rules of private international law show a tendency to rely on residence, rather than on nationality, in order to best attain legal certainty through the consistent application of the same legal framework across borders.[18] The potential of this approach is all the more clear if one bears in mind the opportunities offered to individuals that move across borders on their own will, albeit within the limits set forth by the relevant national legislations. Since the status of regular residents is easier to attain than nationality, by moving across borders aliens may themselves establish – at times even opt for – a given *status civitatis*, freeing themselves from the bond of allegiance with their state of nationality.

Thus, there is a second tendency in international practice, which complements the first one only in part: international law curbs the role of nationality as an exclusive gateway to an individual's civic status. The outcome is coherent with the multi-level approach in which the status of the human being should be currently read. This is a consequence of the fact that the state-centered perspective in which the *status civitatis* was originally forged now suffers some limitations, but has not completely disappeared. The various degrees of protection of the human being relate to the different sources of the corresponding regulation, and find their unitary synthesis around each individual. The criterion used to coordinate these various levels of protection is usually the rule of the most-favourable-treatment. Indeed, international obligations set a minimum standard of protection, whereas states are free to set higher levels of protection that are nonetheless compatible with that standard. This coordination is actually possible, in practice, as long as there is a normative continuity among legal orders: international law sets forth its own legal rules concerning the status of individuals within a given state, whereas states transpose their international obligations into domestic legal rules, making use of the margin of appreciation that international rules leave in this regard. This dialogue takes place among legal systems and rules, since the developments concerning the position of the human being in international law have cast off the complete domination of states over individuals.

Notes

1 P. Franzina, 'The evolving role of nationality in private international law', *supra*, pp. 193–209.
2 A. Vermeer-Künzli, 'Nationality and diplomatic protection: a reapprisal', *supra*, pp. 76–95.
3 H.P. Hestermeyer, '*Staatsvolk* and homogeneity: from Weimar to the *Maastricht* decision of the German Federal Constitutional Court and beyond', *supra*, pp. 1–17.
4 A. Sironi, 'Nationality of individuals in international law: a functional approach', *supra*, pp. 54–75.
5 Sironi, ibid.
6 F. Costamagna, 'Statelessness in the context of state succession: an appraisal under international law', *supra*, pp. 37–53.
7 Sironi, 'Nationality of individuals'.
8 S. Forlati, 'Nationality as a human right', *supra*, pp. 18–36.
9 Ibid., Sironi, 'Nationality of individuals'.
10 Ibid.
11 G. D'Agnone, 'Determining the nationality of companies in ICSID arbitration', *supra*, pp. 153–68.
12 Forlati, 'Nationality as a human right'.
13 D. Rudan, 'Nationality and political rights', *supra*, pp. 117–34; A. Annoni, 'Nationality and social rights', *supra*, pp. 135–52.
14 P. Simone, 'Nationality and regional integration: the case of the European Union', *supra*, pp. 169–92.
15 F. De Vittor, 'Nationality and freedom of movement', *supra*, pp. 96–116.
16 Costamagna, 'Statelessness in the context of state succession'.
17 Annoni, 'Nationality and social rights'.
18 Franzina, 'The evolving role of nationality'.

Index

A/18 case 86–7
Abkhazia 70n24
abuse-of-rights doctrine 54, 69, 69n8,162–3
acquisition of nationality 61–2, 99; by birth 20–3, 28; and interpretation of international legal rules and national legislation 25–6; naturalization 20, 23, 28, 175–6; prohibition of discrimination 24, 28
Advisory Committee on the Framework Convention for the Protection of National Minorities 127
African Charter of Human and Peoples' Rights (ACHPR) 24, 109n2, 120, 123, 125, 129n11, 136, 146n16
African Charter on the Rights and Welfare of the Child (ACRWC) 19, 21, 32n45
African Commission on Human and Peoples' Rights (AComHPR) 60; *Modise v Botswana* 24, 67, 123; *Mouvement Ivoirien des Droits Humains (MIDH) v Côte d'Ivoire* 120, 123
African Committee of Experts on the Rights and Welfare of the Child (ACERWC), *Nubian Children* case 22, 24
Al-Adsani case 91
Albania 119
Albanians in Italy 106
aliens: admission of 22, 96, 97, 105–6; employment 137, 138; expulsion of 98, 100, 107–8; political rights 118, 119–20; preferential treatment 139–40; social security 139; *see also* immigrants; refugees; stateless persons
allegiance, expression of 77, 79
American Convention on Human Rights (ACHR) 19, 20, 21, 30n28, 32n44, 59, 60, 71n36, 98, 109n2, 117, 169–70, 186n6; political rights 121, 125, 126, 129n11; Protocol of San Salvador 136
Amsterdam Treaty 171
Anderson, B. 195
Annoni, A. 135–52
Anzilotti, D. 2
Arab Charter on Human Rights (ArCHR) 19, 20, 30n31, 32n43, 71n36, 98, 120, 131n33, 136, 146n16, 170, 186n8
Aristotle 2
Arendt, H. 37
Asunción, Treaty of 170
asylum seekers 105
Australia, 'Pacific Solution' 115n68
Austro-Hungarian Empire 46
Aziz v Cyprus 122

Badinter Arbitration Committee 62
Bahamas 21
Baltic States 40–1
Bangladesh 45
Barcelona Traction case 154, 160–1, 162
Bedoons 122
Belarus 45, 101
Bhutan 22
bilateral investment treaties (BITs) 159
birth(s): acquisition of nationality by 20–3, 28; registration of 22; statelessness at 55

Böckenförde, E.W. 8
Bogdandy, A. von 8–9
Bolivia 117
bond of nationality 77–80, 210–11
border controls 97, 102, 104, 105–8; externalization of 106–8; maritime 106–8
Bosnia-Herzegovina 46, 62–3
Bronstein v Peru case 59
Brownlie, I. 55
Brubaker, R. 196
Bryde, B.-O. 8

Calvo corporation 161
Canary Islands 106–7
Canevaro case 83, 94n40
Cartagena Declaration on Refugees 125
Catalonia 8
Champion Trading Company v Egypt 63
Chevallier, J. 200
children 20–3, 24, 28, 105, 144, 151n85, 183, 185, 212; born out of wedlock 24, 60; *see also* Convention on the Rights of the Child (CRC)
citizenship 11, 37, 40, 98, 117, 119, 128n4, 169, 170; EU 171–86; German 7; national, and EU citizenship 173–4, 179–80, 184; republican 46; secondary 46; withdrawal of 184
city–state 2
civil rights 135, 212; *see also* International Covenant on Civil and Political Rights (ICCPR)
cognitive studies 9–10
collective statelessness 38, 47
Commission against Racism and Intolerance 124
Committee on Economic, Social and Cultural Rights (CESCR) 137, 138, 143
Committee on the Elimination of Racial Discrimiation (CtERD) 137, 142
Committee on the Rights of the Child (CtRC) 22
Commonwealth of Independent States Convention on Human Rights and Fundamental Freedoms (CIS Convention) 19, 20, 30n29, 120, 130n32
Conference on Security and Cooperation in Europe 101
conflict of laws 194, 197, 199, 203, 205n4, 206–7n17, 209n42
constitutional law 6
Convention on the Avoidance of Statelessness in Relation to State Succession (2006 Convention) 25, 41–2, 43, 44–5, 46, 47, 62, 63, 73n58, n63, n68, 127n2
Convention on Certain Questions relating to the Conflict of Nationality Laws (1930) 18, 38–9, 49n20, 81
Convention on Discrimination in Respect of Employment and Occupation, ILO 136
Convention on the Elimination of All Forms of Discrimination against Women (CEDAW) 24, 34n73, n74, 39, 79
Convention on the Elimination of All Forms of Racial Discrimination (CERD) 24, 34n71, 43, 109n2, 137, 151n78
Convention on Medical Care and Sickness Benefits, ILO 140
Convention on Participation of Foreigners in Public Life at Local Level (1992 Convention) 118, 127, 170
Convention on the Reduction of Statelessness (1961 Convention) 20, 21, 22, 26, 30n32, 31n40, 34n72, 35n94, 36n103, 39, 40, 43, 50n36, 79, 127n3, 183
Convention relating to the Status of Refugees (1951 Convention) 23, 95n65, 104, 105, 115n69, 125, 149n55
Convention relating to the Status of Stateless Persons (1954 Convention) 23, 38, 39, 49n28, 102, 111–12n25, 124, 127, 149n55
Convention on the Rights of the Child (CRC) 19, 20–1, 22, 39, 143
Convention on the Rights of Persons with Disabilities (CRPD) 19, 24, 34n75
Convention on the Settlement of

Investment Disputes (ICSID Convention) 63–4, 153, 155–63, 165n11, n13
Cook Islands 21
corporate nationality 153–68; control test 153, 155–63, 166n17 and 20
Costamagna, F. 37–53
Council of Europe (CoE) 39, 41–2, 62, 103, 117, 118, 124, 127, 136, 170
Council of Europe Convention on Action against Trafficking in Human Beings 103
Covenant on the Rights of the Child in Islam 19
criminal records 44
criteria individuationis 153, 155, 159
Croatia 40, 46, 63
Cuba 101
cultural diversity 204
cultural identity 204
cultural rights 7, 135, 136, 137, 138, 141, 143, 212, 213
Czech Republic 44, 46
Czechoslovakia 40

Danielpour case 88
de facto statelessness 23, 28, 38
de jure statelessness 23, 28, 38
De Vittor, F. 96–116
Decaux, E. 20
Declaration on Friendly Relations 7
democracy 4–5, 6, 9, 124; and political rights 125–6
democratic deficit, EU 171
denationalization 26, 38, 111n21; of minority groups 39, 43–4, 47
Dereci and Others case 180–3, 185–6
Dickson Car Wheel Company case (1931) 91
diplomatic protection 56, 57–8, 76–95, 172, 210–11, 212; of corporate entities 153, 154–5, 156, 161, 162
disabled persons 19, 24, 144
discrimination 118–19; formal 136; indirect 145; racial 24, 43, 123, 137; substantive 136; *see also* non-discrimination
domestic rules on nationality 54, 55–6, 57, 60, 61, 66, 67
domicile *see* residence
dominant/predominant nationality 58, 65–6, 80, 81–3, 85–8, 89, 91, 211
dual nationality 78, 80–9, 91–2, 98, 122, 178–9, 203, 211

economic rights 7, 135, 136, 138, 141, 143
effective link doctrine *see* genuine or effective link
Eisner, K. 4
election(s): free 119, 120; right to stand for 122–4, 125, 127, 170, 172
emigration, control of 97, 102, 107, 108
employment 137–9, 141–2
equal treatment 142, 170, 173, 177, 213
equality 4
equitable geographical distribution, rule of 65
Eritrea 27, 41, 50–1n47, 51n48, 111n21
Eritrea–Ethiopia Claims Commission, *Civilian claims cases* 27, 111n21
Erzberger, M. 4
Esphahanian case 83–4, 85–6
Estonia 40–1, 50n45, n46
Ethiopia 41
ethnic cleansing 40
ethnic engineering 40, 43
European Commission 172
European Commission for Democracy through Law *see* Venice Commission
European Commission of Human Rights (EComHR) 122–3
European Committee of Social Rights (ECSR) 138, 143, 144
European Community, Treaty establishing (TEC) 171, 174, 175, 183, 184
European Convention on Human Rights (ECHR) 22, 25, 48, 50n41, 60, 72n41, 129n17, 150n73, 169, 181, 182, 201, 202; and freedom of movement 97, 100, 108, 180; and political rights 118, 119, 120, 125; and social rights 142, 143

European Convention on Nationality (ECN) 19, 20, 21, 22, 24, 25, 27, 29n18, 31–2n43, 32n52, 33n65, 34n76, 35n94, 36n101, 39, 41, 43, 63, 69n12, 71n36, 92n12, 117, 124, 183–4
European Court of Human Rights (ECtHR) 22, 25, 60, 100, 105–6, 117, 118, 119, 120, 122, 125, 126, 139, 182; *Al-Adsani* case 91; *Aziz v Cyprus* 122; *Genovese v Malta* 24, 60; *Hirsi* case 107, 116n84; *Hirst v the United Kingdom* 121; *Koua Poirrez* case 139; *Kuric and others v Slovenia* 25, 48; *Lucksaz v Poland* 118; *Ponomaryovi* case 140; *Russian Conservative Party of Entrepreneurs v Russia* 121; *Tanase v Moldova* 124; *Xhavara* case 106, 108
European Court of Justice (ECJ) 57, 137, 171, 173; *Dereci and Others* case 180–3, 185–6; *Iida* case 185; *McCarthy* case 178–80, 181, 183, 184, 185, 186; *Micheletti* case 174; *O and S* case 186; *Rottman* case 26, 175–6, 177, 183; *Ruiz Zambrano* case 176–8, 180, 181, 183, 184, 185, 186; *Spain v United Kingdom* 119–20; *Zhu and Chen* case 174–5, 176–7
European identity 1, 9
European integration 8, 171
European Parliament 172
European Social Charter (ESC) 138, 140
European Union (EU) 6, 9, 170–1, 193, 202, 211, 213; Charter of Fundamental Rights 142, 144, 173, 180, 180–3, 185; citizenship 171–86; democratic deficit 171; diplomatic protection 172; freedom of movement 170, 171, 172, 173, 174, 176–83, 184, 185, 213; Global Approach to Migration 102, 106; political rights 117–18, 172; right of residence 171, 173, 176–83, 184, 185; social rights 137–8, 140, 184
exit visas 101, 102
expulsion: of dual or multiple nationals 98; of nationals 97–9; prohibition of 96, 98, 100

fairness 22
family law 197, 201, 203
family life, respect for 105, 106, 115–16n71, n72, 181, 182, 185
Forlati, S. 18–36
foundlings 22
France 80, 143
Franzina, P. 193–209
free elections 119, 120
freedom of expression, association, and assembly 125, 126
freedom of movement 96–116, 170, 171, 172, 173, 174, 176–83, 184, 185, 213
Frontex Hera operations 106–7
functional approach to nationality 55–68

Genovese v Malta 24, 60
genuine or effective link, principle of 45, 46, 54, 68, 72n52, 211; and corporate nationality 161–3, 165n16; and diplomatic protection 57–8, 78–80, 81, 85, 86, 88; and ICSID dispute tribunals 63, 64; and international organizations 66, 67–8; and state succession 61, 62, 68
Georgia 45, 70n24
German Constitutional Court 11, 213; *Lisbon* judgment 11; *Maastricht* judgment 1, 3, 8
Germany: Basic Law 3, 6–7, 8, 11; citizenship 7; immigrant population 6; Nazi 5, 6, 7; *Staatsvolk* and homogeneity 1–9, 11; unification of 44; *Volkszugehörigkeit* 7; Weimar Republic 1, 3–4
globalization 200
Golpira case 87–8
Gonzales v Guyana case 60
Goodwin-Gill, G.S. 103
Greece 5
Greek city-state 2
group formation 9–10
group identification 10, 11

habitual residence 45–6, 62, 82, 84, 85, 90, 92, 193, 195, 200–1, 203
Hague Conference on Private International Law 193

Harvard Draft 81
health care 140, 142–3
Heller, H. 3, 5–6
Helsinki Final Act (1975) 101
Hestermeyer, H.P. 1–17
Hirsi case 107, 116n84
Hirst v the United Kingdom 121
Hitler, A. 4
Holy See 21
homogeneity 1–11
Honduras 117
Hong Kong 121
human rights 11, 18–36, 37, 42, 58–61, 62, 67, 79, 93n26, 97, 101, 104, 126, 137, 140–1, 144, 201, 204, 212
Human Rights Committee (HRC) 19, 22, 24, 59, 60, 96, 98, 99, 101–2, 105, 119, 120, 121–2, 123, 139
Human Rights Council 19, 142
human trafficking 103, 104

identity 11, 204; cultural 204; European 1, 9; national 1; regional 1
Iida case 185
immigrants: acquisition of nationality 99; integration of 6; political participation 127; *see also* irregular migrants; migrant workers
immigration 99, 105–8, 138–9; illegal 97, 102, 103–4, 106–7, 108
Immigration (European Economic Area) Regulations (2000) 175
individualism 199
Institut de Droit International, Rules on Admission and Expulsion of Aliens 97
integration 4; European 8, 171; of immigrants 6; regional 169–92, 202, 203, 204, 213; systemic 21
Inter-American Commission on Human Rights 60
Inter-American Court of Human Rights (IACHR) 19, 59, 117, 126, 142; *Bronstein v Peru* case 59; *Yean and Bosico* case 22, 24, 48–9n12, 60, 67
International Centre for Settlement of Investment Disputes (ICSID) 57, 63–5, 67, 153–68; *Pac Rim Cayman* case 162–3; *Rompetrol* case 157, 158, 159, 160, 162; *Tokios Tokelés* case 157, 158, 159, 160,162
International Convention on the Protection of the Rights of All Migrant Workers and Members of Their Families (ICRMW) 19, 71n36, 109n2, n7, 115–16n72, 139, 140, 141, 143, 145n8, n10, 146n28, 148n40, 150n67, 169, 151n80, 186n4
International Court of Justice (ICJ) 7, 8, 45, 54; *Barcelona Traction* case 154, 160–1, 162; *Nottebohm* case (1955) 18, 23, 61, 63, 77–8, 79, 80, 85, 89, 90, 162
International Covenant on Civil and Political Rights (ICCPR) 7, 19, 20, 21, 22, 30n33, 31n35, 32n48, 35n94, 71n36, 72n41, 97, 99, 100, 101, 102, 103, 104, 107, 109n2, 119, 120, 121, 122, 123, 125, 129n11, 131n37
International Covenant on Economic, Social and Cultural Rights (ICESCR) 7, 129n11, 136, 138, 141, 143, 146n16, n23, n25, 149n48, 151n82
international human rights instruments 19–20, 26, 212
International Labour Organization (ILO) 135–6, 140, 141; Convention on Discrimination in Respect of Employment and Occupation 136; Convention on Medical Care and Sickness Benefits 140; Non-Binding Principles and Guidelines for a Rights-Based Approach to Labour Migration 136
International Law Commission (ILC) 41, 44, 45, 47, 76, 79, 89, 98–9; Draft Articles on Diplomatic Protection (2006) 57–8, 78, 80–2, 89–90, 91, 92, 154, 161, 211; Draft Articles on Nationality of Natural Persons in relation to the Succession of States (1999) 42, 43, 44, 45, 46, 47–8, 61–2
international organizations, staff members 57, 65–6, 67–8

investment disputes 57, 63–5, 67, 153–68
Iran-United States Claims Tribunal 63, 80, 81, 85–8; *A/18* case 86–7; *Danielpour* case 88; *Esphahanian* case 83–4, 85–6; *Golpira* case 87–8; *Malek* case 88
Irish Nationality and Citizenship Act (1956) 175
irregular migrants 140–4, 144–5; employment rights 141; health care rights 142–3; labour rights 141–2; social security 143–4
Isensee, J. 8
Italy 22, 32n52, 80, 119; Albanian immigrants 106
jus cogens 28
jus sanguinis 7, 21, 22, 79, 87
jus soli 7, 21, 60, 79, 87

Japan 22
Jellinek, G. 1–2, 4

Kelsen, H. 4, 5
Kirchhof, P. 8
Kosovo 8, 45
Koua Poirrez case 139
Kuric and others v Slovenia 25, 48, 72n48
Kuwait 122

labour rights 141–2
labour standards 135–6
laissez-passer 102
Landinelli Silva v Uruguay 121–2
Latvia 40–1, 50n45 and 46, 117
law: sources of 201
laws: conflict of 83, 194, 197, 199, 203, 205n4, 206–7n17, 209n42
legal positivism 4, 194
Leibholz, H. 54
Leichtensztejn case 102
lex patriae 196, 201, 202
Liebknecht, K. 4
life, right to 142, 144
Lisbon case 11
Lisbon Treaty 172, 184
Lithuania 50n42, 157
Litt, T. 4
Lucksaz v Poland 118
Luxemburg, R. 4

Maastricht case 1, 3, 8
Maastricht Treaty 171, 173
McCarthy case 178–80, 181, 183, 184, 185, 186
Macedonia, Former Yugoslav Republic of 46
Machiavelli, N. 5
mailbox companies 162
Malek case 88
Malta 24, 60
Mancini, P.S. 194
maritime border controls 106–8
Maslov case 100
Mathison case 83
Mercosur 170, 186n9
Mergé case 81, 84–5
Methodenstreit 3–6
Mexico 10, 117, 128n5, 142
Mexico, Constitution (1917) 5
Micheletti case 174
Micula v Romania 64
migrant workers 136, 140, 169, 170; human rights 140; labour rights 141–2; social security 143–4
migration 96; *see also* emigration; immigration
minority groups, denationalization of 39, 43–4, 47
mixed-claims commissions 80, 81, 95n73
Modise v Botswana 24, 67, 123
Mogos v Romania case 27
Moldova 114n52, 124
Monaco 20–1, 31n37
Montesquieu, Baron de 5
Montevideo Convention on Rights and Duties of States (1933) 2
Morocco 18, 93n22, 114n52
most favourable treatment, principle of 119, 214
Mouvement Ivoirien des Droits Humains (MIDH) v Côte d'Ivoire 120, 123
multinational corporations 200
multiple nationality 42, 54, 58, 65, 67, 80–9, 98, 211

nation-state *see* state(s)

national identity 1
national rules on nationality 54, 55–6, 57, 60, 61, 66, 67
nationality: acquisition of *see* acquisition; bond of xi, 77–80, 210–11; as a connecting factor 197–8, 200; corporate 153–68; decline of 198–203;
deprivation of 20, 57, 175–6, 183–4; arbitrary 26, 27, 28, 34n72, 38, 39, 59, 60; by predecessor states 47; dominant/predominant nationality 58, 65–6, 80, 81–3, 85–8, 89, 91, 211; dual 78, 80–9, 91–2, 98, 122, 178–9, 203, 211; effective *see* genuine or effective link; forced conferral of 55; and freedom of movement 96–116; functional approach to 55–68; as head of jurisdiction 194, 197–8, 200; horizontal dimension of 196; as a human right 18–36, 42, 58–61, 67, 79; multiple 42, 54, 58, 65, 67, 80–9, 98, 211; and political rights 37, 117–34; and private international law (PIL) 193–209; renunciation of 23, 27, 55, 60, 62; right to retain and change 20, 26–7, 55; and social rights 135-
152; technical advantages of 202–3; vertical dimension of 196
Nationality Decrees in Tunis and Morocco (1923) 18
nationality-of-claims rule 58, 76–92
nationality shopping 23
naturalization 20, 23, 28, 77, 82, 175–6
Nazi Germany 5, 6, 7
negative rights 135
Nepal 101
Netherlands 93n16
New Zealand 125
non-discrimination, principle of 24, 28, 42, 55, 60, 66, 118, 146n16, 212; EU citizens 170, 172, 173; and freedom of movement 105, 106, 172; and social rights 136, 137, 138, 143; and state succession 43–4
non-governmental organizations 200
non-*refoulement*, principle of 104, 105, 106
non-responsibility rule 81, 87, 89, 91
Nottebohm case (1955) 18, 23, 61, 63, 77–8, 79, 80, 85, 89, 90, 162
Nubian Children case 22, 24

O and S case 186
O'Connell, D.P. 62
Okonkwo against Austria case 27
Oman 20–1, 22, 31n37
Oppenheim, L. 54
option, right of 62
Organization of American States 126, 193

Pac Rim Cayman case 162–3
Panevezys-Saldutiskis Railway case 77, 78
passport delivery procedures 101–2
'passportization' practices 23, 70n24
Permanent Court of International Justice (PCIJ) 77; *Nationality Decrees in Tunis and Morocco* (1923) 18; *Panevezys-Saldutiskis Railway* case 77, 78
Pernice, I. 8
Plato 2
pluralism 5–6, 124, 126, 199
Poiares Maduro, M. 183
Polis 2
political participation 84
political parties 126
political rights 37, 117–34, 135, 171, 172, 212, 213; *see also* International Covenant on Civil and Political Rights (ICCPR)
Ponomaryovi case 140
positivism, legal 4, 194
post-modern states 200–2
predominant/dominant nationality 58, 65–6, 80, 81–3, 85–8, 89, 91, 211
preferential treatment 139–40
prisoners, political rights 121
private international law (PIL) 193–209; flexibilization of 199–200; individualist turn in 199; materialization of 199
private life, respect for 105, 106, 112n30, 181, 182
proportionality, principle of 26, 27, 103, 144, 176, 184

Protocol against the Smuggling of Migrants by Land, Sea and Air 104
Protocol to Prevent, Suppress and Punish Trafficking in Persons 103
Protocol relating to Certain Cases of Statelessness (1930) 18, 31n41, 39

Qatar 101
quasi-political rights 125, 127

racial discrimination 24, 43, 123, 137
Rathenau, W. 4
refugees 23, 26, 37, 99, 104, 105, 106, 213; diplomatic protection of 76, 89–91, 92; political rights 124–5, 127; preferential treatment of 140
regional identity 1
regional integration 169–92, 202, 203, 204, 213
remittances, transfer of 170
Renan, E. 5
renunciation of nationality 23, 27, 55, 60, 62
Reparation of Injuries case 81
residence 83, 210, 213; habitual 45–6, 62, 82, 84, 85, 90, 92, 193, 195, 200–1, 203; lawful 90, 92, 178; right of 171, 173, 176–83, 184, 185
retention centres 104
right to leave a country 96–7, 100–4, 105, 107, 108
'Robbers Grave Experiment' 10
Roma 44
Rompetrol case 157, 158, 159, 160, 162
Rottman case 26, 175–6, 177, 183
Rudan, D. 117–34
Ruiz Zambrano case 176–8, 180, 181, 183, 184, 185, 186
Russia 45, 70n24
Russian Conservative Party of Entrepreneurs v Russia 121

Saint-Germain-en-Laye, Treaty of 46
Salerno, F. 210–14
Saudi Arabia 101
Savigny, F.C. von 194
Schmitt, C. 3, 4, 5, 6
Schneidermann, P. 4
Schreuer, C.H. 156
self-determination 7–8, 62–3
self-identification 9, 10, 11, 88, 92
Serrano Saenz v Ecuador case 60
Sharpston, E. 177–8
ships' crews 76, 89, 95n63
Siag v Egypt 64
Singapore 21
Sironi, A. 54–75
Sloane, R.D. 55
Slovakia 46
Slovenia 25, 40, 46
Smend, R. 4
smuggling of migrants 104
social groups, formation of 9–10
social justice 135
social rights 7, 37, 135–52, 184, 212, 213
social security 135, 136, 138, 139, 140, 143–4, 170
Soufraki v the United Arab Emirates 64
sources of law 201
South Ossetia 70n24
South Sudan 46–7, 52–3n84, n85, n86
Southern African Development Community (SADC) 170
Southern Common Market (Mercosur) 170, 186n9
sovereignty *see* state(s), sovereignty
Soviet Union 40
Spain v United Kingdom 119–20
spouses 23, 105, 178–9
Staatsvolk, and homogeneity 1–9, 11
state succession 212; defining states' responsibilities in relation to 44–7, 61–3, 68; statelessness and 25, 38, 40–8, 55, 57, 61–2
stateless persons 23, 39, 76, 89–90, 91, 99; political rights 124; preferential treatment of 140; social rights 137; *see also* Convention relating to the Status of Stateless Persons
statelessness 18, 19, 26, 27, 28, 31n41, 37, 38–53, 184; at birth 55; collective 38, 47; de facto 23,38; de jure 23, 38; and state succession 25, 38, 40–8, 55, 57, 61–2
state(s) 1–2, 6, 8, 9, 195; dissolution of 44; domestic rules on nationality 54, 55–6, 57, 60, 61, 66, 67; geo-

political identity of 196; homogeneity and 10–11; post-modern 200–2; predecessor 42,44, 45, 46, 47; separation of part of territory 44; sovereignty 6, 78, 79, 81, 170–1, 194, 210 (change of 40, 45); transfer of territory 44; unification of 44
status Germans 7
stereotypes 9, 10
Stewart v Canada 99
subrogate motherhood 26, 35n90
Sudan 46–7
supranationality 6, 9, 204
systemic integration, principle of 21

Tanase v Moldova 124
Tizzano, A. 174
Tokios Tokelés case 157, 158, 159, 160, 162
Tomuschat, C. 9
torture, prohibition of 142, 144
trade unions 135, 140, 141
Treaty on European Union (TEU) 172, 173–4, 180, 184, 185
Treaty on the Functioning of the European Union (TFEU) 172, 173, 175, 177, 181, 183, 184, 185, 186
Trianon, Treaty of 46
Trstenjak, V. 185
Tunisia 18
Turkey 5

Ukraine 101, 157
United Arab Emirates (UAE) 21
United Kingdom 30–1n34, 122, 125
United Nations (UN) 39, 48, 136; Charter 7; Declaration on Friendly Relations 7; staff members 65–6
United Nations Administrative Tribunal (UNAT) 65
United Nations Convention against Transnational Organized Crime 103, 114n58, n60
United Nations Declaration on the Human Rights of Individuals Who Are Not Nationals of the Country in Which They Live 140
United Nations High Commissioner for Refugees (UNHCR) 21, 37, 125
United Nations Sub-Commission on the Promotion and Protection of Human Rights 119
United Nations Working Group on Minorities 119
United States (US) 5, 31n35; Court of Appeal 23
Universal Declaration of Human Rights (UDHR) 19, 20, 27, 39, 42, 71n36, 96, 117, 120, 136, 149n48, 169
Uruguay 121–2
Uzbekistan 101

Van Panhuys, H.F. 55
Vasak, K. 135
veil piercing 154, 157, 161
Venice Commission 41, 47, 124, 127; Declaration on the Consequences of State Succession for Nationality of Natural Persons 42
Vermeer-Künzli, A. 76–95
Vienna Convention on the Law of Treaties (VCLT) 64, 151n84, 158, 166n26
voting rights 117, 118, 119–22, 125, 126–7, 172, 173

Weil, P. 158, 159
Weiler, J. 9
women 24, 39, 79
World Bank 64

Xhavara case 106, 108

Yean and Bosico case 22, 24, 48–9n12, 60, 67
Yemen 44
Yugoslavia 40, 62

Zhu and Chen case 174–5, 176–7

For Product Safety Concerns and Information please contact our EU
representative GPSR@taylorandfrancis.com
Taylor & Francis Verlag GmbH, Kaufingerstraße 24, 80331 München, Germany

www.ingramcontent.com/pod-product-compliance
Ingram Content Group UK Ltd.
Pitfield, Milton Keynes, MK11 3LW, UK
UKHW022026061126
477531UK00002B/58

* 9 7 8 0 4 1 5 5 3 5 4 5 8 *